WOW —

KOYOHARU GOTOUGE

Volume 2 is out! Thank you! I'm troubling a lot of people, but I'll keep doing my best. On the way to the convenience store in my neighborhood, I came across vomit on the ground three times, but I'll keep doing my best.

DEMON SLAYER:
KIMETSU NO YAIBA
VOLUME 2
Shonen Jump Edition

Story and Art by
KOYOHARU GOTOUGE

TRANSLATION John Werry
ENGLISH ADAPTATION Stan!
TOUCH-UP ART & LETTERING John Hunt
DESIGN Adam Grano
EDITOR Mike Montesa

Printed in Italy

Published by VIZ Media, LLC
P.O. Box 77010
San Francisco, CA 94107

10 9
First printing, September 2018
Ninth printing, April 2021

ratings.viz.com
RATED T TEEN

PARENTAL ADVISORY
DEMON SLAYER: KIMETSU NO YAIBA is rated T for Teen and recommended for ages 13 and up. This volume contains realistic and fantasy violence.

VIZ MEDIA
viz.com

SHONEN JUMP

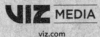

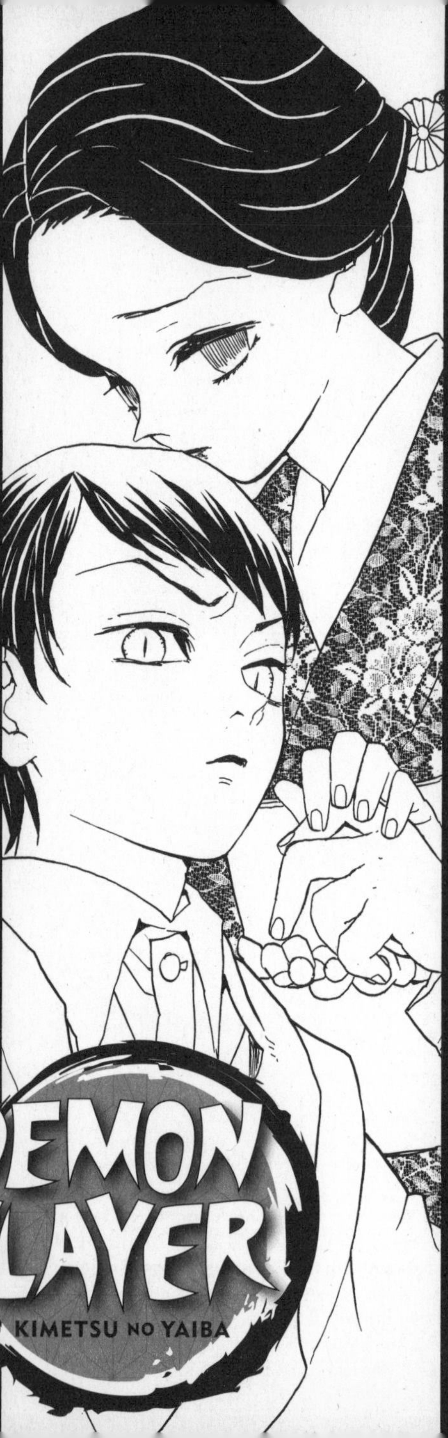
DEMON SLAYER
KIMETSU NO YAIBA

2

IT WAS YOU

KOYOHARU GOTOUGE

CHARACTERS

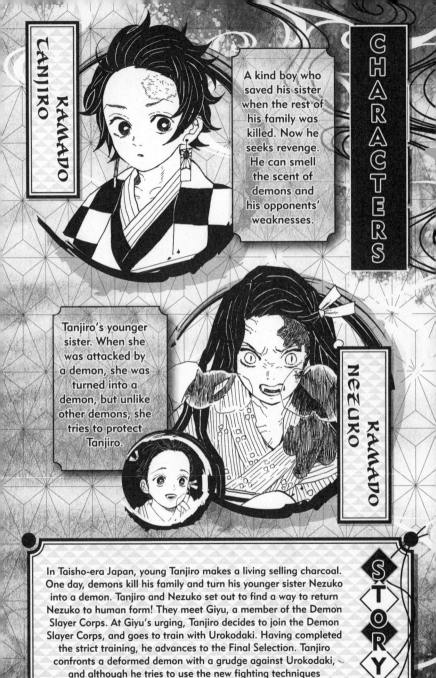

KAMADO TANJIRO

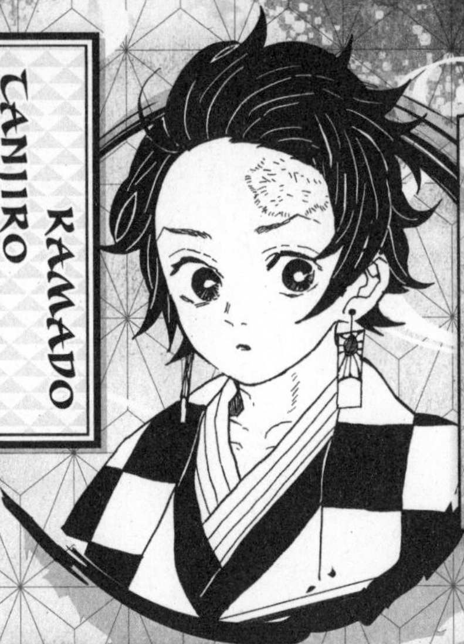

A kind boy who saved his sister when the rest of his family was killed. Now he seeks revenge. He can smell the scent of demons and his opponents' weaknesses.

KAMADO NEZUKO

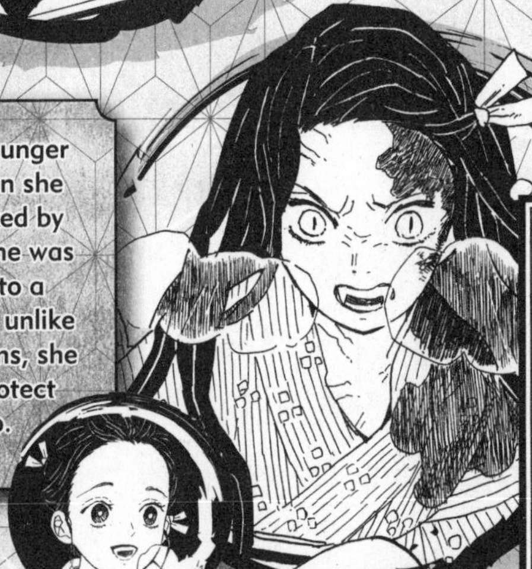

Tanjiro's younger sister. When she was attacked by a demon, she was turned into a demon, but unlike other demons, she tries to protect Tanjiro.

STORY

In Taisho-era Japan, young Tanjiro makes a living selling charcoal. One day, demons kill his family and turn his younger sister Nezuko into a demon. Tanjiro and Nezuko set out to find a way to return Nezuko to human form! They meet Giyu, a member of the Demon Slayer Corps. At Giyu's urging, Tanjiro decides to join the Demon Slayer Corps, and goes to train with Urokodaki. Having completed the strict training, he advances to the Final Selection. Tanjiro confronts a deformed demon with a grudge against Urokodaki, and although he tries to use the new fighting techniques he has learned, they may not be enough...

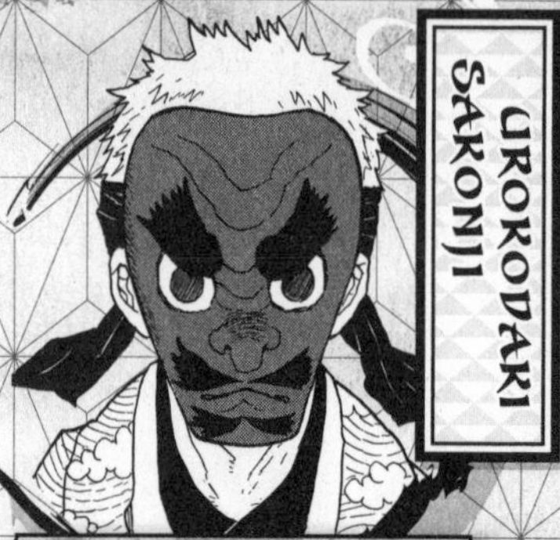
UROKODAKI SAKONJI

A trainer in the Demon Slayer Corps and Tanjiro's master.

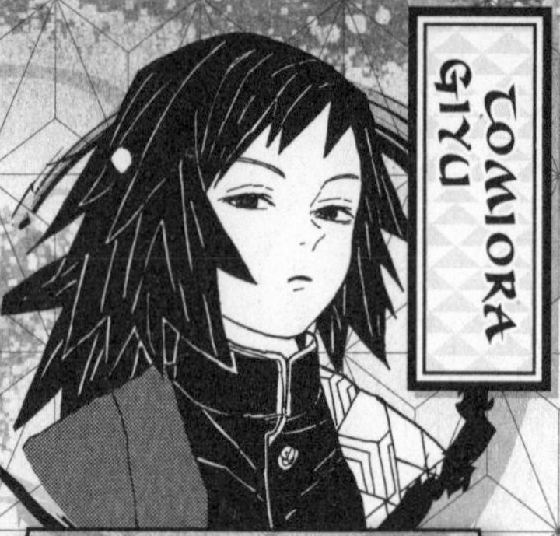
TOMIOKA GIYU

A member of the Demon Slayer Corps and the one who led Tanjiro to them.

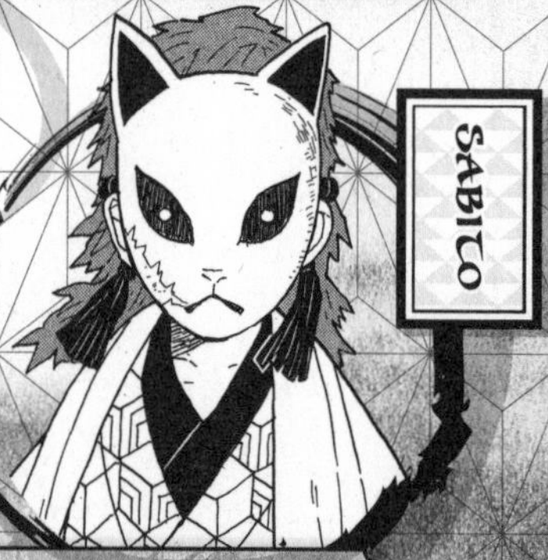
SABITO

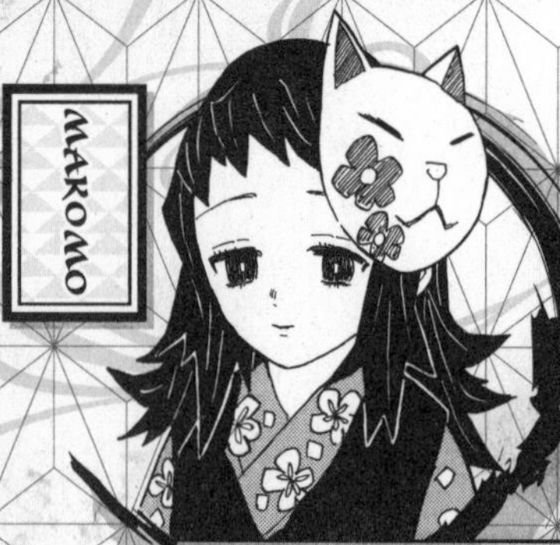
MAKOMO

Former pupils of Urokodaki. They assist with Tanjiro's training.

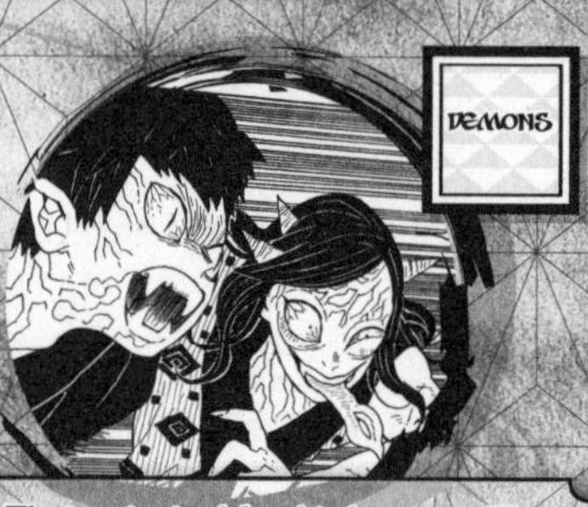
DEMONS

Their principal food is humans. They have powerful physical capabilities and their wounds heal quickly. Some demons can transform and have supernatural abilities. Only sunlight or beheading with a special sword can kill them.

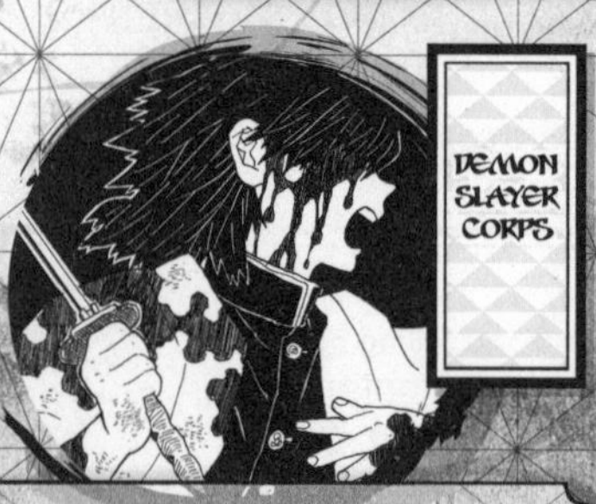
DEMON SLAYER CORPS

An organization of a few hundred members and not officially recognized by the government. They hunt demons, but details such as who their leader is remain shrouded in mystery.

CONTENTS

DEMON SLAYER
KIMETSU NO YAIBA

2

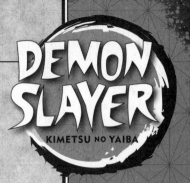

IT WAS YOU

CHAPTER 8: BIG BROTHER

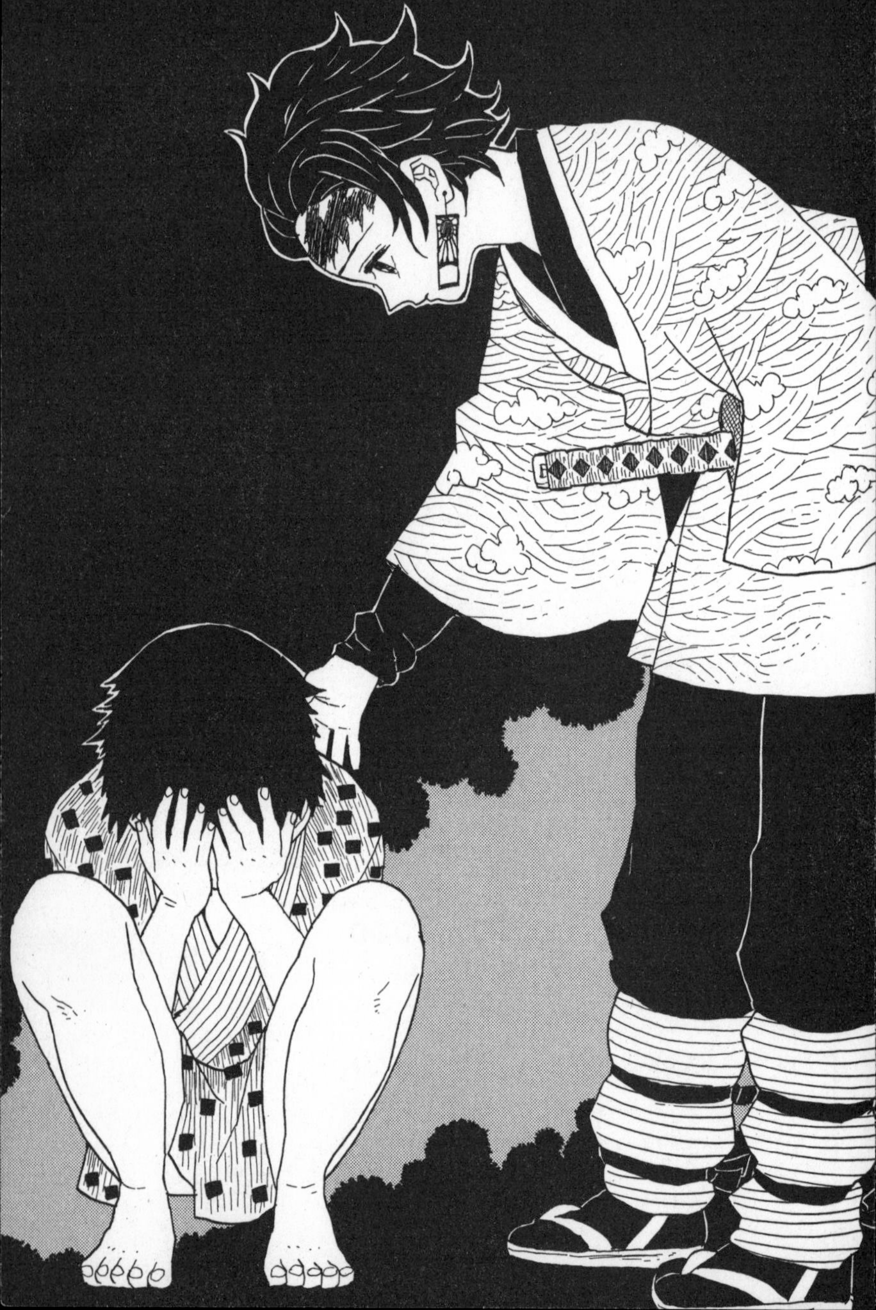

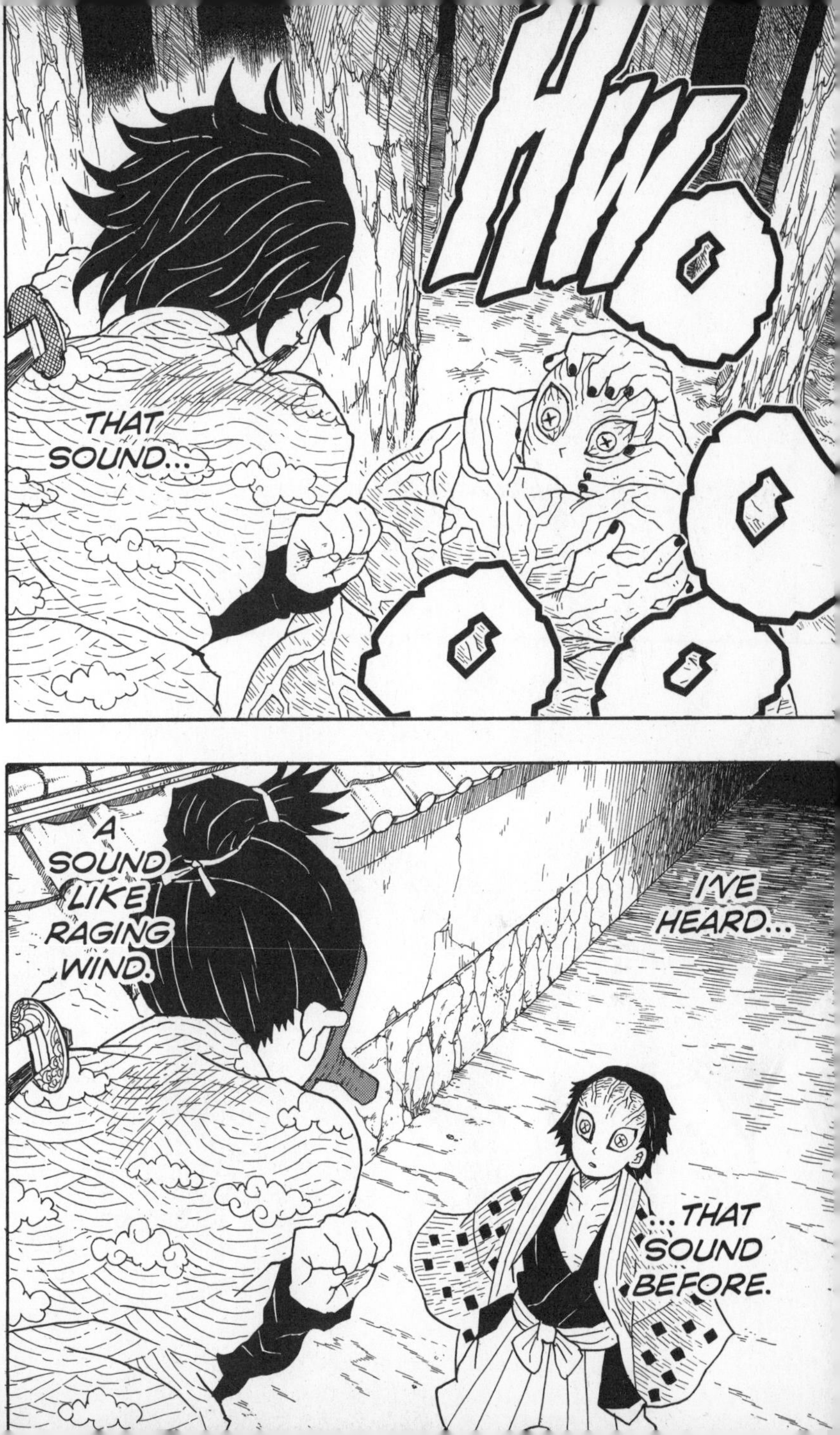
HWOOOO
THAT SOUND...
I'VE HEARD...
...THAT SOUND BEFORE.
A SOUND LIKE RAGING WIND.

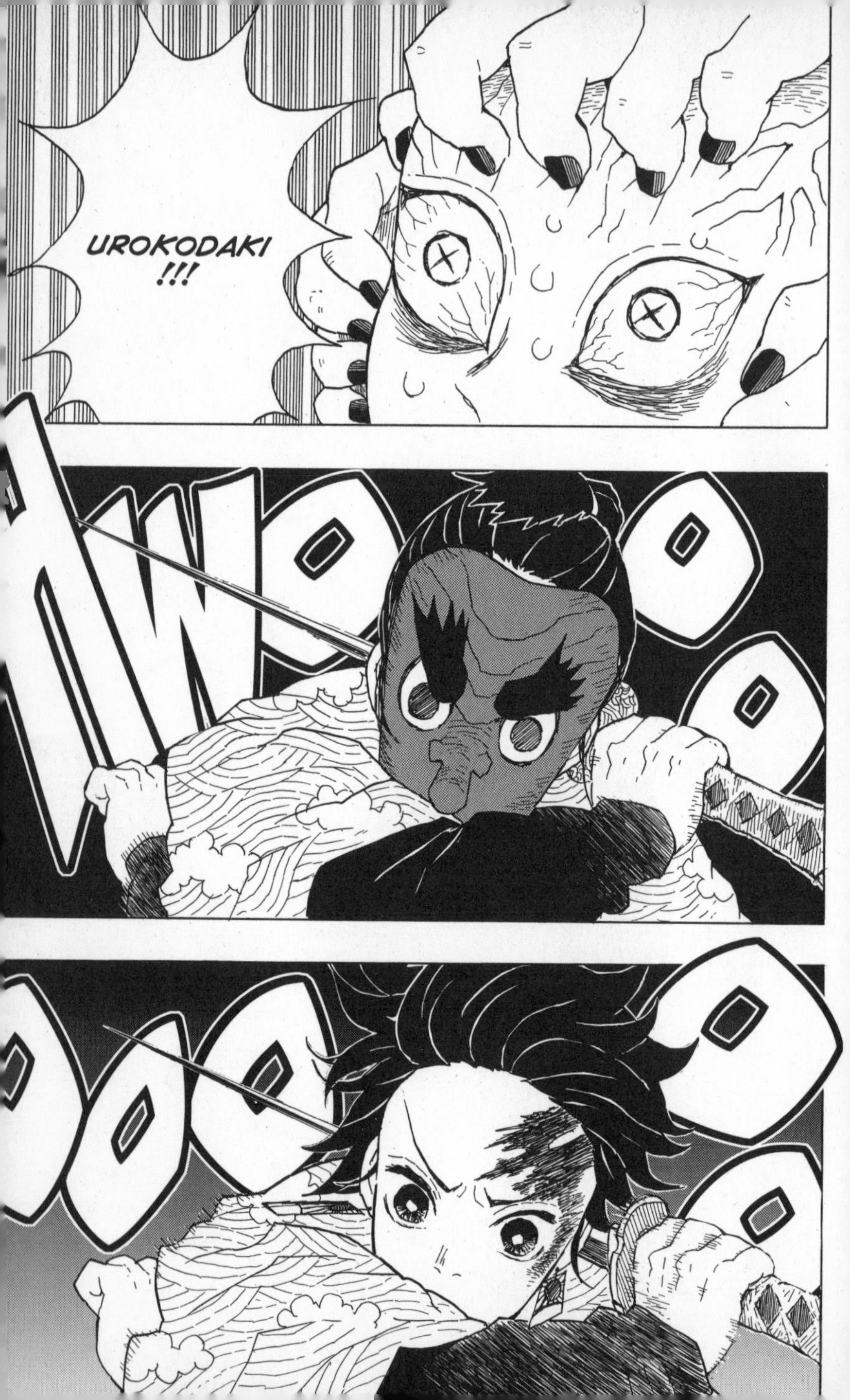
UROKODAKI !!!

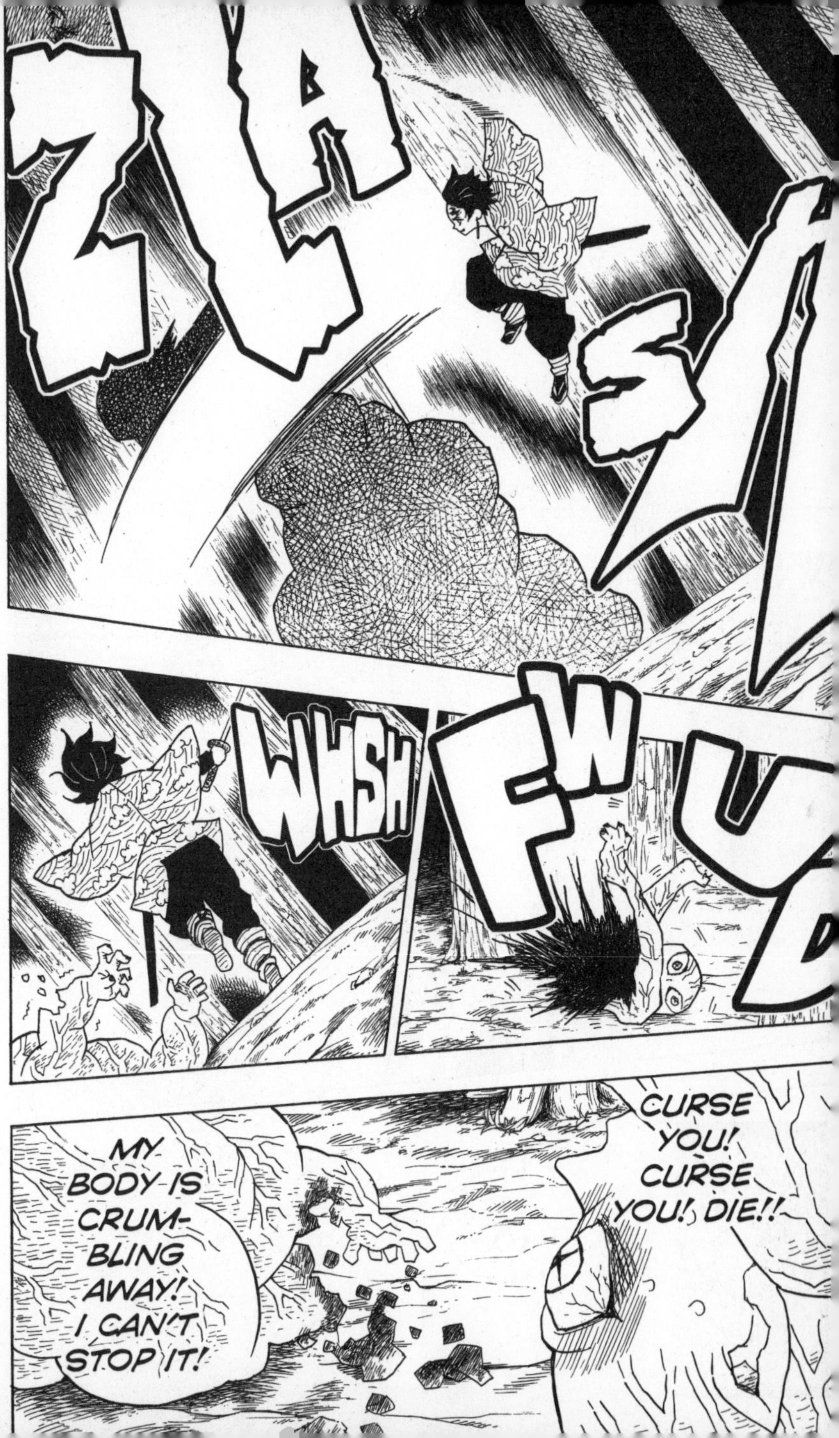
ZA
FWUD
WHSH
CURSE YOU! CURSE YOU! DIE!!
MY BODY IS CRUMBLING AWAY! I CAN'T STOP IT!

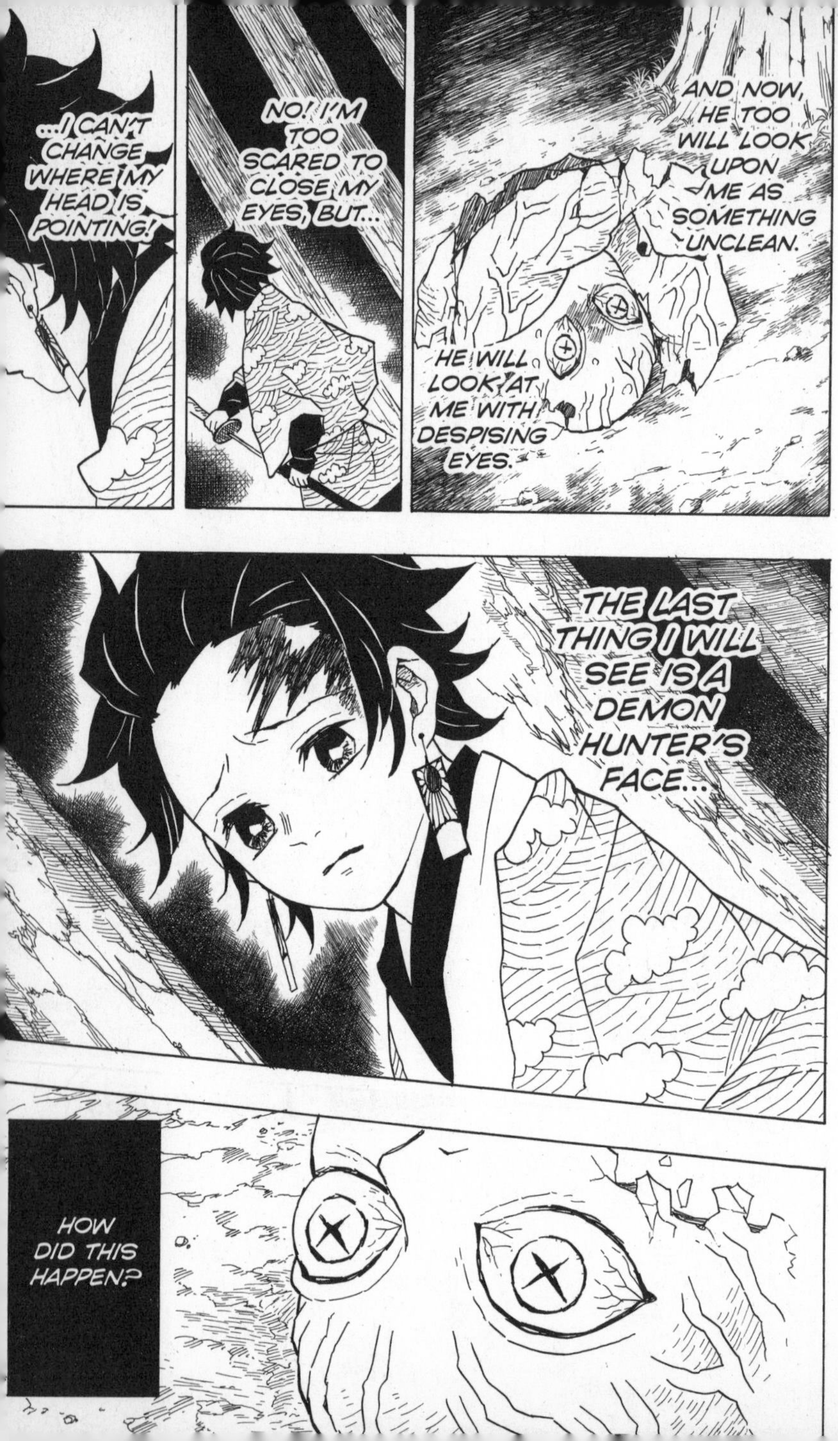
AND NOW, HE TOO WILL LOOK UPON ME AS SOMETHING UNCLEAN.
HE WILL LOOK AT ME WITH DESPISING EYES.
NO! I'M TOO SCARED TO CLOSE MY EYES, BUT...
...I CAN'T CHANGE WHERE MY HEAD IS POINTING!
THE LAST THING I WILL SEE IS A DEMON HUNTER'S FACE...
HOW DID THIS HAPPEN?

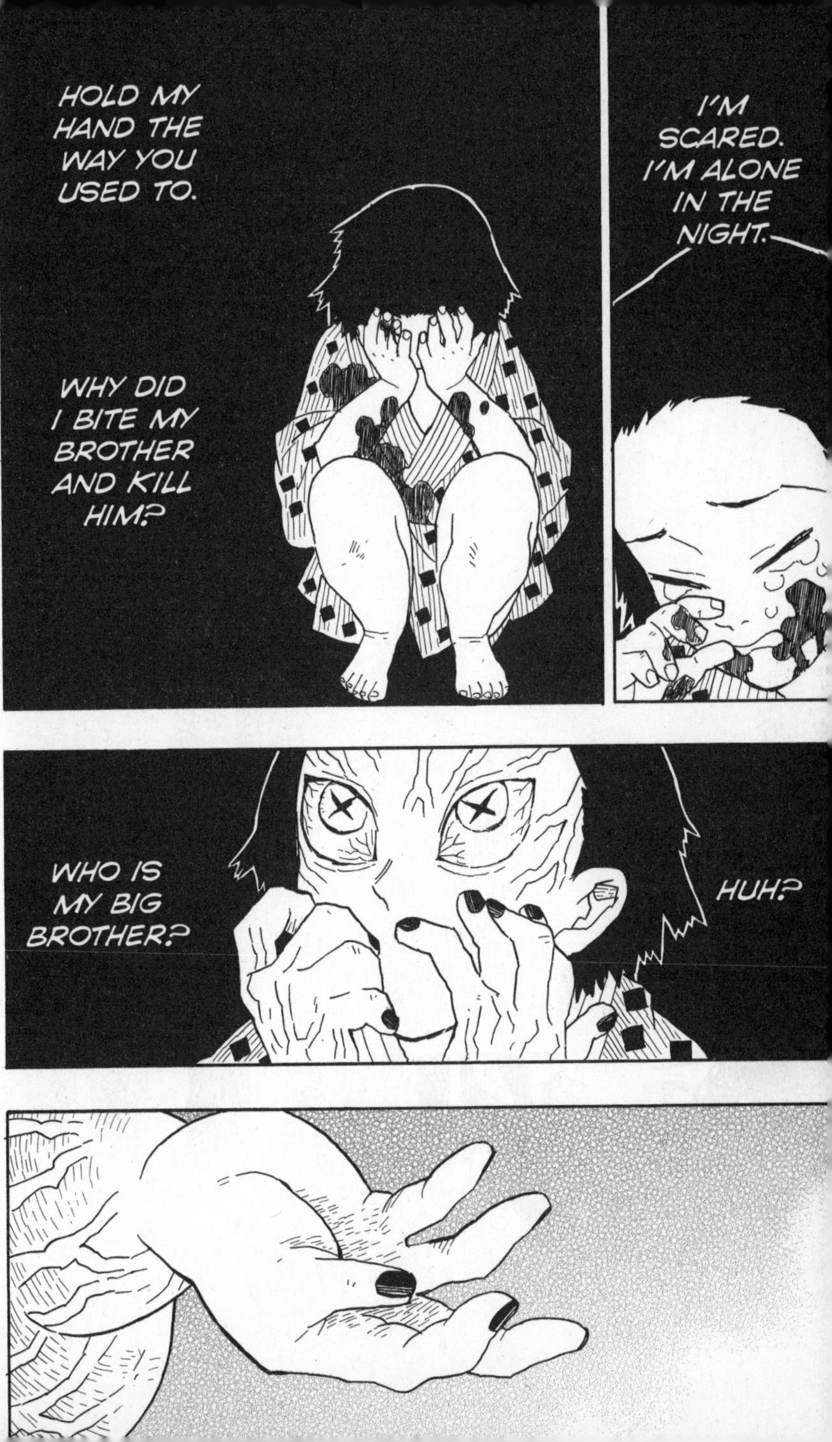
I'M SCARED. I'M ALONE IN THE NIGHT.
HOLD MY HAND THE WAY YOU USED TO.
WHY DID I BITE MY BROTHER AND KILL HIM?
HUH?
WHO IS MY BIG BROTHER?

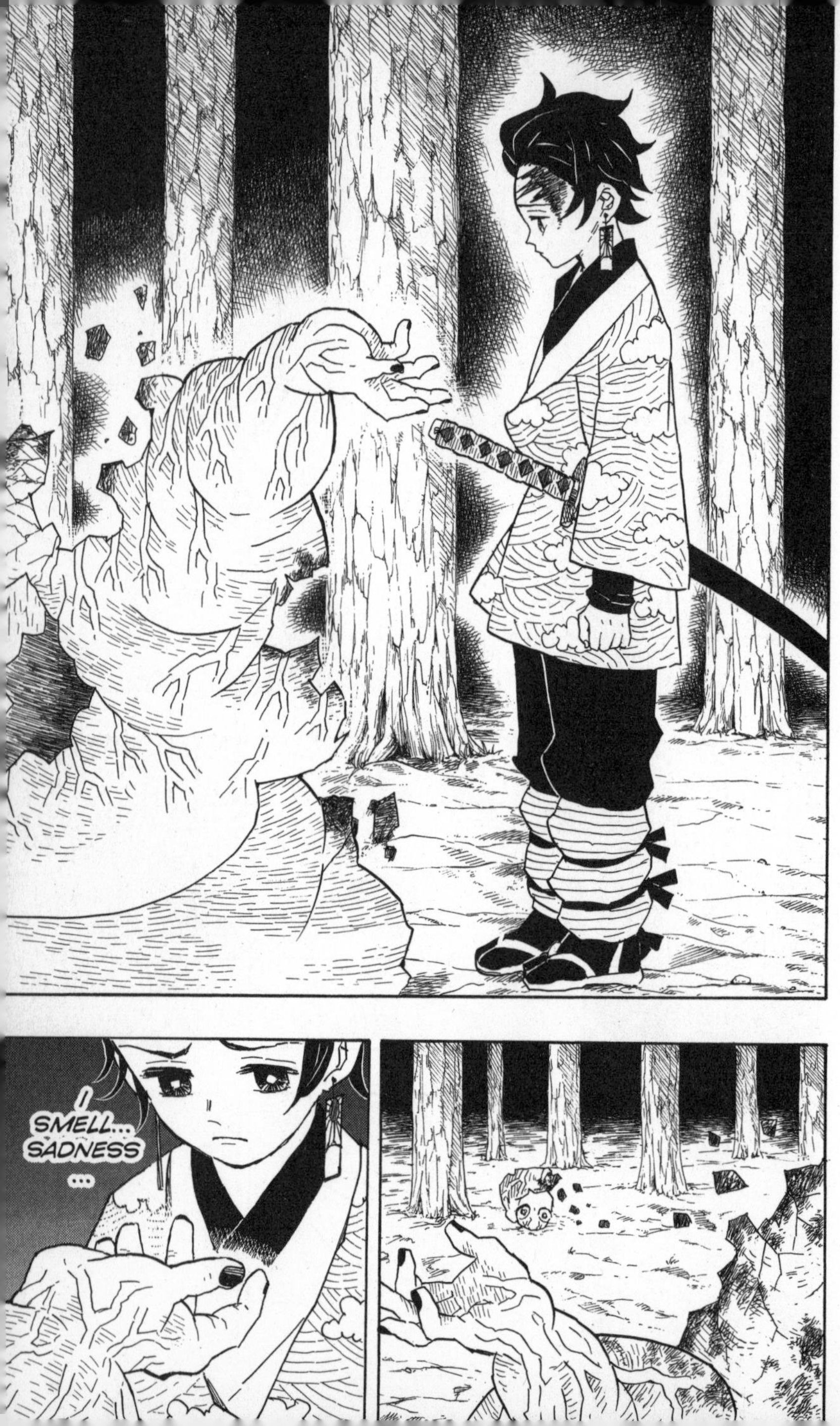
I SMELL... SADNESS ...

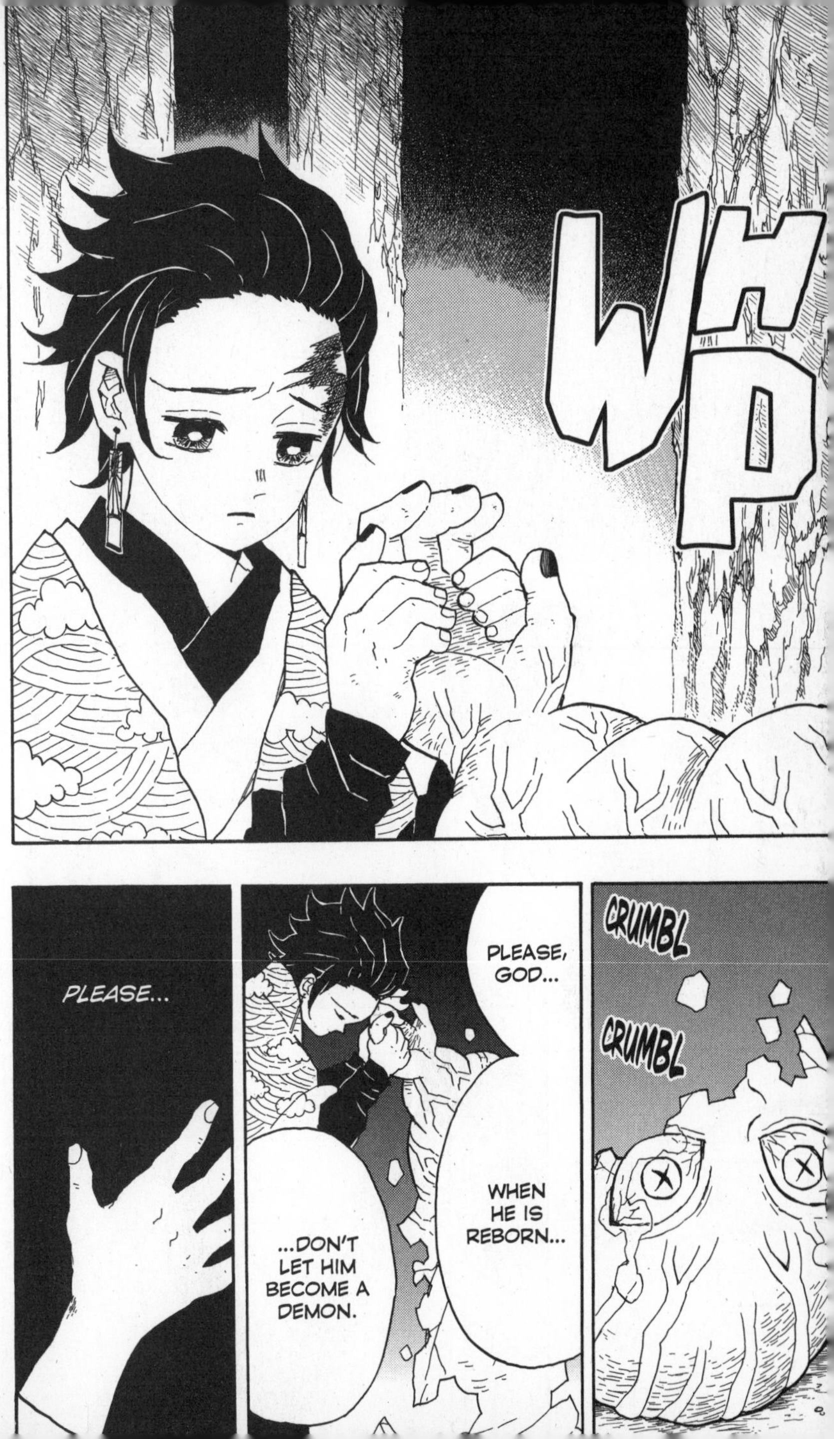
WHP
CRUMBL
CRUMBL
PLEASE, GOD...
WHEN HE IS REBORN...
...DON'T LET HIM BECOME A DEMON.
PLEASE...

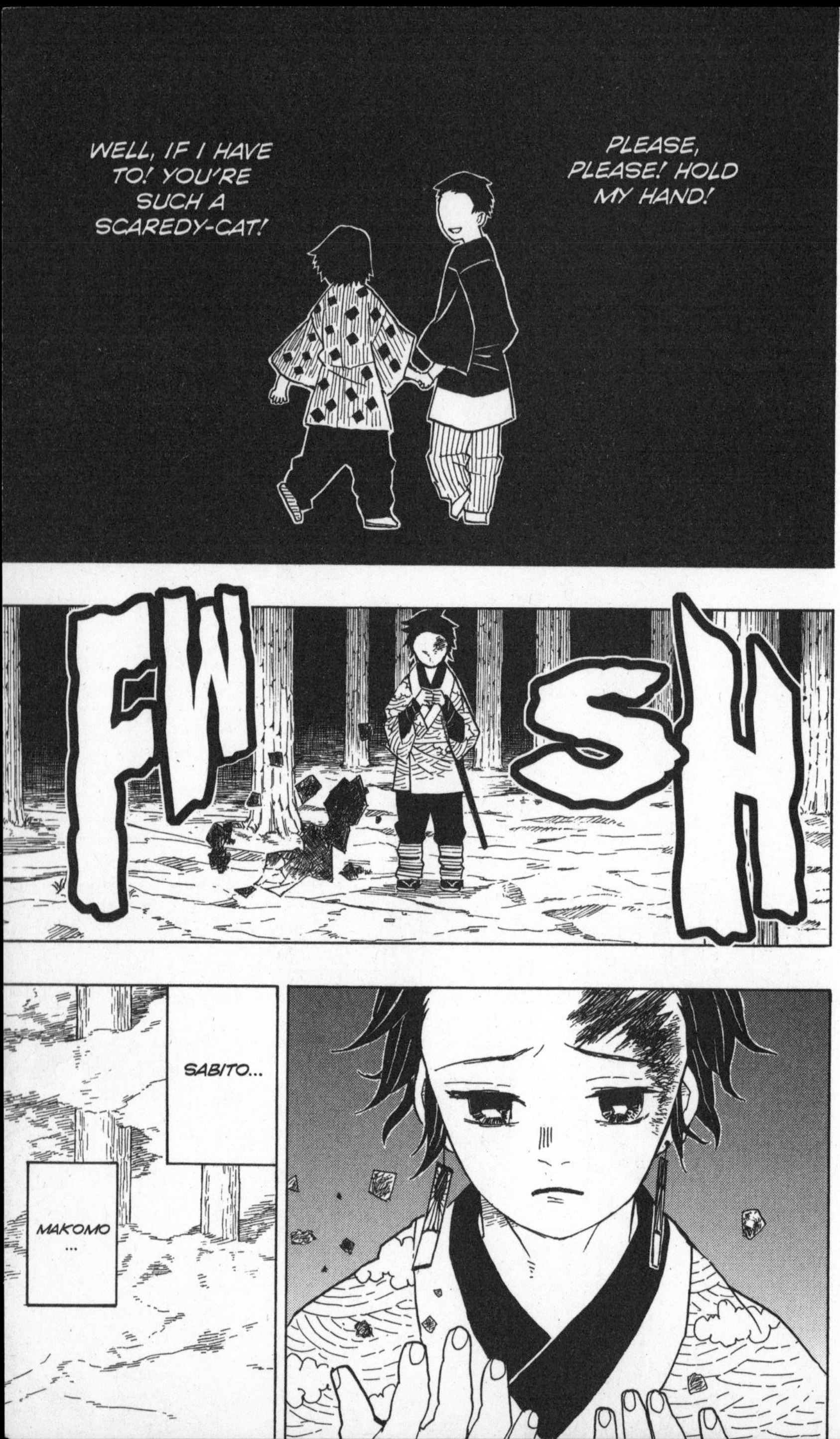
PLEASE, PLEASE! HOLD MY HAND!
WELL, IF I HAVE TO! YOU'RE SUCH A SCAREDY-CAT!
FWSH
SABITO...
MAKOMO ...

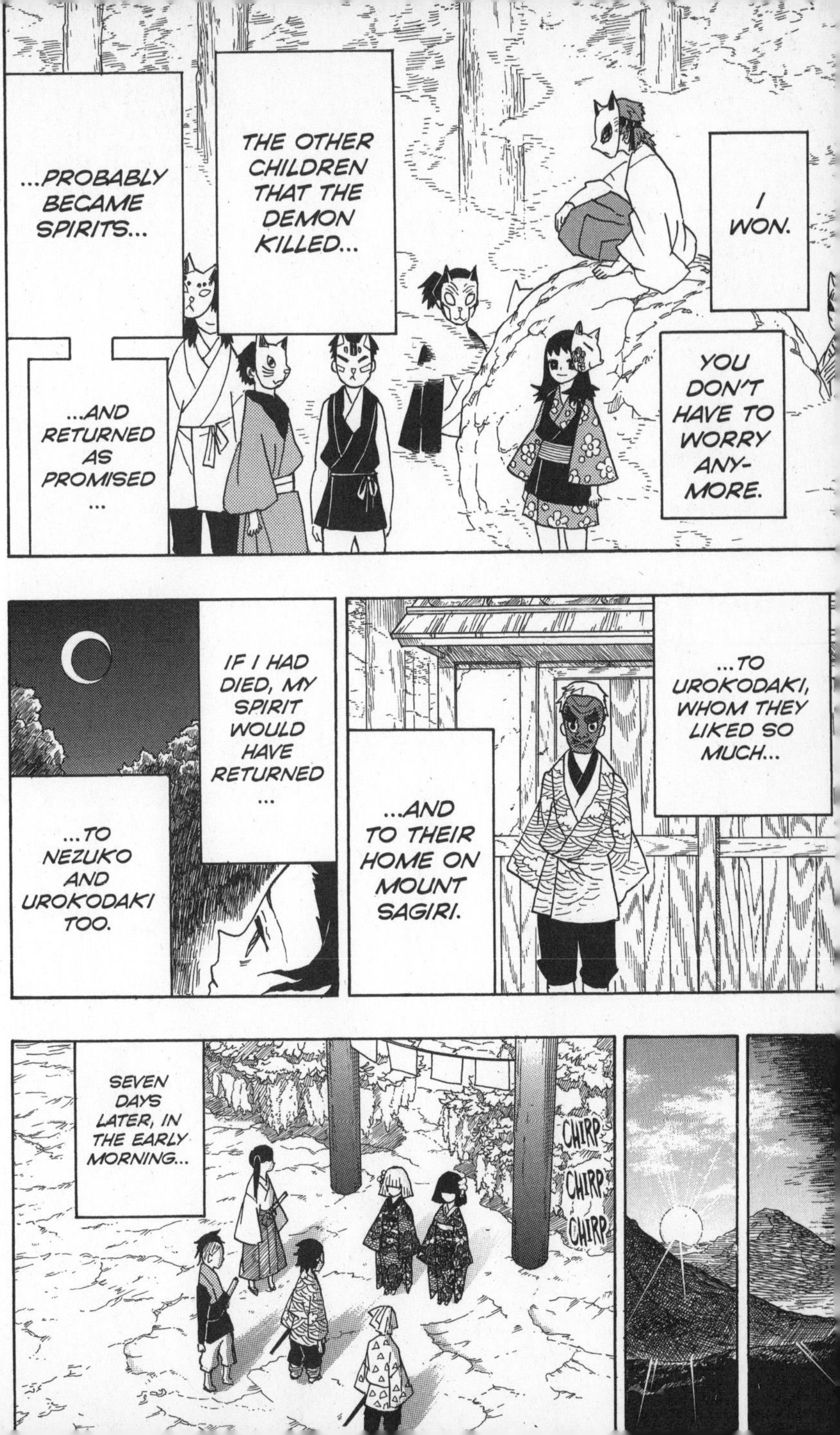
I WON.
YOU DON'T HAVE TO WORRY ANY-MORE.
THE OTHER CHILDREN THAT THE DEMON KILLED...
...PROBABLY BECAME SPIRITS...
...AND RETURNED AS PROMISED...
...TO UROKODAKI, WHOM THEY LIKED SO MUCH...
...AND TO THEIR HOME ON MOUNT SAGIRI.
IF I HAD DIED, MY SPIRIT WOULD HAVE RETURNED...
...TO NEZUKO AND UROKODAKI TOO.
SEVEN DAYS LATER, IN THE EARLY MORNING...
CHIRP
CHIRP
CHIRP

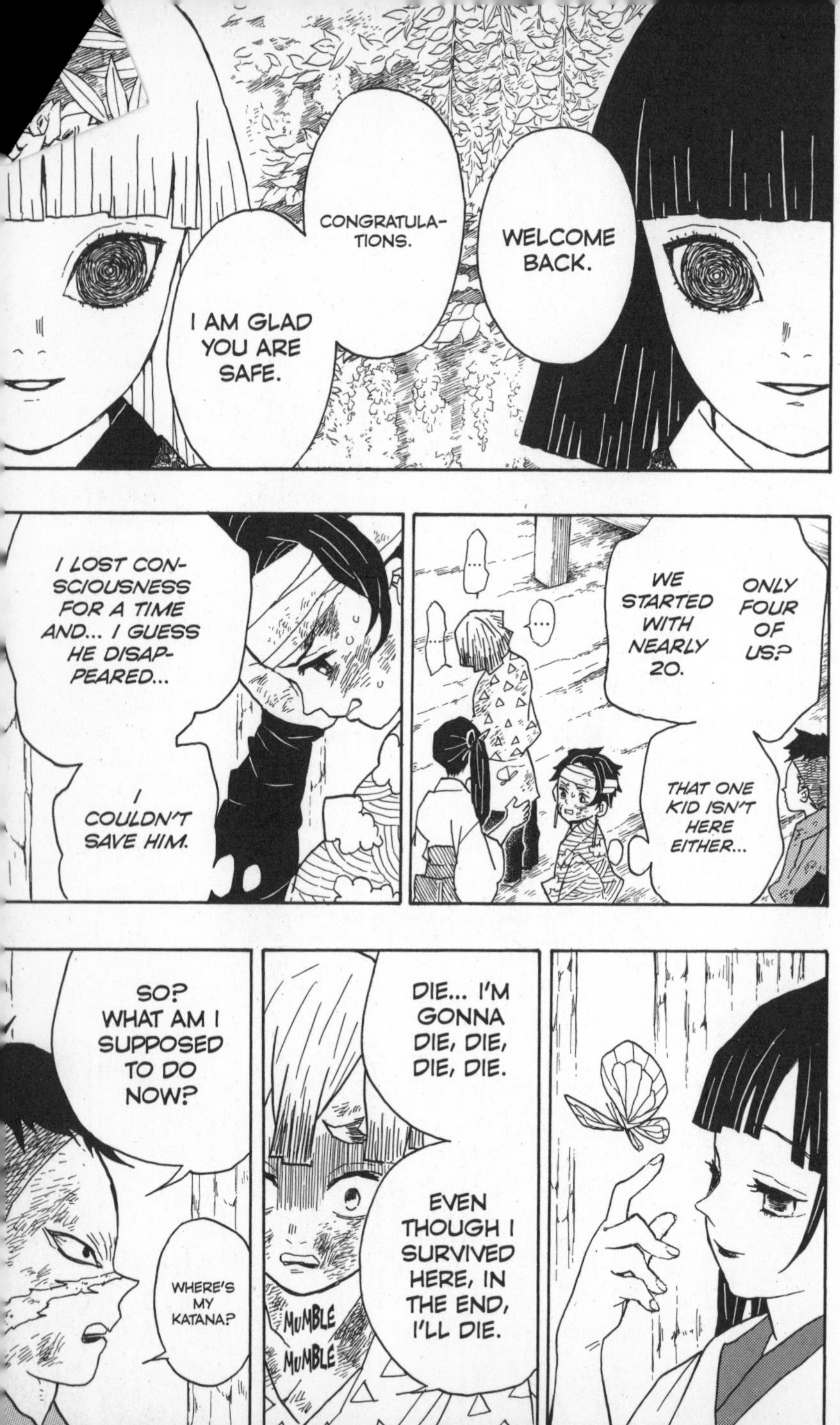
WELCOME BACK.
CONGRATULATIONS.
I AM GLAD YOU ARE SAFE.
ONLY FOUR OF US?
WE STARTED WITH NEARLY 20.
....
...
....
THAT ONE KID ISN'T HERE EITHER...
I LOST CONSCIOUSNESS FOR A TIME AND... I GUESS HE DISAPPEARED...
I COULDN'T SAVE HIM.
DIE... I'M GONNA DIE, DIE, DIE, DIE.
EVEN THOUGH I SURVIVED HERE, IN THE END, I'LL DIE.
MUMBLE
MUMBLE
SO? WHAT AM I SUPPOSED TO DO NOW?
WHERE'S MY KATANA?

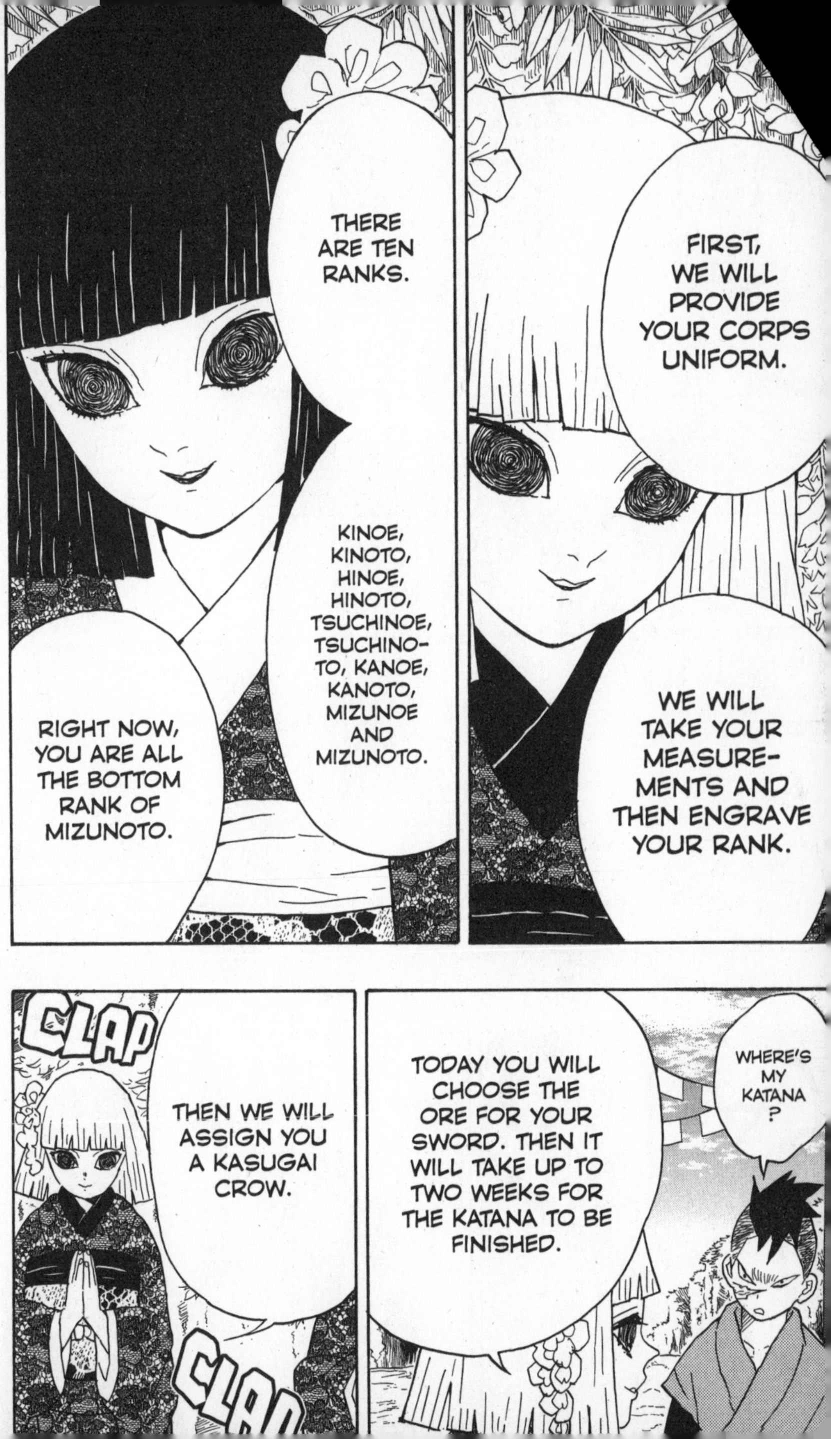
FIRST, WE WILL PROVIDE YOUR CORPS UNIFORM.
WE WILL TAKE YOUR MEASUREMENTS AND THEN ENGRAVE YOUR RANK.
THERE ARE TEN RANKS.
KINOE, KINOTO, HINOE, HINOTO, TSUCHINOE, TSUCHINOTO, KANOE, KANOTO, MIZUNOE AND MIZUNOTO.
RIGHT NOW, YOU ARE ALL THE BOTTOM RANK OF MIZUNOTO.
WHERE'S MY KATANA?
TODAY YOU WILL CHOOSE THE ORE FOR YOUR SWORD. THEN IT WILL TAKE UP TO TWO WEEKS FOR THE KATANA TO BE FINISHED.
CLAP
THEN WE WILL ASSIGN YOU A KASUGAI CROW.

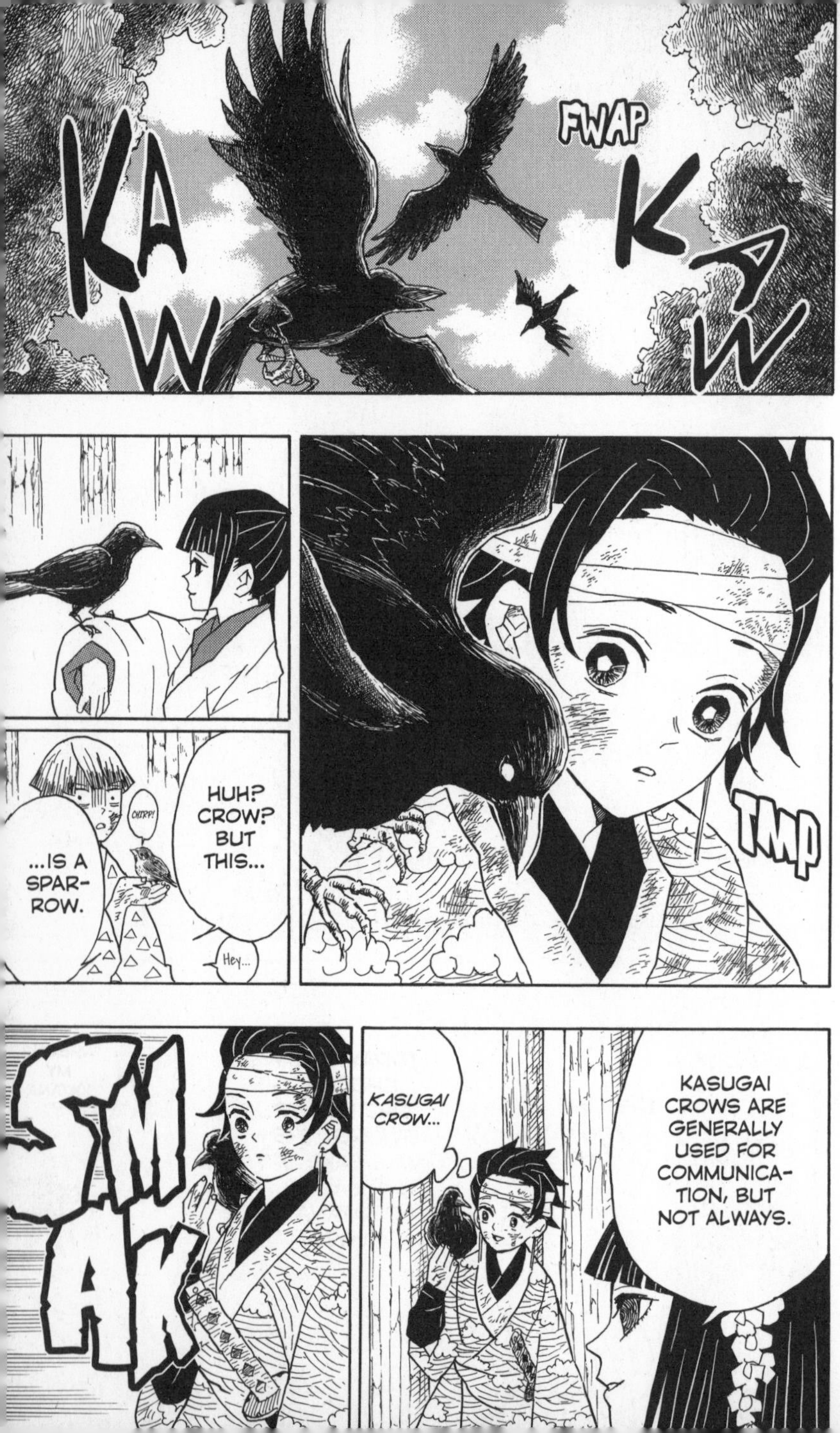
FWAP
KAW
KAW
TMP
HUH? CROW? BUT THIS...
CHIRP!
...IS A SPARROW.
Hey...
KASUGAI CROWS ARE GENERALLY USED FOR COMMUNICATION, BUT NOT ALWAYS.
KASUGAI CROW...
SMAK

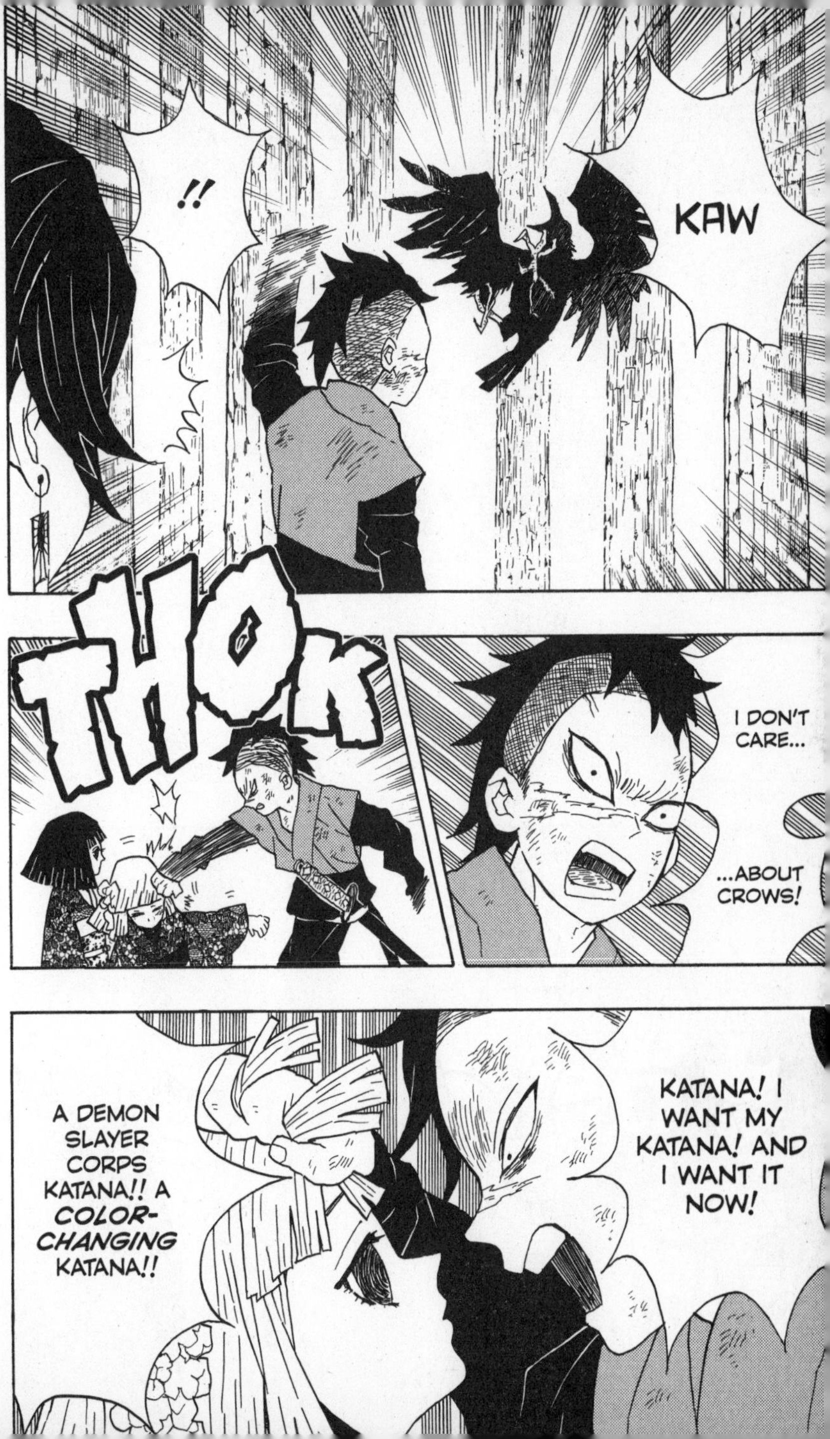
KAW
!!
I DON'T CARE...
...ABOUT CROWS!
THOK
KATANA! I WANT MY KATANA! AND I WANT IT NOW!
A DEMON SLAYER CORPS KATANA!! A *COLOR-CHANGING* KATANA!!

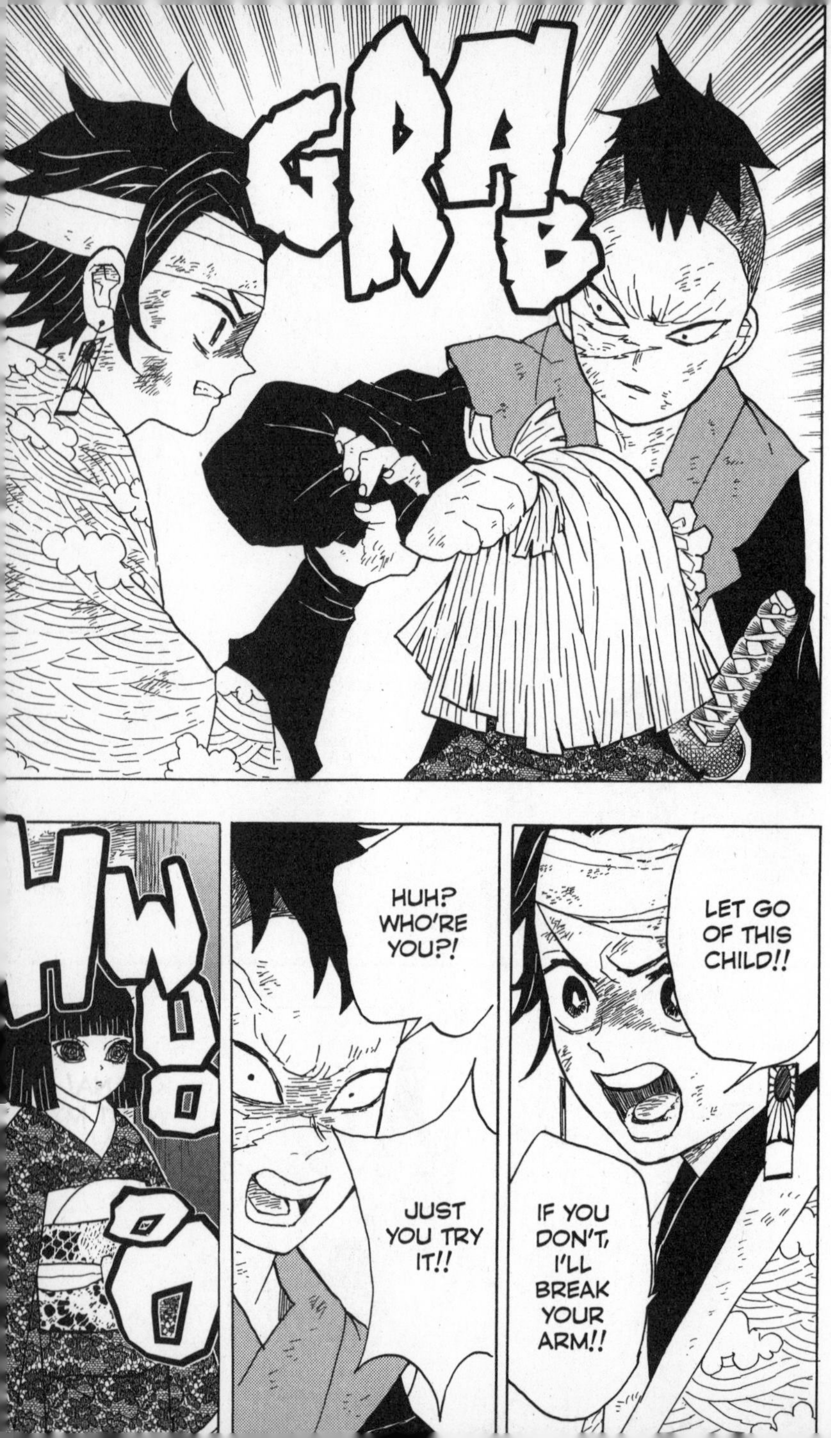
GRAB
LET GO OF THIS CHILD!!
IF YOU DON'T, I'LL BREAK YOUR ARM!!
HUH? WHO'RE YOU?!
JUST YOU TRY IT!!
HWOOOO

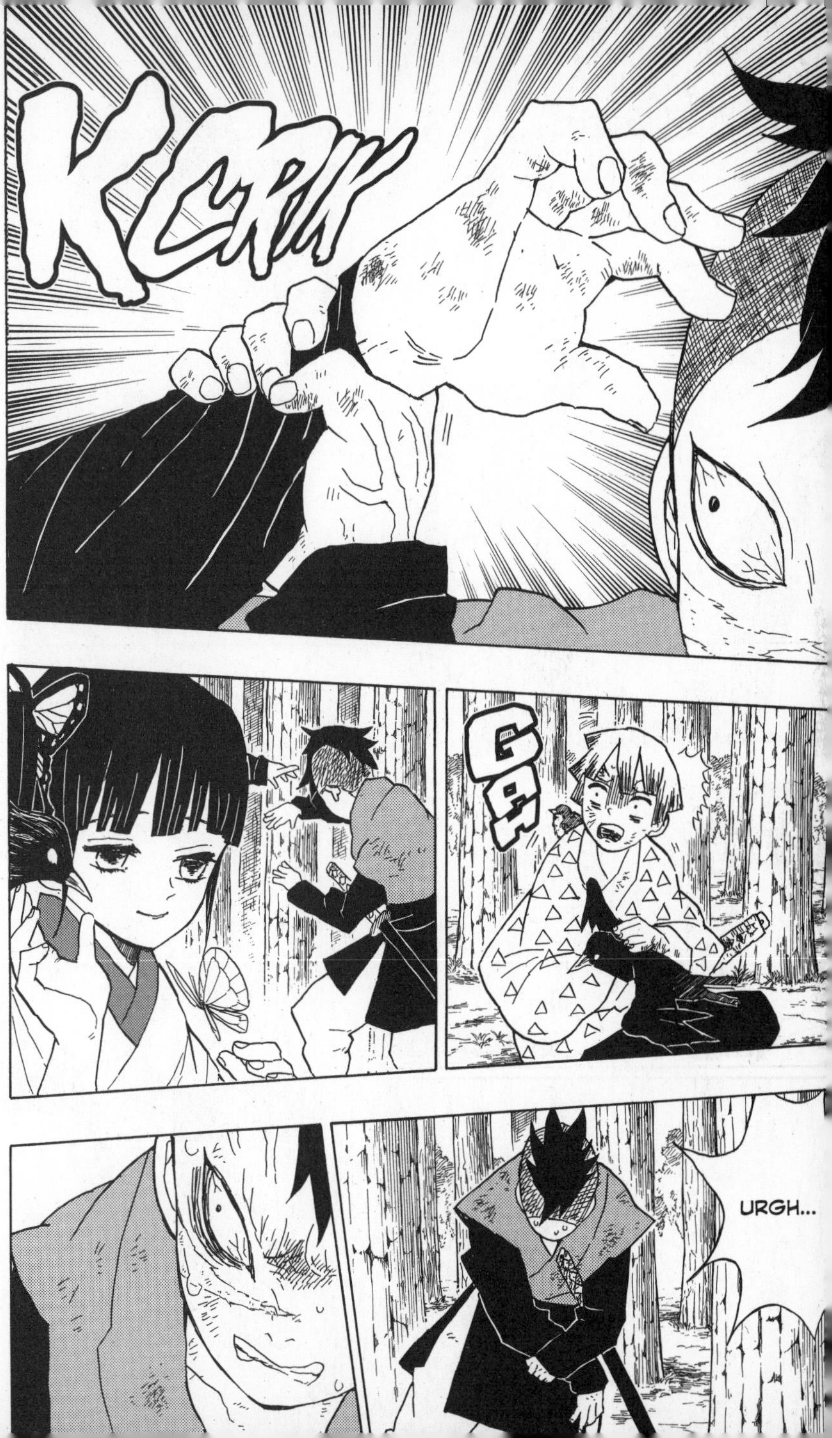
KCRIK
GASP
URGH...

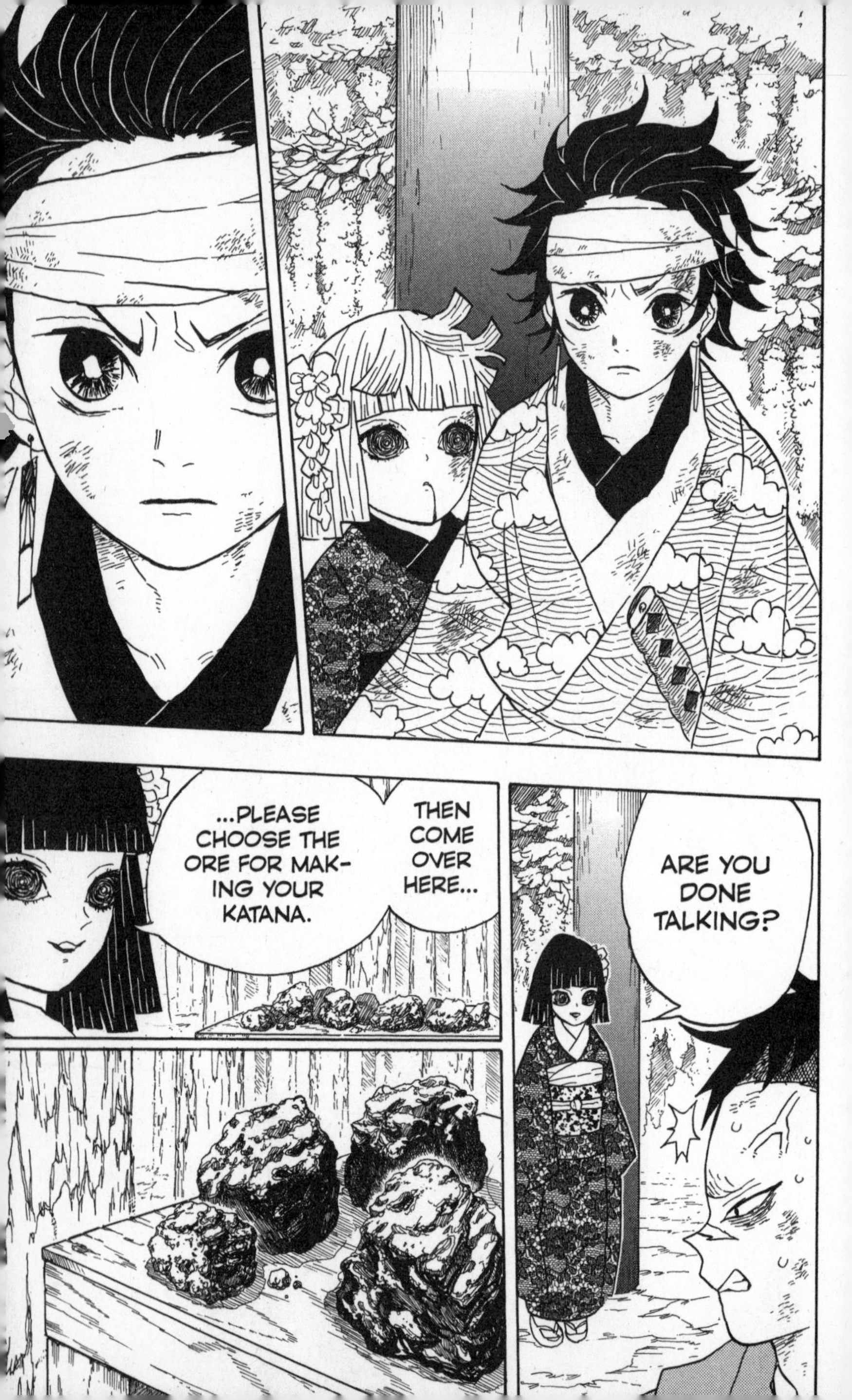
ARE YOU DONE TALKING?
THEN COME OVER HERE...
...PLEASE CHOOSE THE ORE FOR MAK-ING YOUR KATANA.

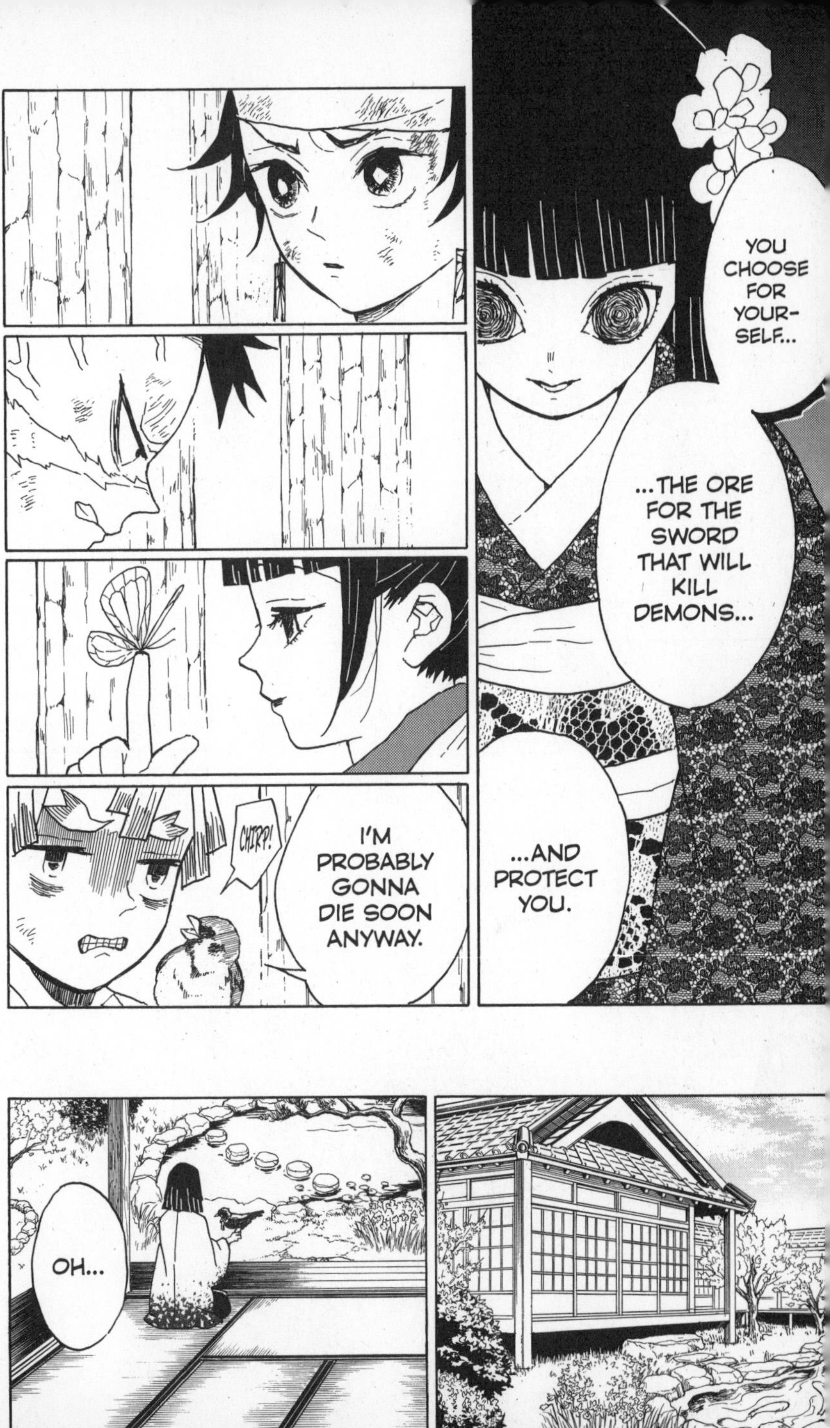
YOU CHOOSE FOR YOURSELF...
...THE ORE FOR THE SWORD THAT WILL KILL DEMONS...
...AND PROTECT YOU.
I'M PROBABLY GONNA DIE SOON ANYWAY.
CHIRP!
OH...

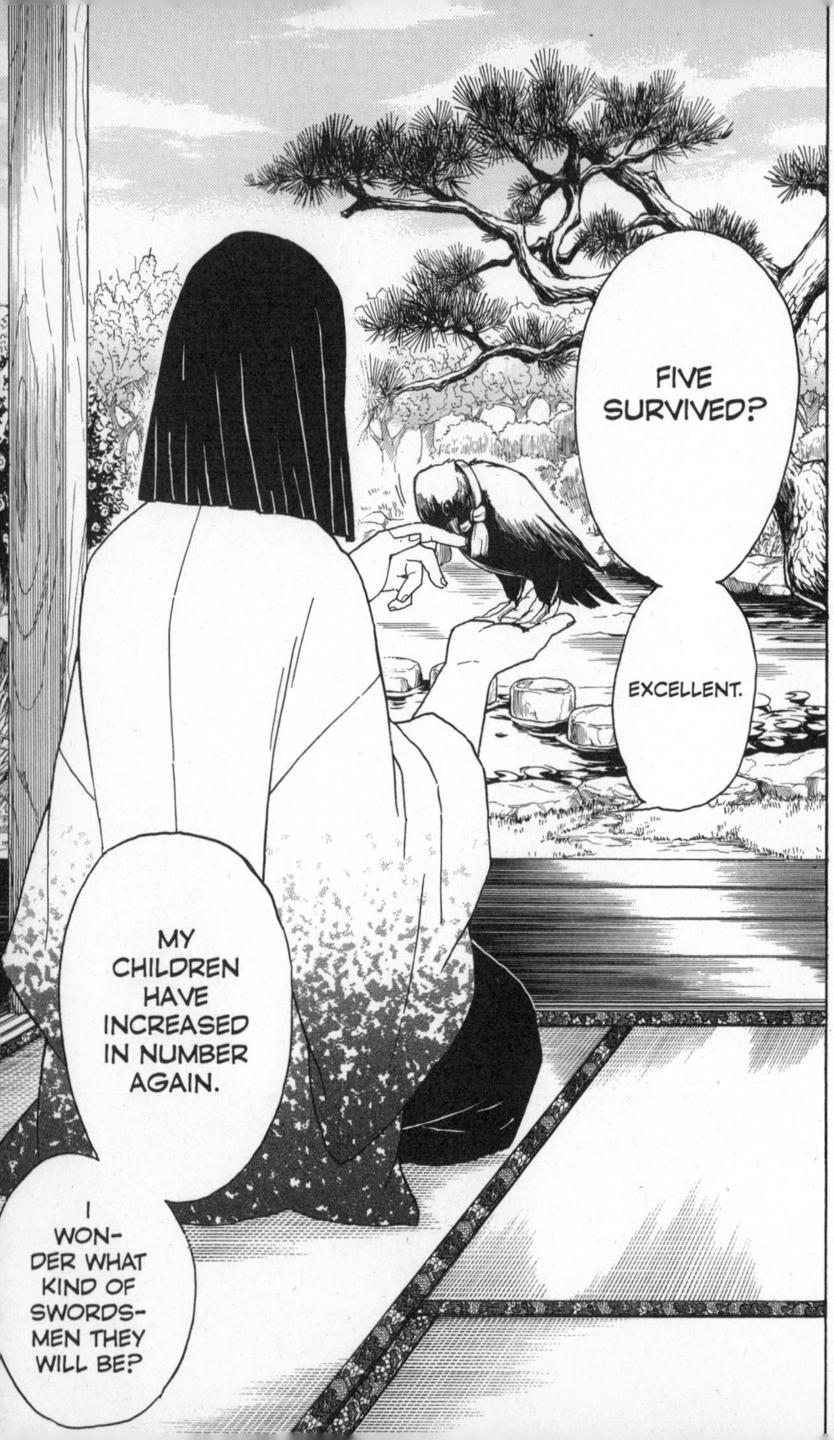
FIVE SURVIVED?
EXCELLENT.
MY CHILDREN HAVE INCREASED IN NUMBER AGAIN.
I WON-DER WHAT KIND OF SWORDS-MEN THEY WILL BE?

ORIGINAL ART FOR USE AS A SURVEY PRIZE
REGIONAL-THEMED ILLUSTRATION
    I. TANJIRO (AS NAMAHAGE, AKITA PREFECTURE)

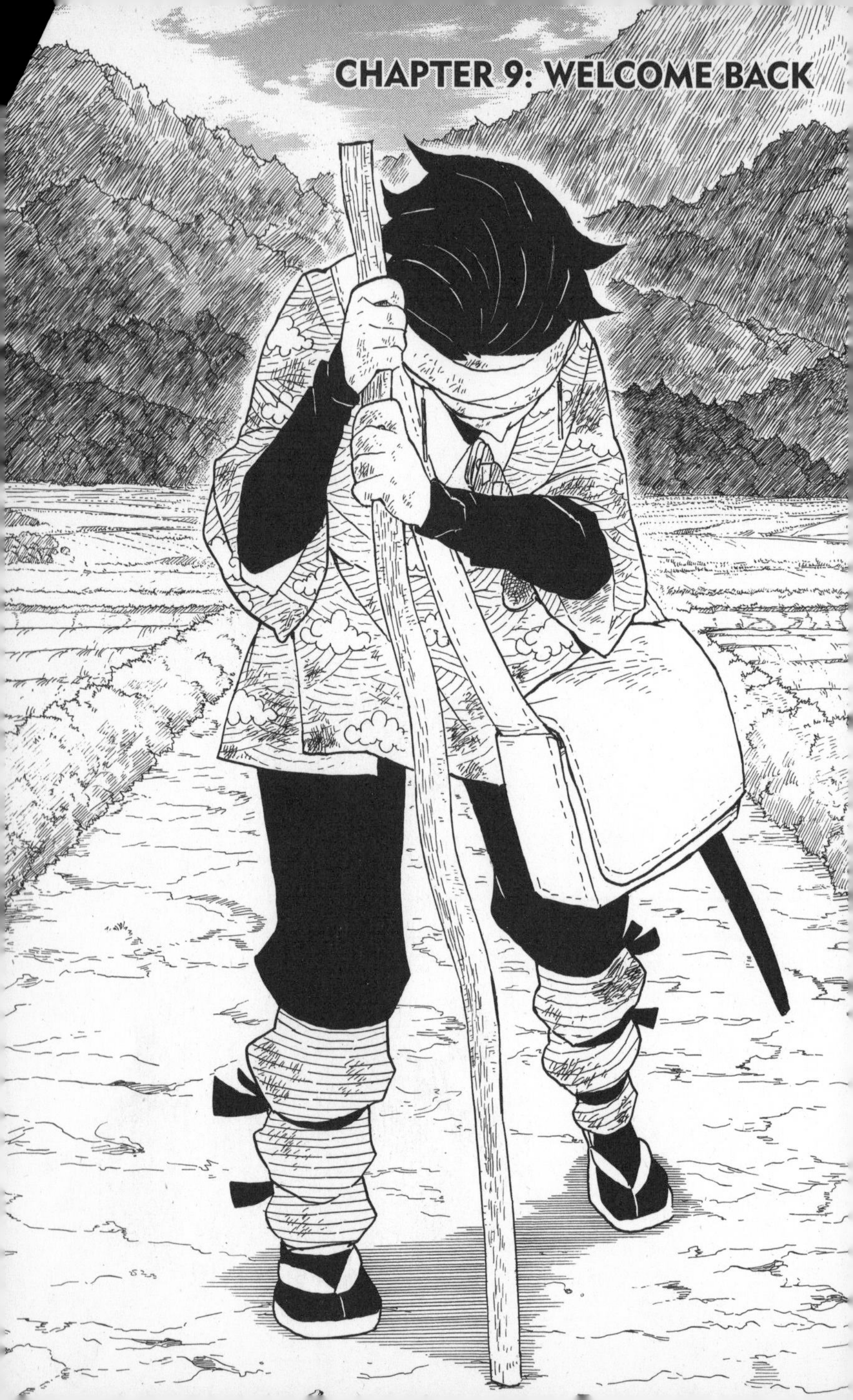
CHAPTER 9: WELCOME BACK

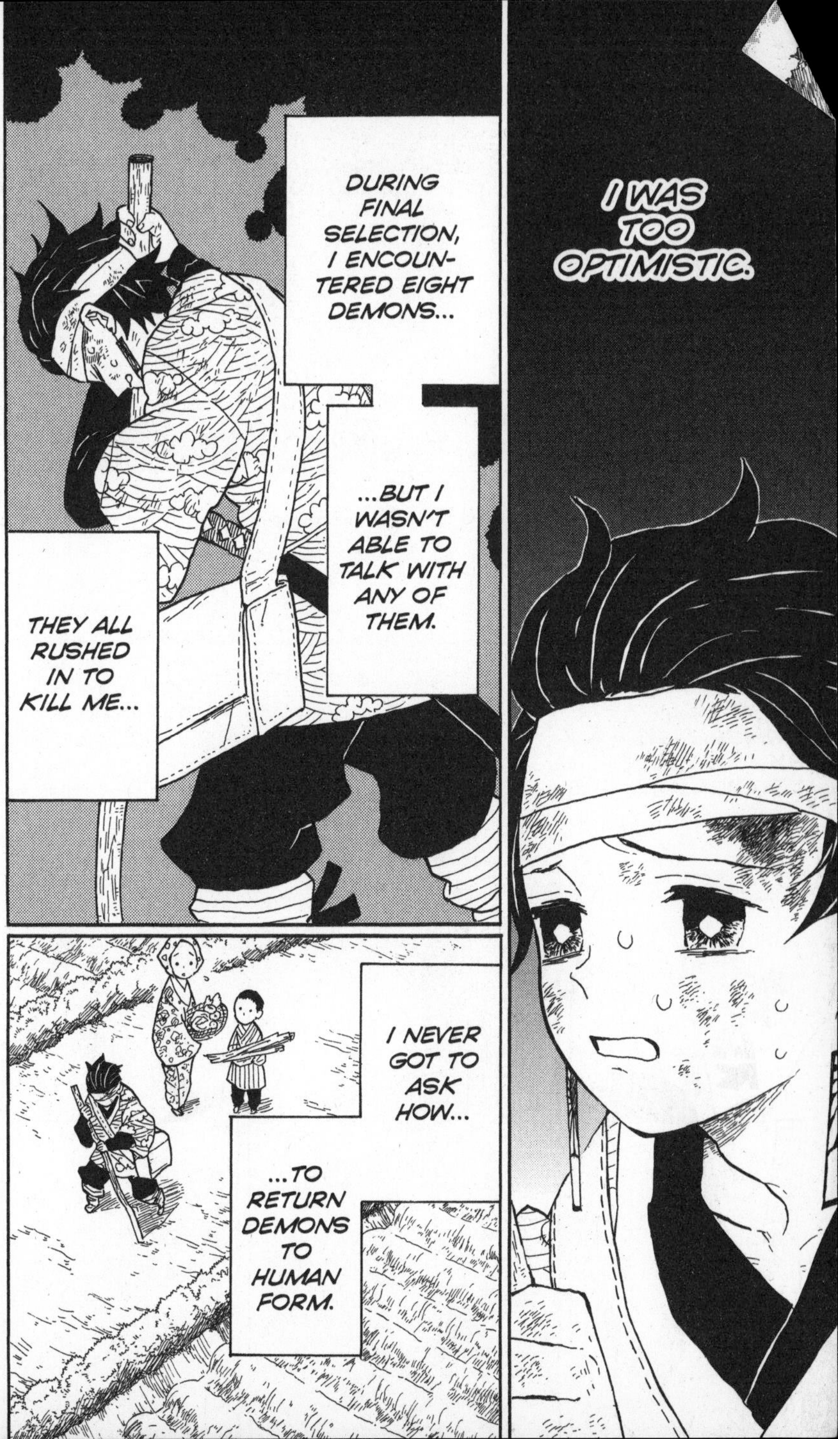
I WAS TOO OPTIMISTIC.
DURING FINAL SELECTION, I ENCOUNTERED EIGHT DEMONS...
...BUT I WASN'T ABLE TO TALK WITH ANY OF THEM.
THEY ALL RUSHED IN TO KILL ME...
I NEVER GOT TO ASK HOW...
...TO RETURN DEMONS TO HUMAN FORM.

I'M SORRY.

I'M SORRY, NEZUKO.

EVER SINCE I STARTED COMING DOWN MOUNT FUJIKASANE, I'VE BEEN OVERWHELMED BY A HORRIBLE EXHAUSTION.

I WANT TO GO BACK AS SOON AS POSSIBLE, BUT MY WHOLE BODY HURTS, SO I CAN'T.

EVEN MY UNIFORM FEELS HEAVY.

KRRRK

UROKO-DAKI... NEZUKO...

I MADE IT.

AH... THE SUN IS ALREADY SETTING.

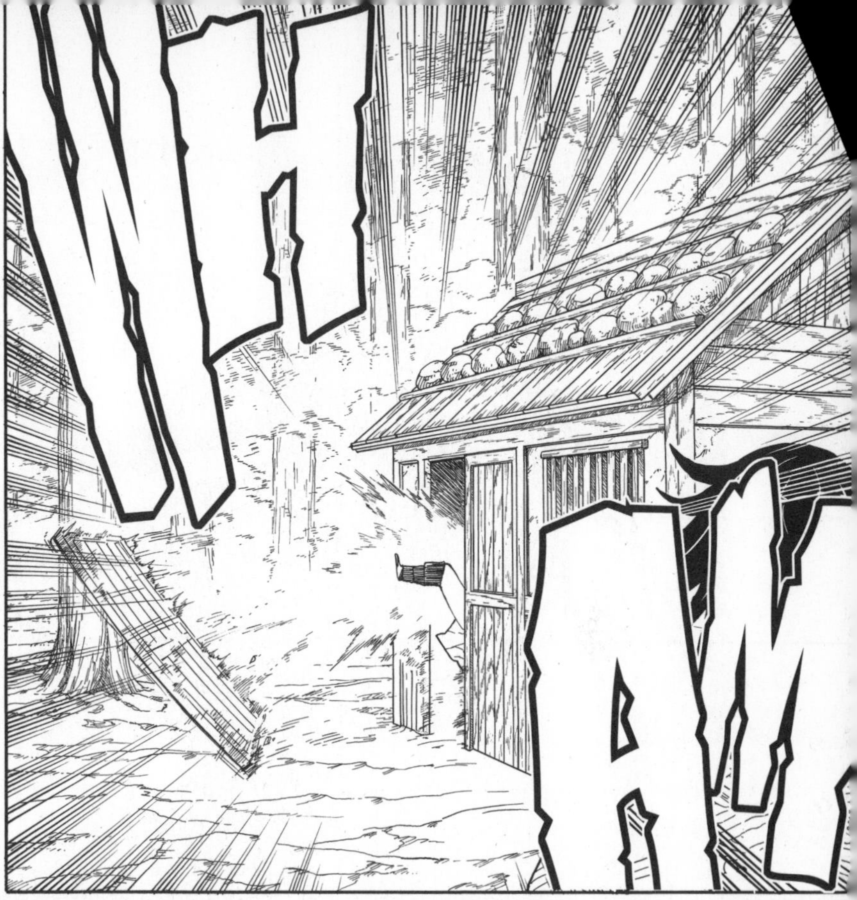
WHAM

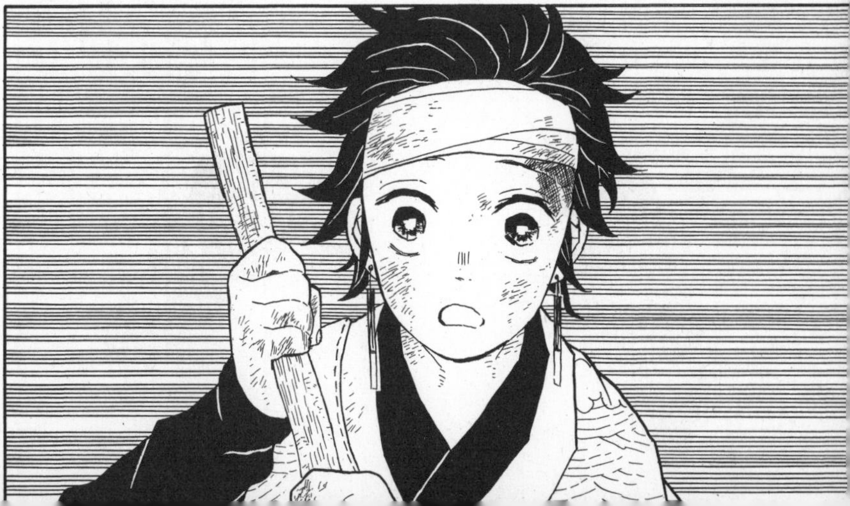

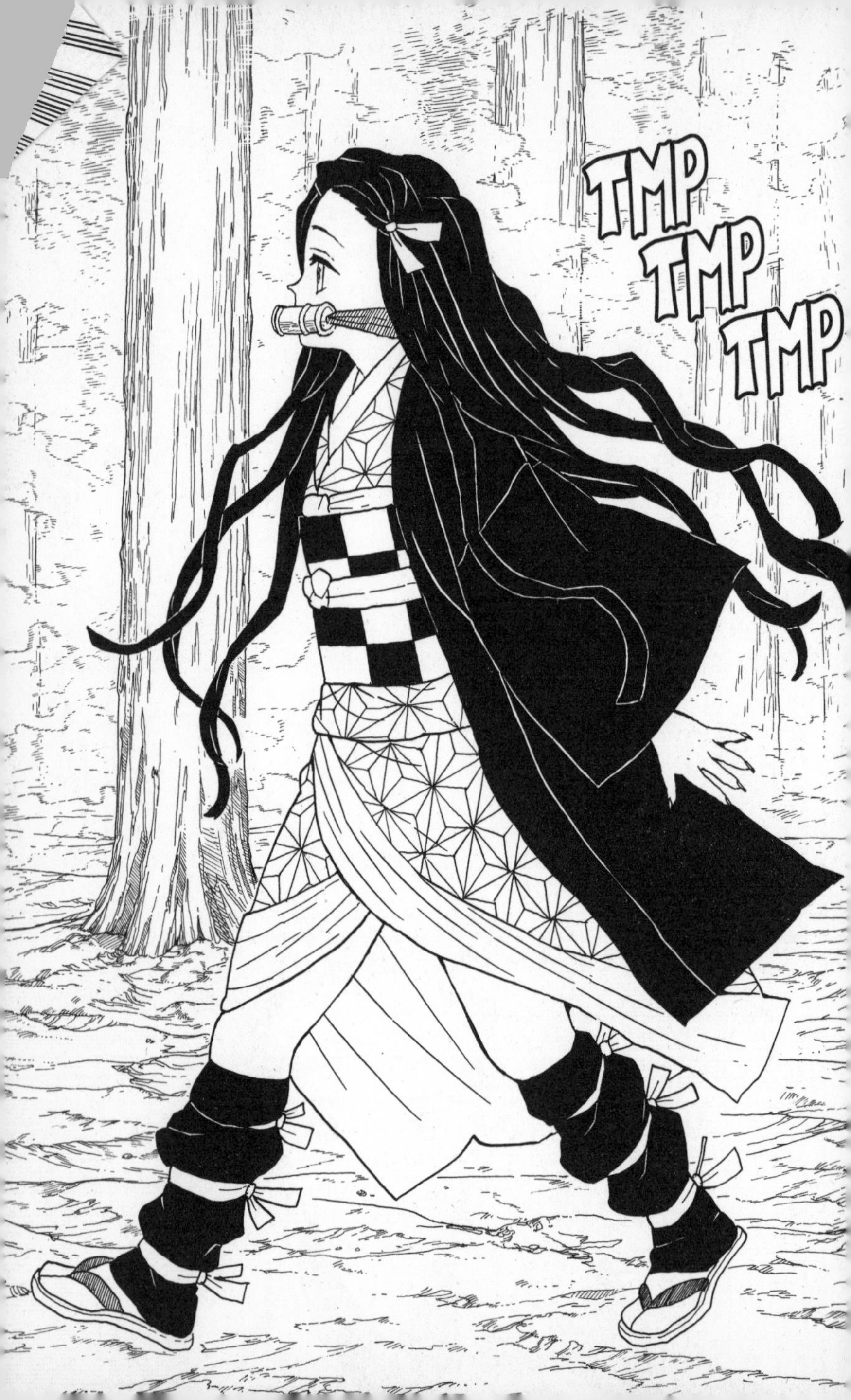
TMP TMP TMP

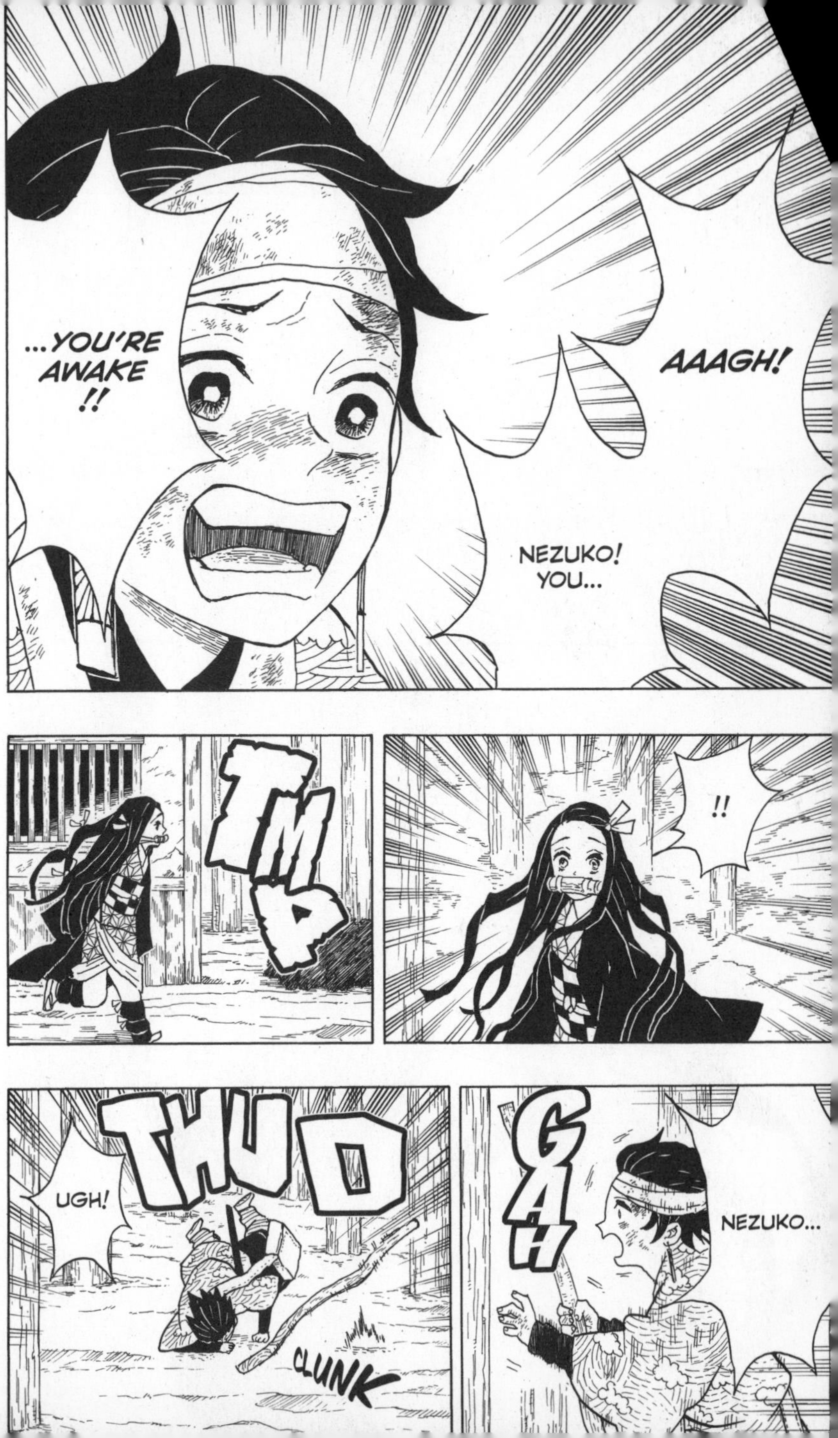
AAAGH!
NEZUKO! YOU...
...YOU'RE AWAKE !!
!!
TMP
NEZUKO...
GAH
THUD
UGH!
CLUNK

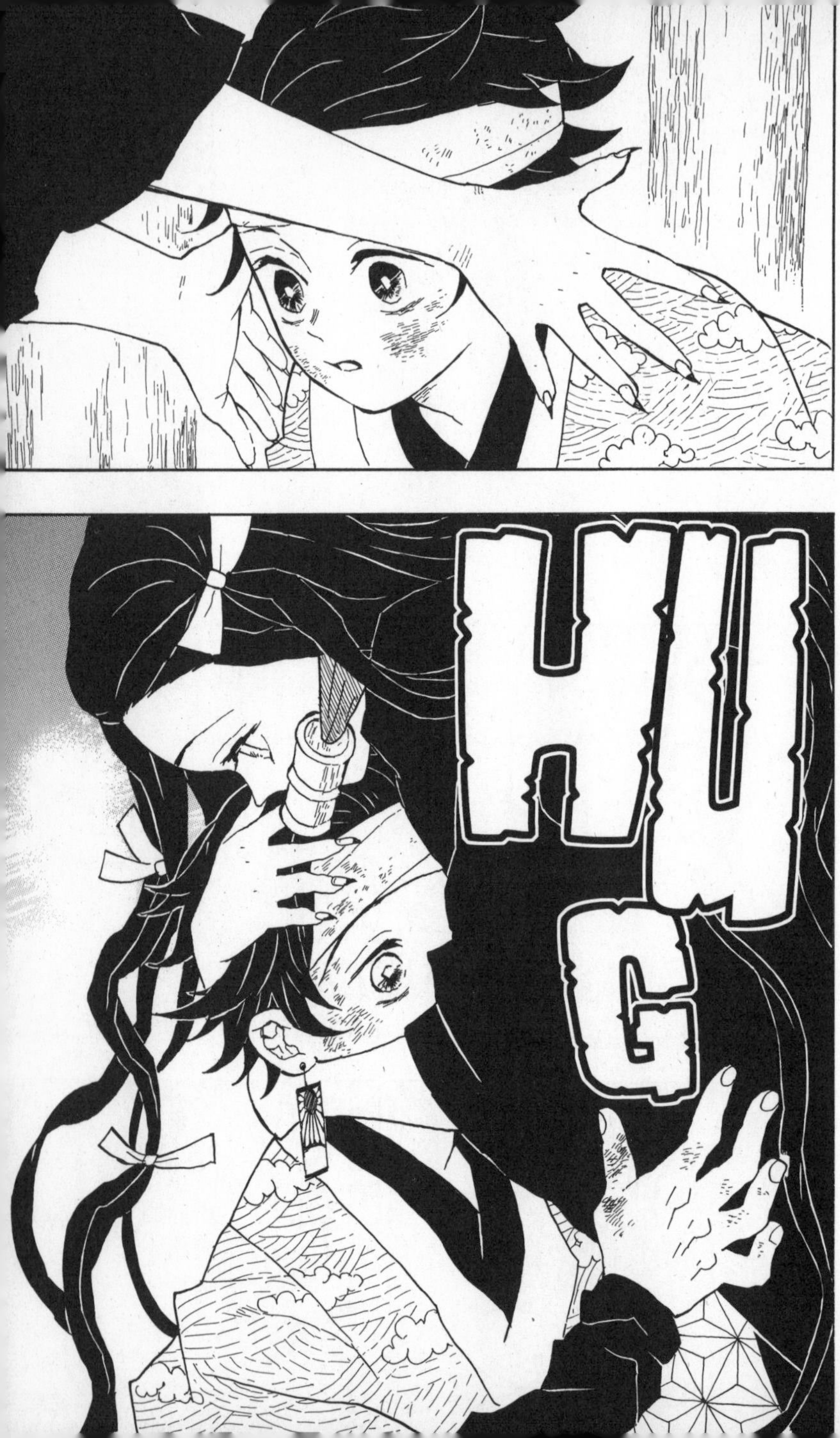
HUG

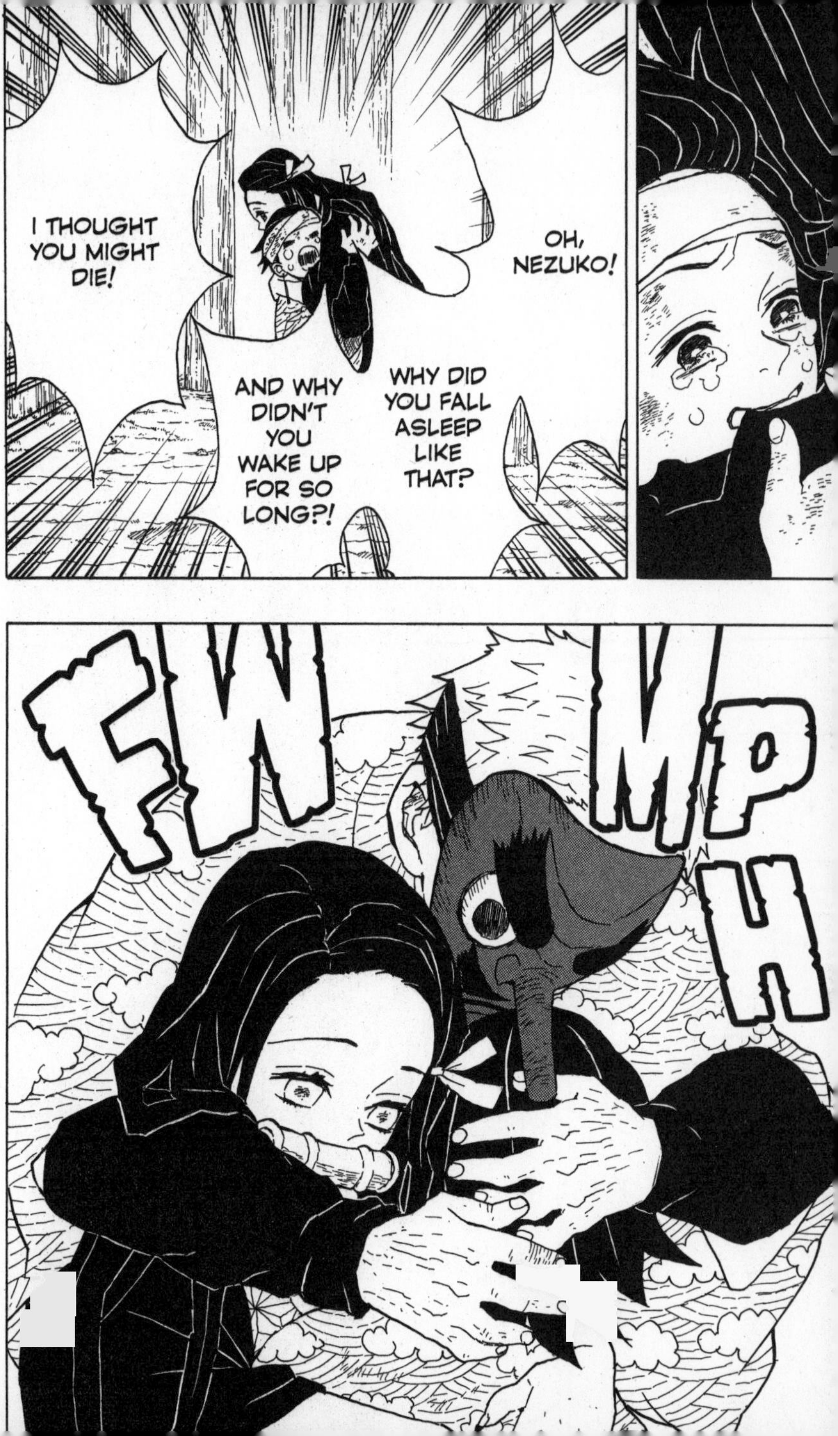
OH, NEZUKO!
WHY DID YOU FALL ASLEEP LIKE THAT?
AND WHY DIDN'T YOU WAKE UP FOR SO LONG?!
I THOUGHT YOU MIGHT DIE!
FWMPH

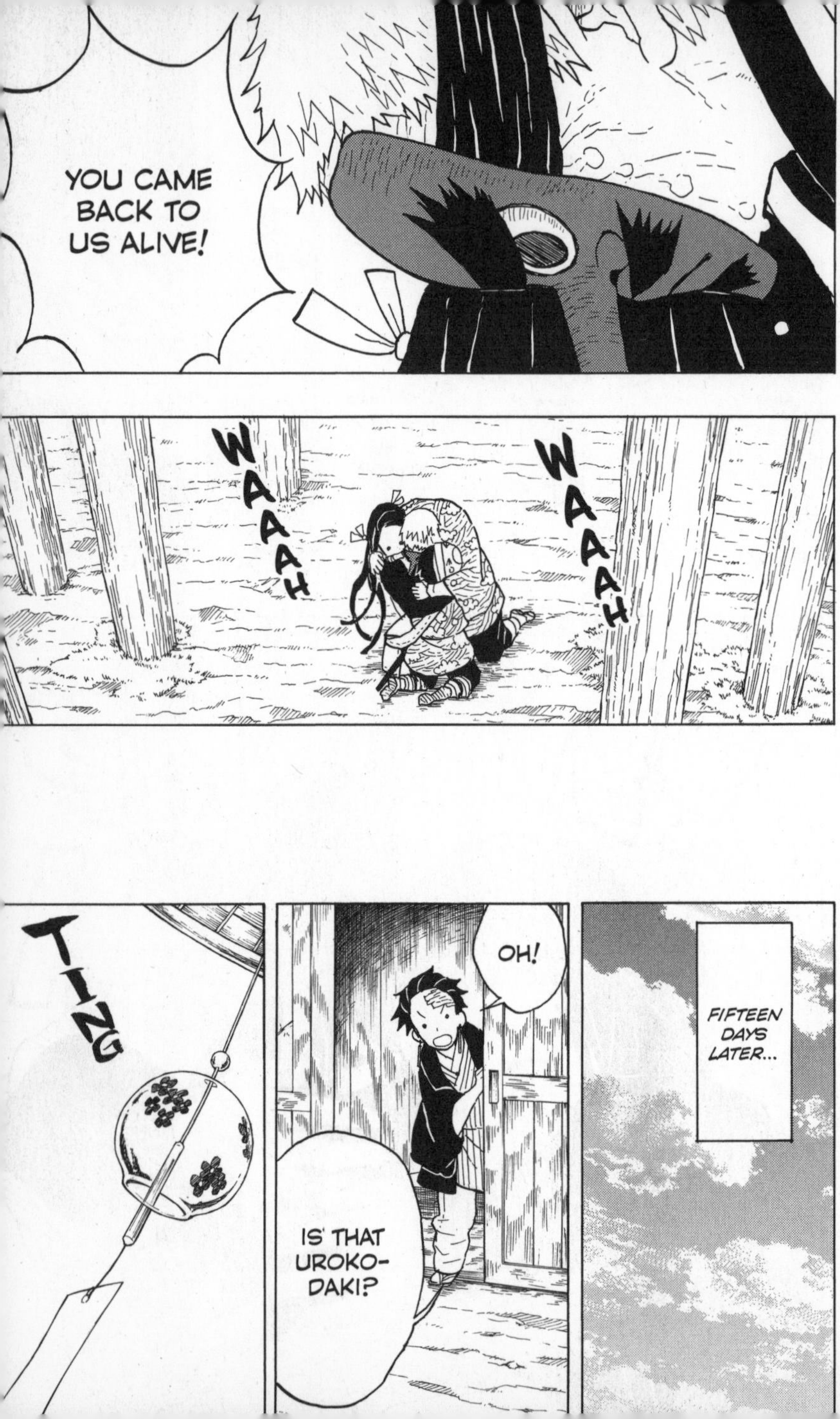
YOU CAME BACK TO US ALIVE!
WAAAH
WAAAH
FIFTEEN DAYS LATER...
OH!
IS THAT UROKO-DAKI?
TING

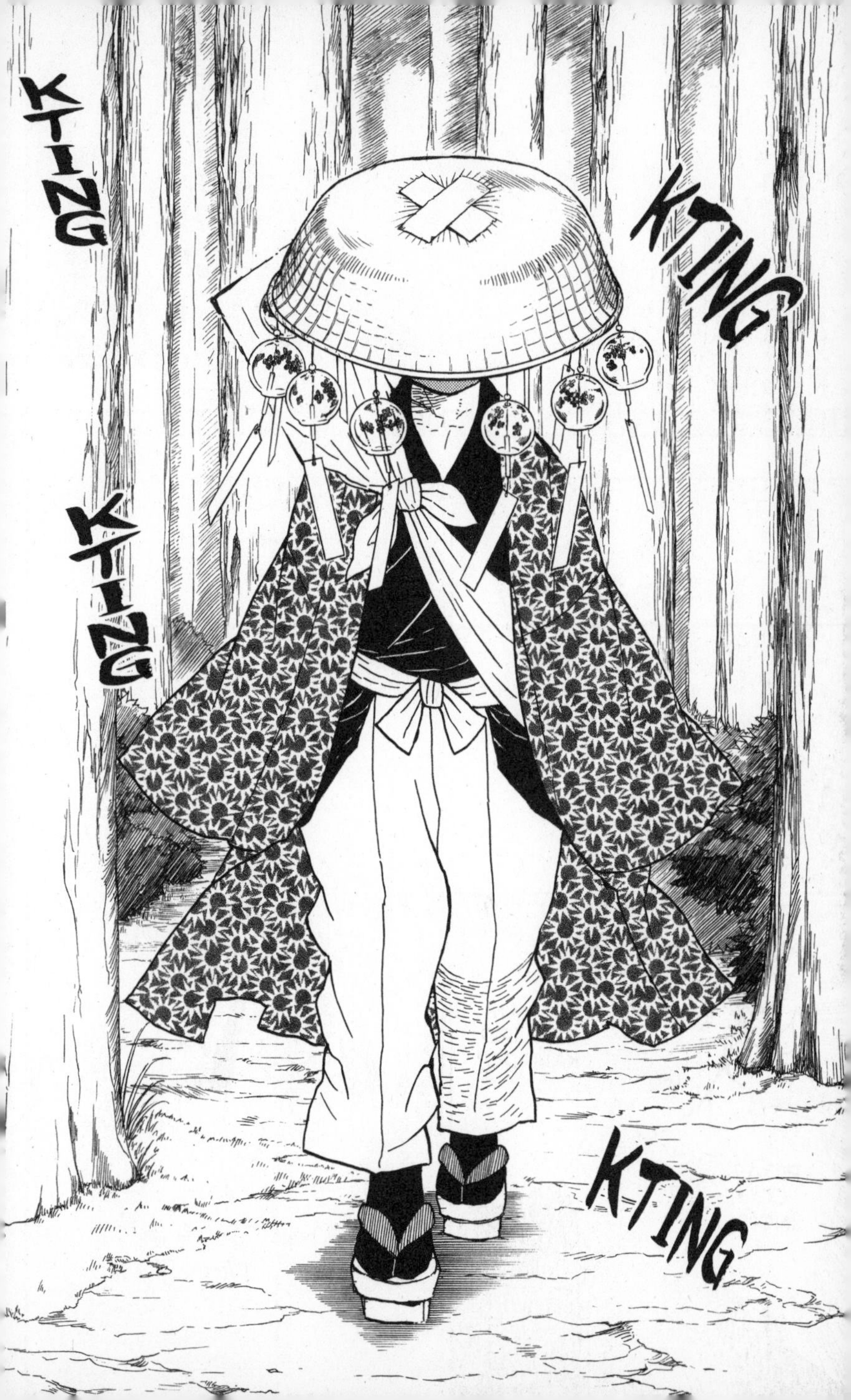
KTING
KTING
KTING
KTING

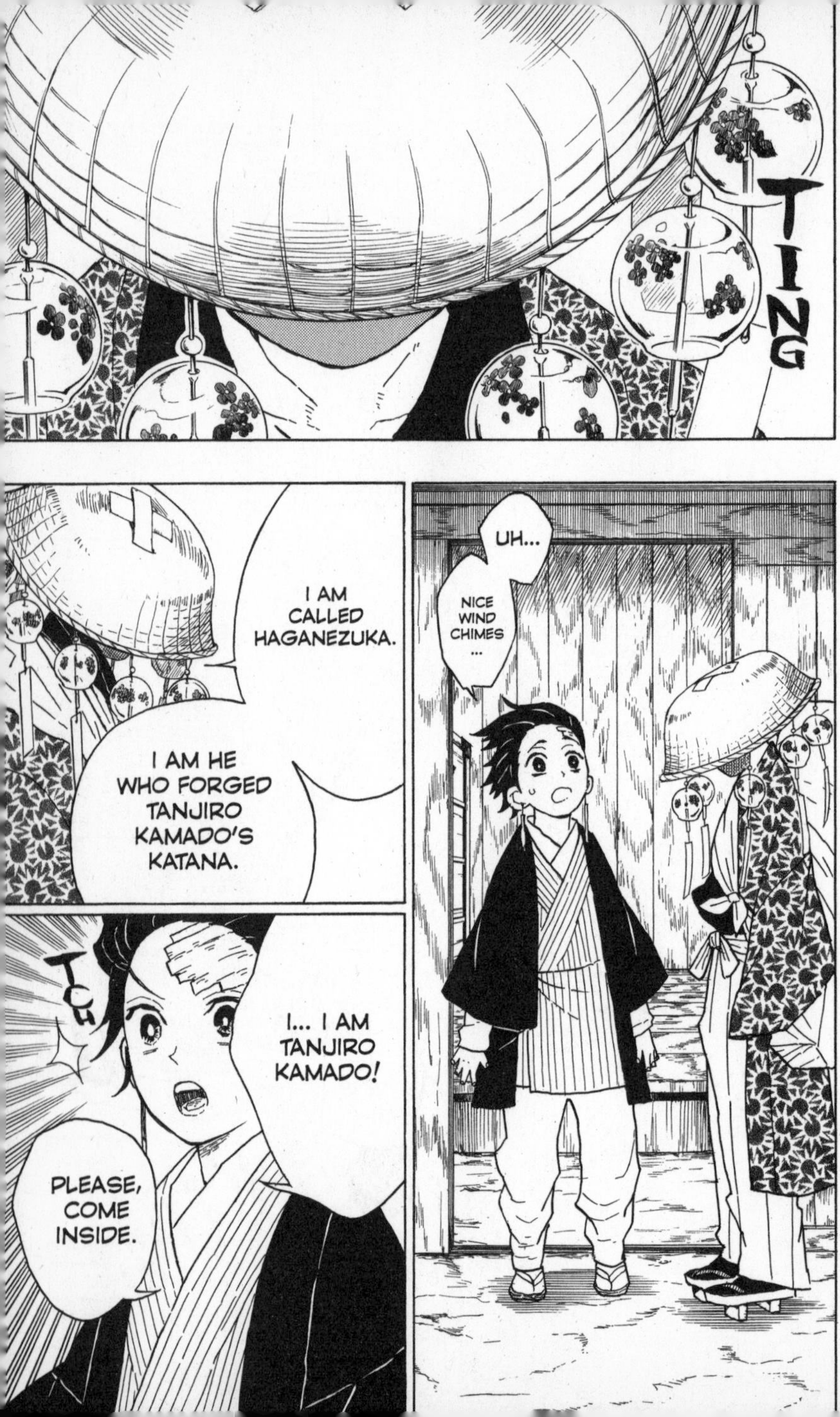
TING
UH...
NICE WIND CHIMES ...
I AM CALLED HAGANEZUKA.
I AM HE WHO FORGED TANJIRO KAMADO'S KATANA.
I... I AM TANJIRO KAMADO!
TCH
PLEASE, COME INSIDE.

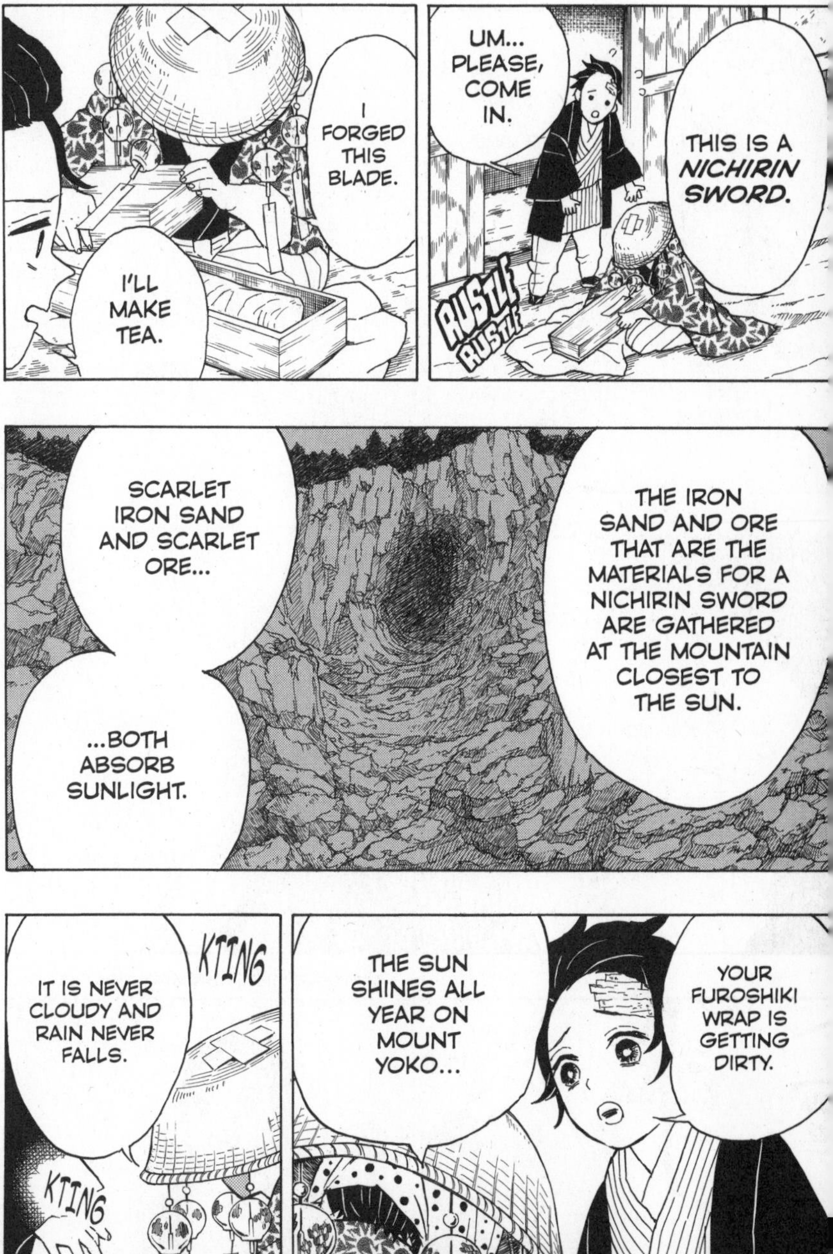
THIS IS A *NICHIRIN SWORD.*
UM... PLEASE, COME IN.
RUSTLE RUSTLE
I FORGED THIS BLADE.
I'LL MAKE TEA.
THE IRON SAND AND ORE THAT ARE THE MATERIALS FOR A NICHIRIN SWORD ARE GATHERED AT THE MOUNTAIN CLOSEST TO THE SUN.
SCARLET IRON SAND AND SCARLET ORE...
...BOTH ABSORB SUNLIGHT.
YOUR FUROSHIKI WRAP IS GETTING DIRTY.
THE SUN SHINES ALL YEAR ON MOUNT YOKO...
KTING
IT IS NEVER CLOUDY AND RAIN NEVER FALLS.
KTING

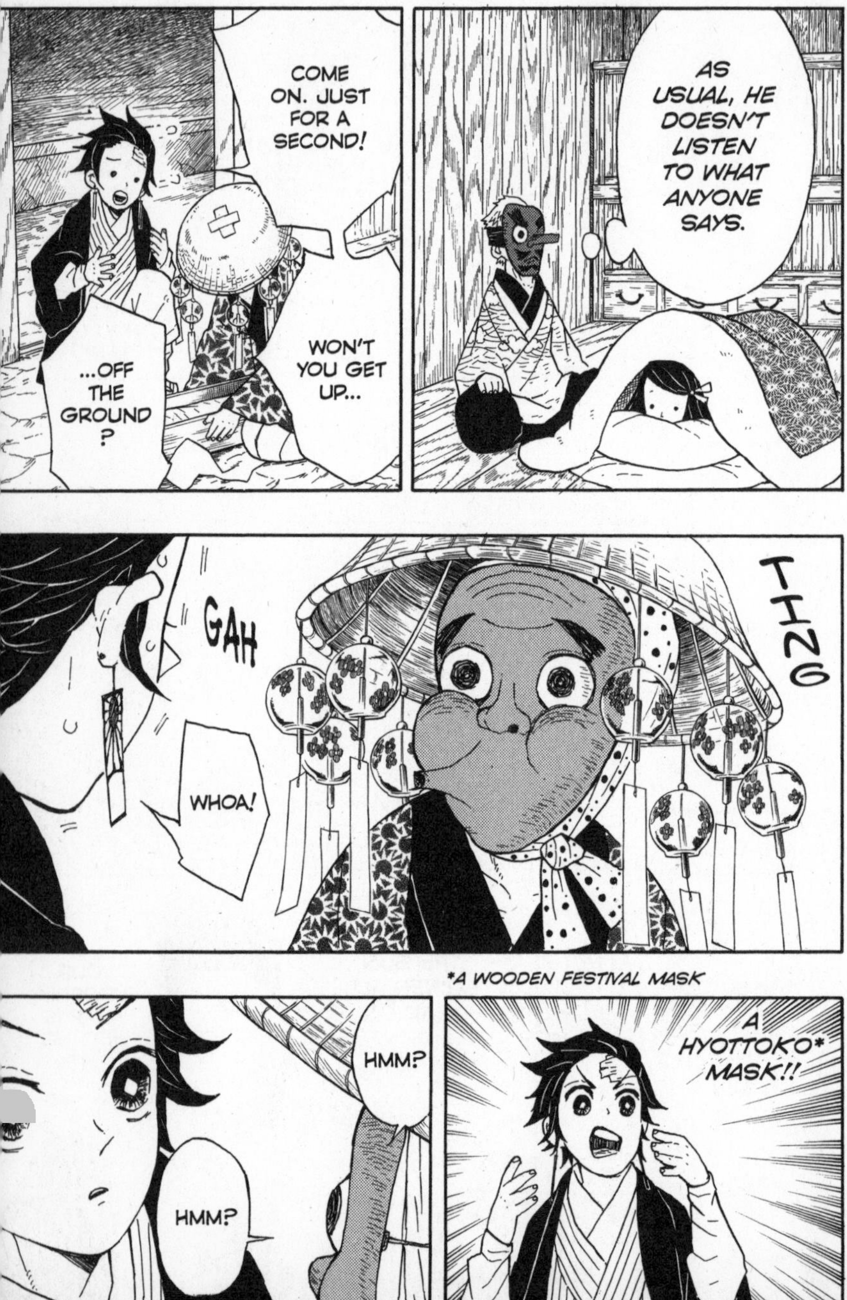
AS USUAL, HE DOESN'T LISTEN TO WHAT ANYONE SAYS.
COME ON. JUST FOR A SECOND!
WON'T YOU GET UP...
...OFF THE GROUND?
TING
GAH
WHOA!
A HYOTTOKO* MASK!!
HMM?
HMM?

*A WOODEN FESTIVAL MASK

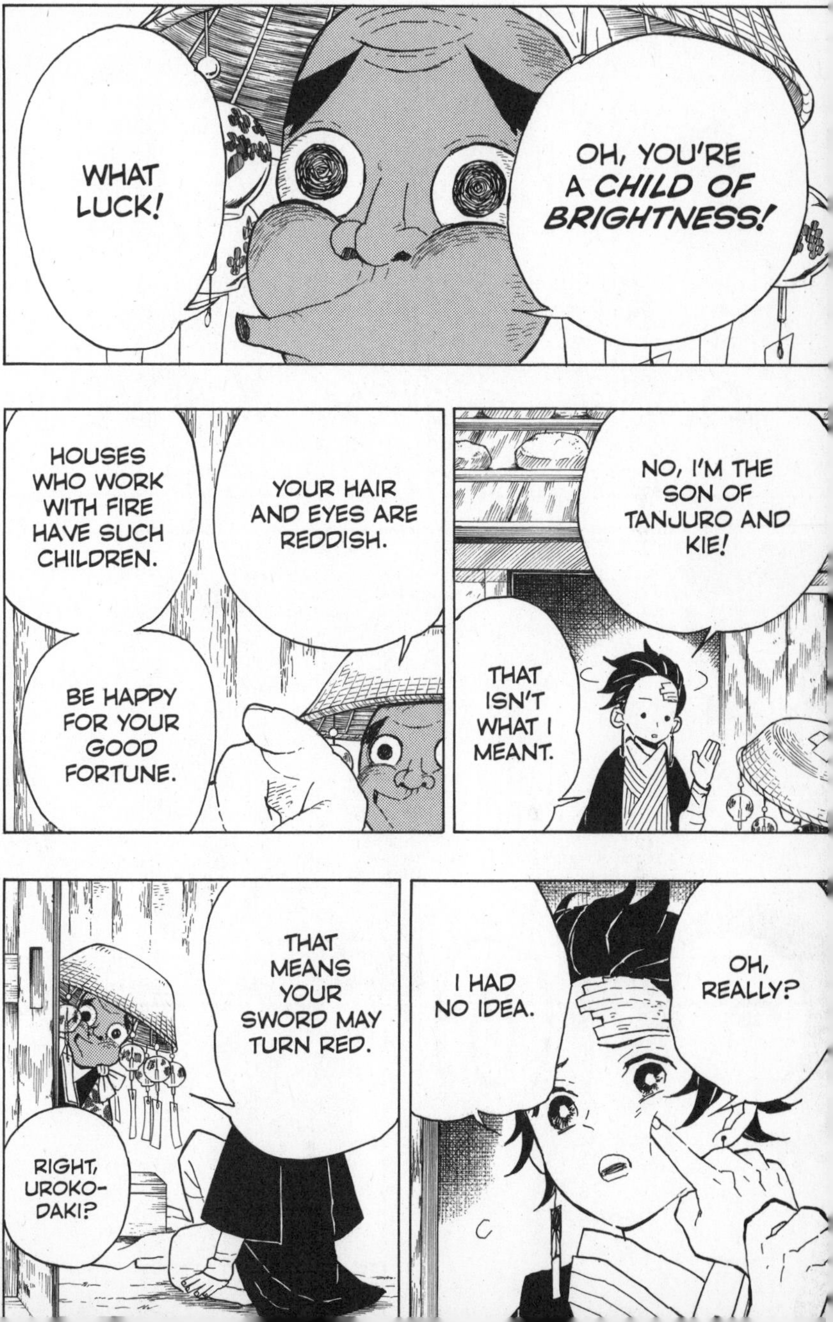
OH, YOU'RE A *CHILD OF BRIGHTNESS!*
WHAT LUCK!
NO, I'M THE SON OF TANJURO AND KIE!
THAT ISN'T WHAT I MEANT.
YOUR HAIR AND EYES ARE REDDISH.
HOUSES WHO WORK WITH FIRE HAVE SUCH CHILDREN.
BE HAPPY FOR YOUR GOOD FORTUNE.
OH, REALLY?
I HAD NO IDEA.
THAT MEANS YOUR SWORD MAY TURN RED.
RIGHT, UROKO-DAKI?

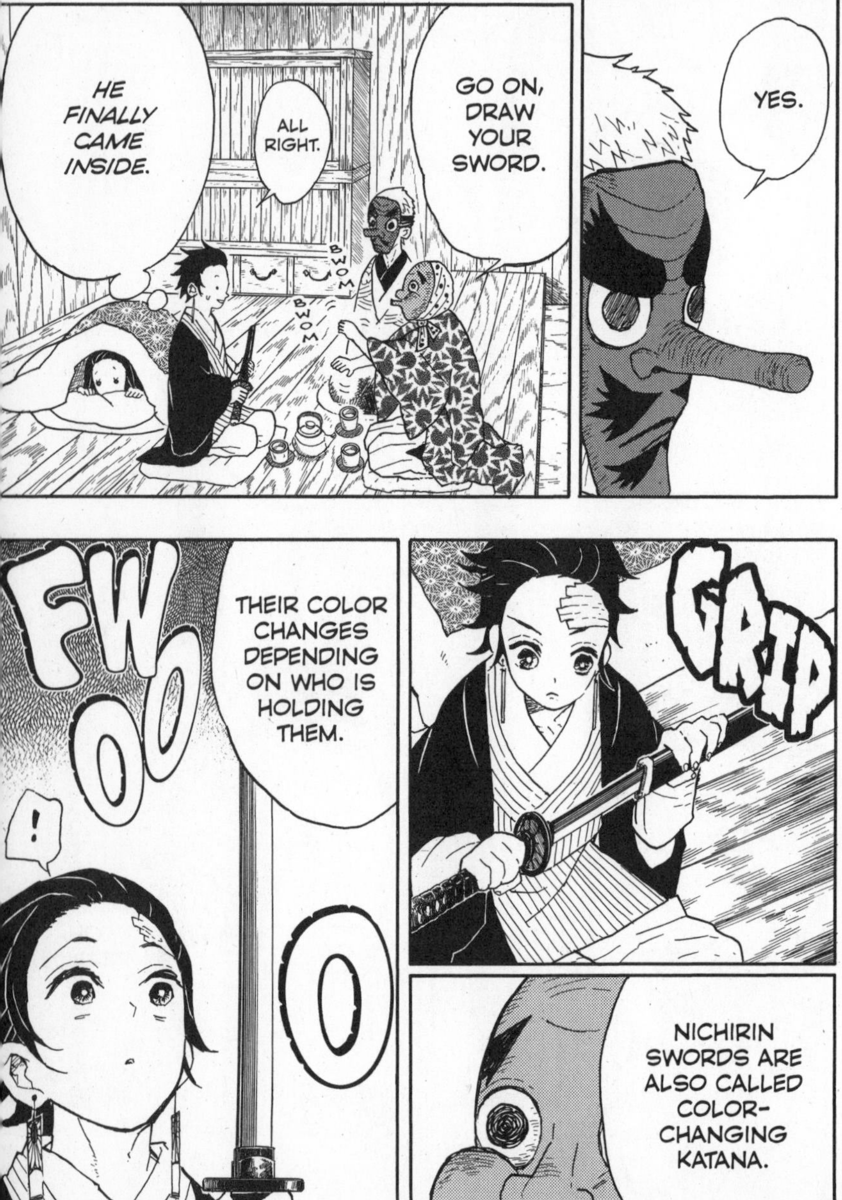
YES.
GO ON, DRAW YOUR SWORD.
ALL RIGHT.
BWOM
BWOM
HE FINALLY CAME INSIDE.
GRIP
NICHIRIN SWORDS ARE ALSO CALLED COLOR-CHANGING KATANA.
THEIR COLOR CHANGES DEPENDING ON WHO IS HOLDING THEM.
FWOOOO
!

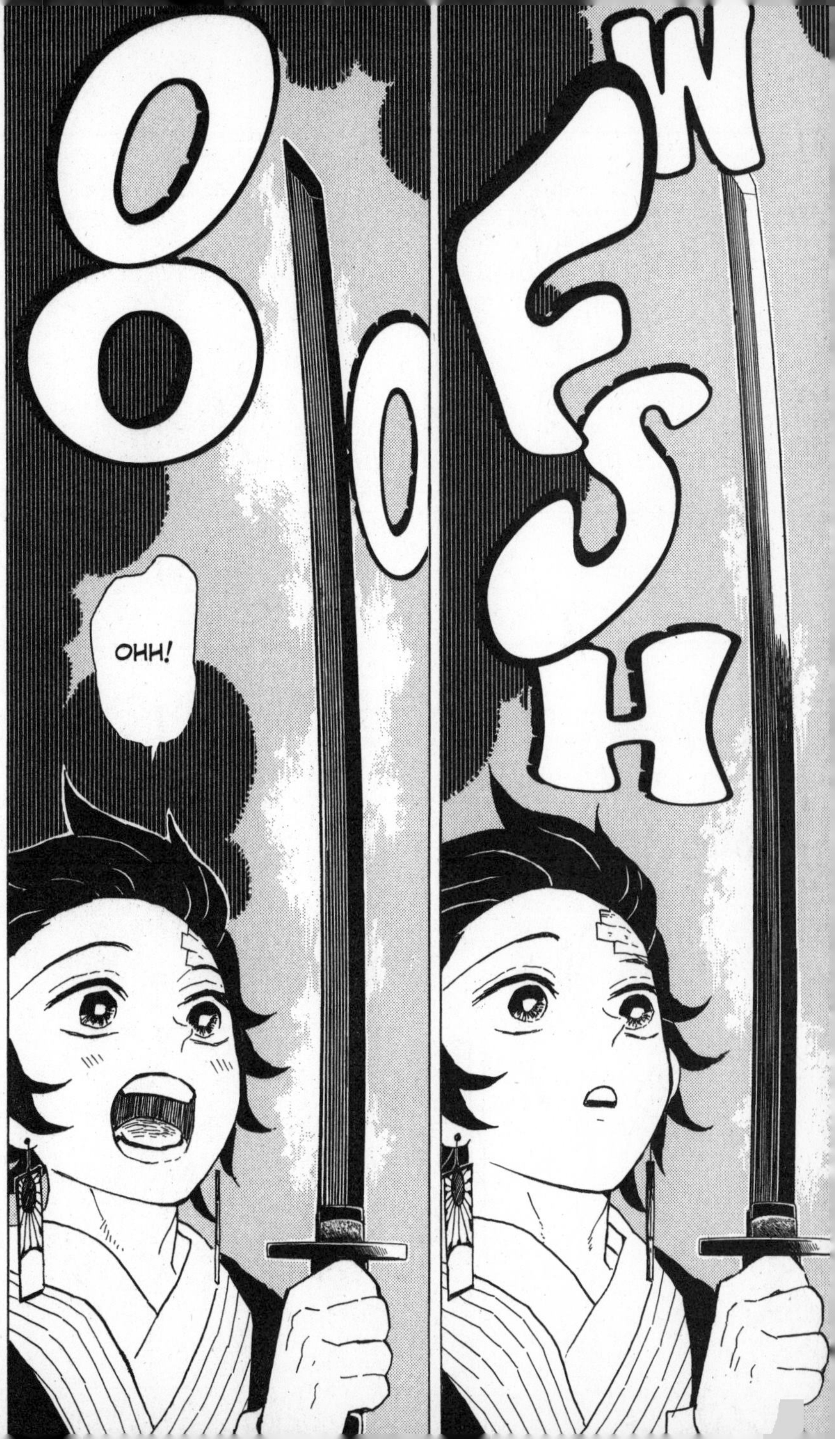
WOOOOSH
OHH!

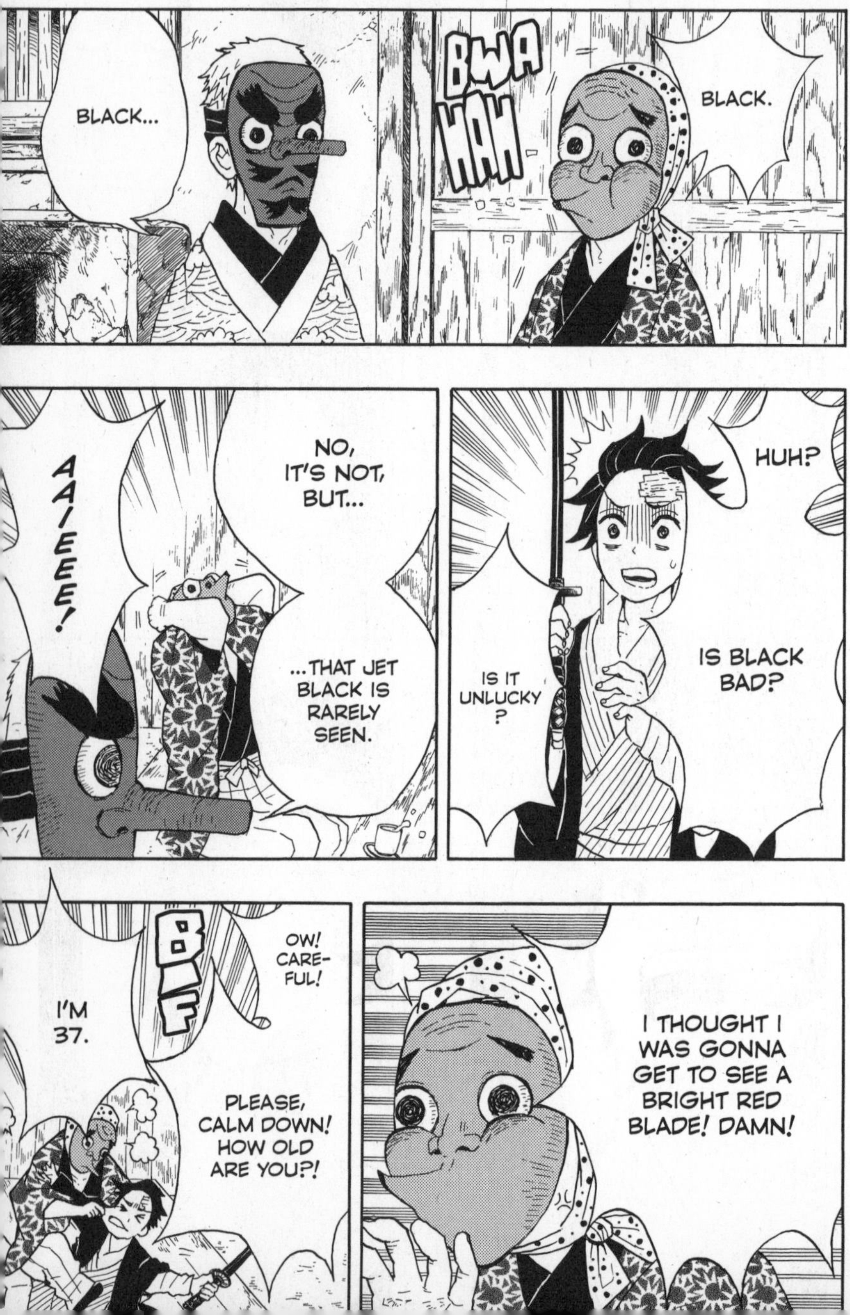
BLACK.
BWA HAH
BLACK...
HUH?
IS BLACK BAD?
IS IT UNLUCKY?
NO, IT'S NOT, BUT...
...THAT JET BLACK IS RARELY SEEN.
AAIEEE!
I THOUGHT I WAS GONNA GET TO SEE A BRIGHT RED BLADE! DAMN!
OW! CARE-FUL!
BIF
I'M 37.
PLEASE, CALM DOWN! HOW OLD ARE YOU?!

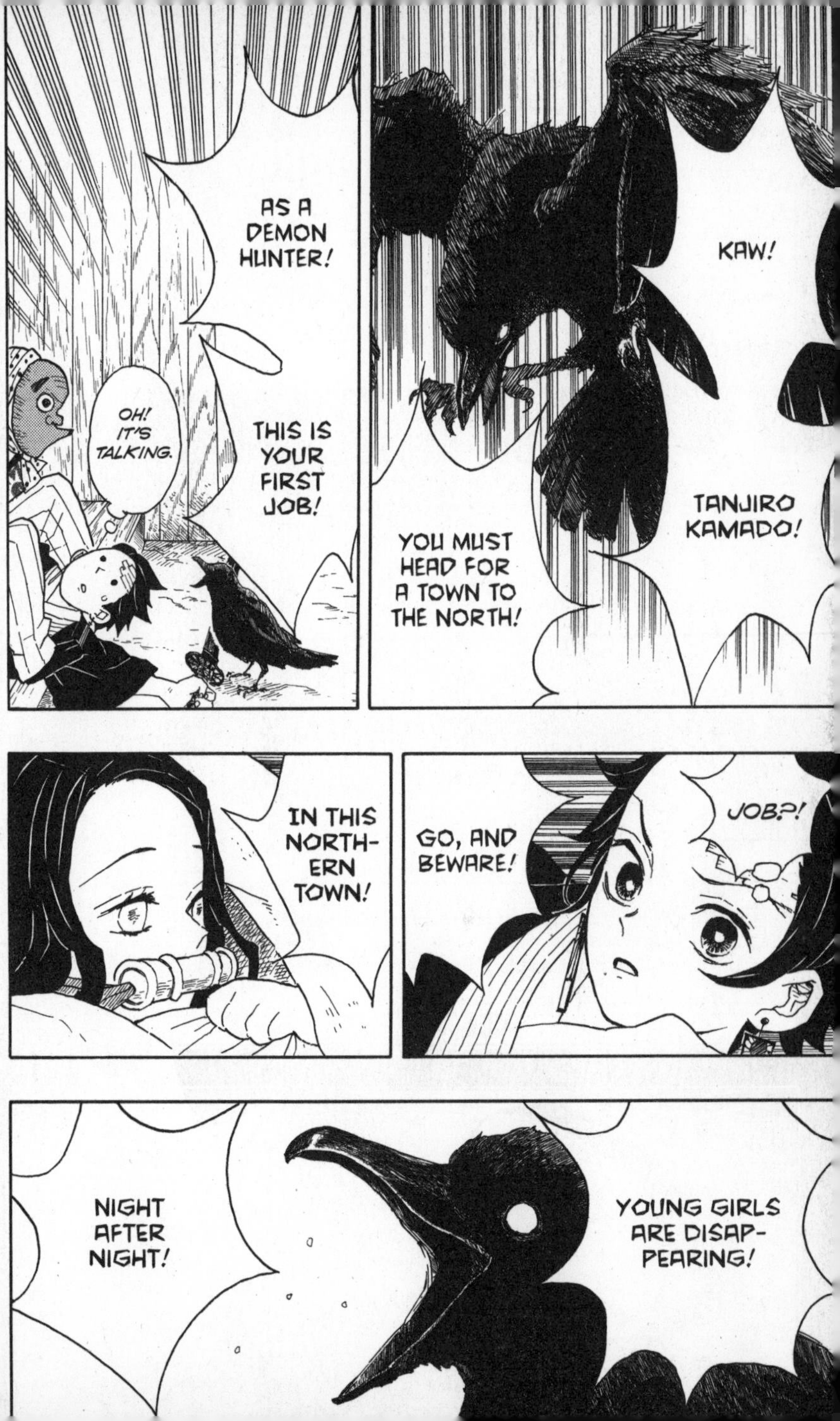
KAW!
TANJIRO KAMADO!
YOU MUST HEAD FOR A TOWN TO THE NORTH!
AS A DEMON HUNTER!
THIS IS YOUR FIRST JOB!
OH! IT'S TALKING.
JOB?!
GO, AND BEWARE!
IN THIS NORTH-ERN TOWN!
YOUNG GIRLS ARE DISAP-PEARING!
NIGHT AFTER NIGHT!

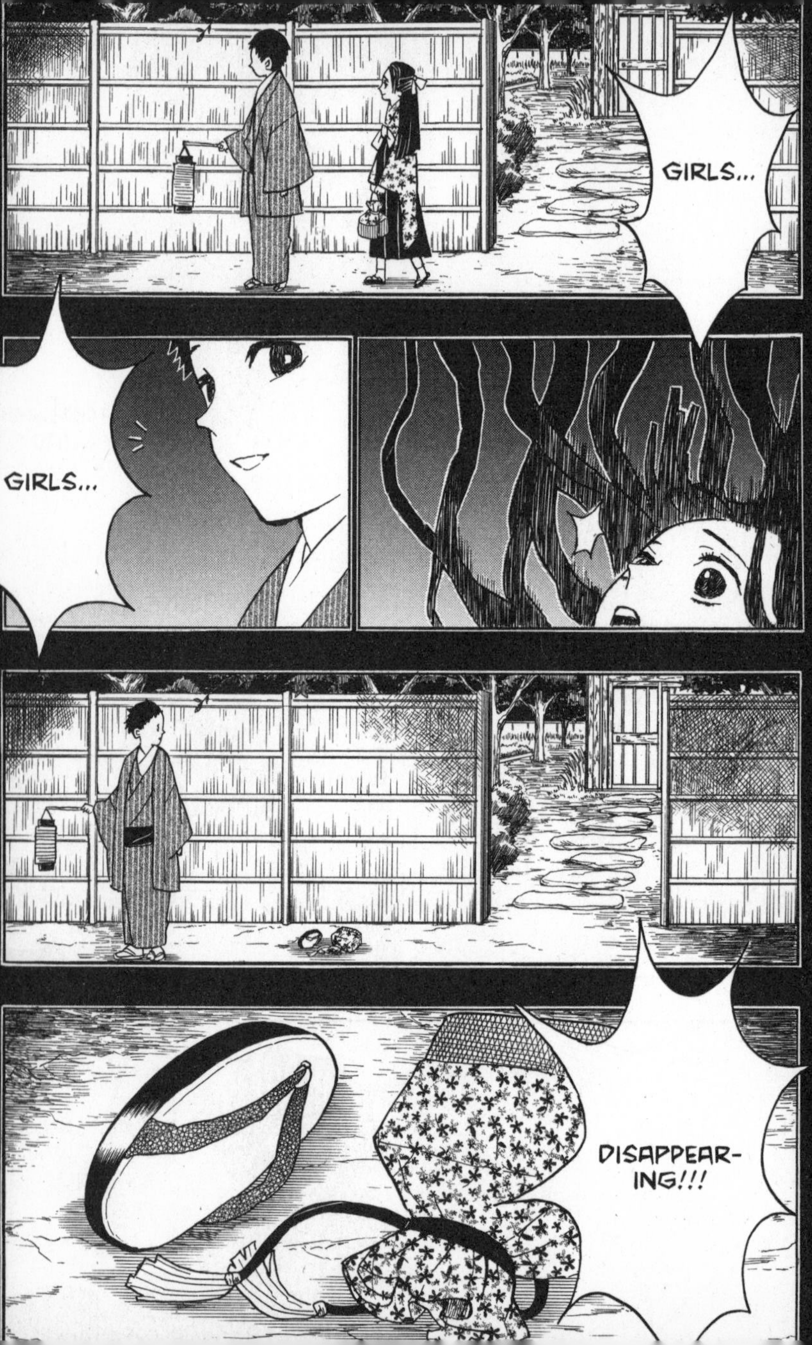
GIRLS...
GIRLS...
DISAPPEAR-
ING!!!

ORIGINAL GOODS FOR USE AS A SURVEY PRIZE
REGIONAL-THEMED ILLUSTRATION
2. NEZUKO (UDON, KAGAWA PREFECTURE)

CHAPTER 10: KIDNAPPER'S BOG

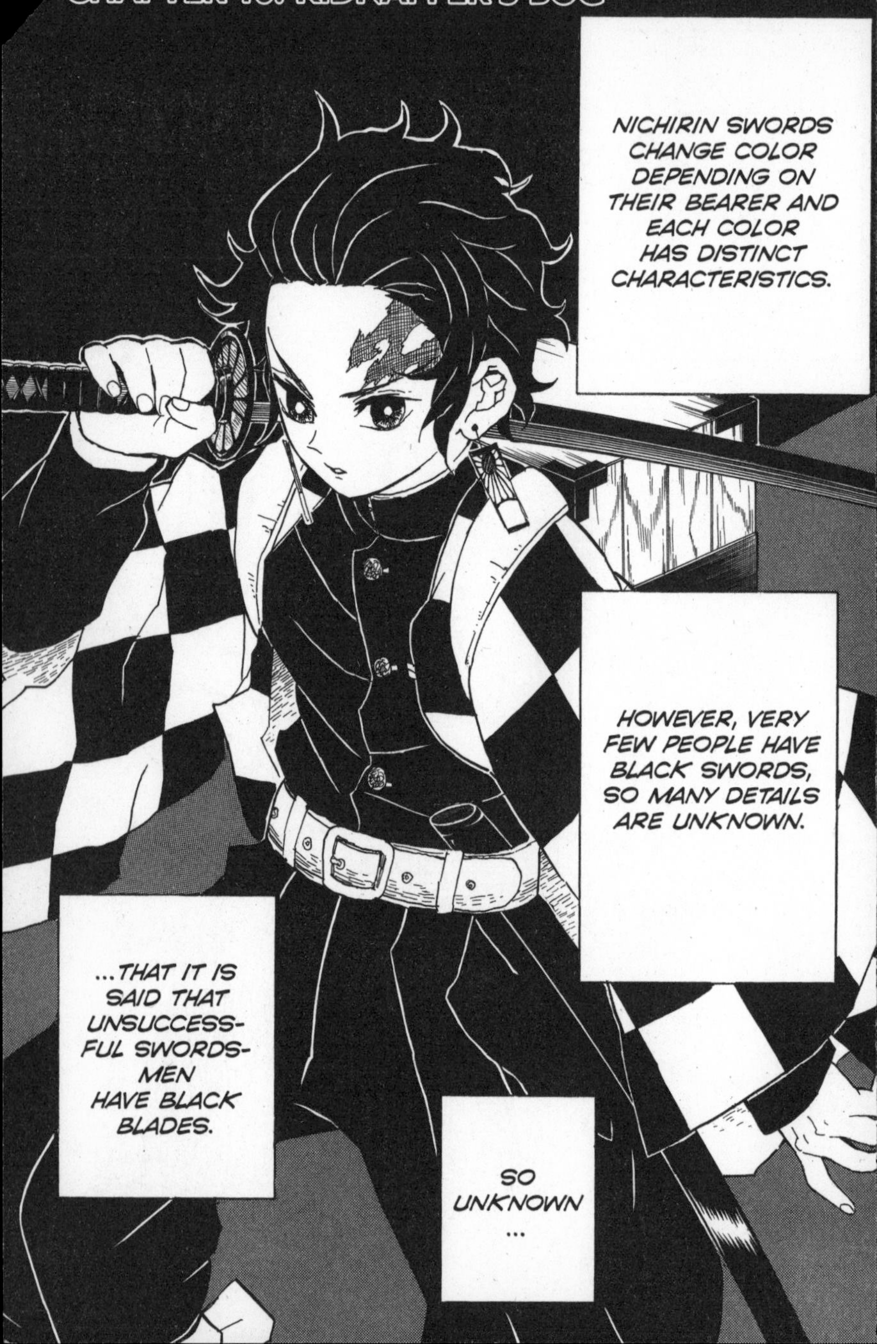
NICHIRIN SWORDS CHANGE COLOR DEPENDING ON THEIR BEARER AND EACH COLOR HAS DISTINCT CHARACTERISTICS.
HOWEVER, VERY FEW PEOPLE HAVE BLACK SWORDS, SO MANY DETAILS ARE UNKNOWN.
...THAT IT IS SAID THAT UNSUCCESS-FUL SWORDS-MEN HAVE BLACK BLADES.
SO UNKNOWN ...

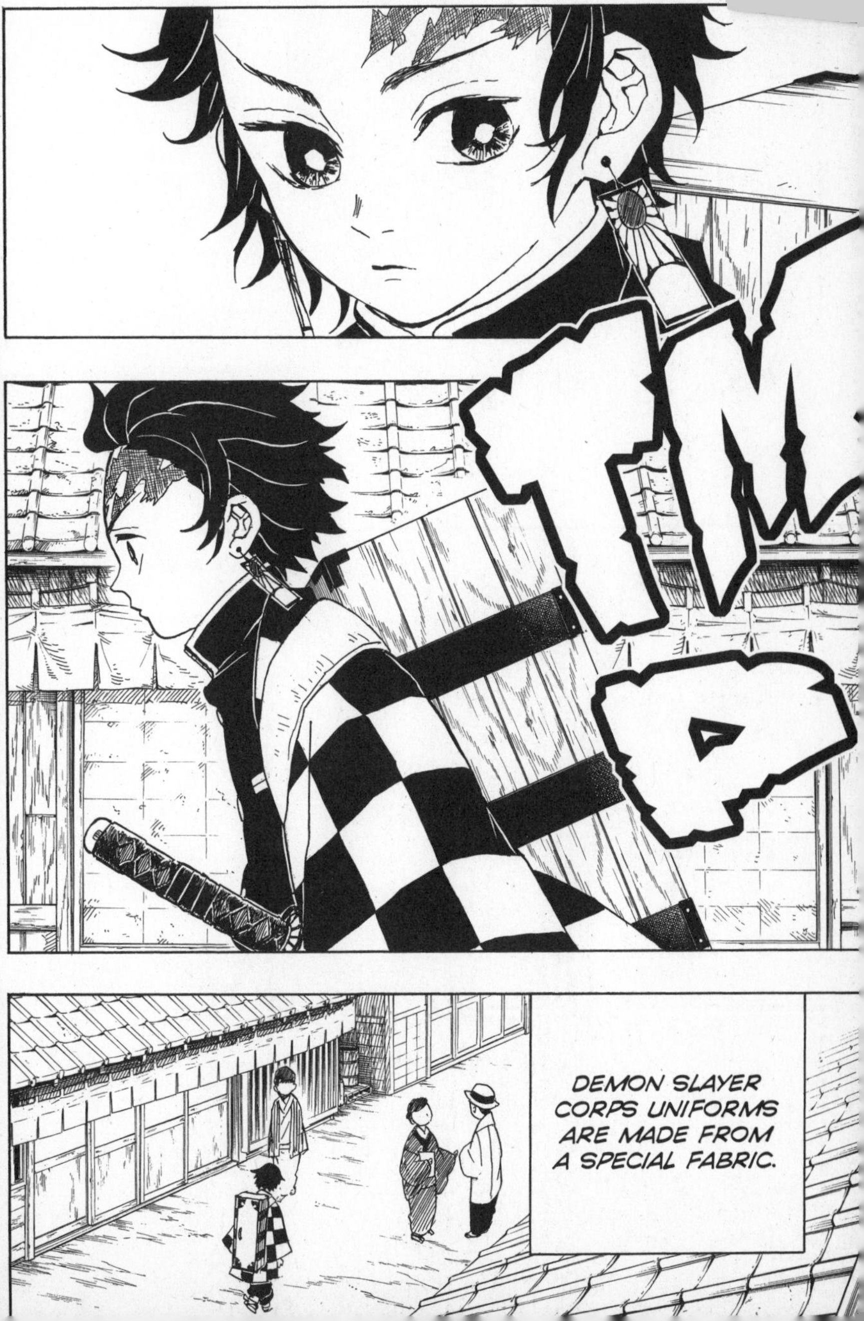
DEMON SLAYER CORPS UNIFORMS ARE MADE FROM A SPECIAL FABRIC.

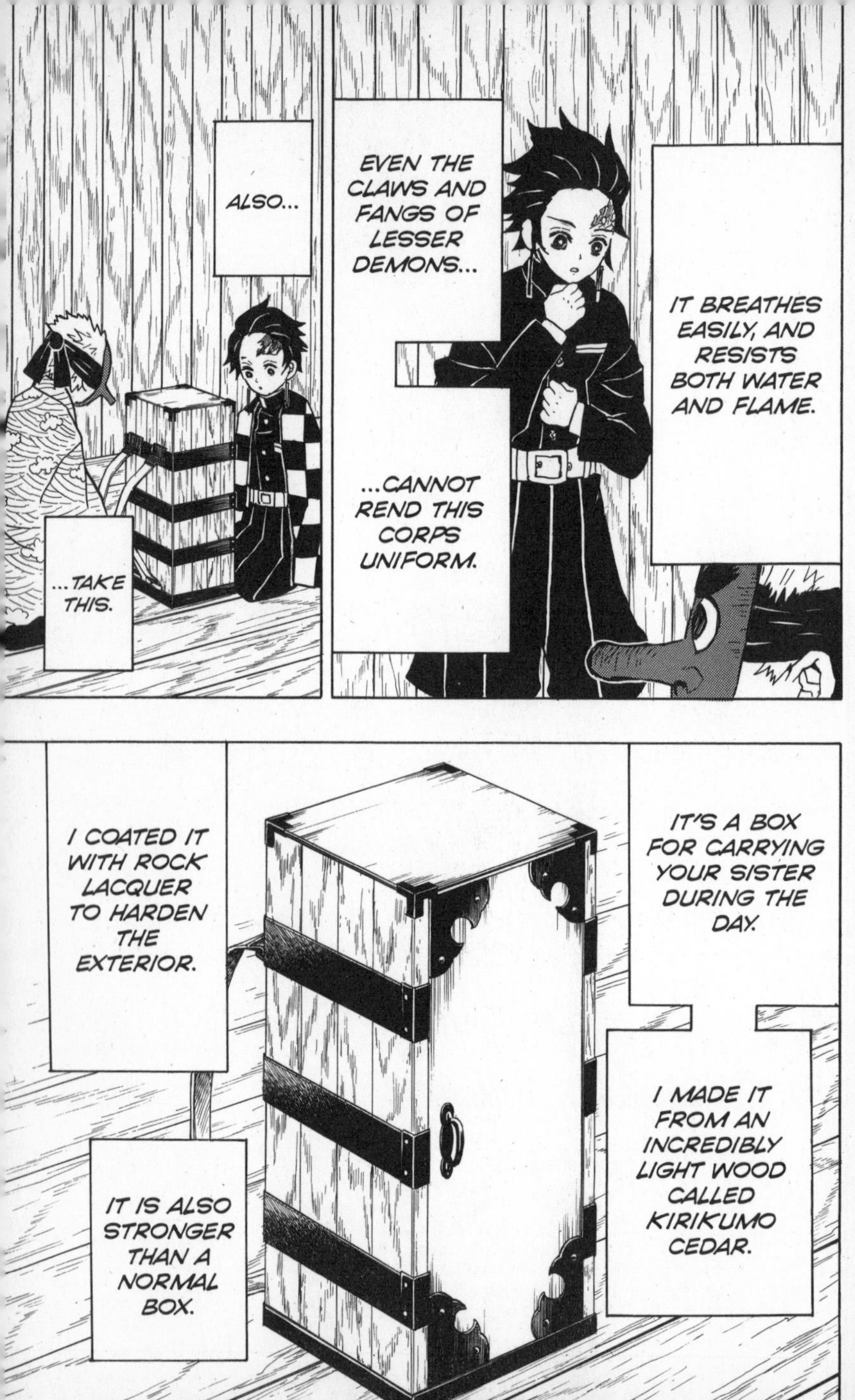
EVEN THE CLAWS AND FANGS OF LESSER DEMONS...
...CANNOT REND THIS CORPS UNIFORM.
IT BREATHES EASILY, AND RESISTS BOTH WATER AND FLAME.
ALSO...
...TAKE THIS.
IT'S A BOX FOR CARRYING YOUR SISTER DURING THE DAY.
I MADE IT FROM AN INCREDIBLY LIGHT WOOD CALLED KIRIKUMO CEDAR.
I COATED IT WITH ROCK LACQUER TO HARDEN THE EXTERIOR.
IT IS ALSO STRONGER THAN A NORMAL BOX.

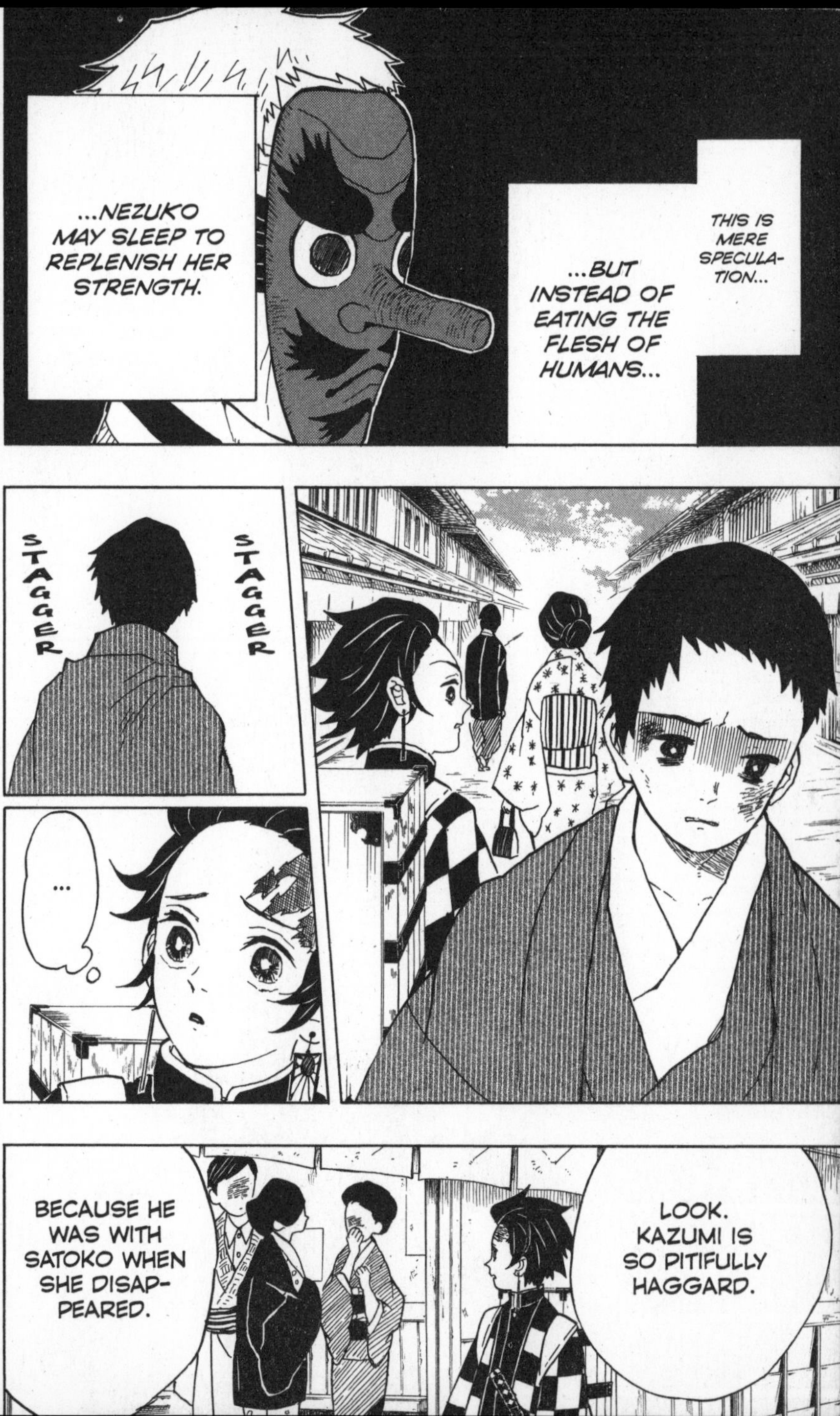
THIS IS MERE SPECULATION...
...BUT INSTEAD OF EATING THE FLESH OF HUMANS...
...NEZUKO MAY SLEEP TO REPLENISH HER STRENGTH.
STAGGER
STAGGER
...
LOOK. KAZUMI IS SO PITIFULLY HAGGARD.
BECAUSE HE WAS WITH SATOKO WHEN SHE DISAPPEARED.

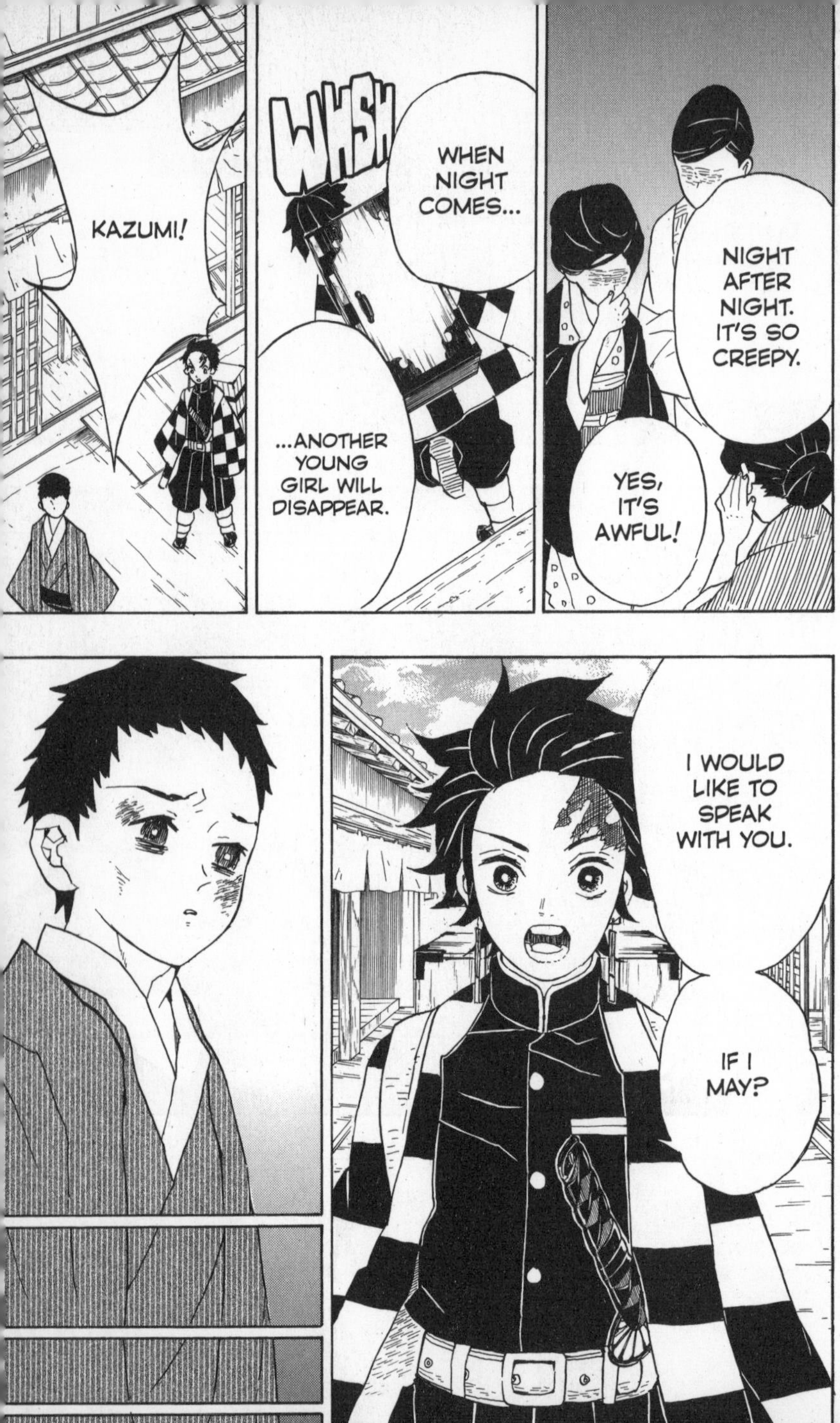
NIGHT AFTER NIGHT. IT'S SO CREEPY.
YES, IT'S AWFUL!
WHEN NIGHT COMES...
WHSH
...ANOTHER YOUNG GIRL WILL DISAPPEAR.
KAZUMI!
I WOULD LIKE TO SPEAK WITH YOU.
IF I MAY?

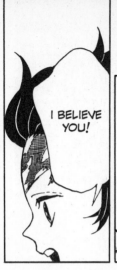

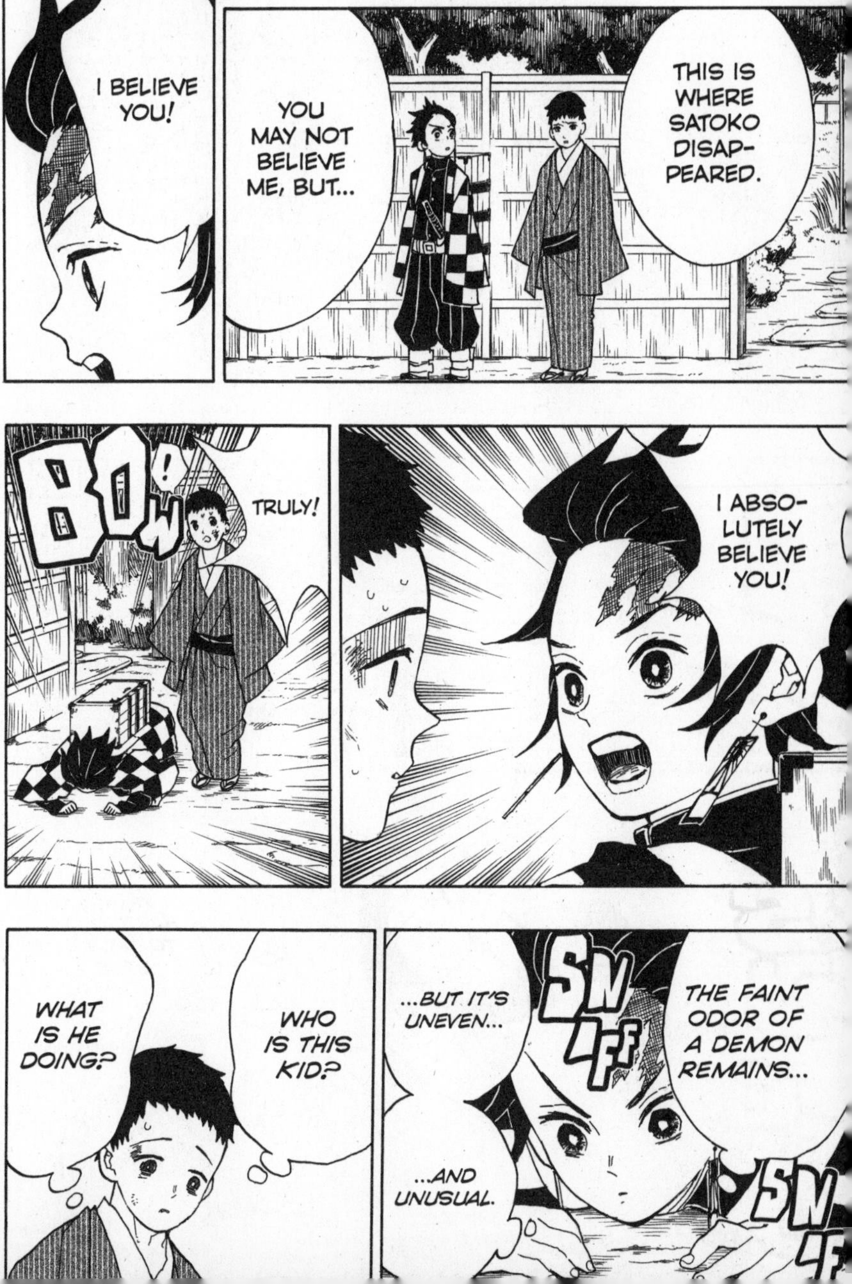
THIS IS WHERE SATOKO DISAPPEARED.
YOU MAY NOT BELIEVE ME, BUT...
I BELIEVE YOU!
I ABSOLUTELY BELIEVE YOU!
TRULY!
!
BOW
THE FAINT ODOR OF A DEMON REMAINS...
SNIFF
...BUT IT'S UNEVEN...
...AND UNUSUAL.
SNIF
WHO IS THIS KID?
WHAT IS HE DOING?

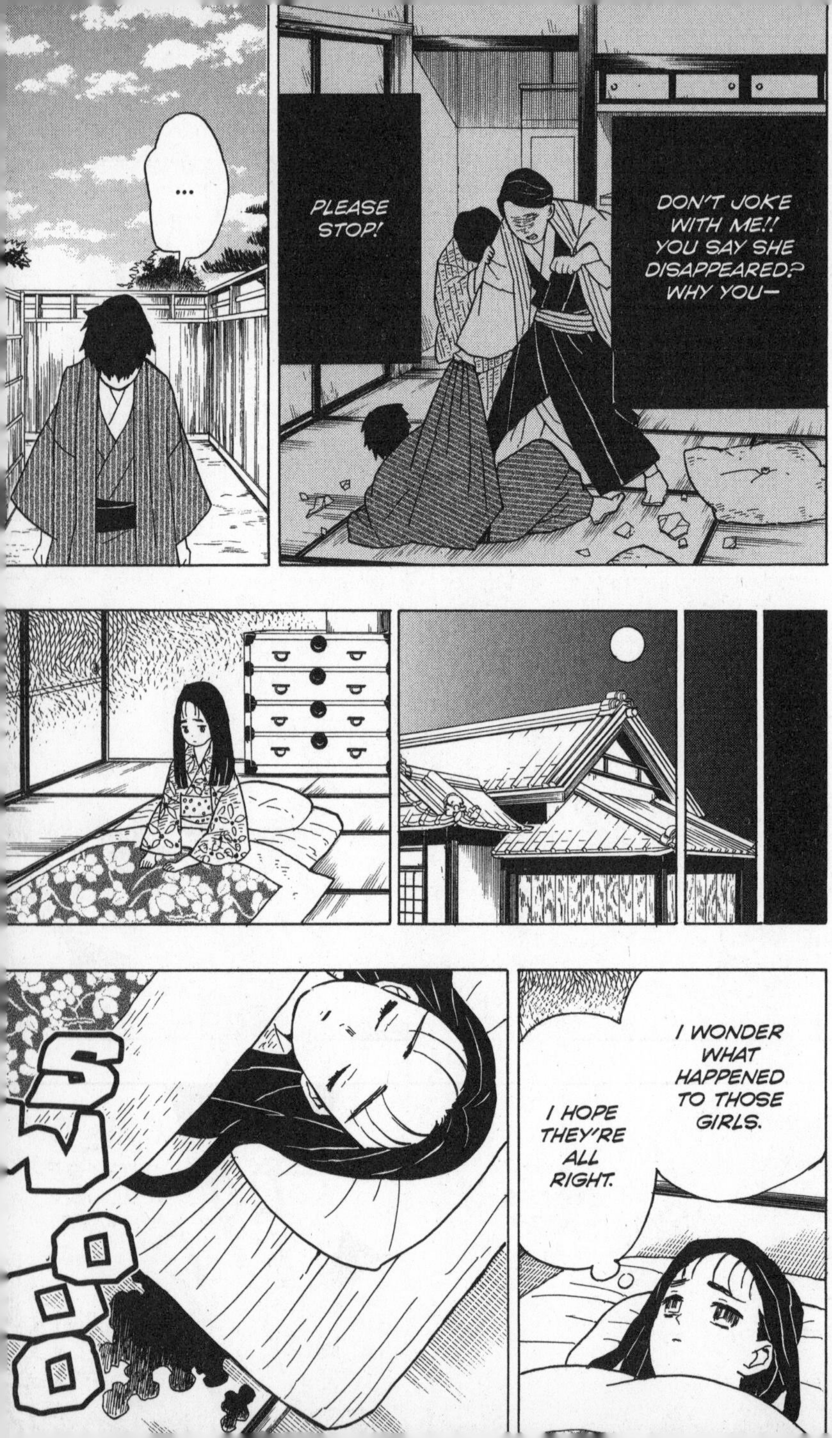
DON'T JOKE WITH ME!! YOU SAY SHE DISAPPEARED? WHY YOU—
PLEASE STOP!
...
I WONDER WHAT HAPPENED TO THOSE GIRLS.
I HOPE THEY'RE ALL RIGHT.

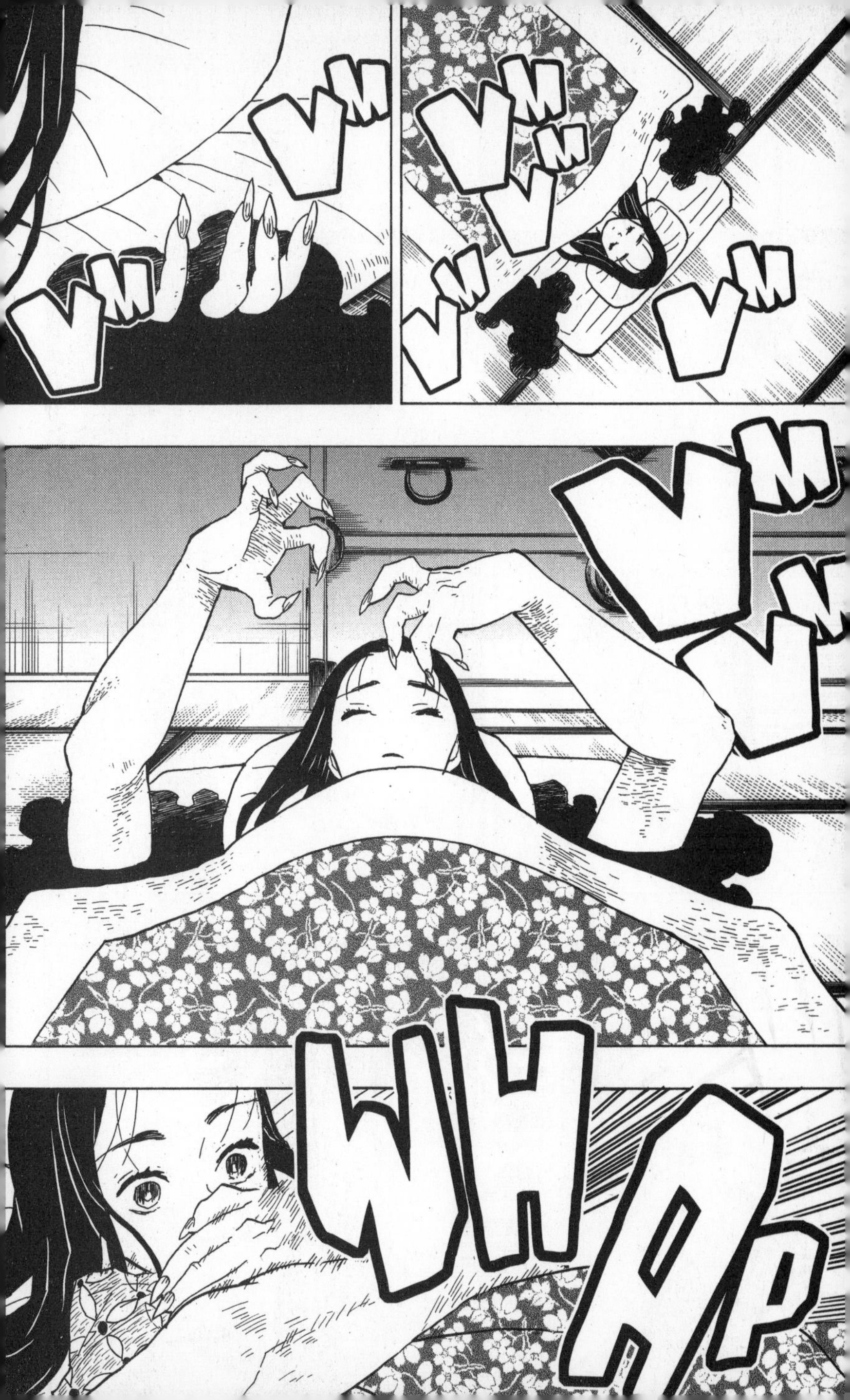
VM
VM
VM
VM
VM
VM
VM
VM
WHAP

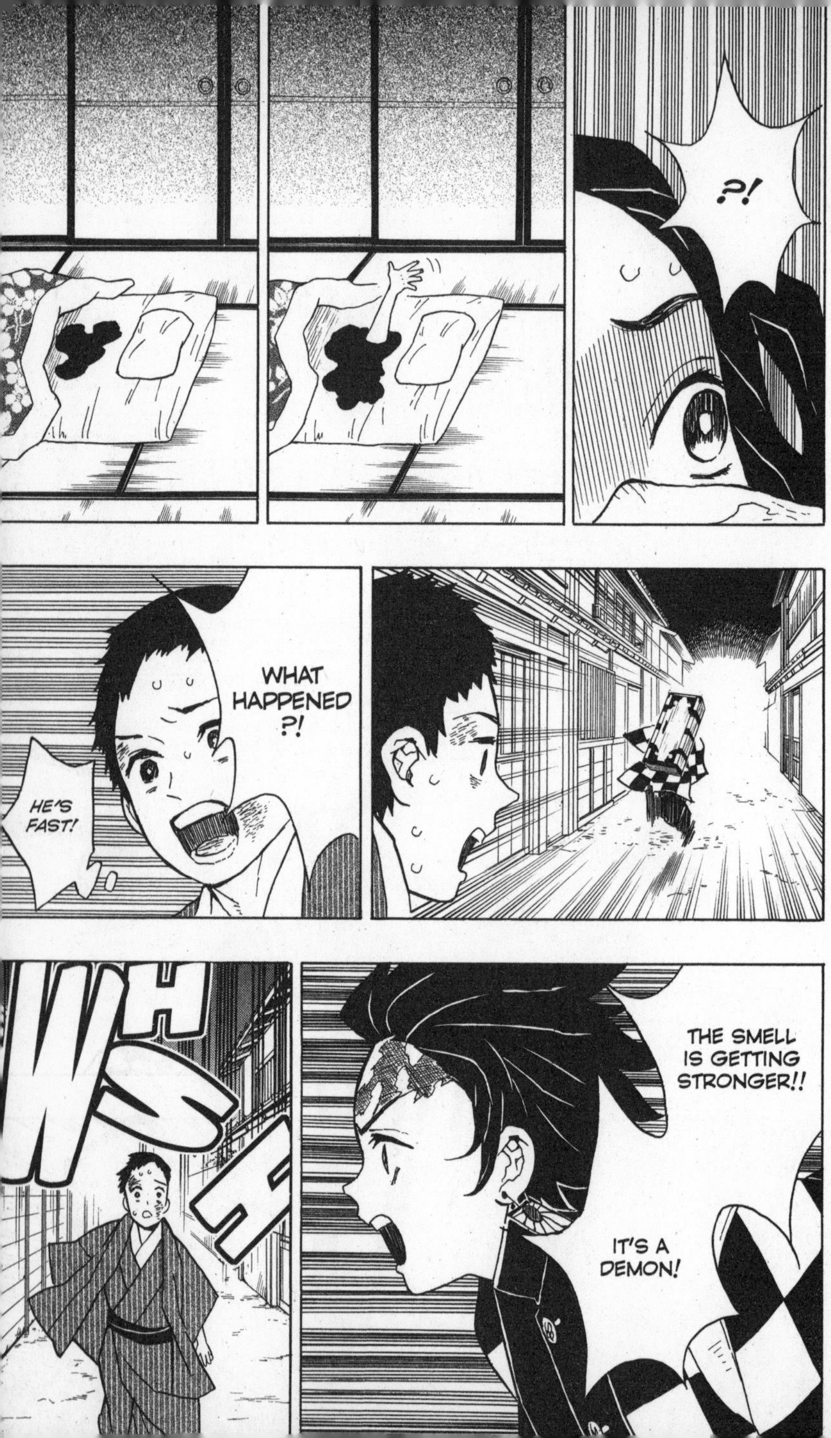
?!
WHAT HAPPENED?!
HE'S FAST!
THE SMELL IS GETTING STRONGER!!
IT'S A DEMON!
WHSH

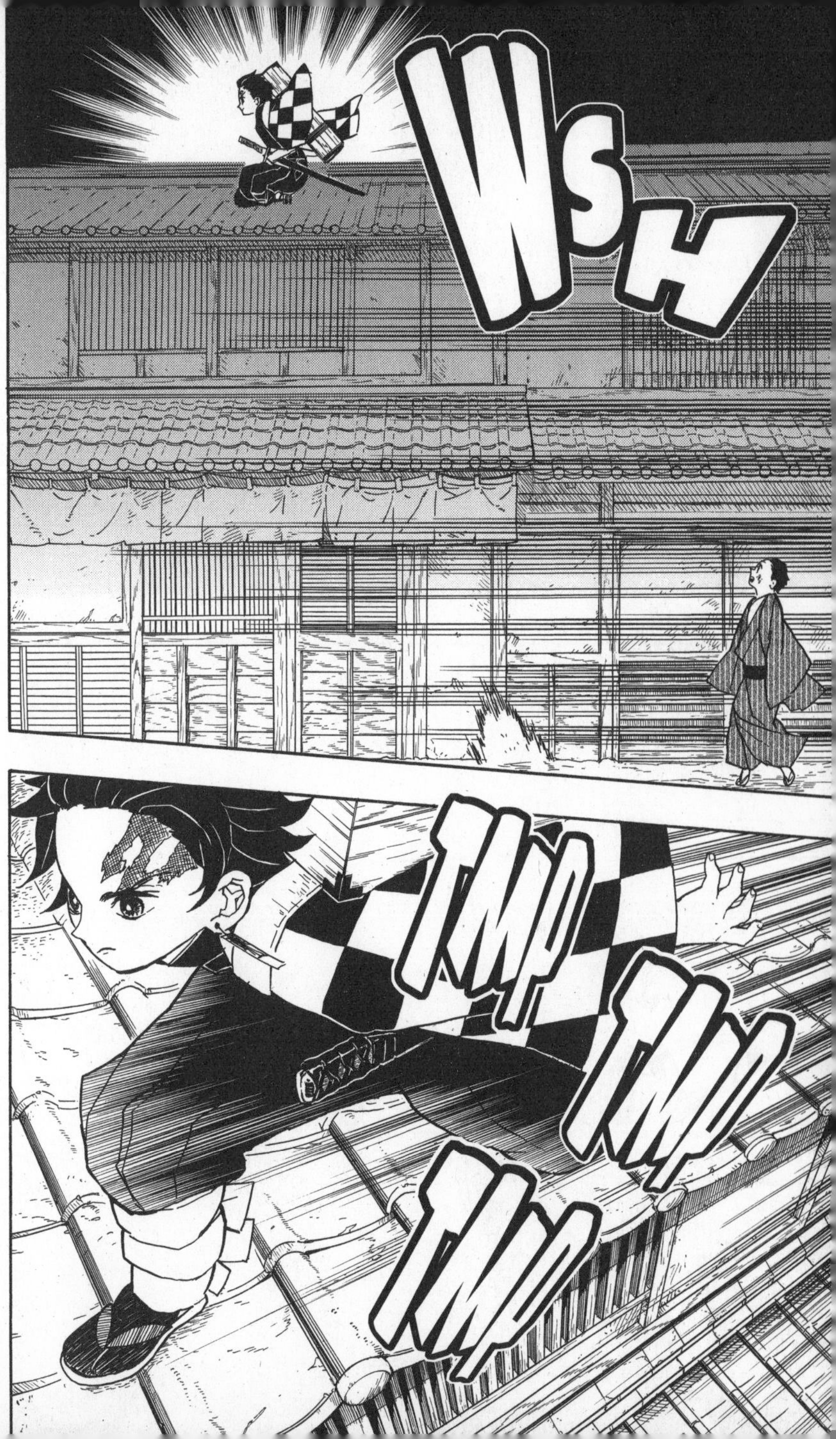
WSH
TMP
TMP
TMP

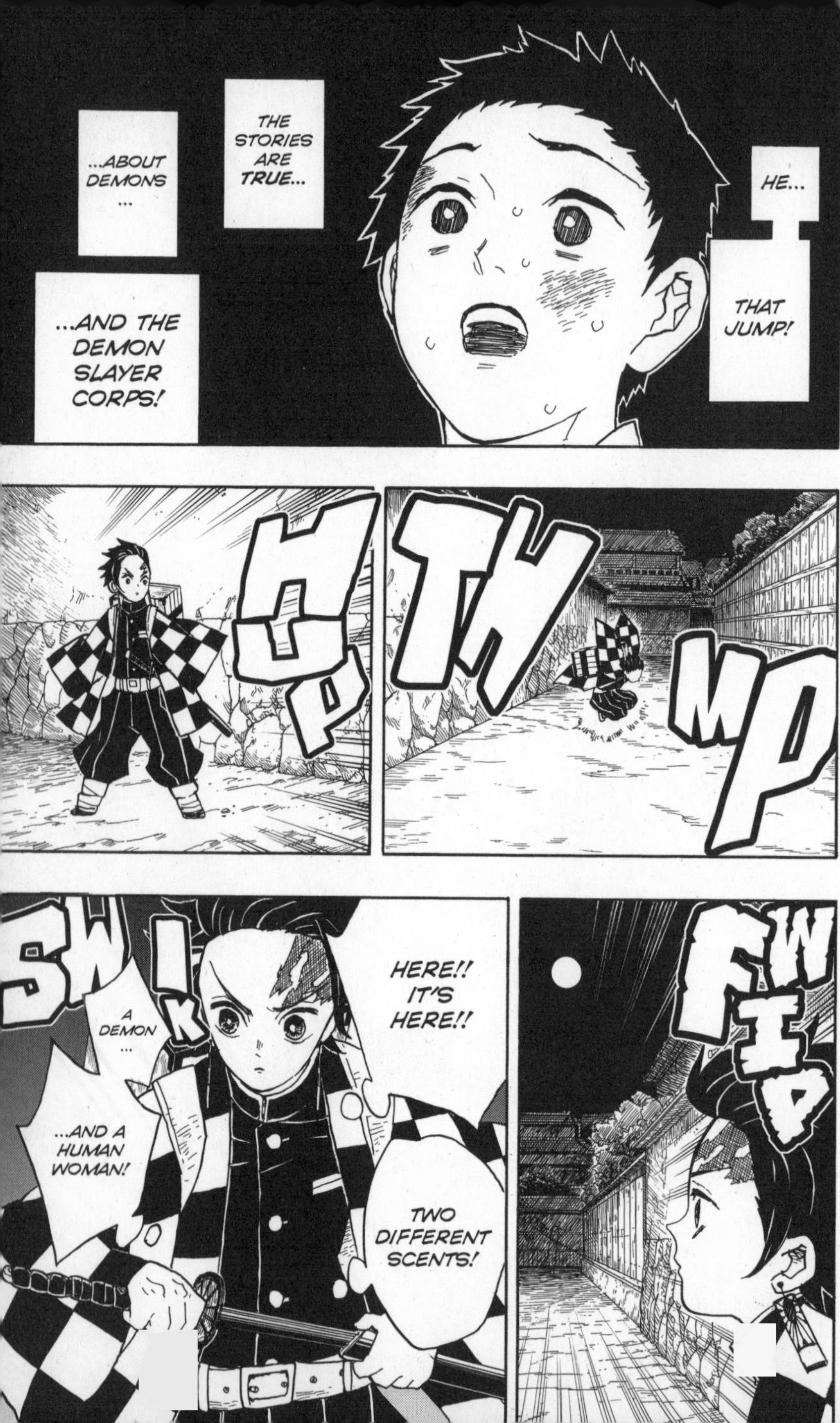
HE...
THAT JUMP!
THE STORIES ARE TRUE...
...ABOUT DEMONS ...
...AND THE DEMON SLAYER CORPS!
THMP
HOP
FWIP
SWIK
HERE!! IT'S HERE!!
A DEMON ...
...AND A HUMAN WOMAN!
TWO DIFFERENT SCENTS!

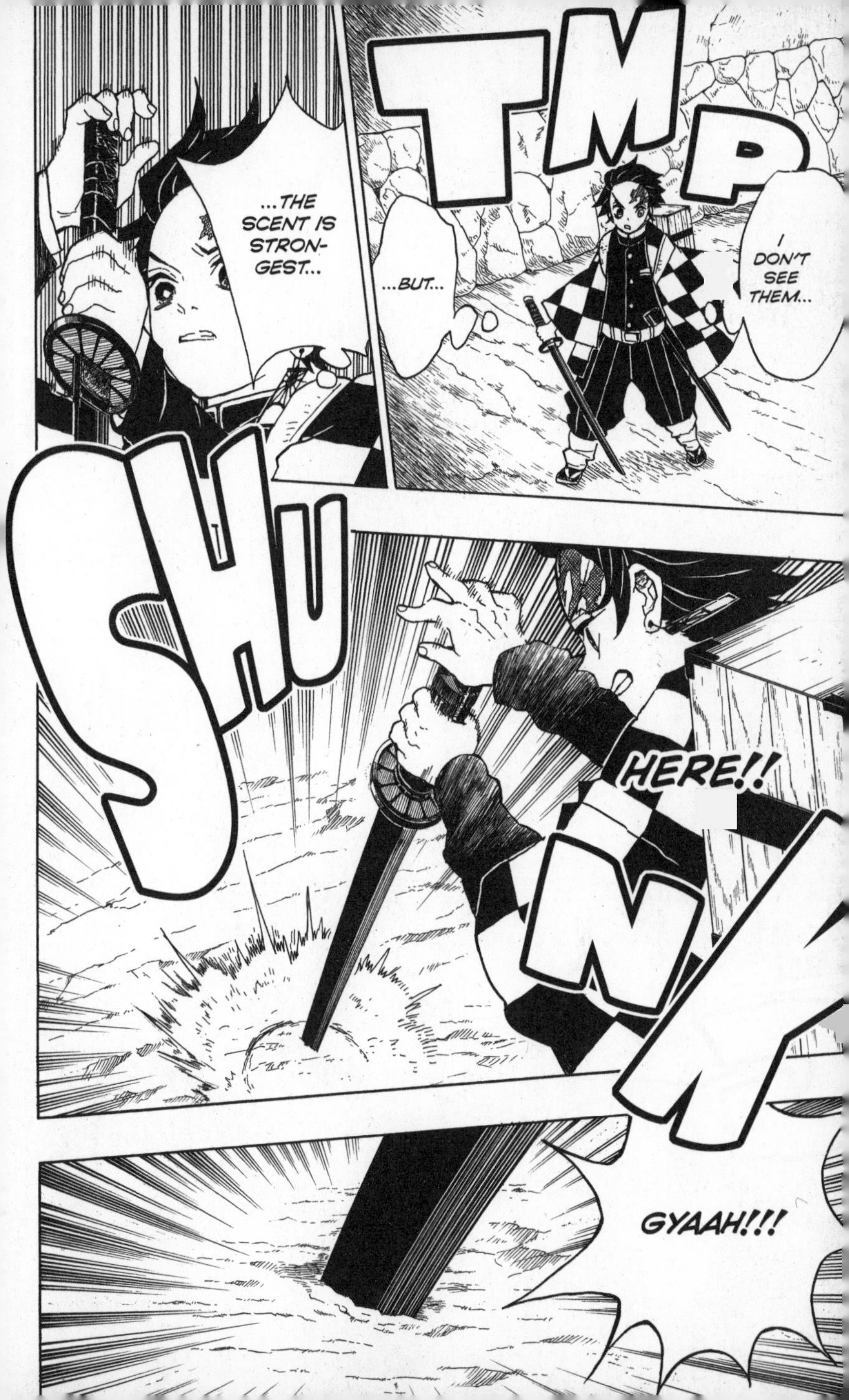
TMP
I DON'T SEE THEM...
...BUT...
...THE SCENT IS STRONGEST...
HERE!!
SHU
NK
GYAAH!!!

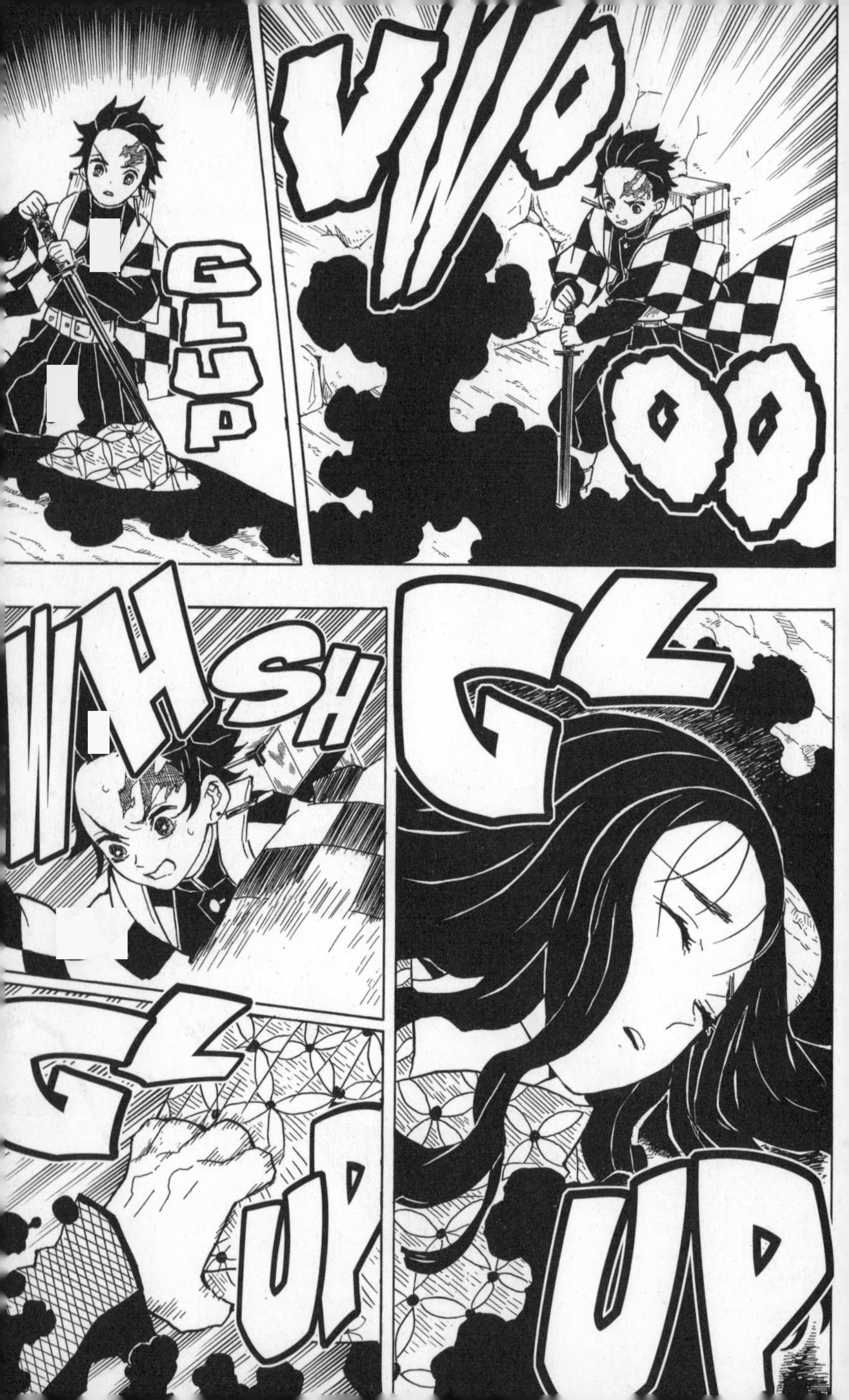
VWO
OO
GLUP
GL
UP
WHSH
GL
UP

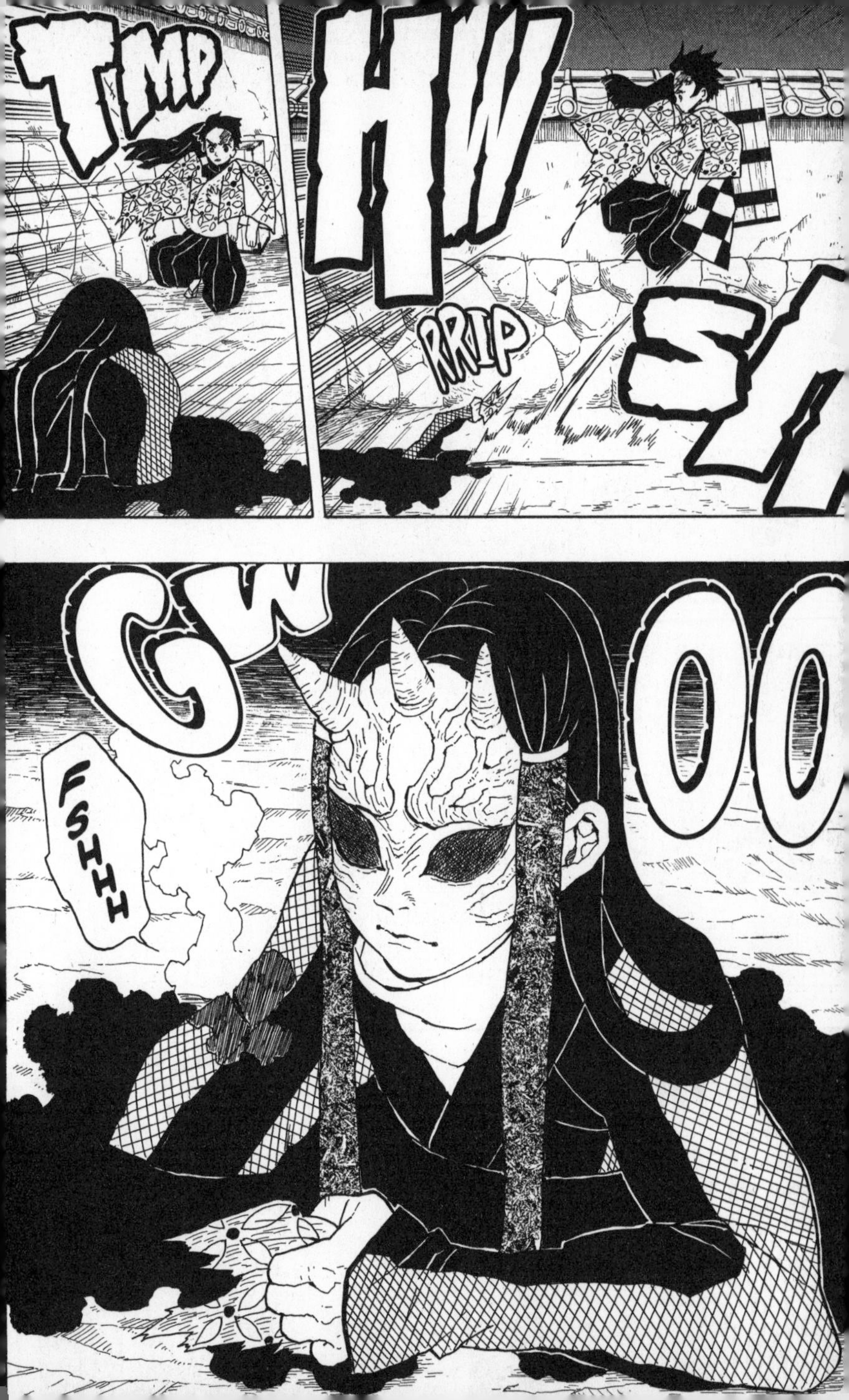
HW
SL
RRIP
TMP
OO
GW
FSHHH

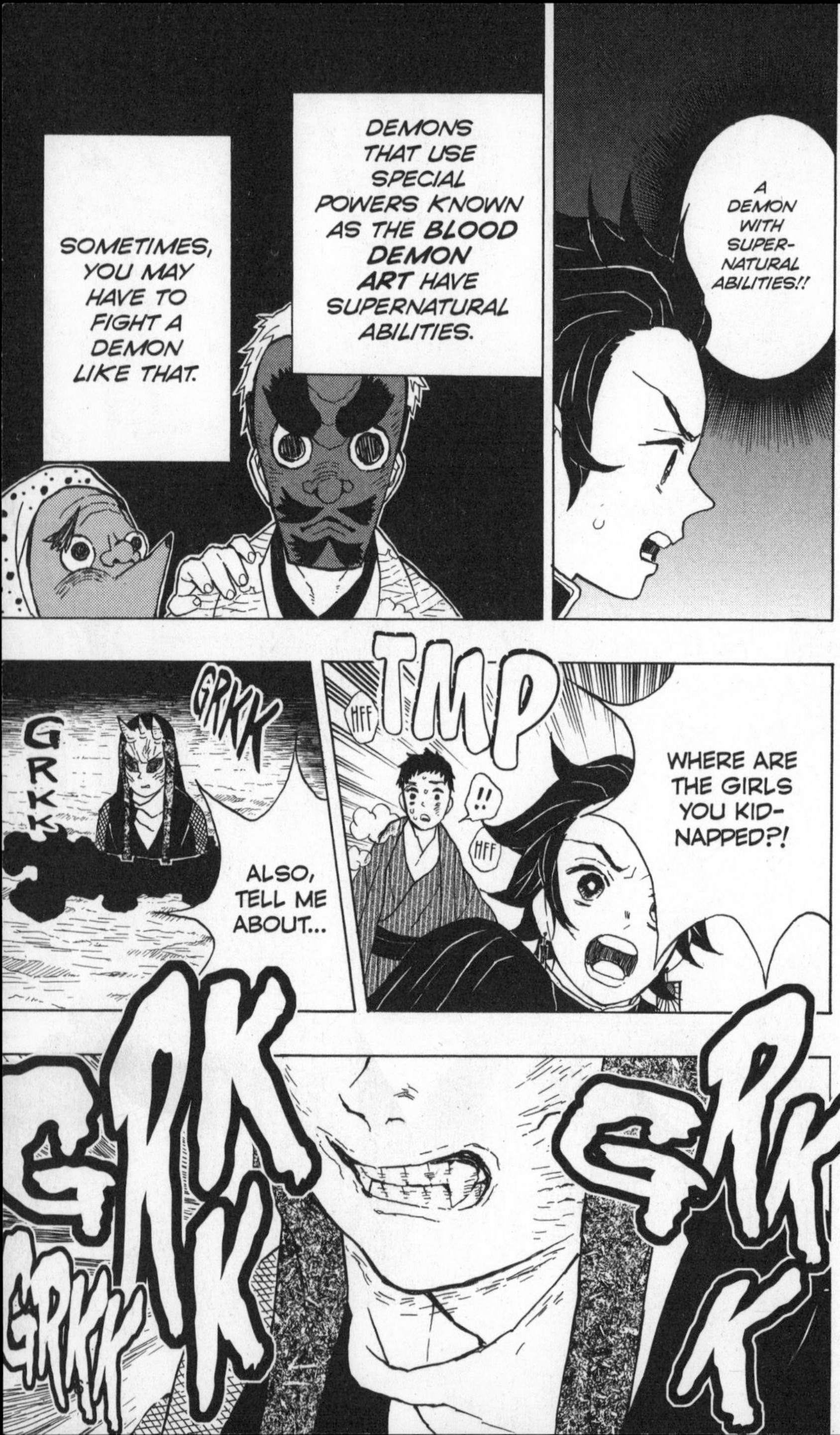
A DEMON WITH SUPER-NATURAL ABILITIES!!
DEMONS THAT USE SPECIAL POWERS KNOWN AS THE BLOOD DEMON ART HAVE SUPERNATURAL ABILITIES.
SOMETIMES, YOU MAY HAVE TO FIGHT A DEMON LIKE THAT.
TMP
WHERE ARE THE GIRLS YOU KID-NAPPED?!
HFF
!!
HFF
GRKK
GRKK
ALSO, TELL ME ABOUT...
GRK
GRK
GRKK

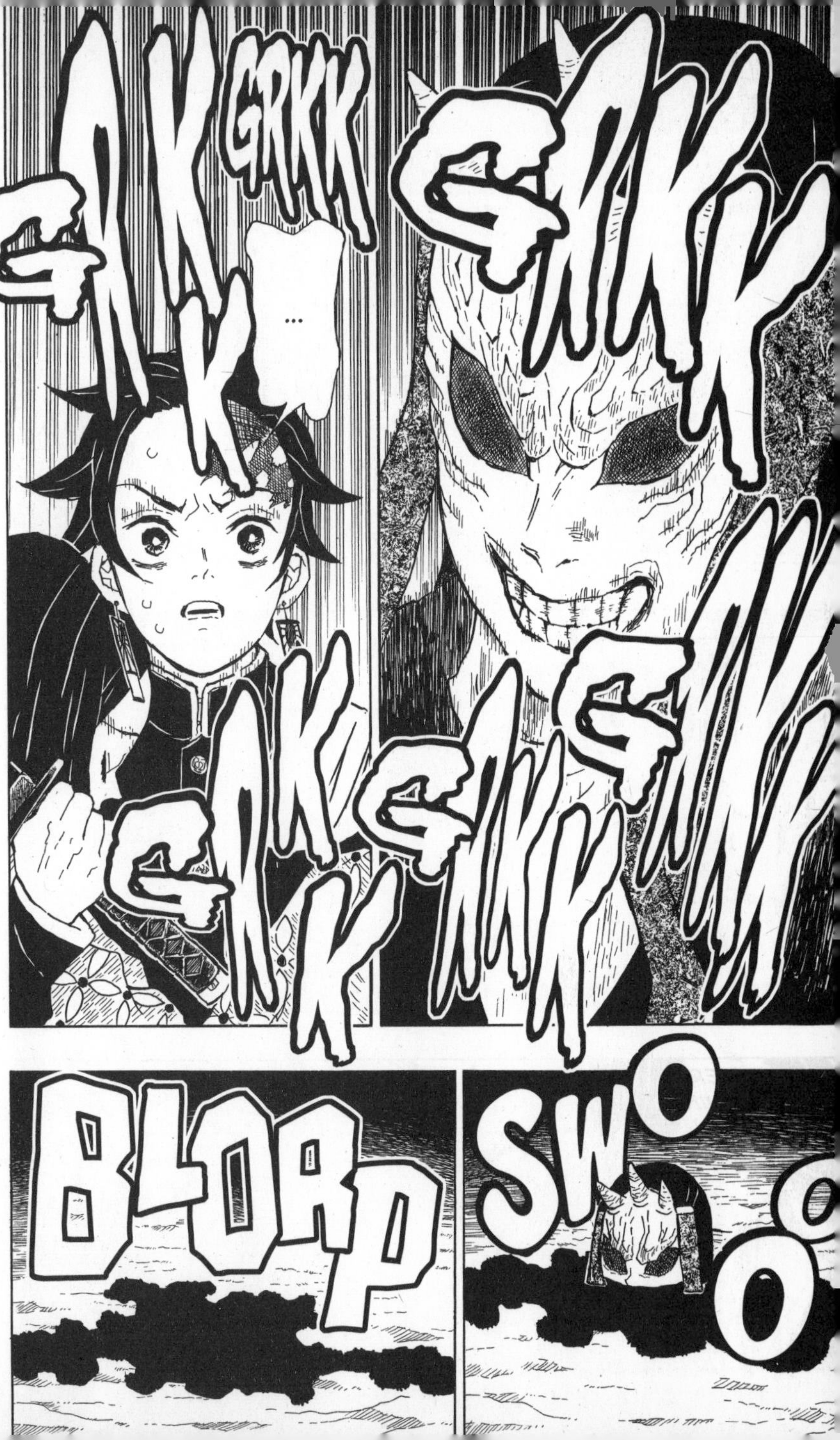
GAKK
GAKKK
GAKK
GRKK
...
GAKK
SWOOO
BLORP

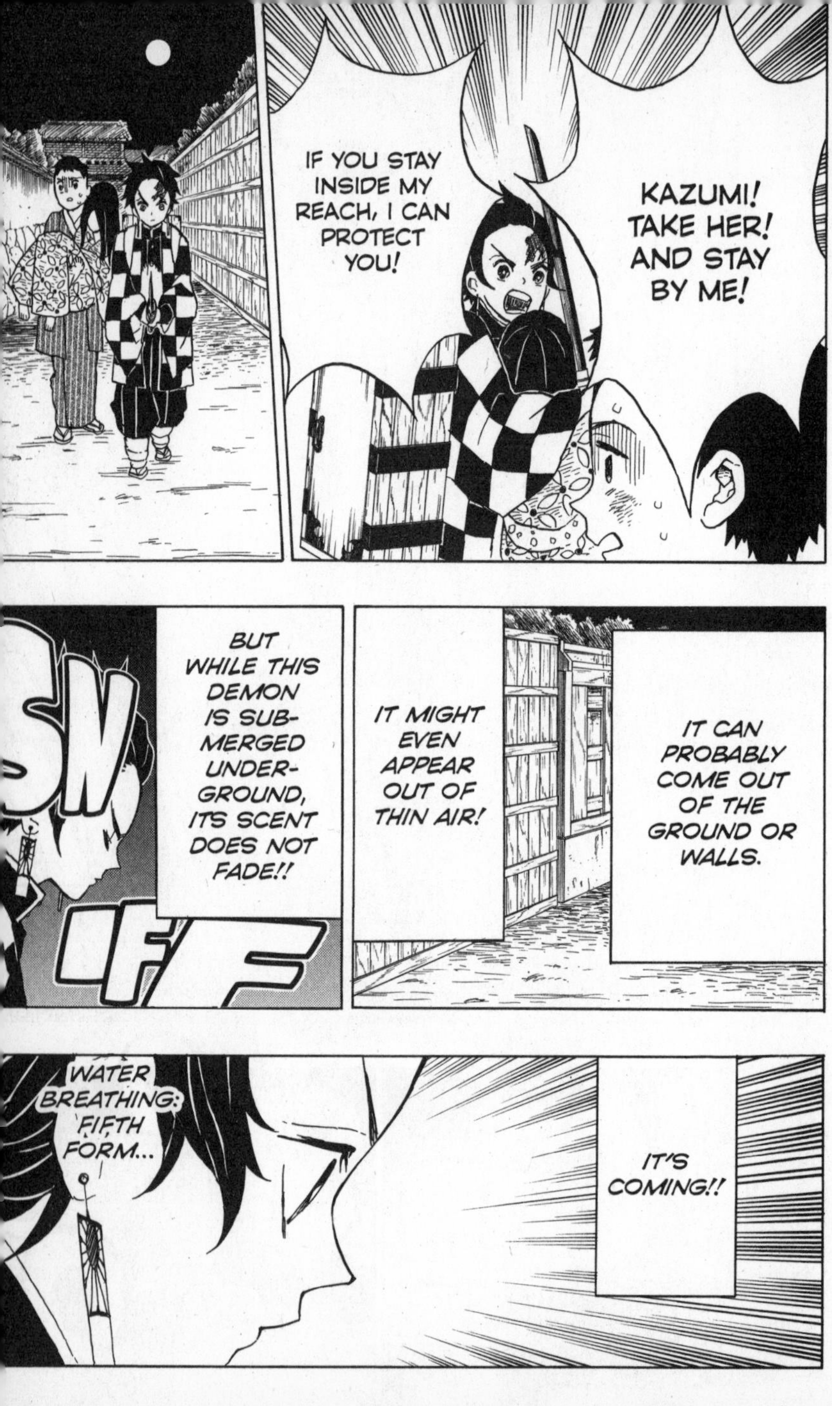
KAZUMI! TAKE HER! AND STAY BY ME!
IF YOU STAY INSIDE MY REACH, I CAN PROTECT YOU!
IT CAN PROBABLY COME OUT OF THE GROUND OR WALLS.
IT MIGHT EVEN APPEAR OUT OF THIN AIR!
BUT WHILE THIS DEMON IS SUB-MERGED UNDER-GROUND, ITS SCENT DOES NOT FADE!!
SNIFF
IT'S COMING!!
WATER BREATHING: FIFTH FORM...

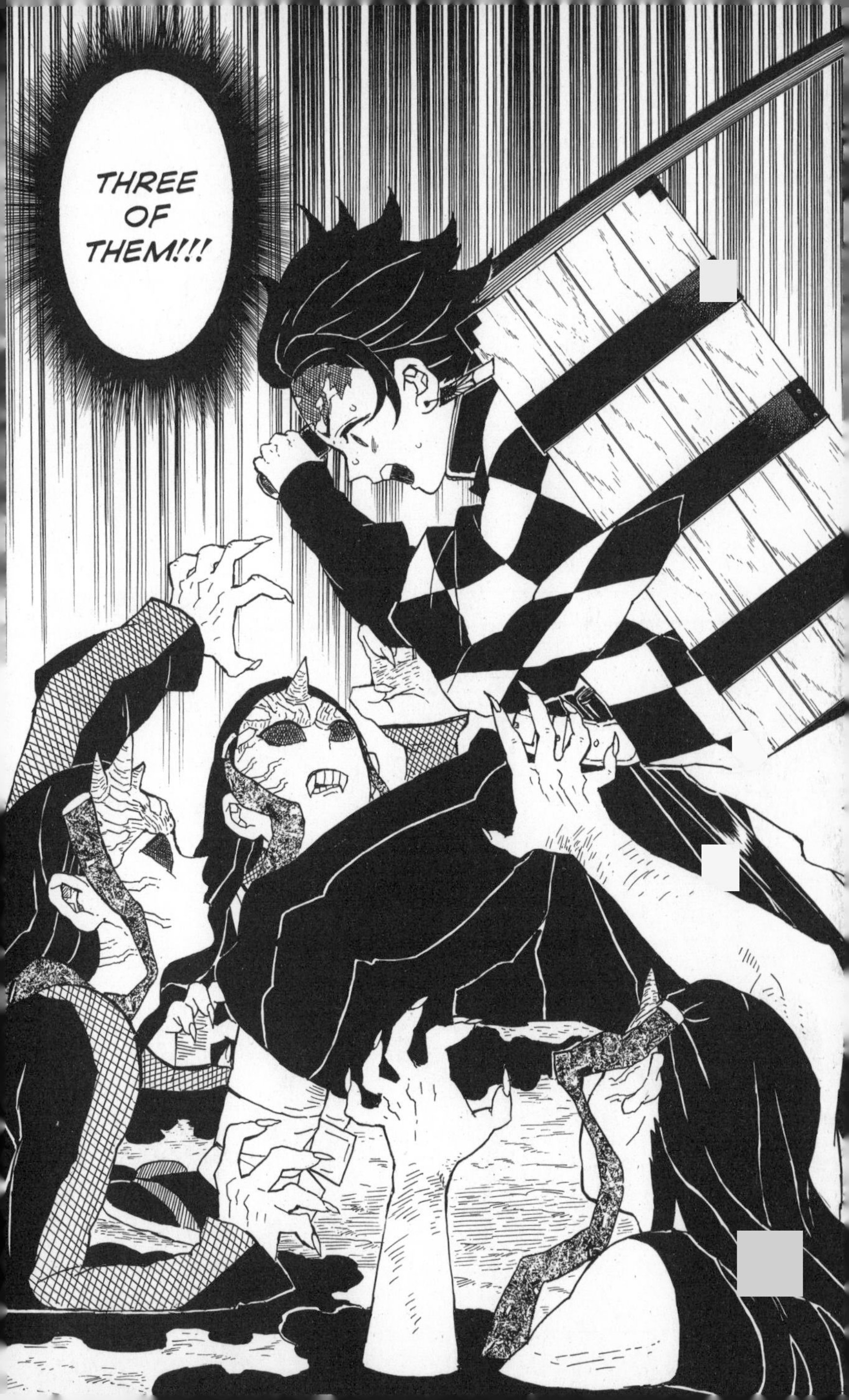
THREE OF THEM!!!

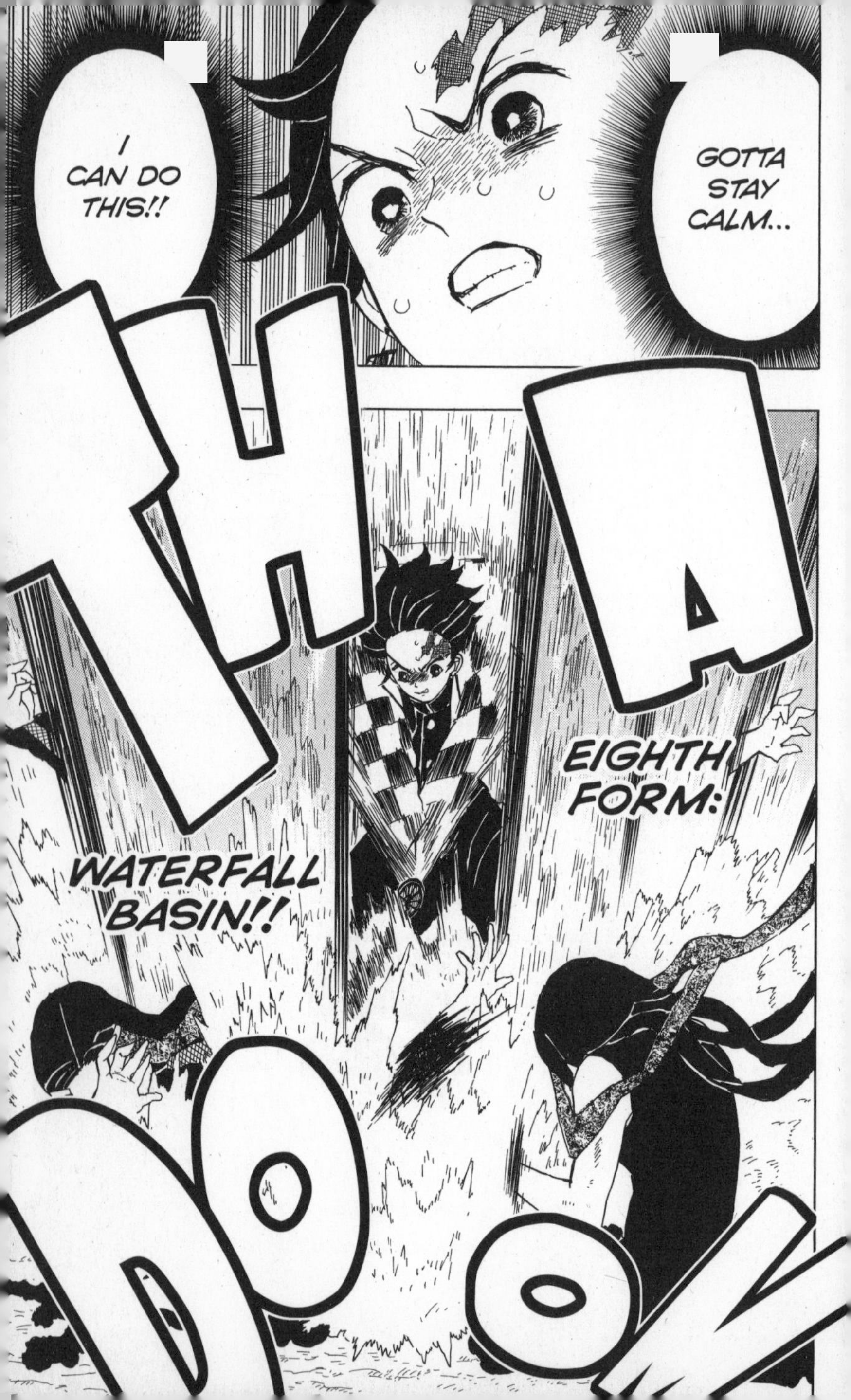
GOTTA STAY CALM...
I CAN DO THIS!!
EIGHTH FORM:
WATERFALL BASIN!!

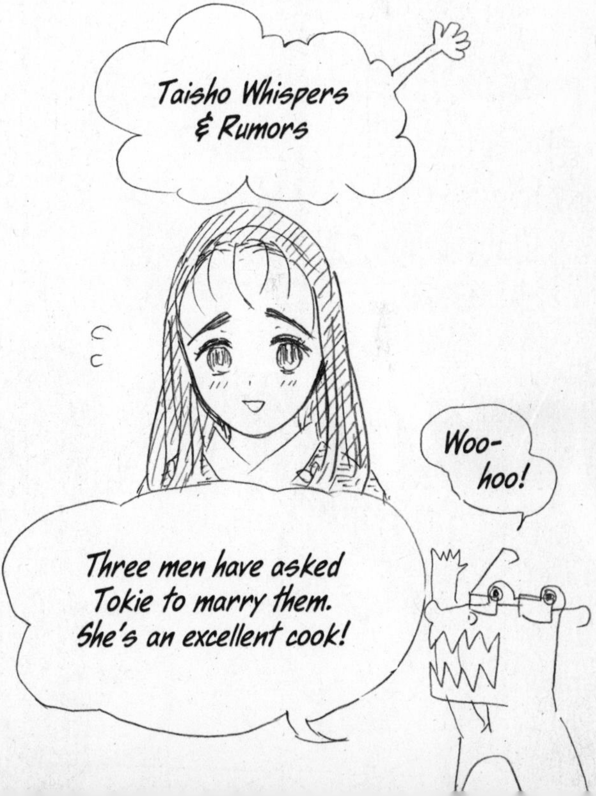
Taisho Whispers & Rumors
Woo-hoo!
Three men have asked Tokie to marry them. She's an excellent cook!

CHAPTER 11: SUGGESTION

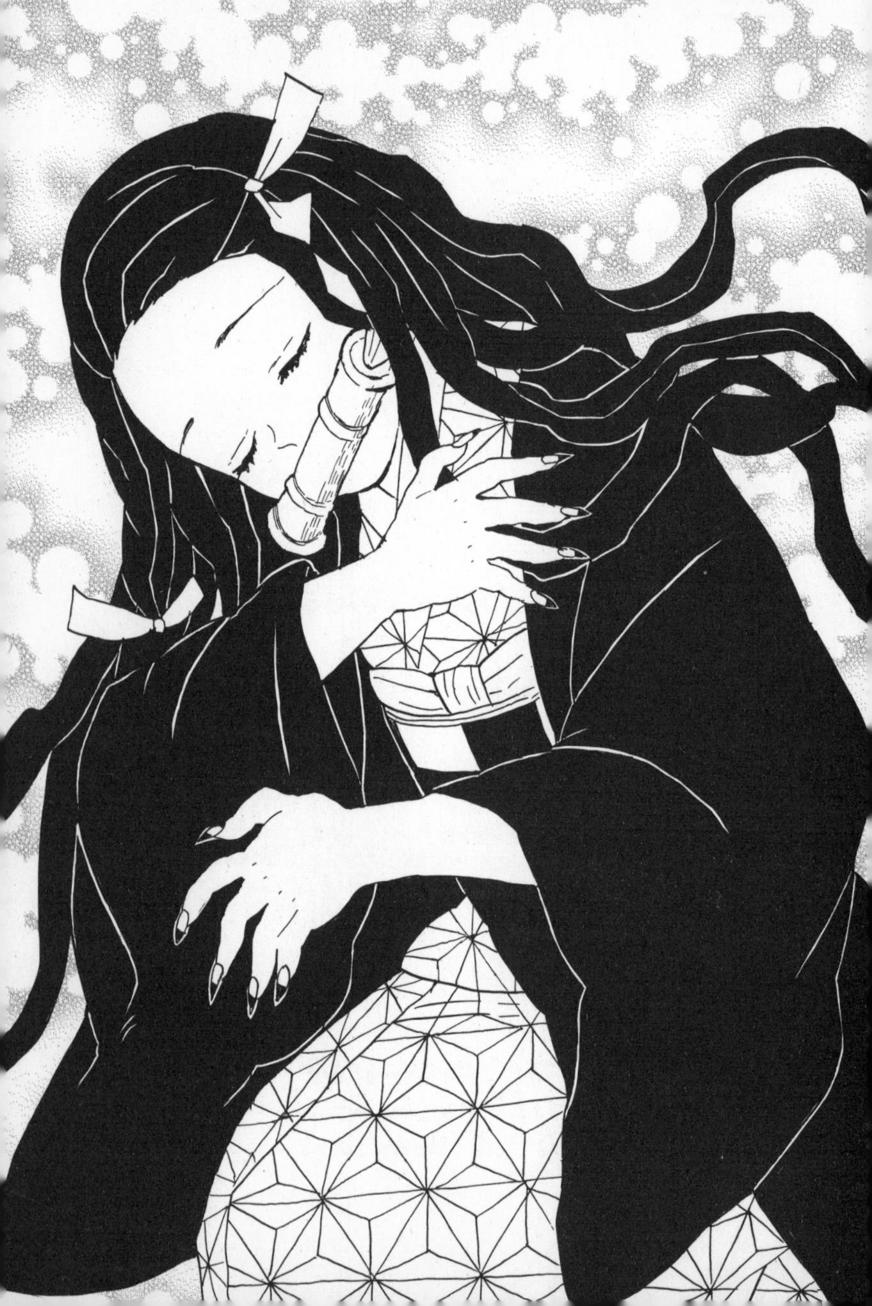

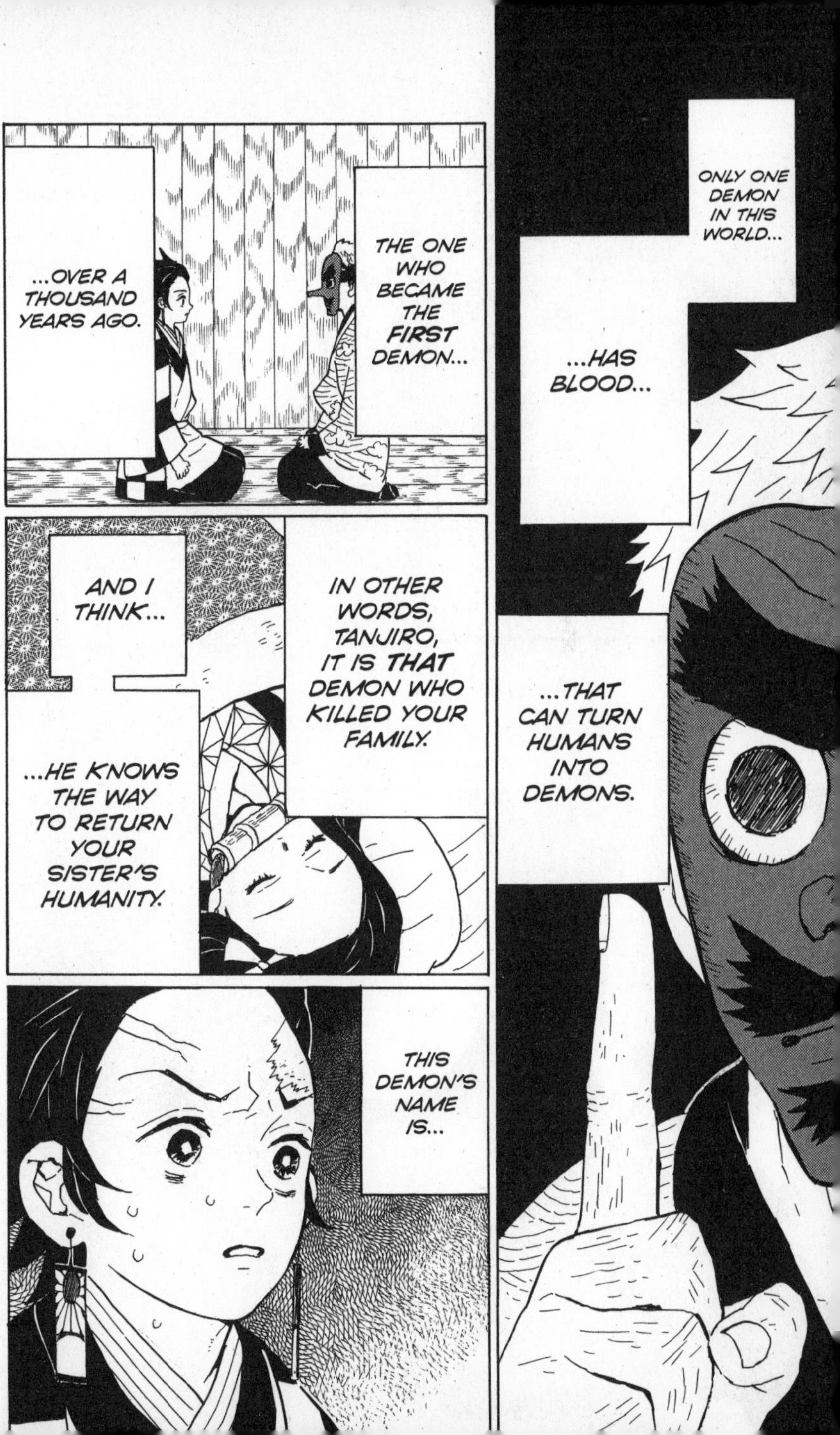
ONLY ONE DEMON IN THIS WORLD...
...HAS BLOOD...
...THAT CAN TURN HUMANS INTO DEMONS.
THE ONE WHO BECAME THE FIRST DEMON...
...OVER A THOUSAND YEARS AGO.
IN OTHER WORDS, TANJIRO, IT IS THAT DEMON WHO KILLED YOUR FAMILY.
AND I THINK...
...HE KNOWS THE WAY TO RETURN YOUR SISTER'S HUMANITY.
THIS DEMON'S NAME IS...

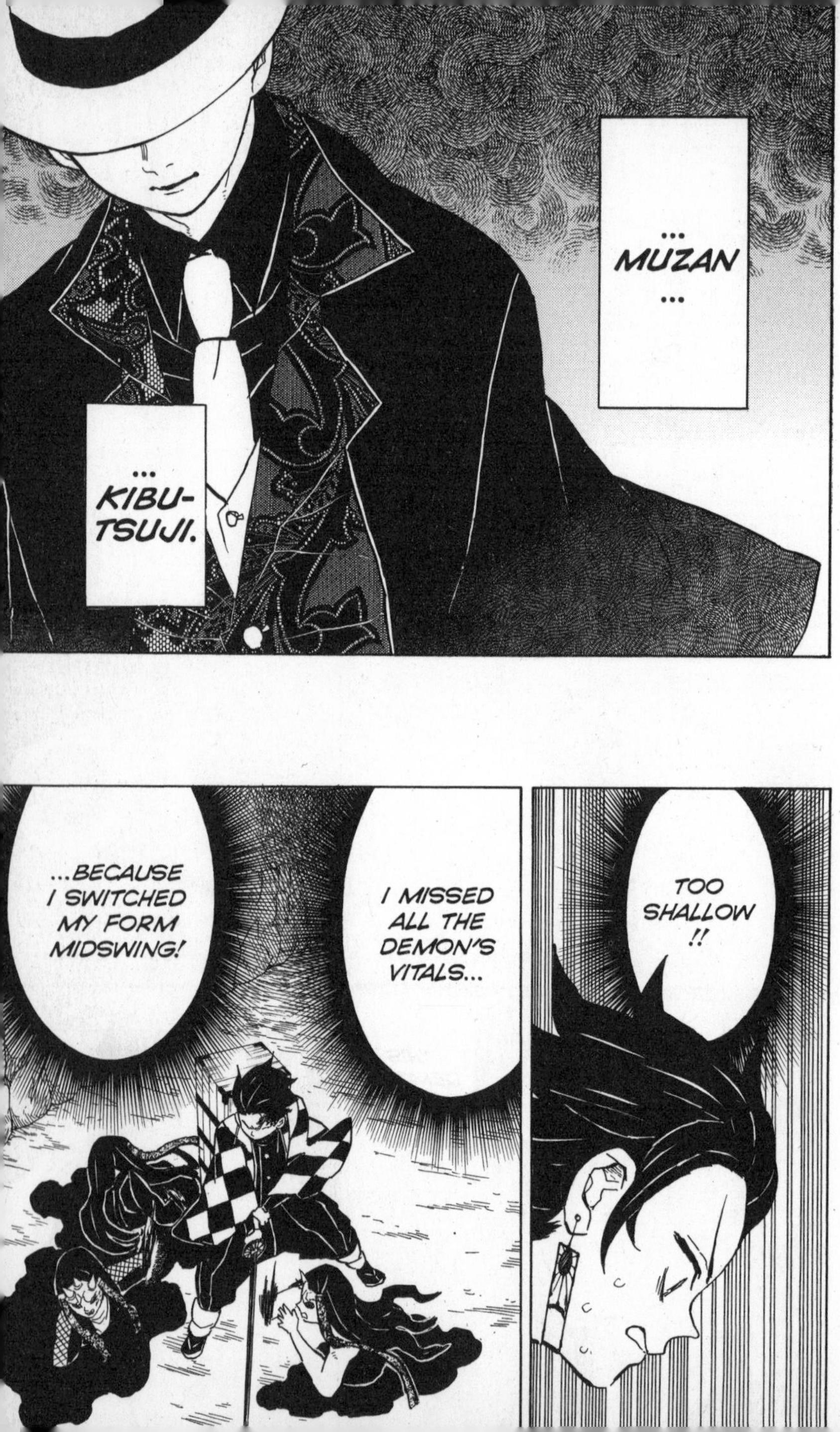
...
MUZAN
...
...
KIBU-
TSUJI.
TOO SHALLOW!!
I MISSED ALL THE DEMON'S VITALS...
...BECAUSE I SWITCHED MY FORM MIDSWING!

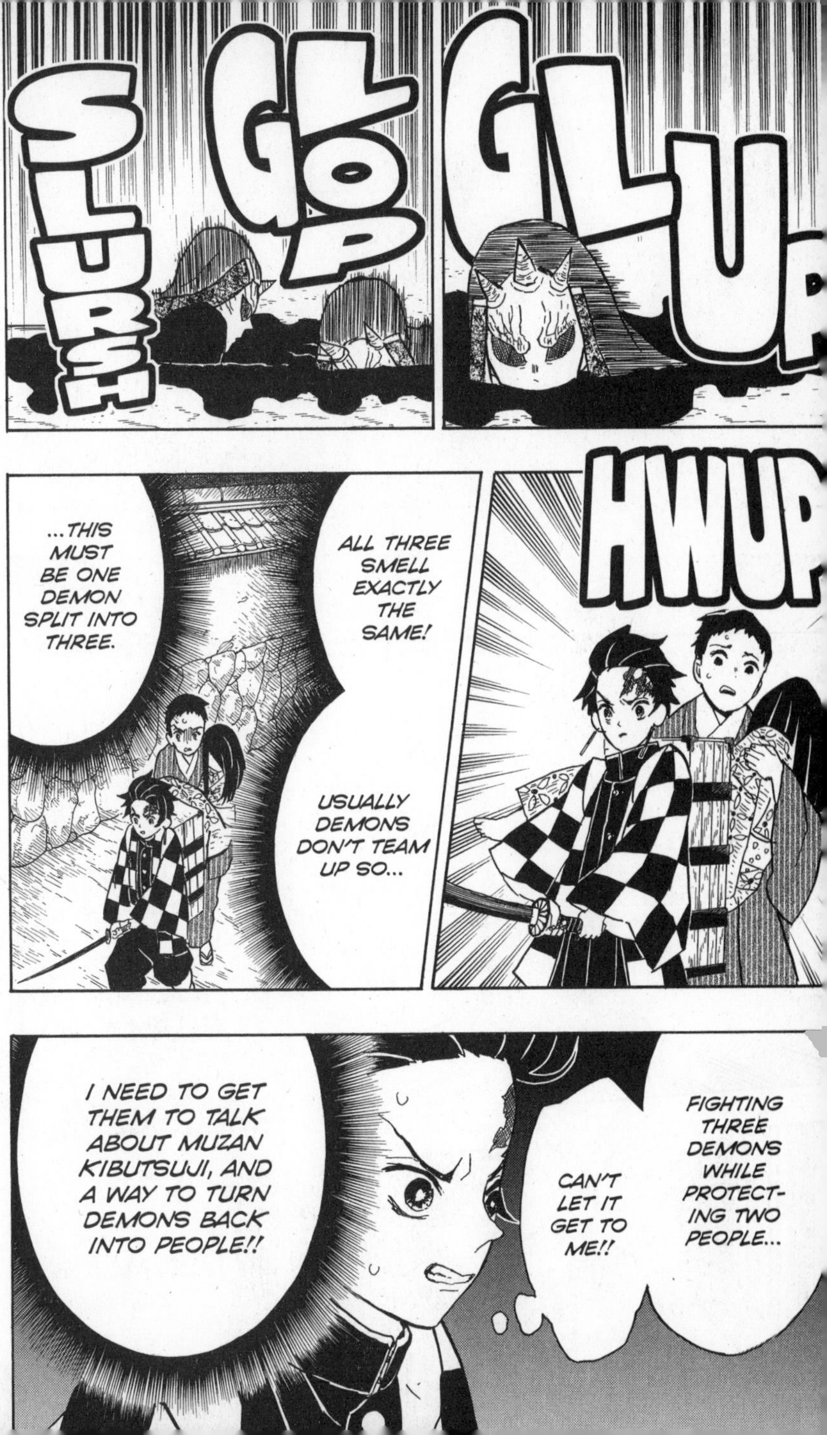
GLUP
GLOP
SLURSH
HWUP
ALL THREE SMELL EXACTLY THE SAME!
USUALLY DEMONS DON'T TEAM UP SO...
...THIS MUST BE ONE DEMON SPLIT INTO THREE.
FIGHTING THREE DEMONS WHILE PROTECT-ING TWO PEOPLE...
CAN'T LET IT GET TO ME!!
I NEED TO GET THEM TO TALK ABOUT MUZAN KIBUTSUJI, AND A WAY TO TURN DEMONS BACK INTO PEOPLE!!

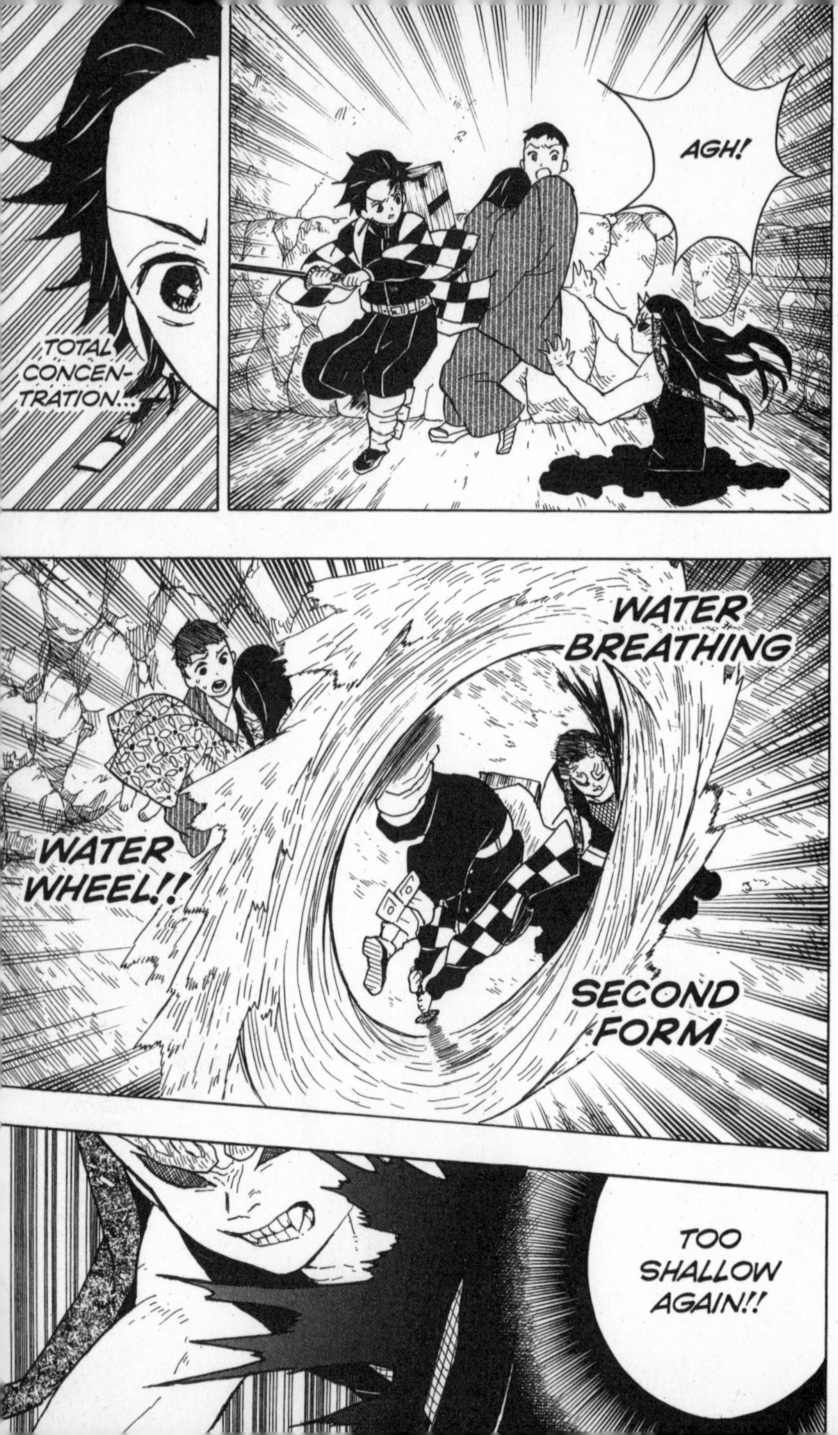
AGH!
TOTAL CONCENTRATION...
WATER BREATHING
SECOND FORM
WATER WHEEL!!
TOO SHALLOW AGAIN!!

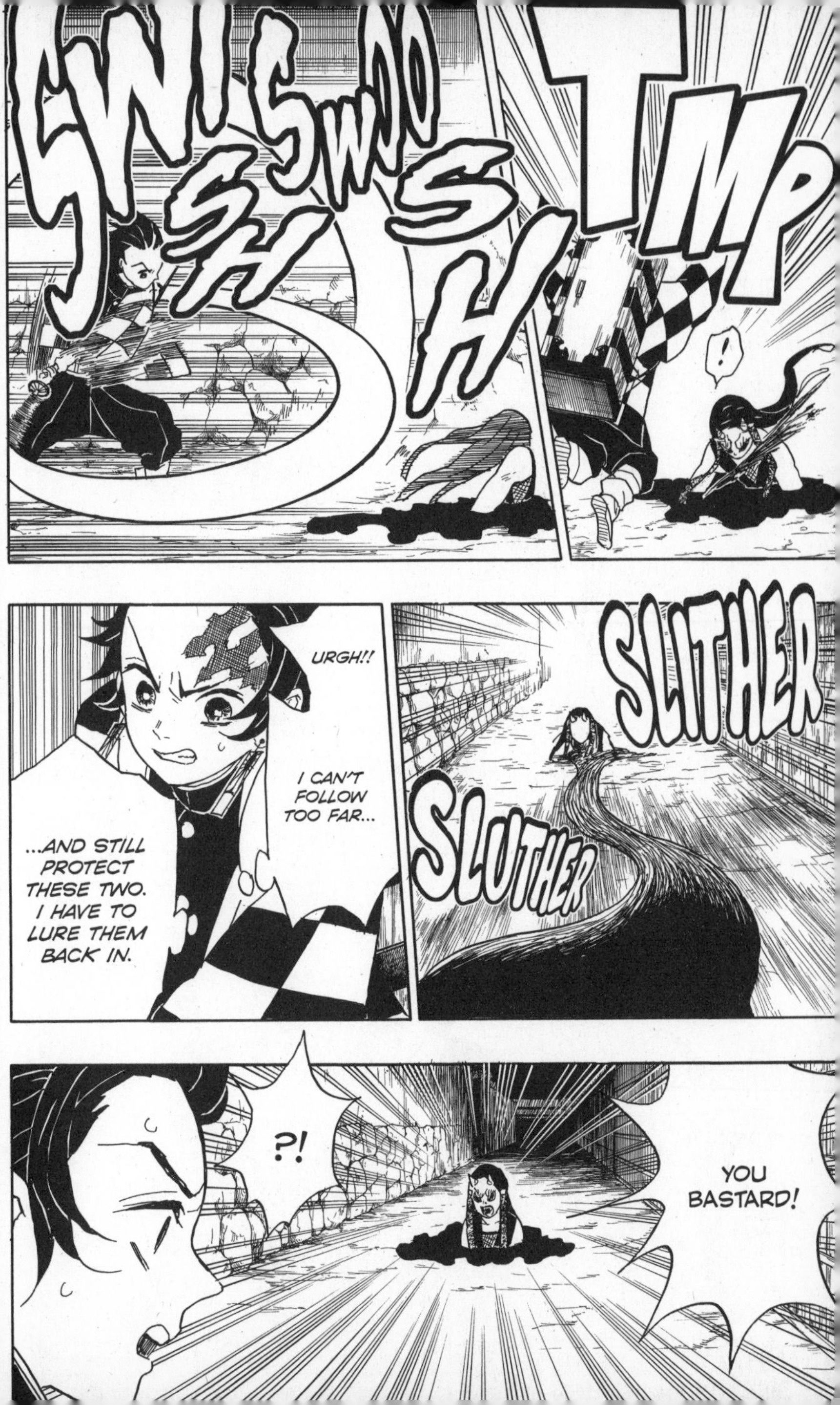
TMP
!
SWOOSH
SWOOSH
SLITHER
SLITHER
URGH!!
I CAN'T FOLLOW TOO FAR...
...AND STILL PROTECT THESE TWO. I HAVE TO LURE THEM BACK IN.
YOU BASTARD!
?!

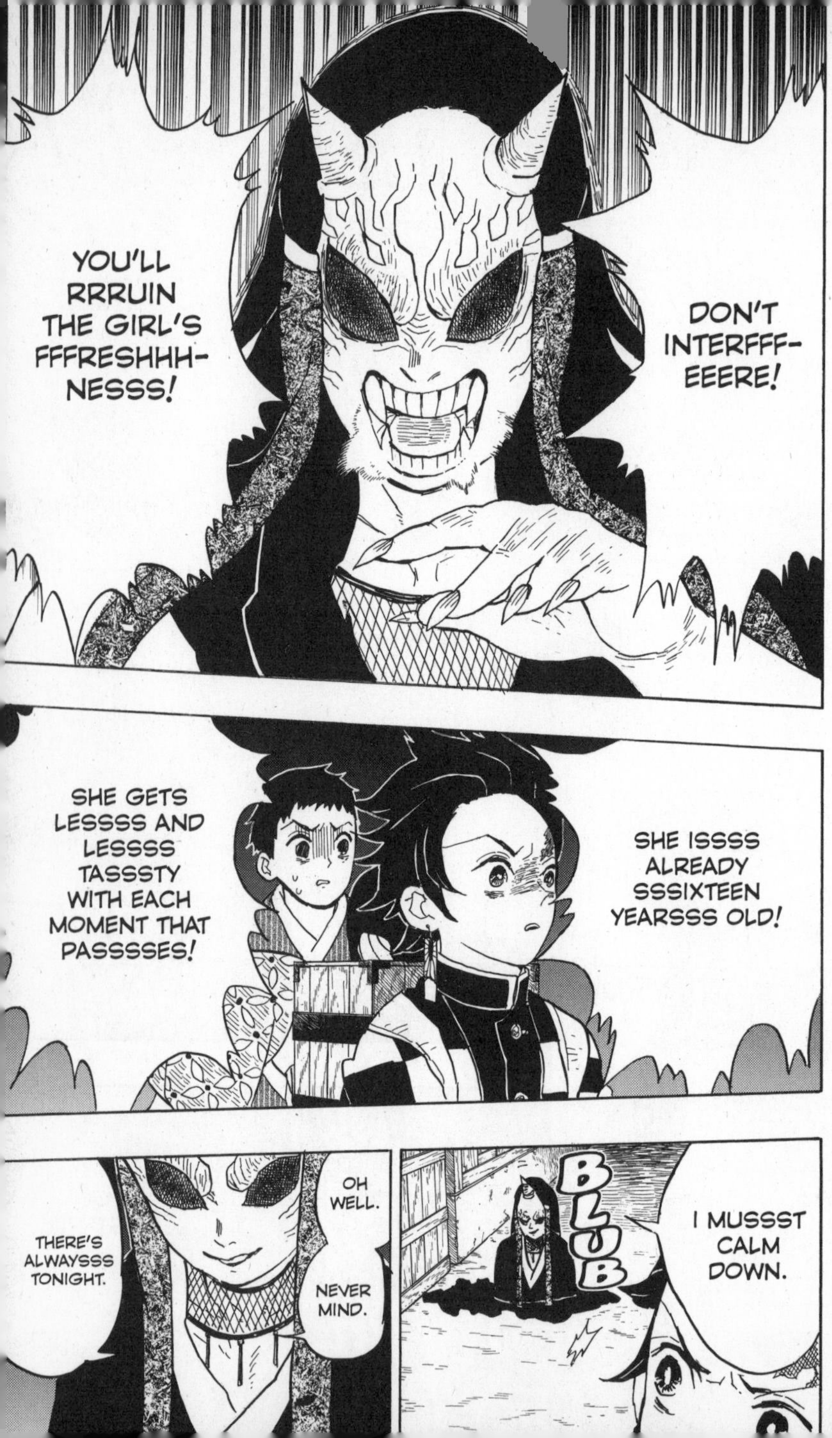
DON'T INTERFFF-EEERE!
YOU'LL RRRUIN THE GIRL'S FFFRESHHH-NESSS!
SHE ISSSS ALREADY SSSIXTEEN YEARSSS OLD!
SHE GETS LESSSS AND LESSSS TASSSTY WITH EACH MOMENT THAT PASSSSES!
I MUSSST CALM DOWN.
BLUB
OH WELL.
NEVER MIND.
THERE'S ALWAYSSS TONIGHT.

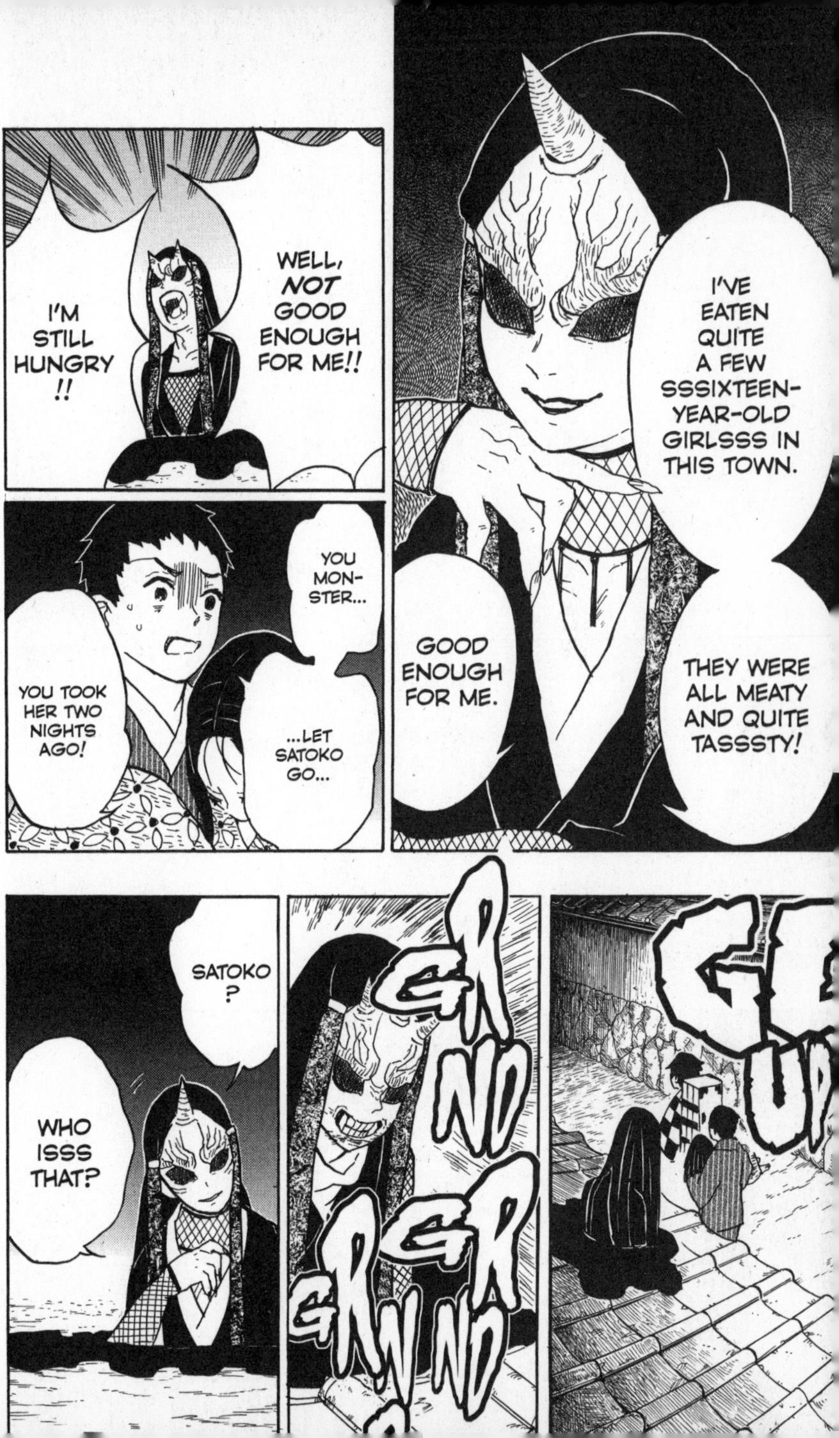
I'VE EATEN QUITE A FEW SSSIXTEEN-YEAR-OLD GIRLSSS IN THIS TOWN.
THEY WERE ALL MEATY AND QUITE TASSSTY!
GOOD ENOUGH FOR ME.
WELL, *NOT* GOOD ENOUGH FOR ME!!
I'M STILL HUNGRY!!
YOU MONSTER...
...LET SATOKO GO...
YOU TOOK HER TWO NIGHTS AGO!
SATOKO?
WHO ISSS THAT?

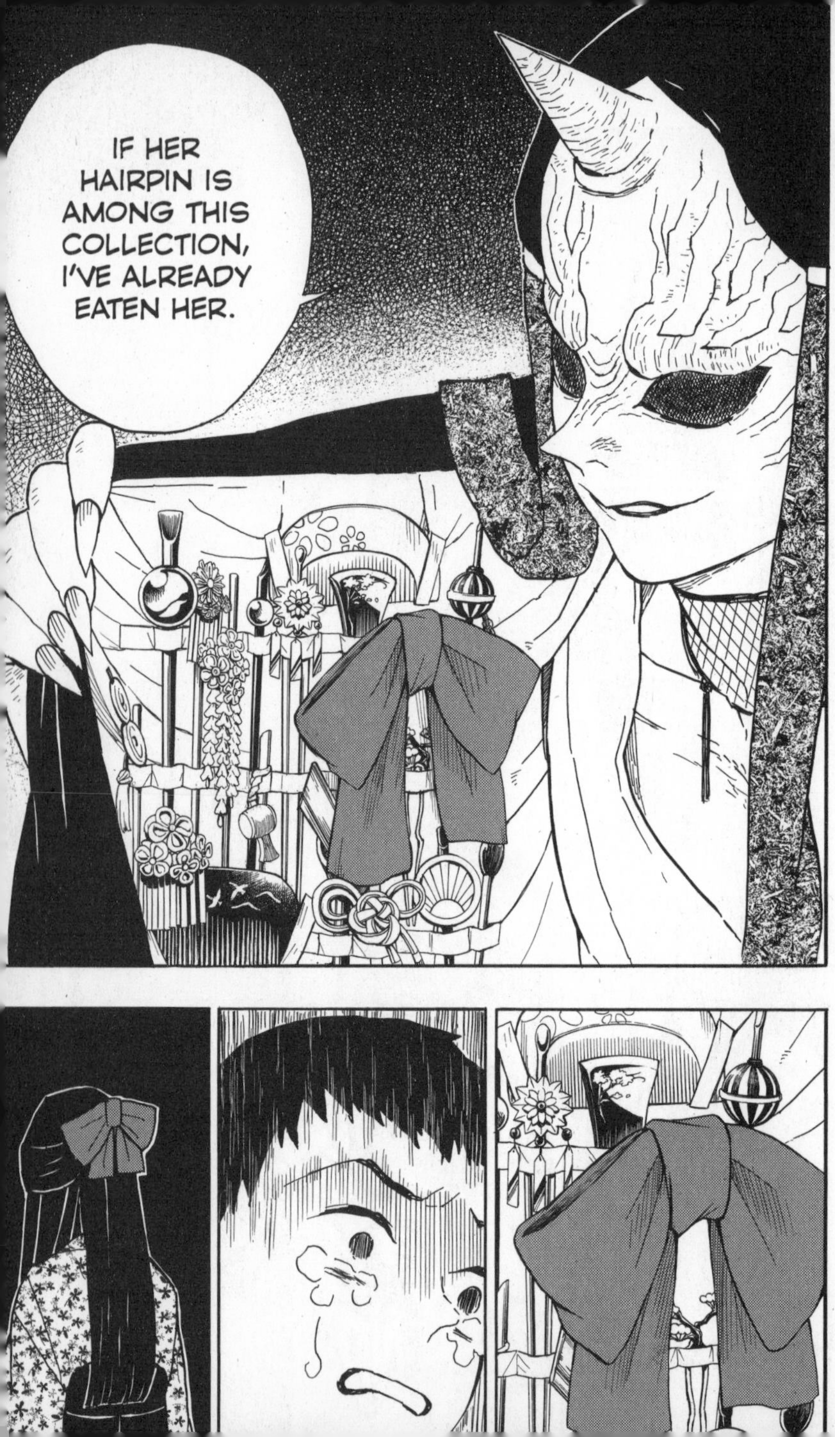
IF HER HAIRPIN IS AMONG THIS COLLECTION, I'VE ALREADY EATEN HER.

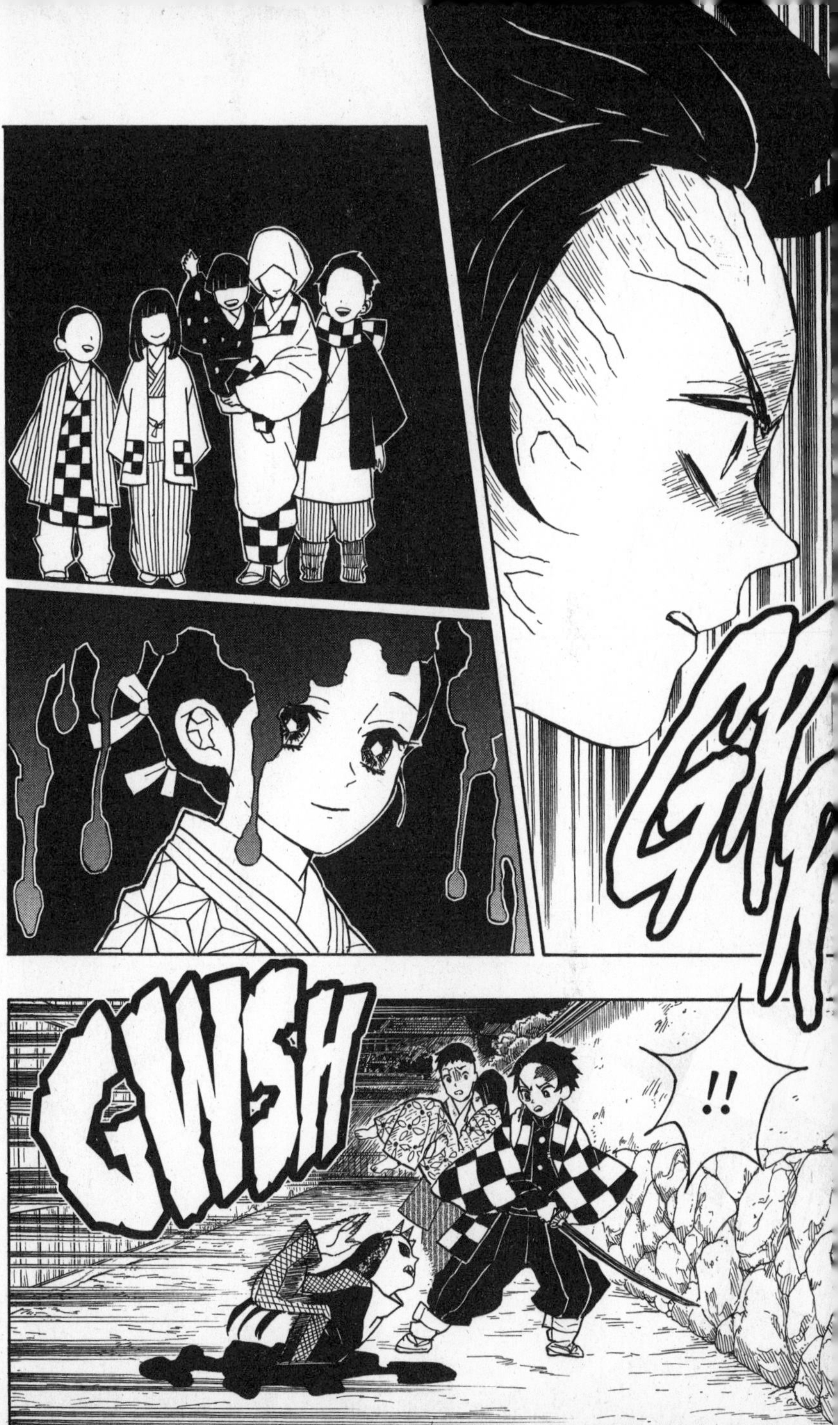
!!

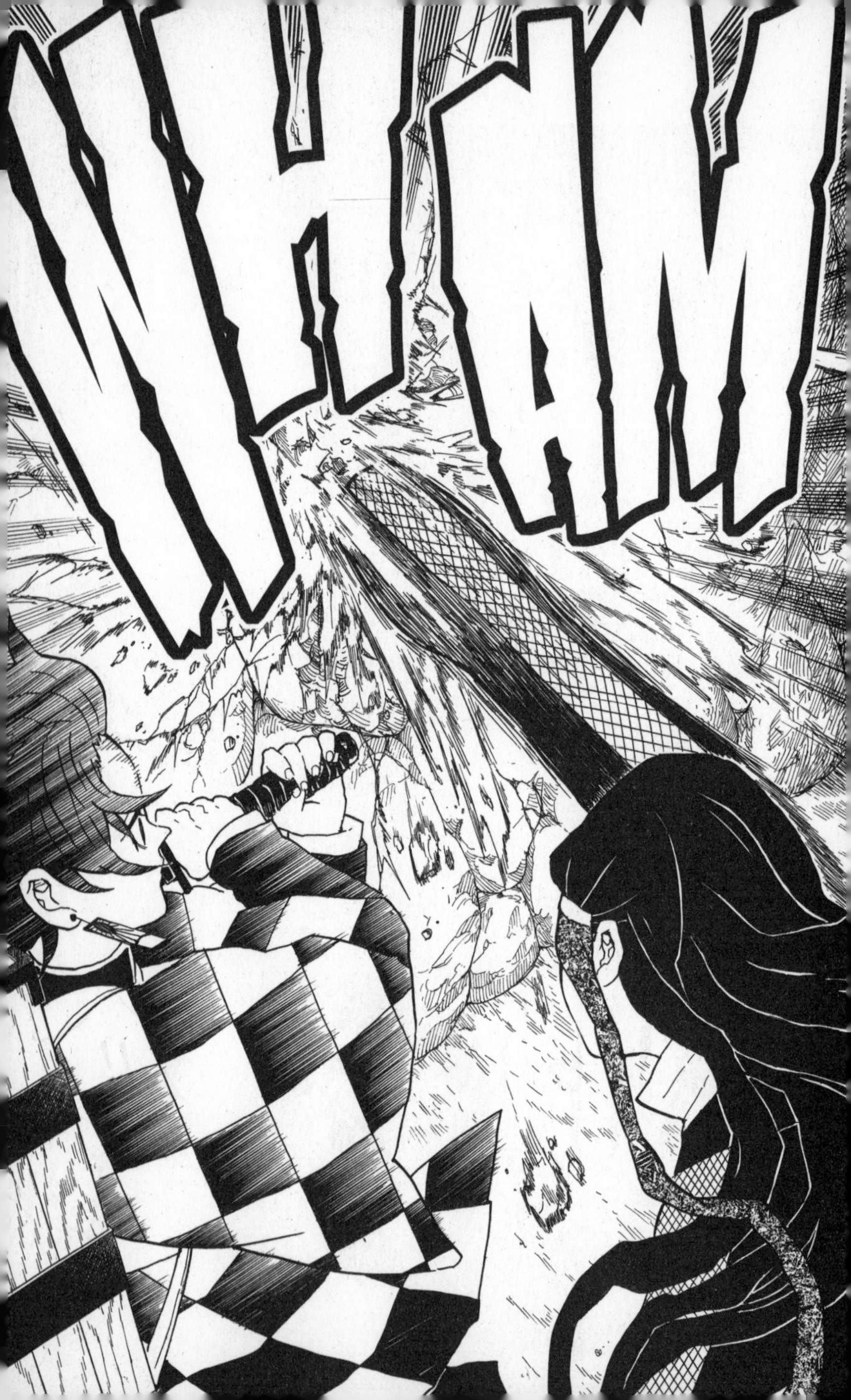
WHAM

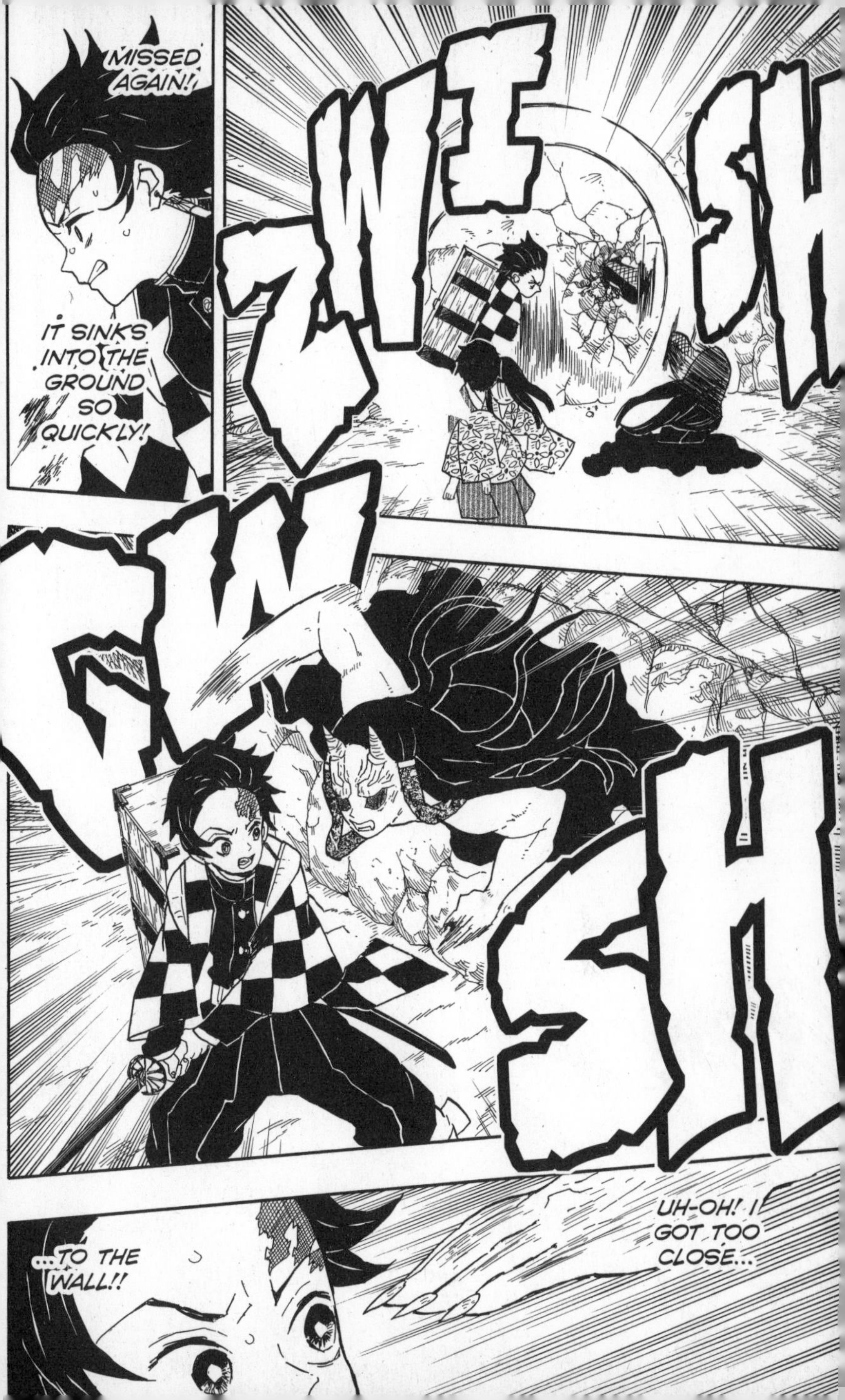
MISSED AGAIN!
IT SINKS INTO THE GROUND SO QUICKLY!
UH-OH! I GOT TOO CLOSE...
...TO THE WALL!!

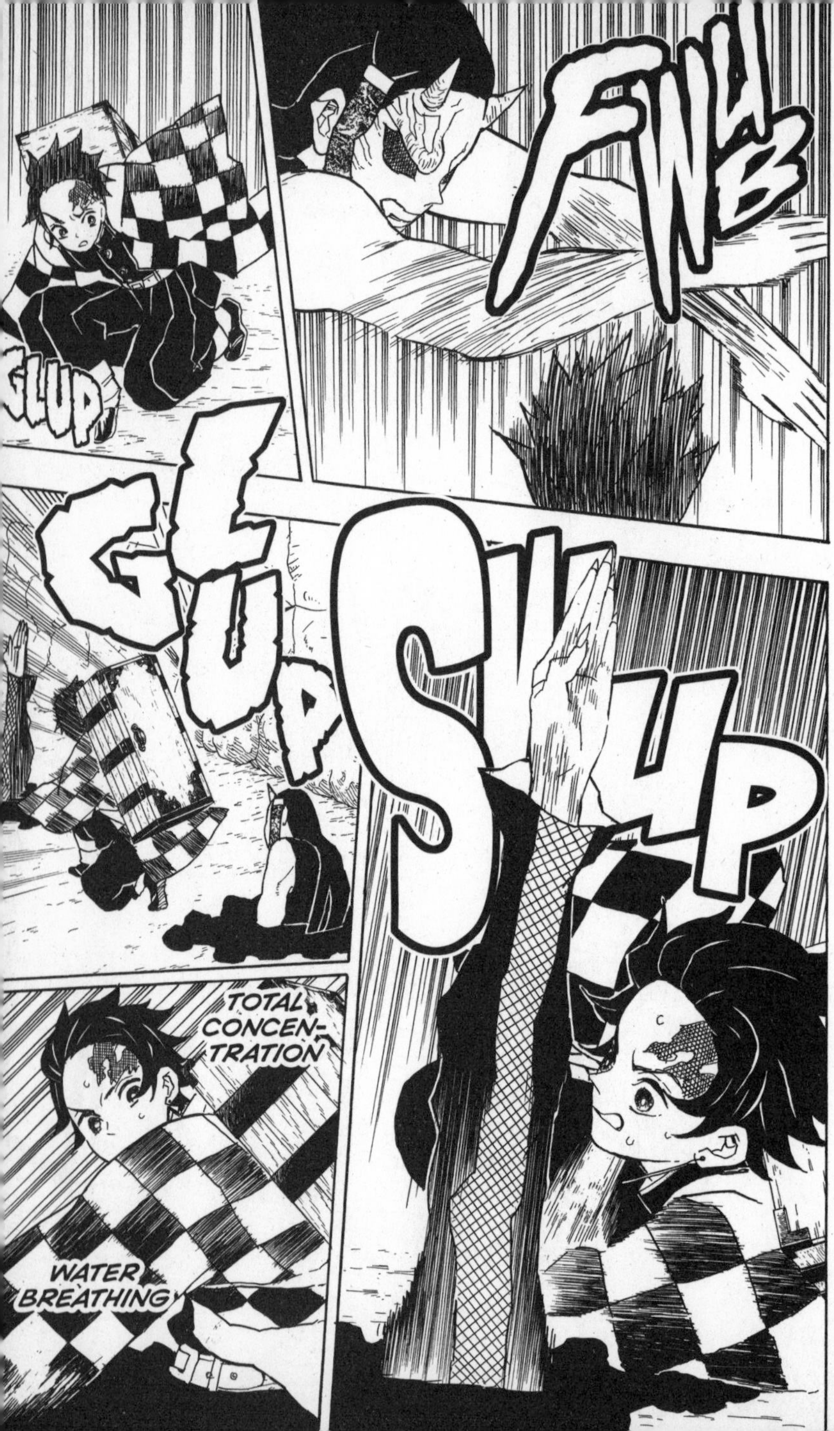
FWUB
GLUP
SHUP
GLUP
TOTAL CONCEN-TRATION
WATER BREATHING

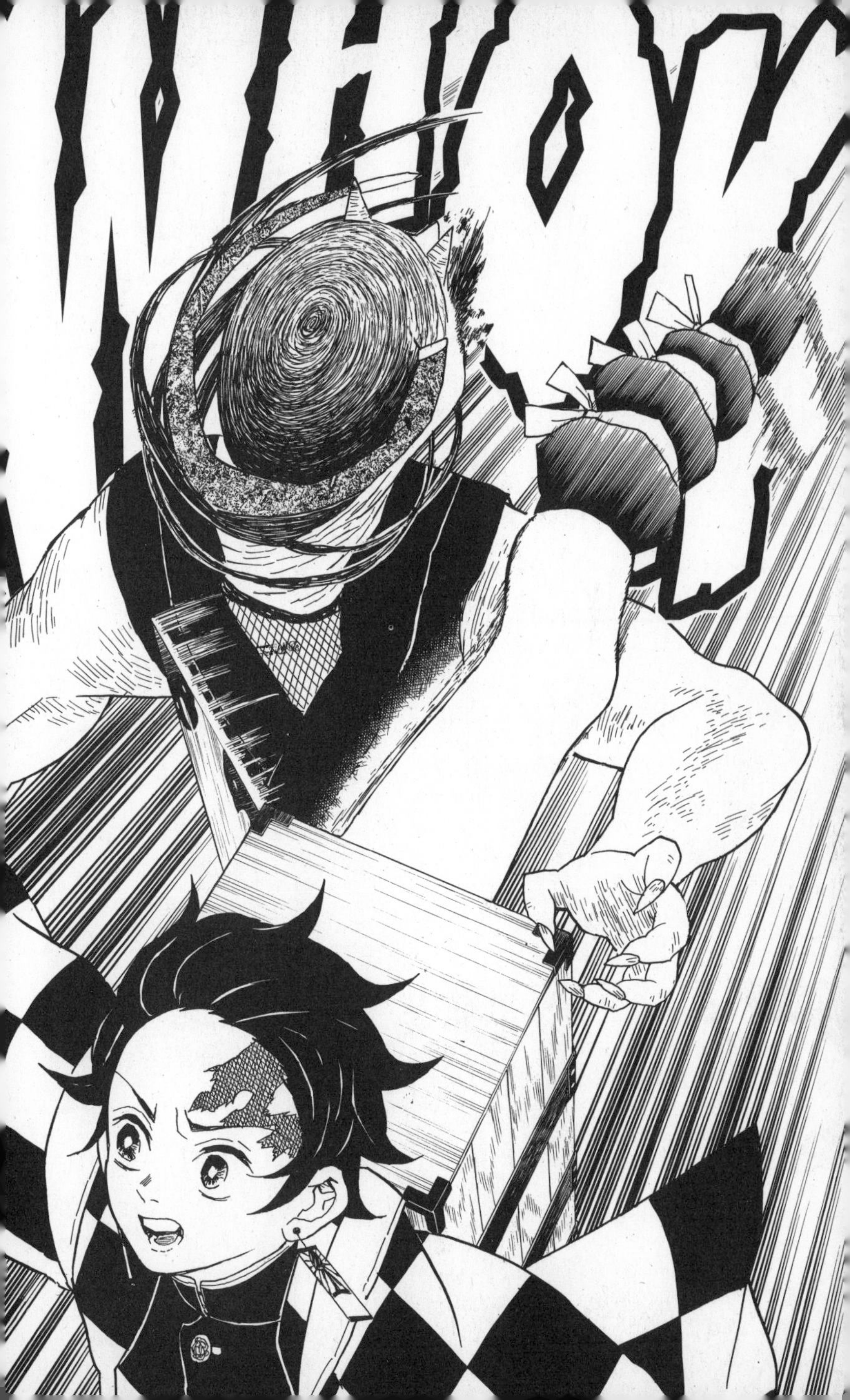

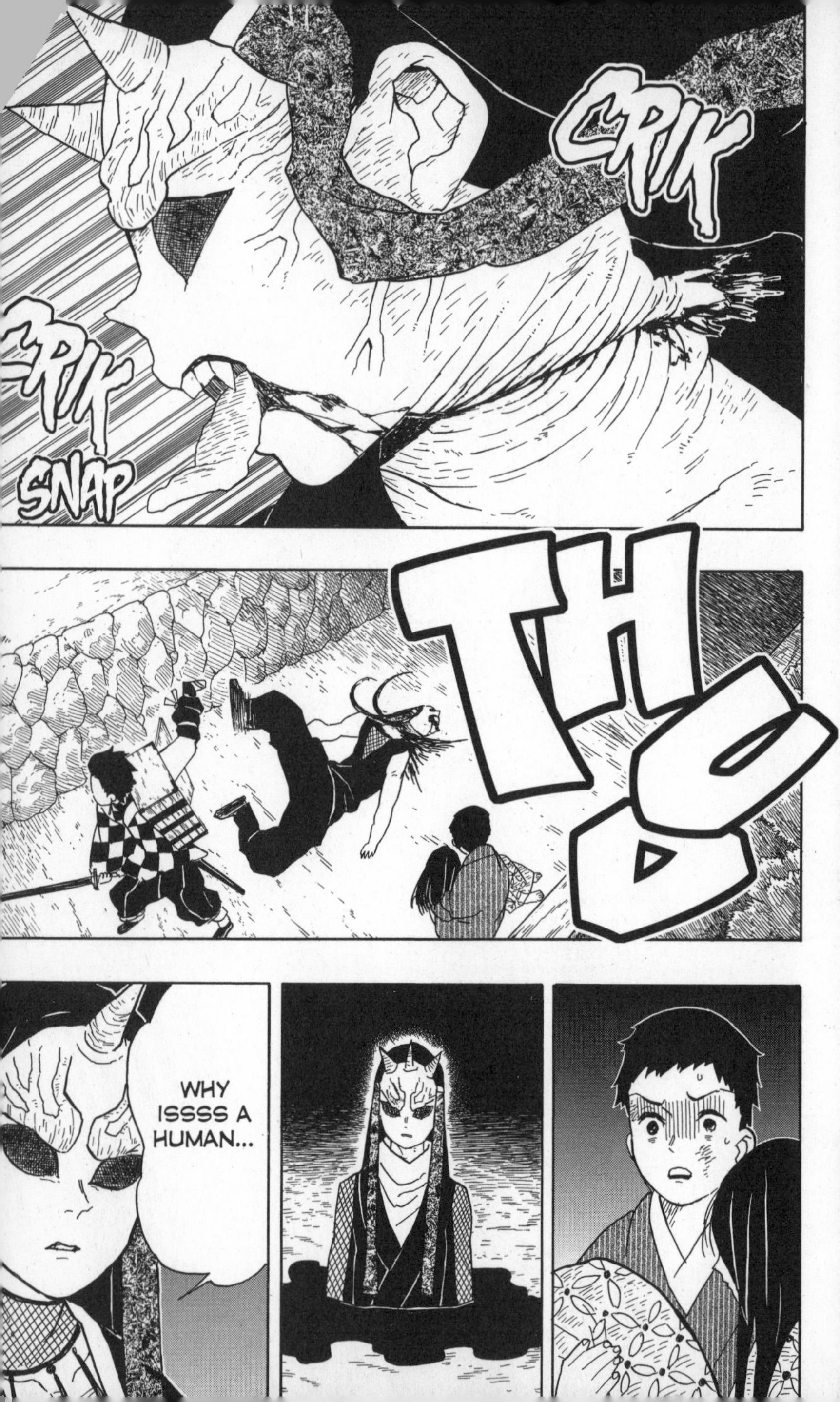
CRIK
CRIK
SNAP
THUD
WHY ISSSS A HUMAN...

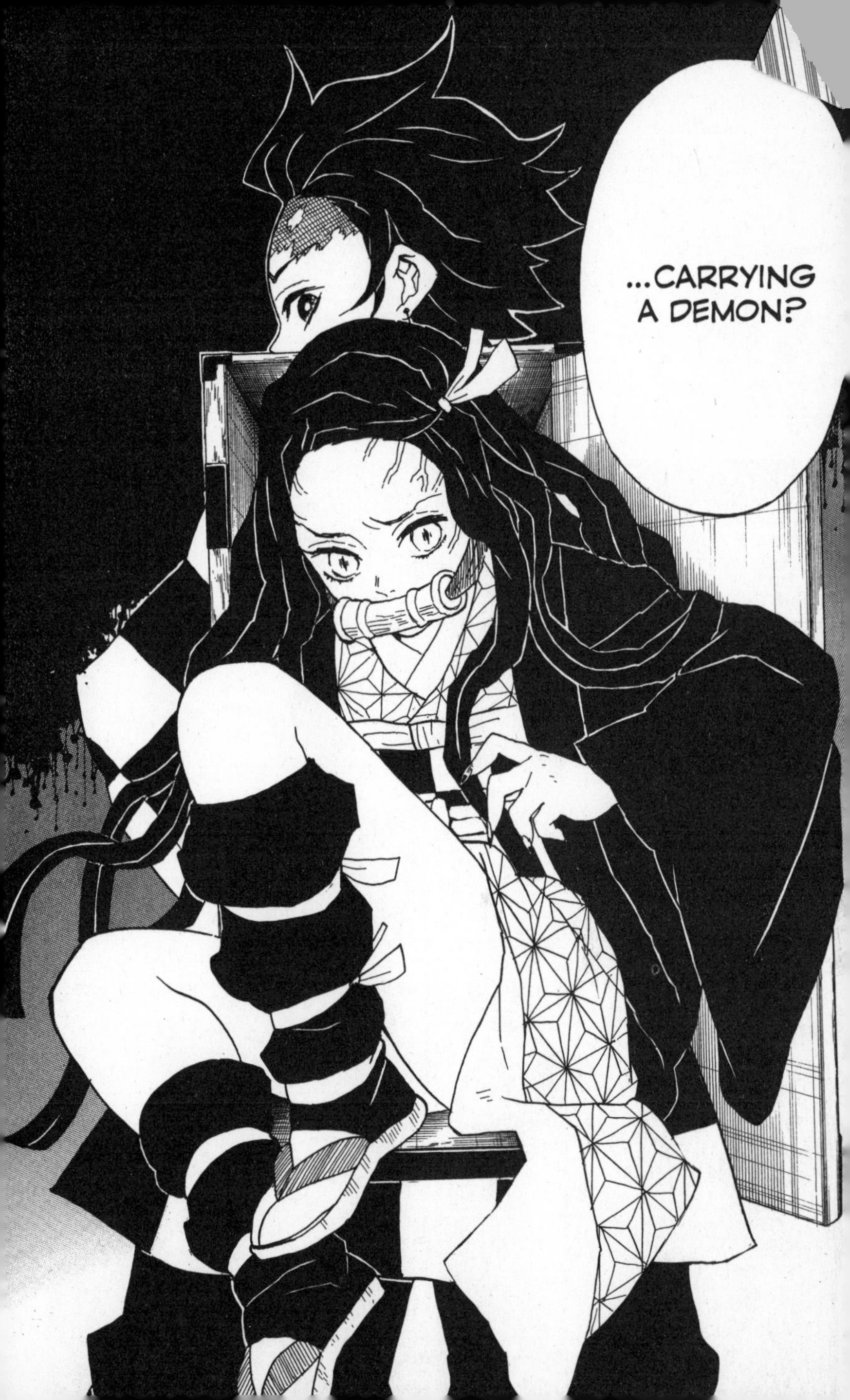
...CARRYING A DEMON?

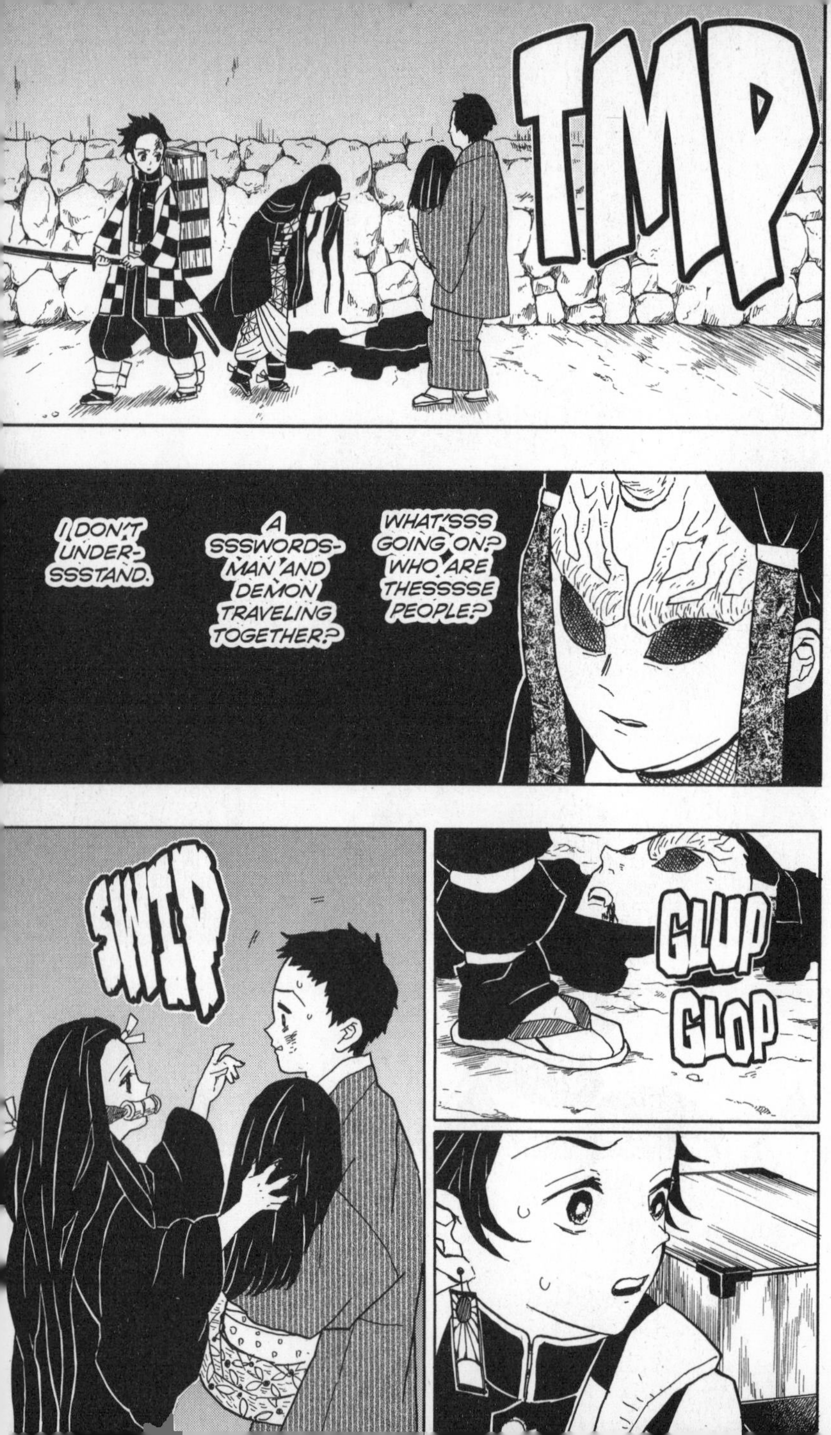
TMP
WHAT'SSS GOING ON? WHO ARE THESSSSE PEOPLE?
A SSSWORDS-MAN AND DEMON TRAVELING TOGETHER?
I DON'T UNDER-SSSTAND.
GLUP
GLOP
SWTP

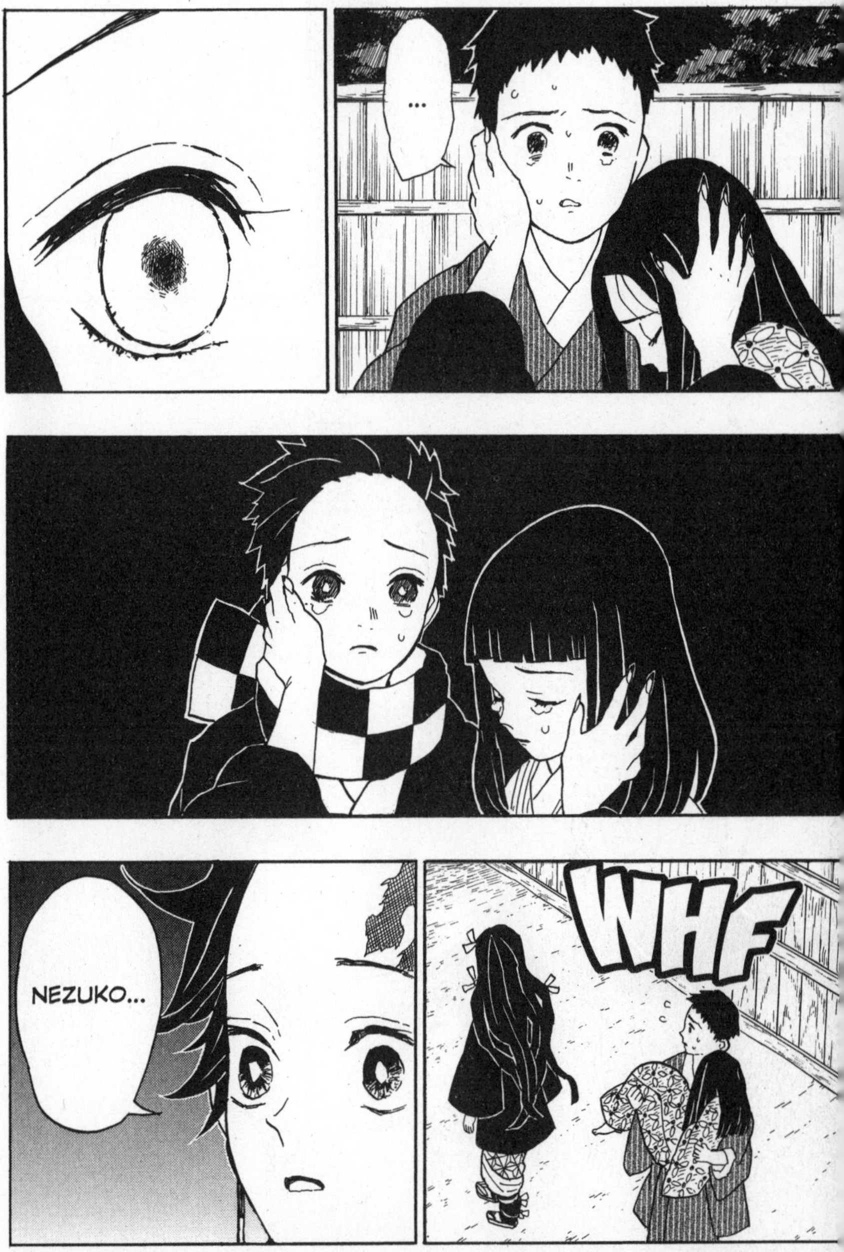
...
WHF
NEZUKO...

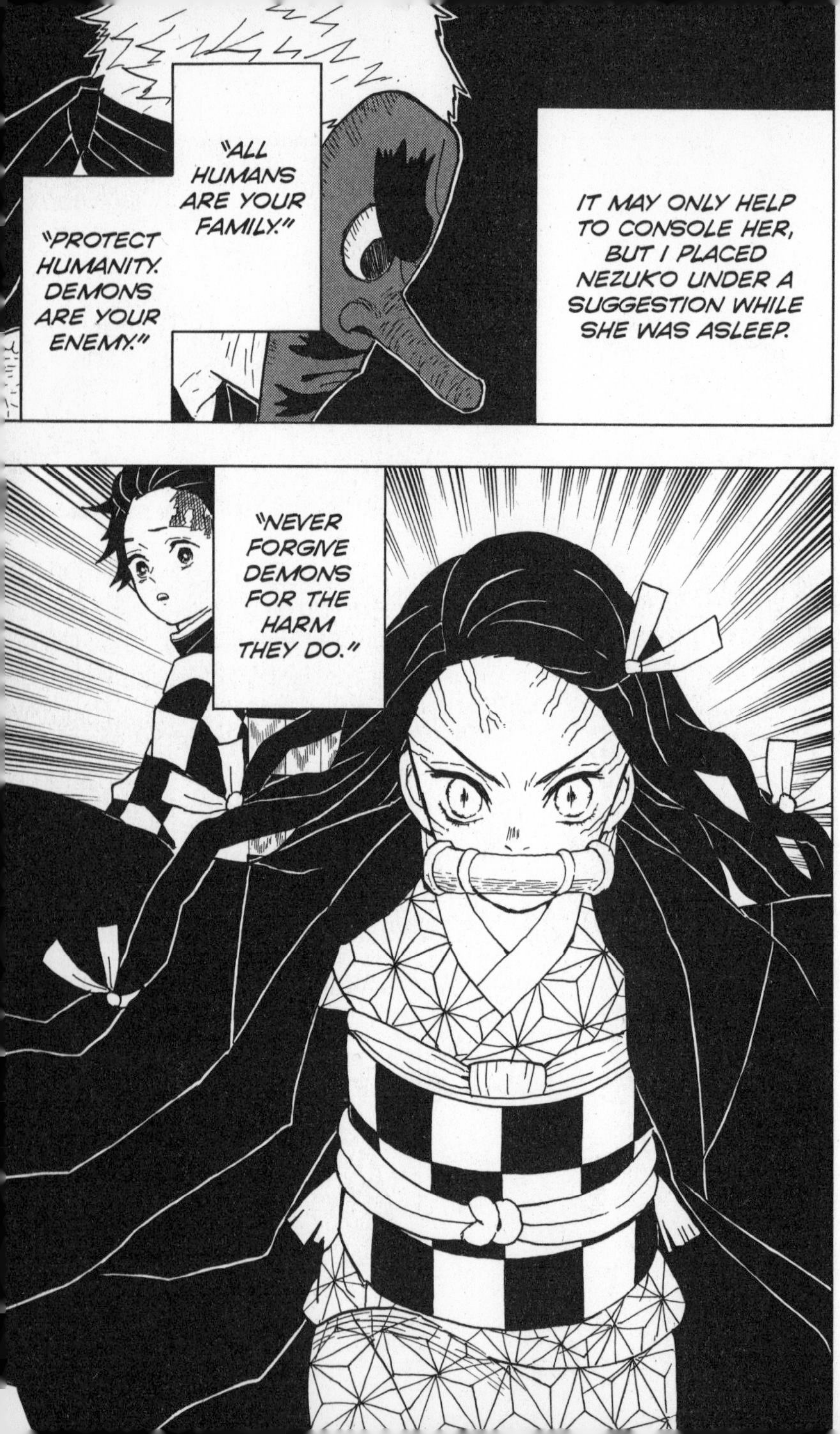
IT MAY ONLY HELP TO CONSOLE HER, BUT I PLACED NEZUKO UNDER A SUGGESTION WHILE SHE WAS ASLEEP.
"ALL HUMANS ARE YOUR FAMILY."
"PROTECT HUMANITY. DEMONS ARE YOUR ENEMY."
"NEVER FORGIVE DEMONS FOR THE HARM THEY DO."

EARLY STAGE

Tanjiro / Nezuko
(The first time I drew these two.)

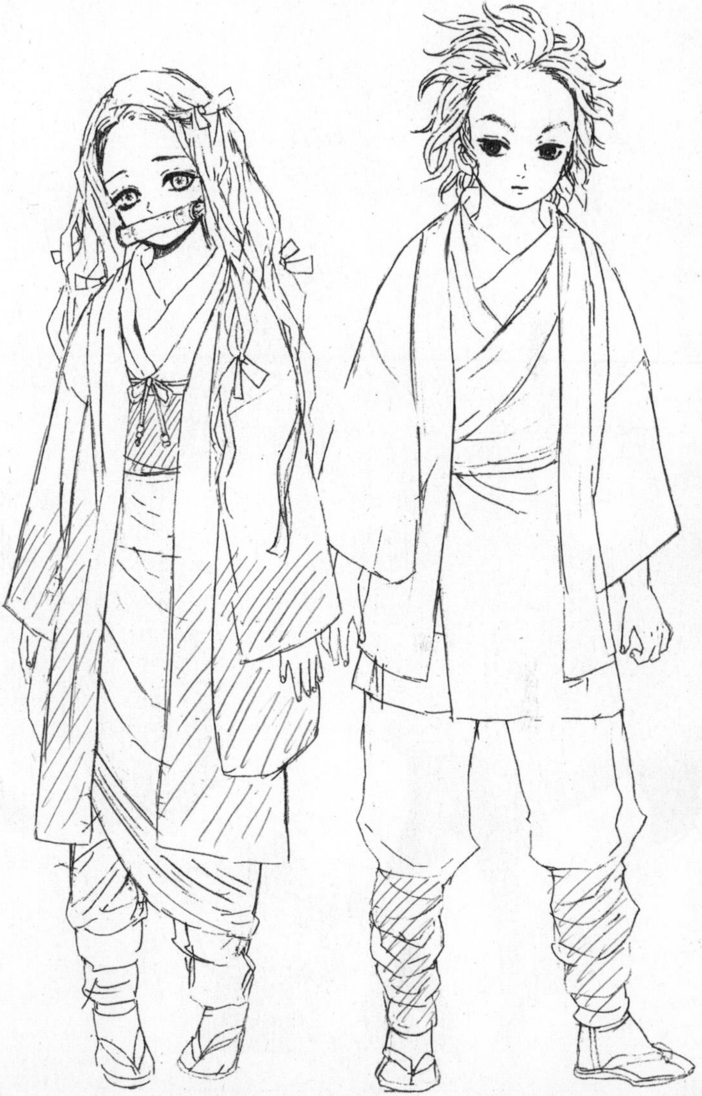

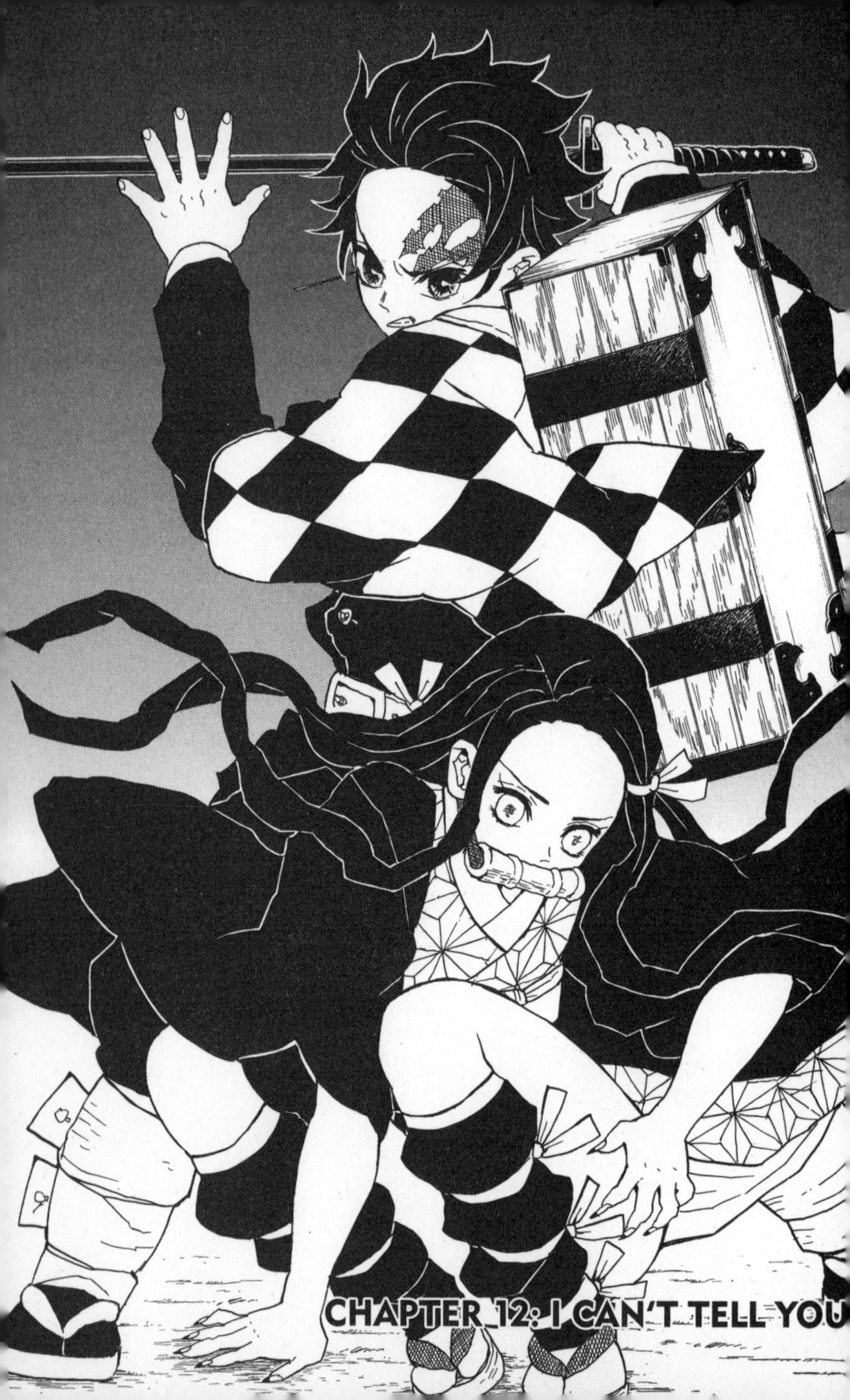
CHAPTER 12: I CAN'T TELL YOU

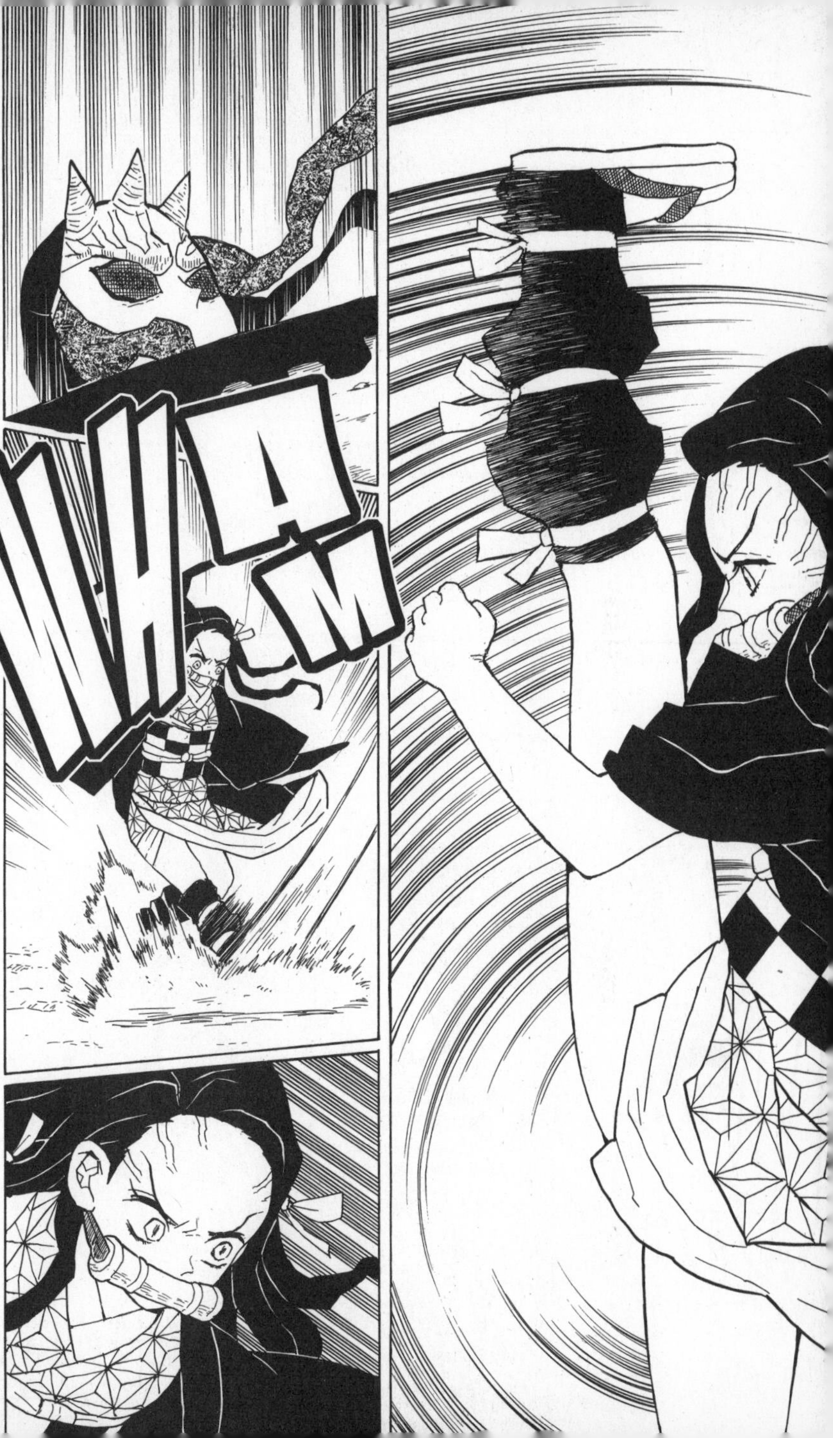
WHAM

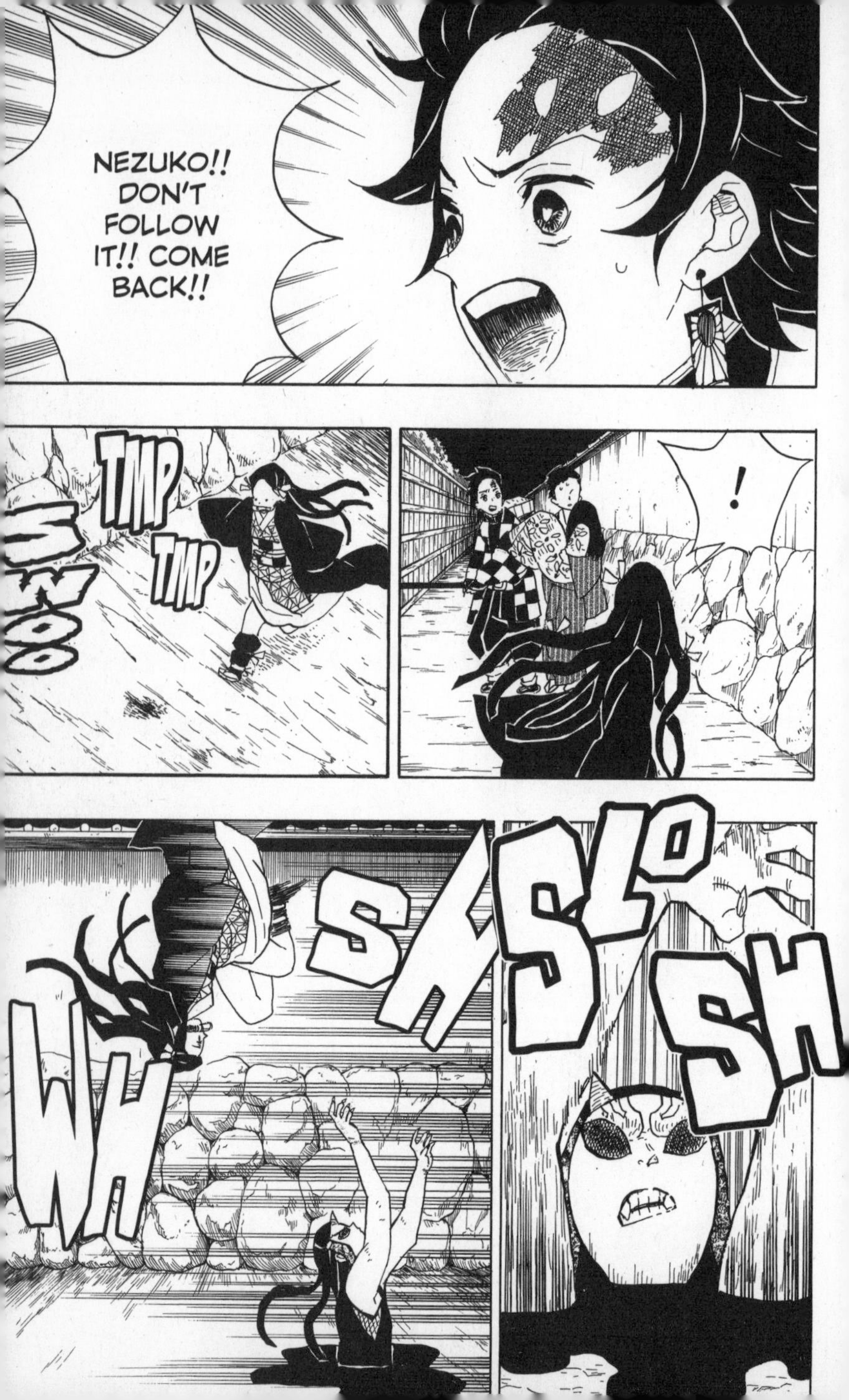
NEZUKO!! DON'T FOLLOW IT!! COME BACK!!
!
TMP
TMP
SLOSH

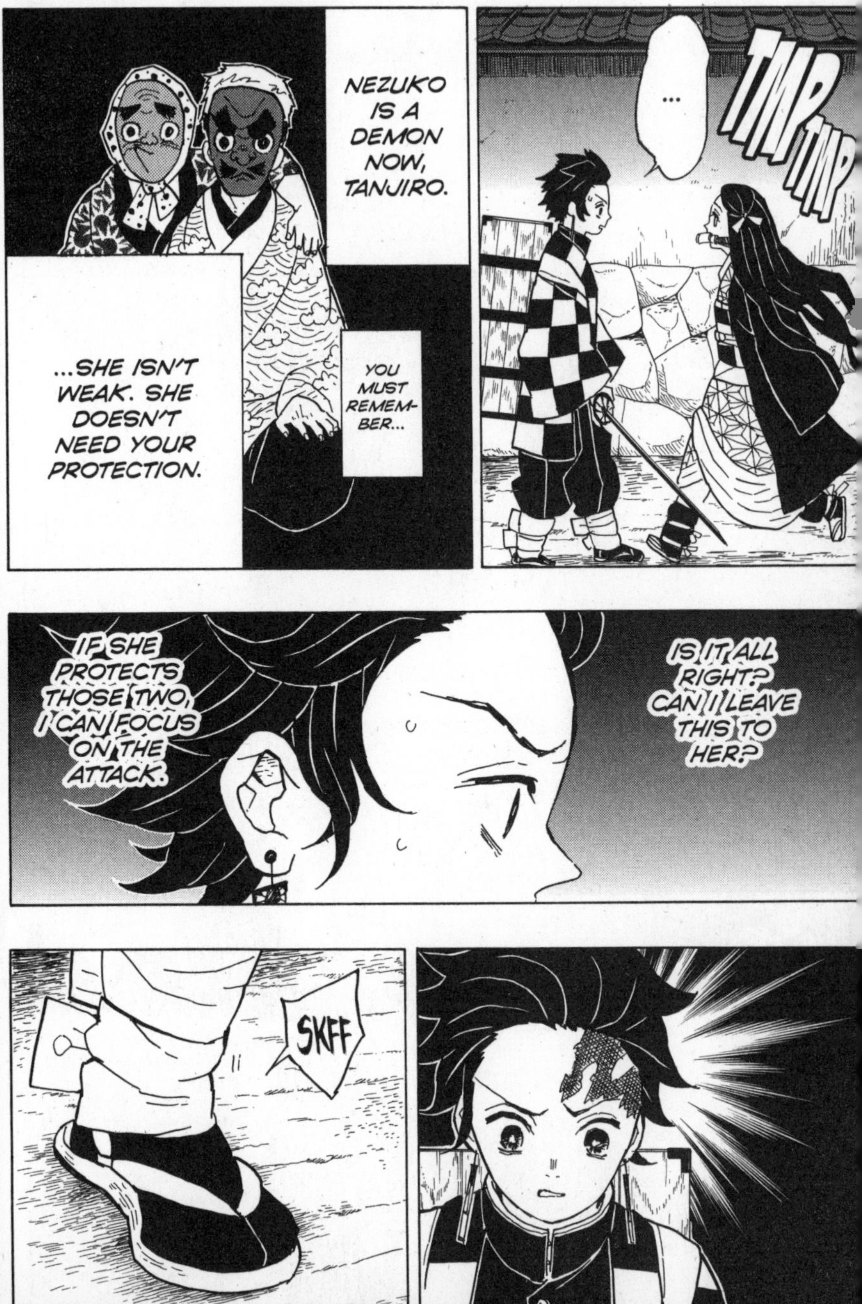
...
TMP TMP
NEZUKO IS A DEMON NOW, TANJIRO.
YOU MUST REMEMBER...
...SHE ISN'T WEAK. SHE DOESN'T NEED YOUR PROTECTION.
IS IT ALL RIGHT? CAN I LEAVE THIS TO HER?
IF SHE PROTECTS THOSE TWO, I CAN FOCUS ON THE ATTACK.
SKFF

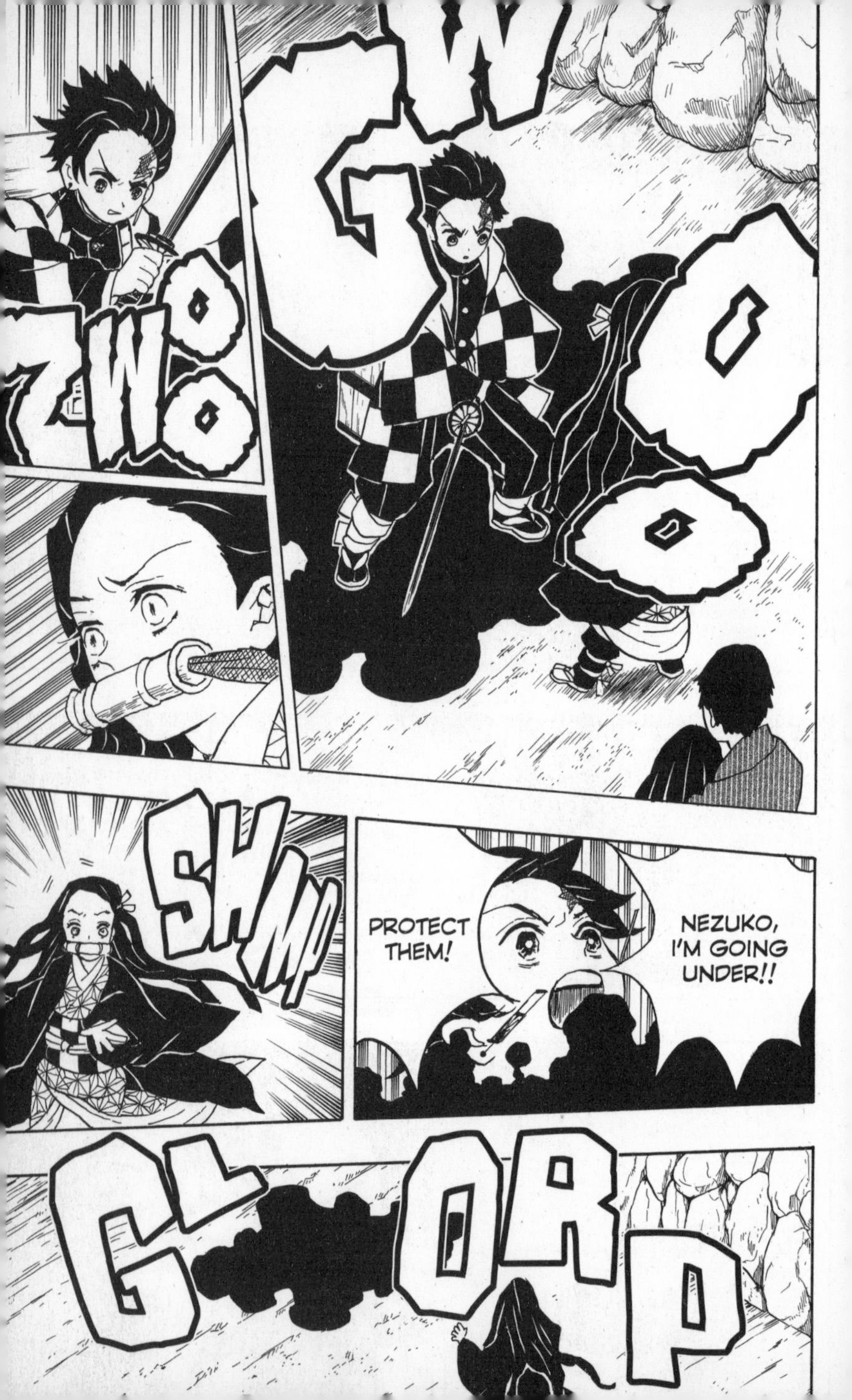

NEZUKO, I'M GOING UNDER!!
PROTECT THEM!
SHMP

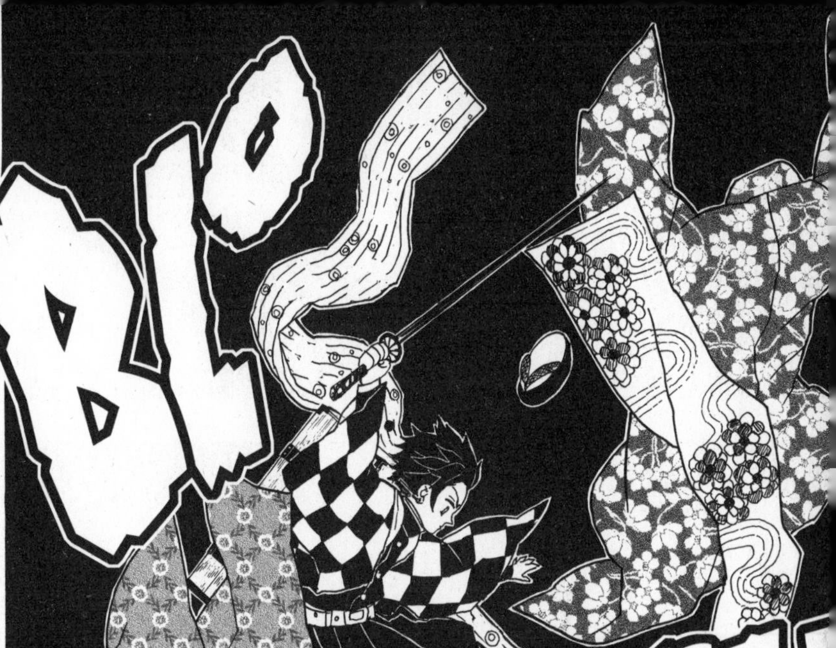
BLO
OSH
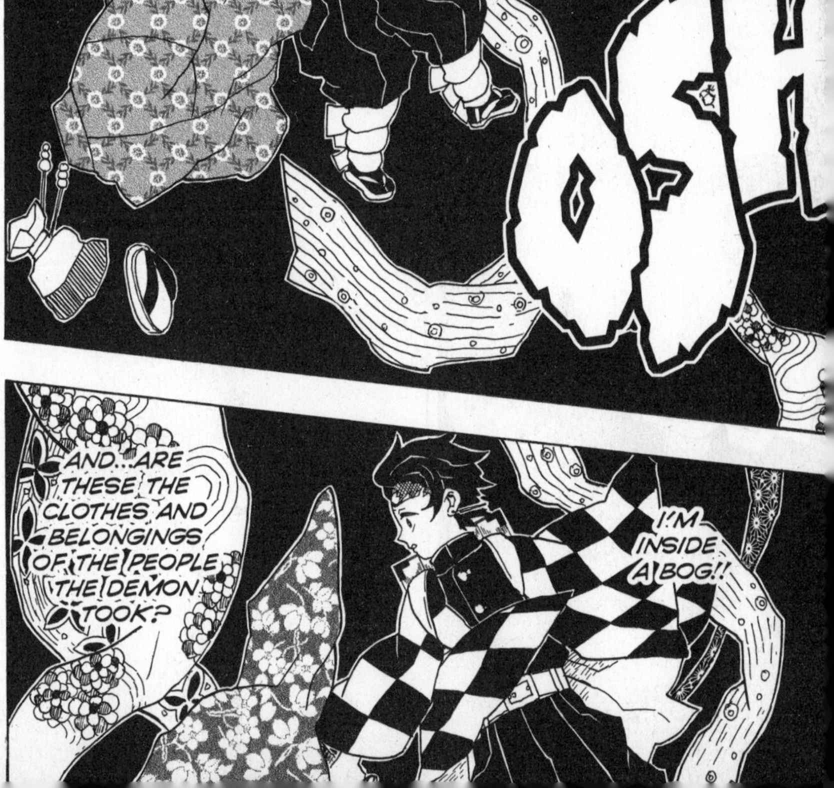
I'M INSIDE A BOG!!
AND...ARE THESE THE CLOTHES AND BELONGINGS OF THE PEOPLE THE DEMON TOOK?

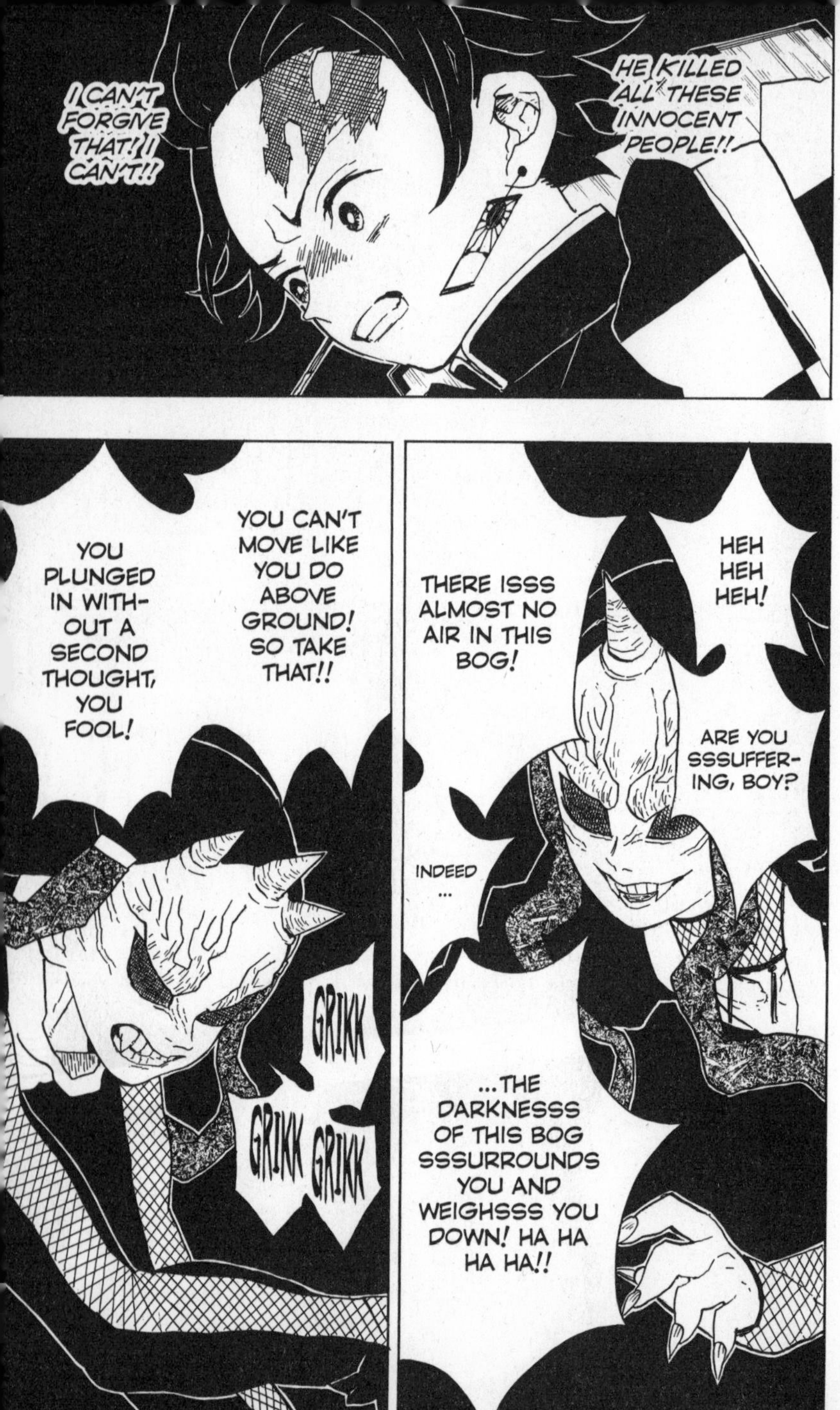
HE KILLED ALL THESE INNOCENT PEOPLE!!
I CAN'T FORGIVE THAT! I CAN'T!!
HEH HEH HEH!
THERE ISSS ALMOST NO AIR IN THIS BOG!
ARE YOU SSSUFFERING, BOY?
INDEED ...
...THE DARKNESSS OF THIS BOG SSSURROUNDS YOU AND WEIGHSSS YOU DOWN! HA HA HA HA!!
YOU CAN'T MOVE LIKE YOU DO ABOVE GROUND! SO TAKE THAT!!
YOU PLUNGED IN WITH-OUT A SECOND THOUGHT, YOU FOOL!
GRIKK
GRIKK GRIKK

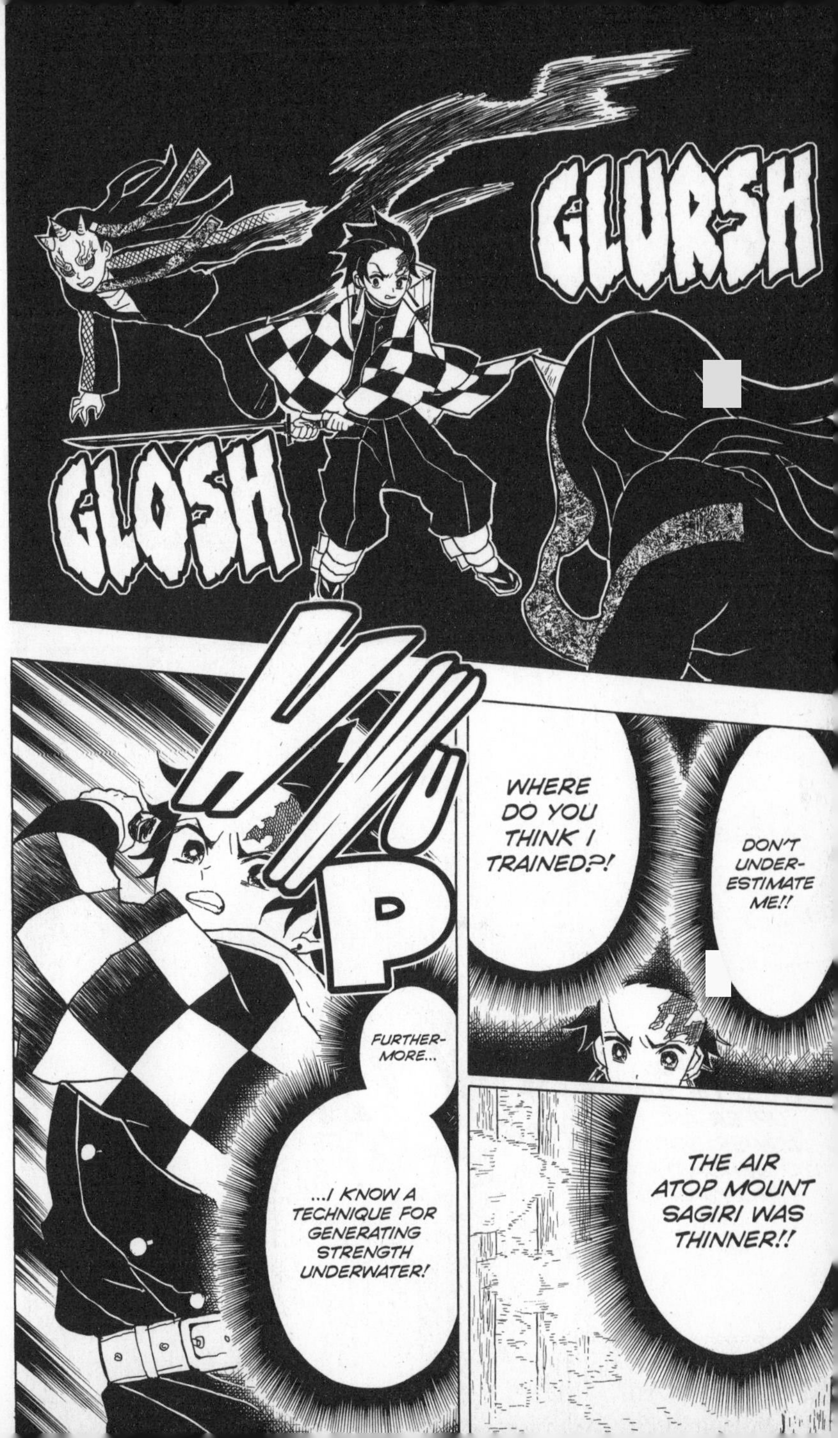
GLURSH
GLOSH
DON'T UNDER-ESTIMATE ME!!
WHERE DO YOU THINK I TRAINED?!
THE AIR ATOP MOUNT SAGIRI WAS THINNER!!
WHUP
FURTHER-MORE...
...I KNOW A TECHNIQUE FOR GENERATING STRENGTH UNDERWATER!

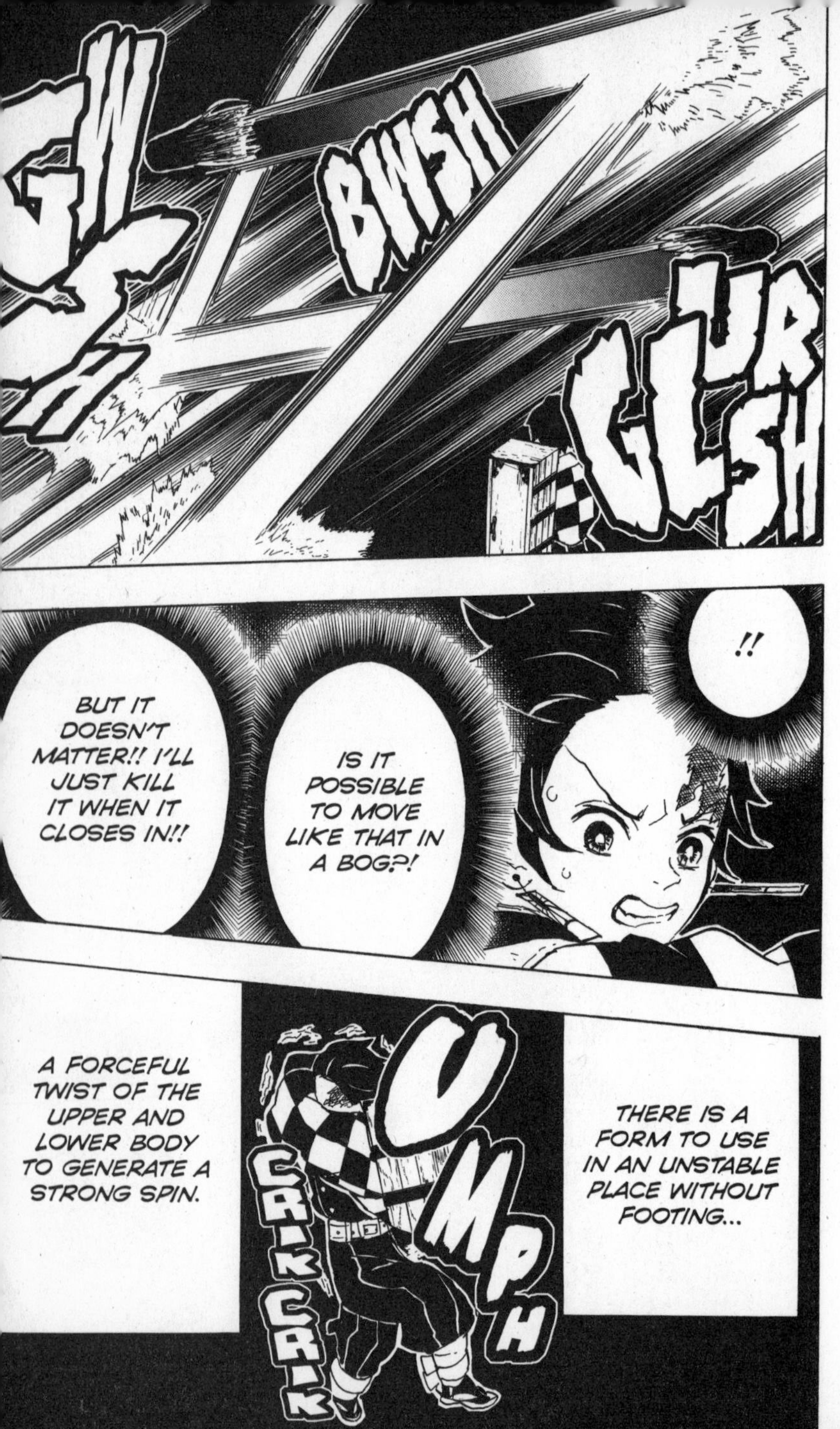
GURGLSH
BWSH
!!
IS IT POSSIBLE TO MOVE LIKE THAT IN A BOG?!
BUT IT DOESN'T MATTER!! I'LL JUST KILL IT WHEN IT CLOSES IN!!
THERE IS A FORM TO USE IN AN UNSTABLE PLACE WITHOUT FOOTING...
UMPH
CRIK CRIK CRIK
A FORCEFUL TWIST OF THE UPPER AND LOWER BODY TO GENERATE A STRONG SPIN.

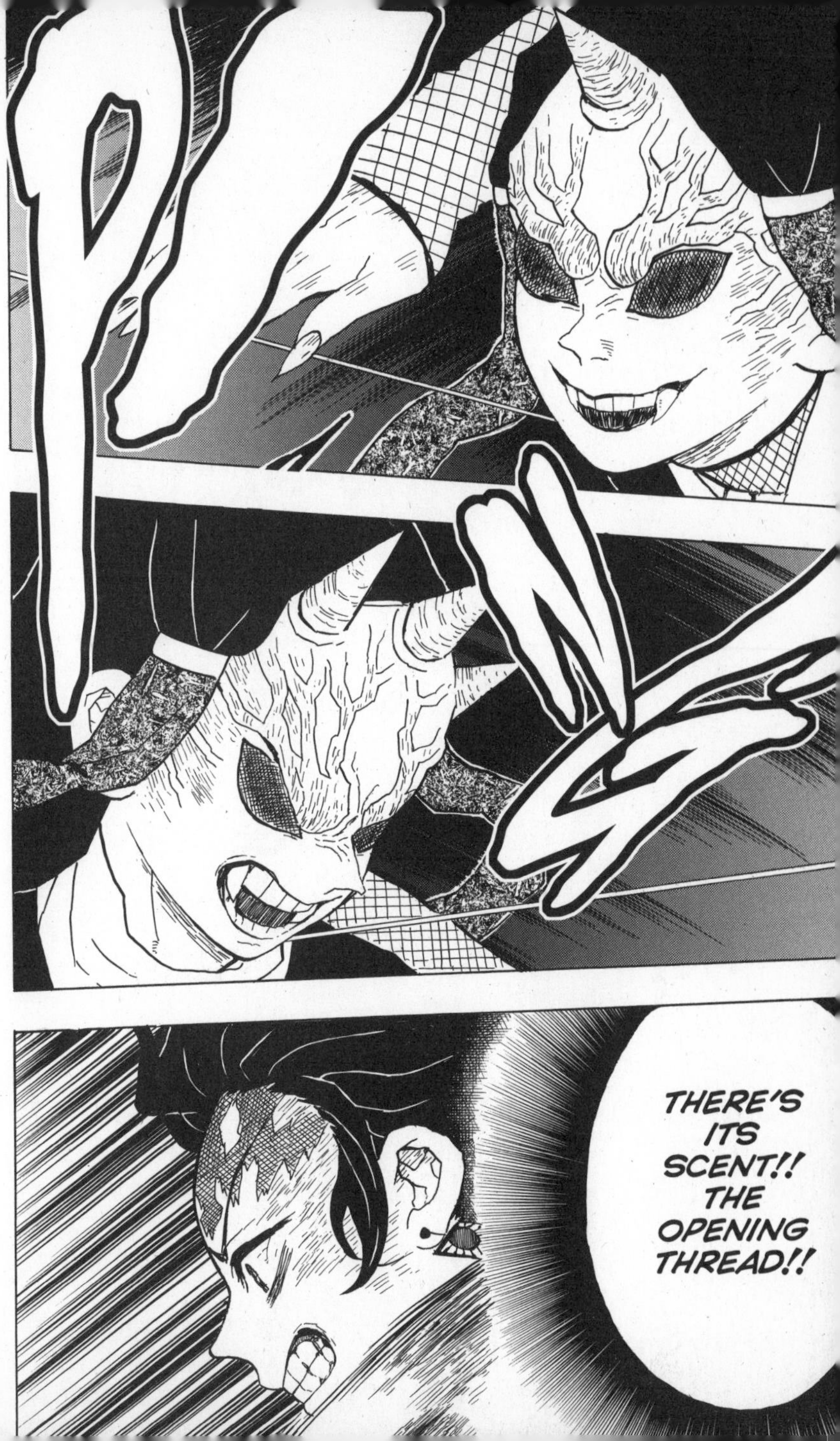
THERE'S ITS SCENT!! THE OPENING THREAD!!

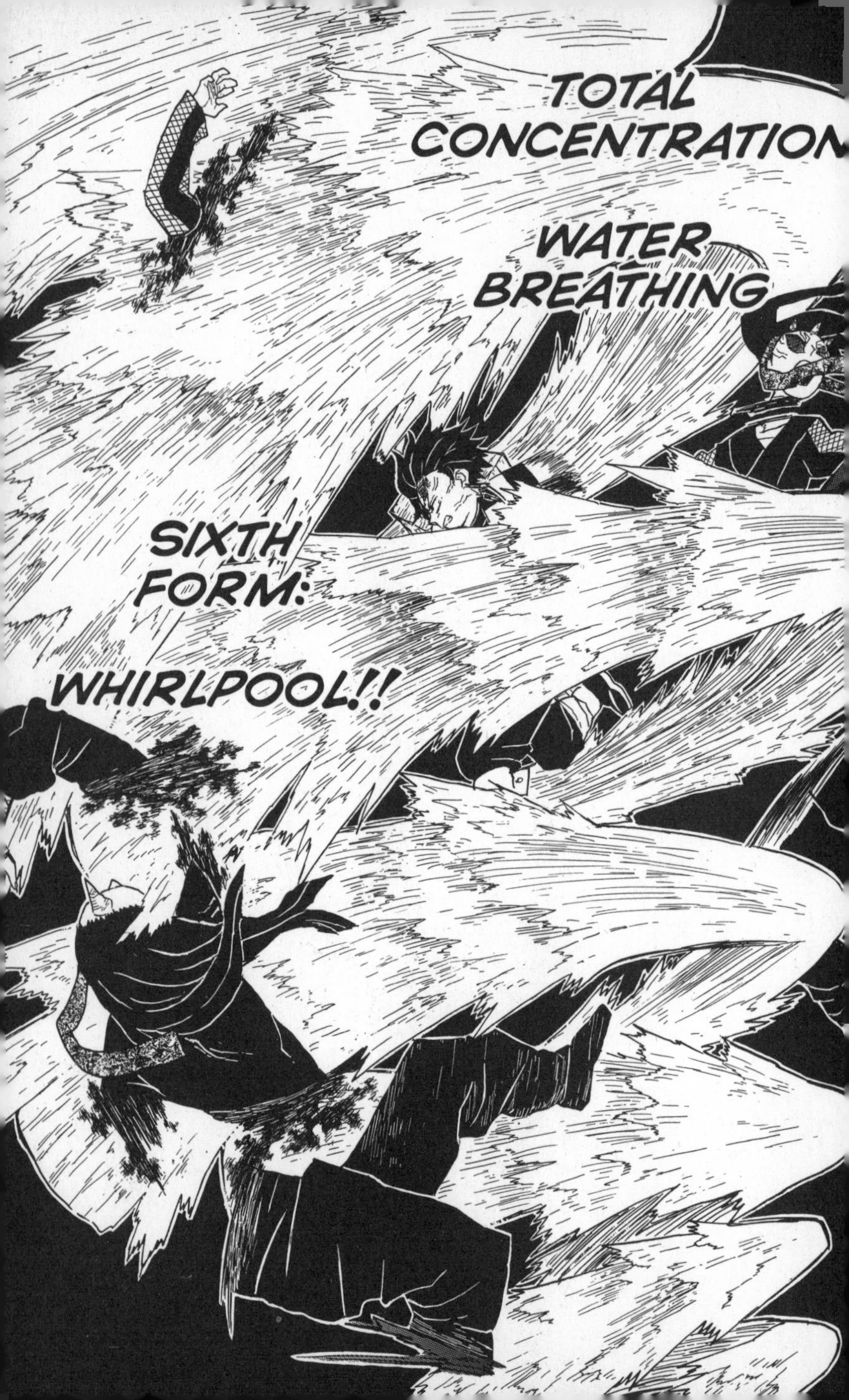
TOTAL CONCENTRATION
WATER BREATHING
SIXTH FORM:
WHIRLPOOL!!

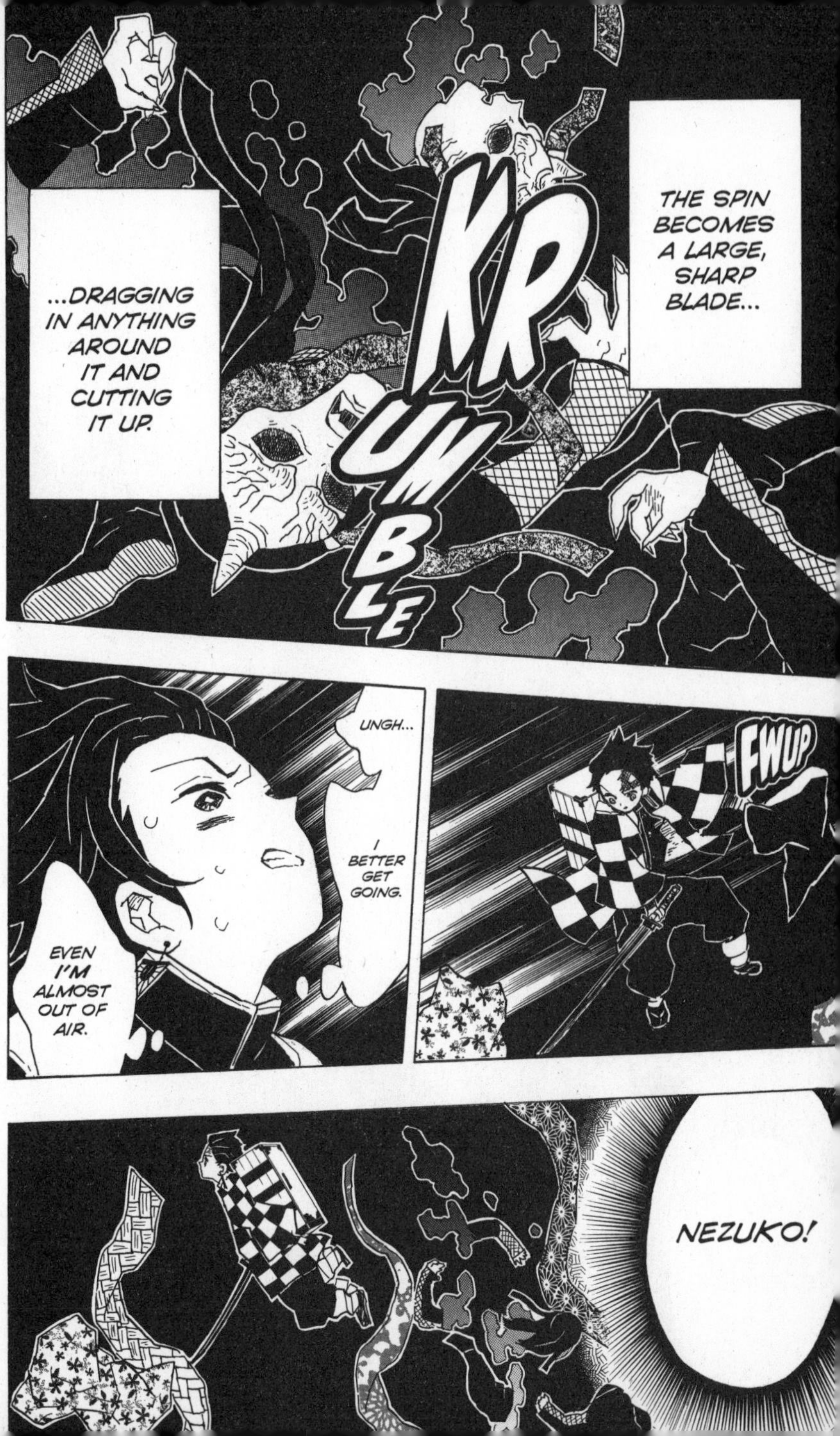
THE SPIN BECOMES A LARGE, SHARP BLADE...
KRUMBLE
...DRAGGING IN ANYTHING AROUND IT AND CUTTING IT UP.
FWUP
UNGH...
I BETTER GET GOING.
EVEN I'M ALMOST OUT OF AIR.
NEZUKO!

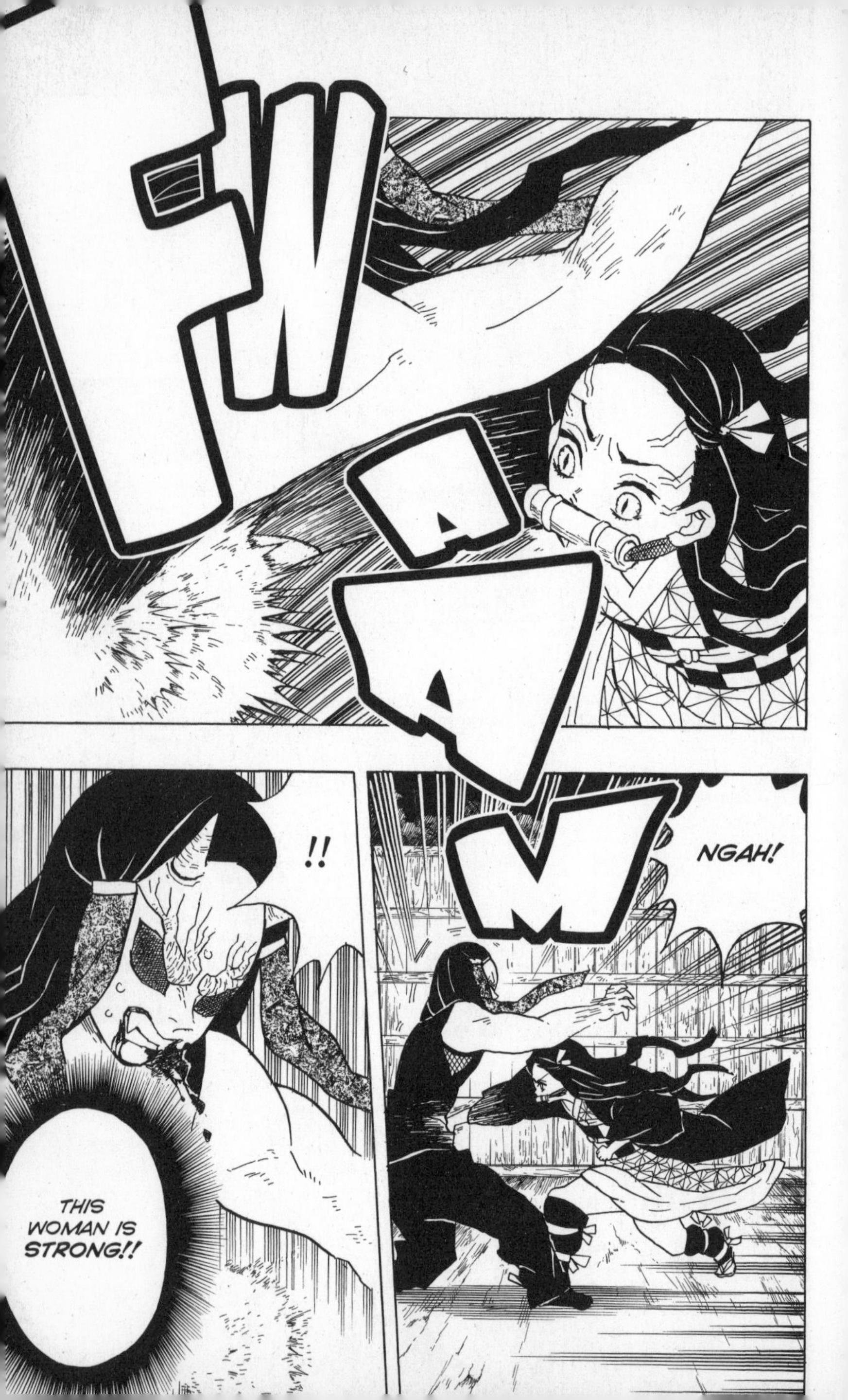
NGAH!
!!
THIS WOMAN IS STRONG!!

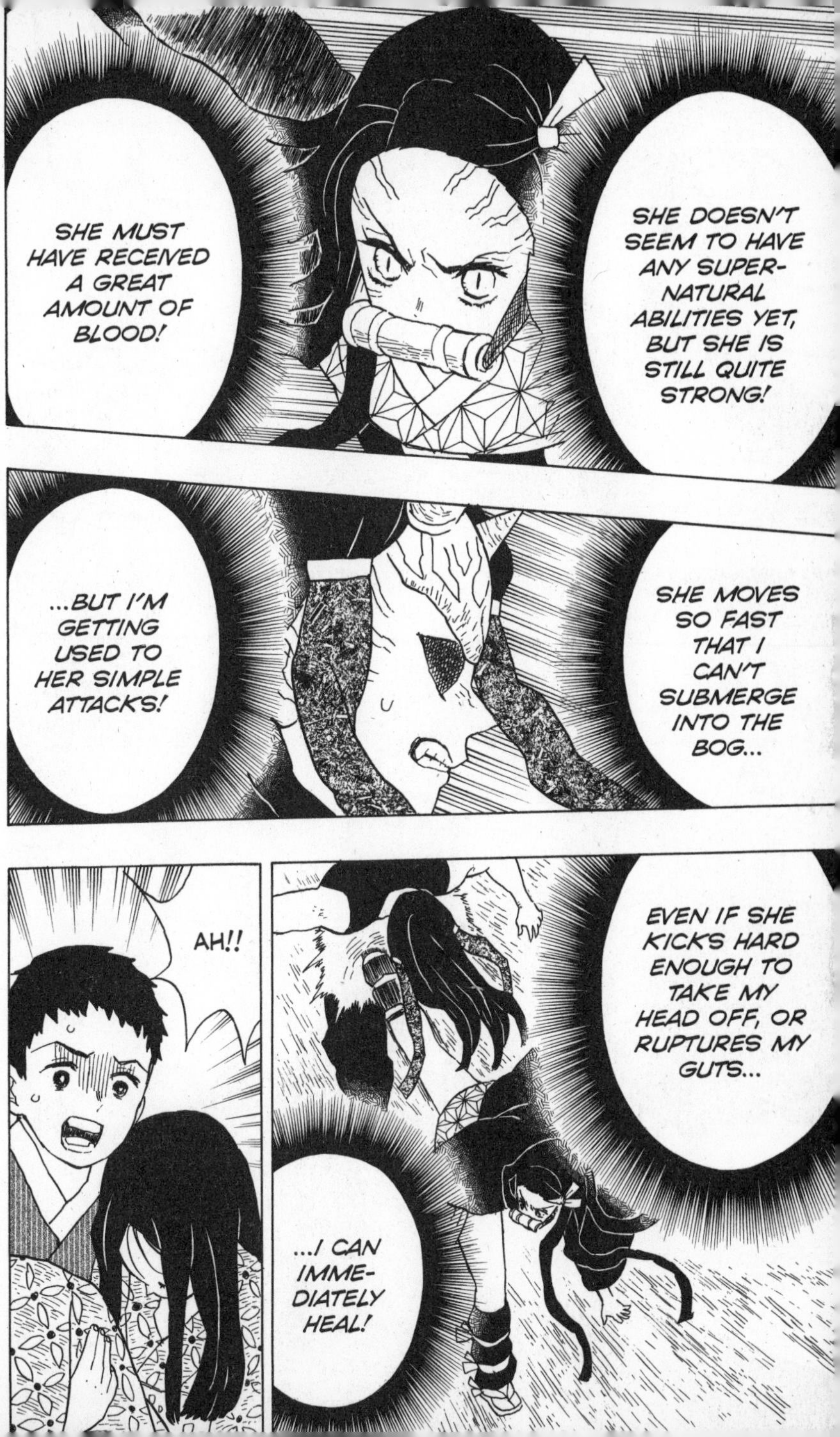
SHE DOESN'T SEEM TO HAVE ANY SUPER-NATURAL ABILITIES YET, BUT SHE IS STILL QUITE STRONG!
SHE MUST HAVE RECEIVED A GREAT AMOUNT OF BLOOD!
SHE MOVES SO FAST THAT I CAN'T SUBMERGE INTO THE BOG...
...BUT I'M GETTING USED TO HER SIMPLE ATTACKS!
EVEN IF SHE KICKS HARD ENOUGH TO TAKE MY HEAD OFF, OR RUPTURES MY GUTS...
...I CAN IMME-DIATELY HEAL!
AH!!

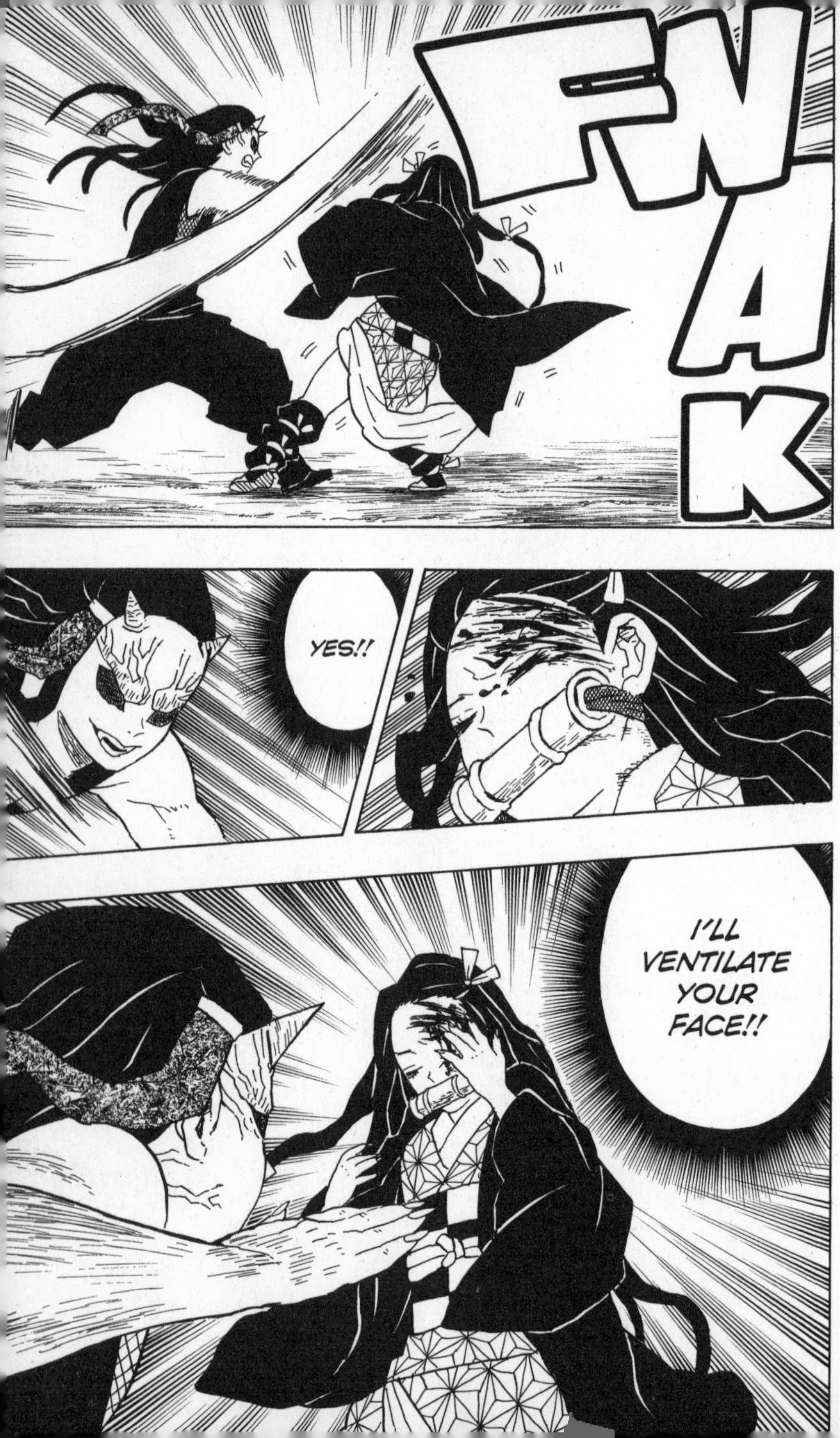
FWAK
YES!!
I'LL VENTILATE YOUR FACE!!

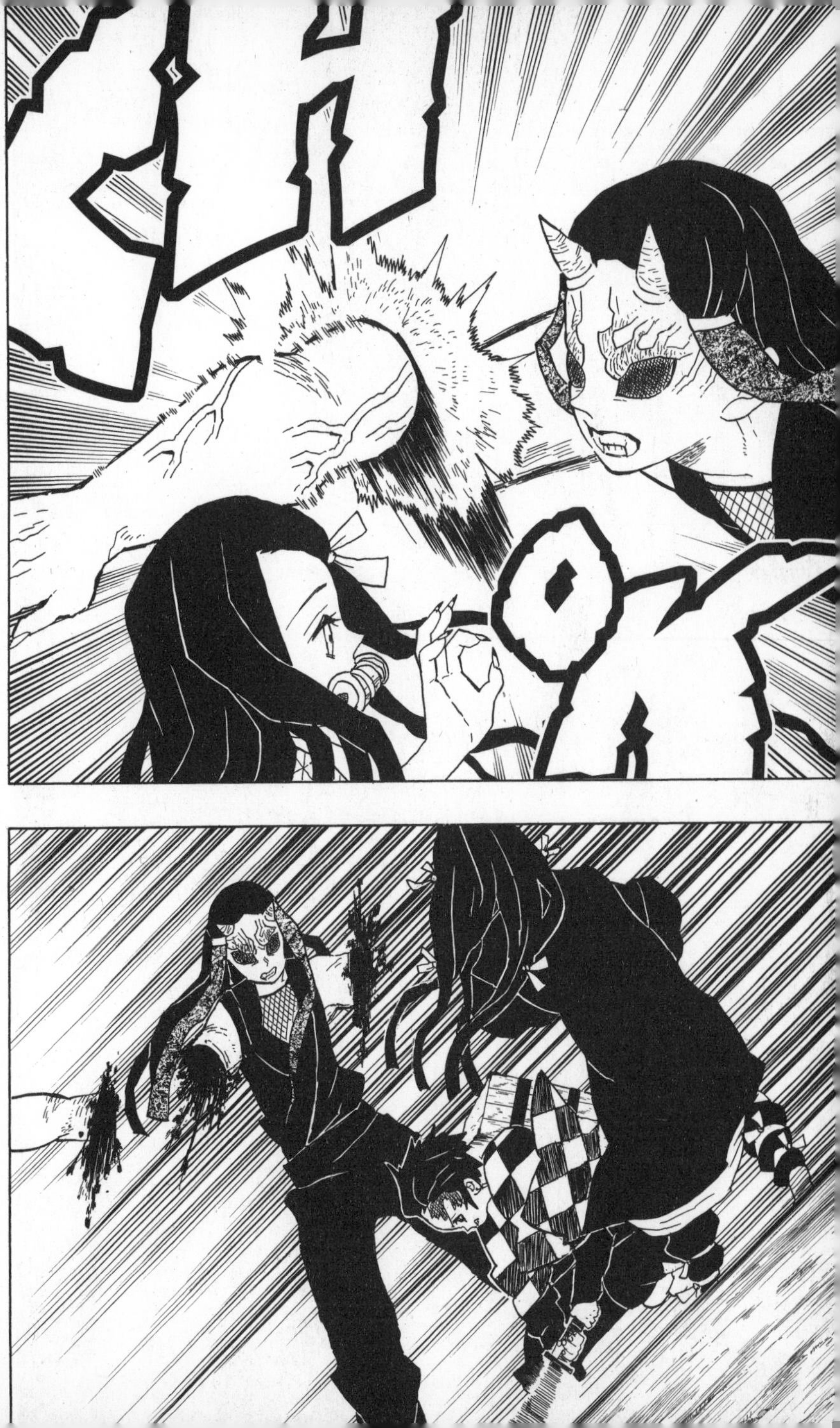

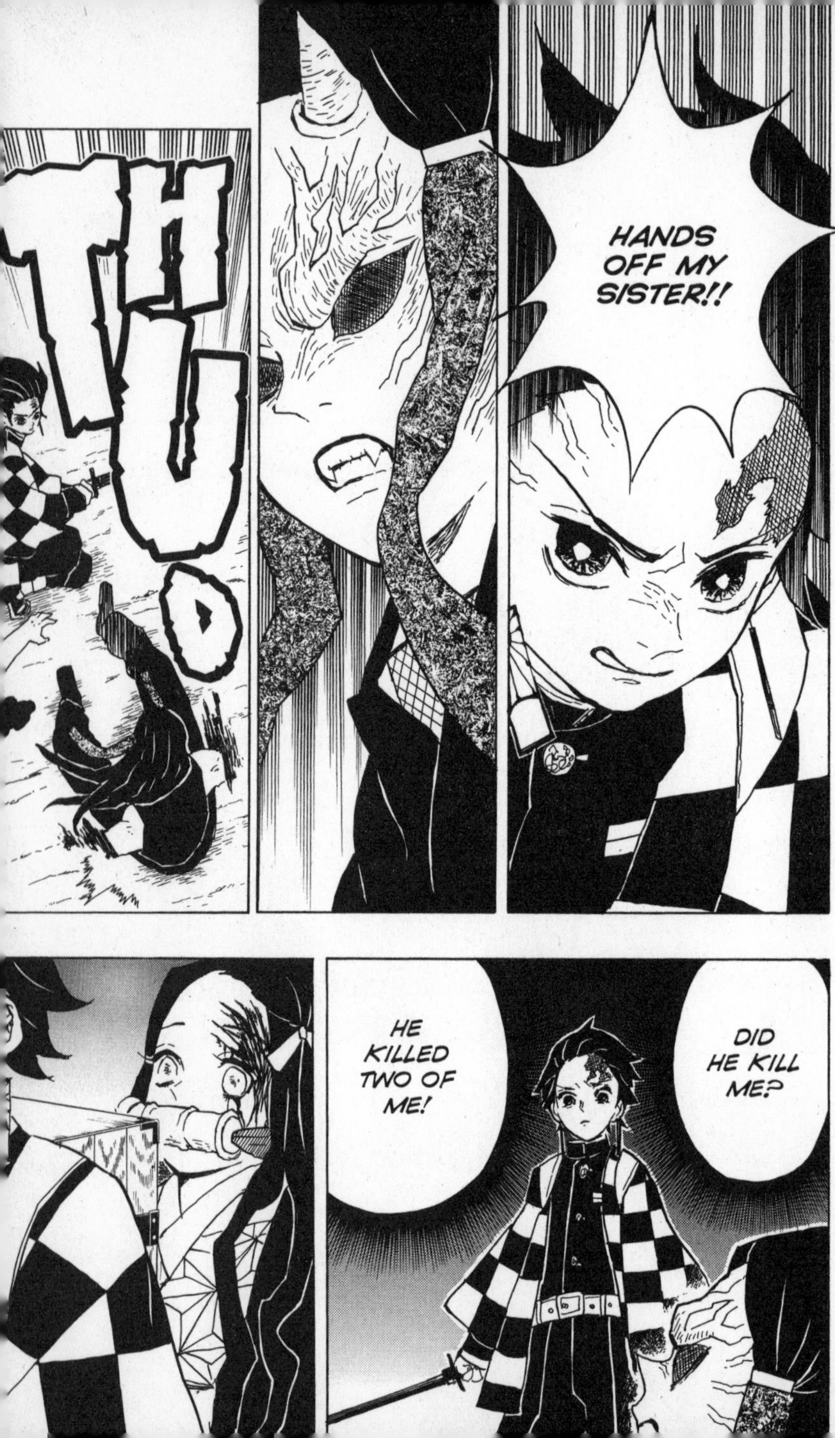
HANDS OFF MY SISTER!!
THUD
DID HE KILL ME?
HE KILLED TWO OF ME!

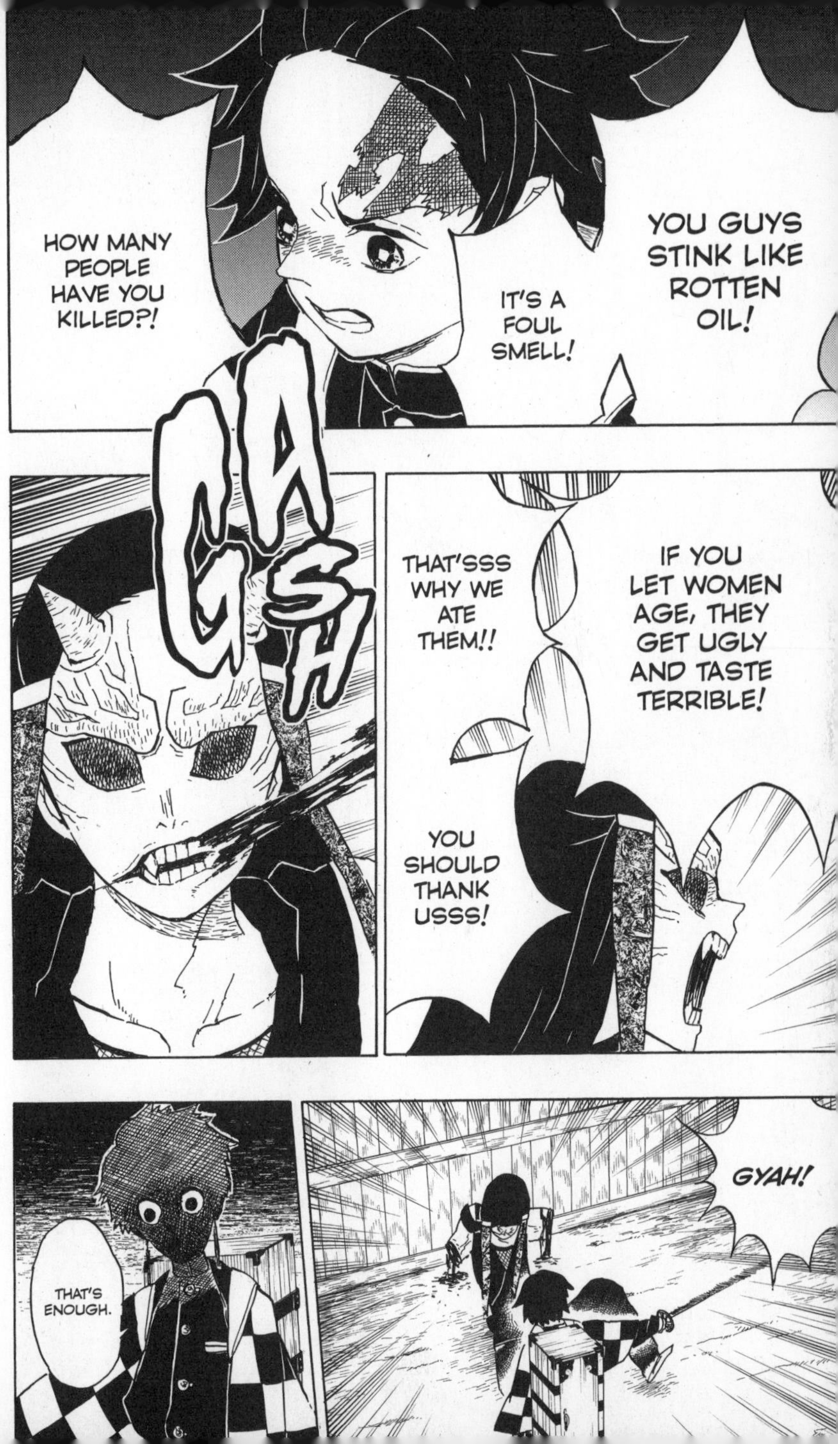
YOU GUYS STINK LIKE ROTTEN OIL!
IT'S A FOUL SMELL!
HOW MANY PEOPLE HAVE YOU KILLED?!
IF YOU LET WOMEN AGE, THEY GET UGLY AND TASTE TERRIBLE!
THAT'SSS WHY WE ATE THEM!!
YOU SHOULD THANK USSS!
GASH
GYAH!
THAT'S ENOUGH.

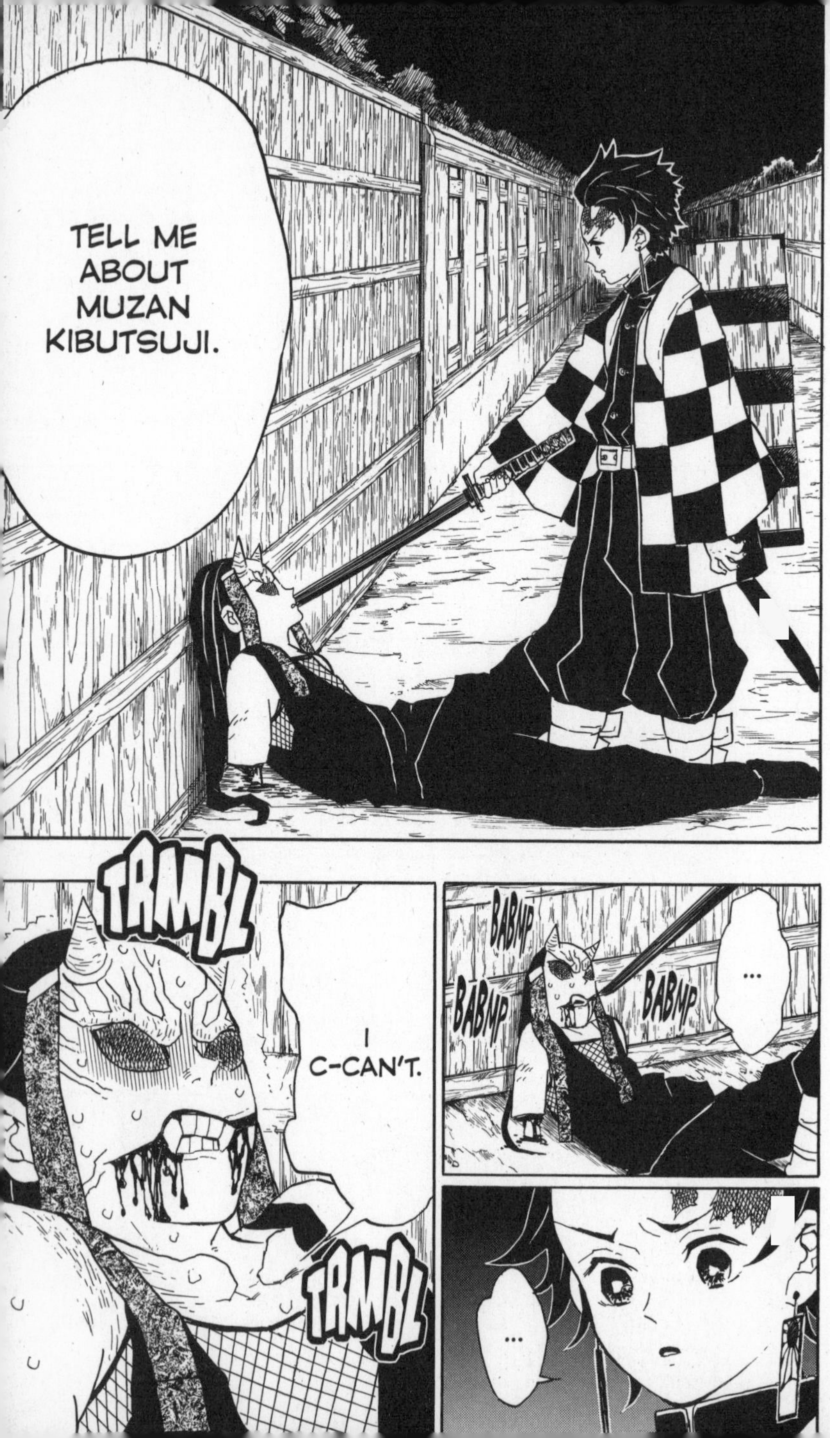
TELL ME ABOUT MUZAN KIBUTSUJI.
BABMP
BABMP
BABMP
...
...
TRMBL
I C-CAN'T.
TRMBL

From the cover of the Shonen Jump 21/22 double issue, 2016.

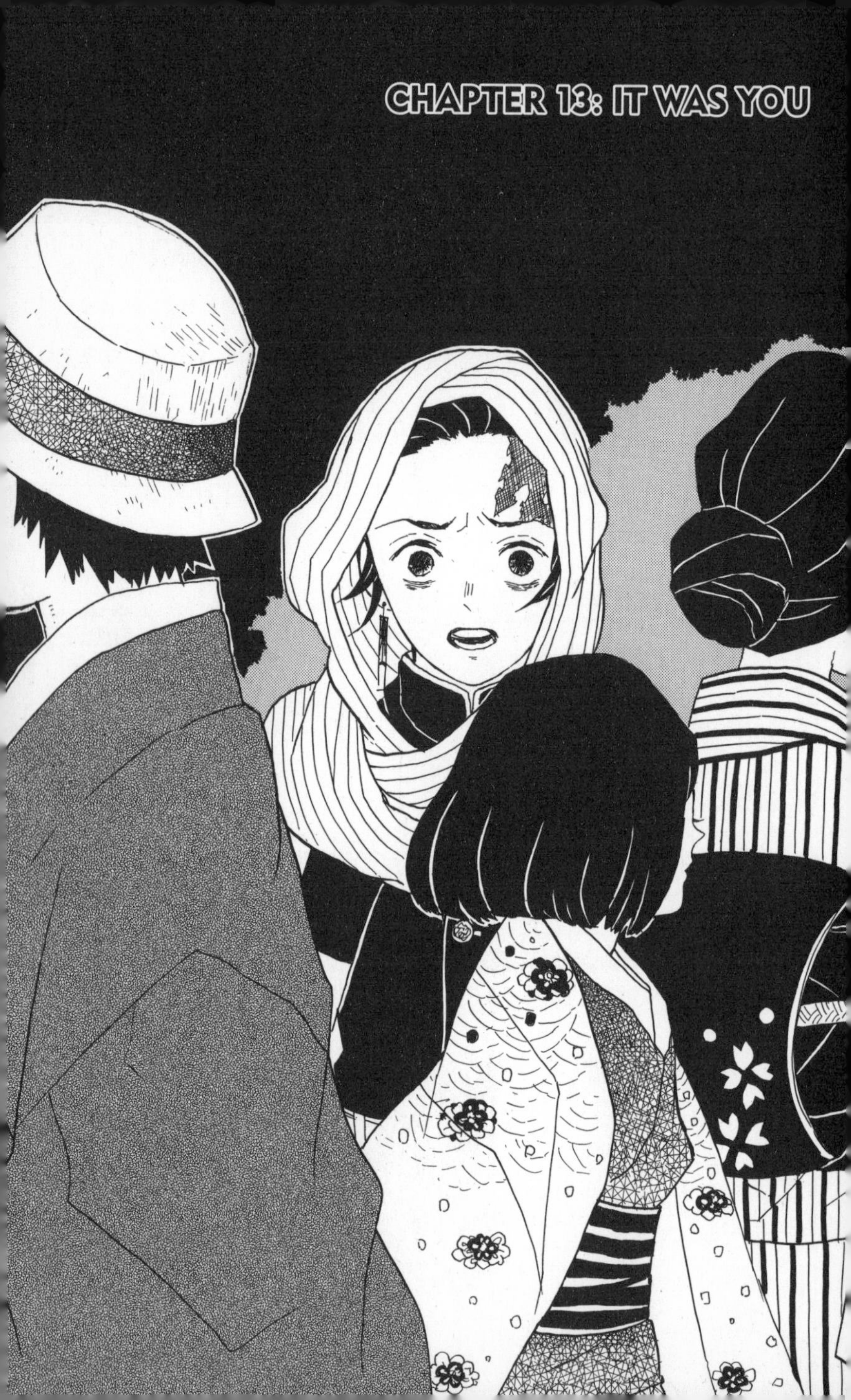
CHAPTER 13: IT WAS YOU

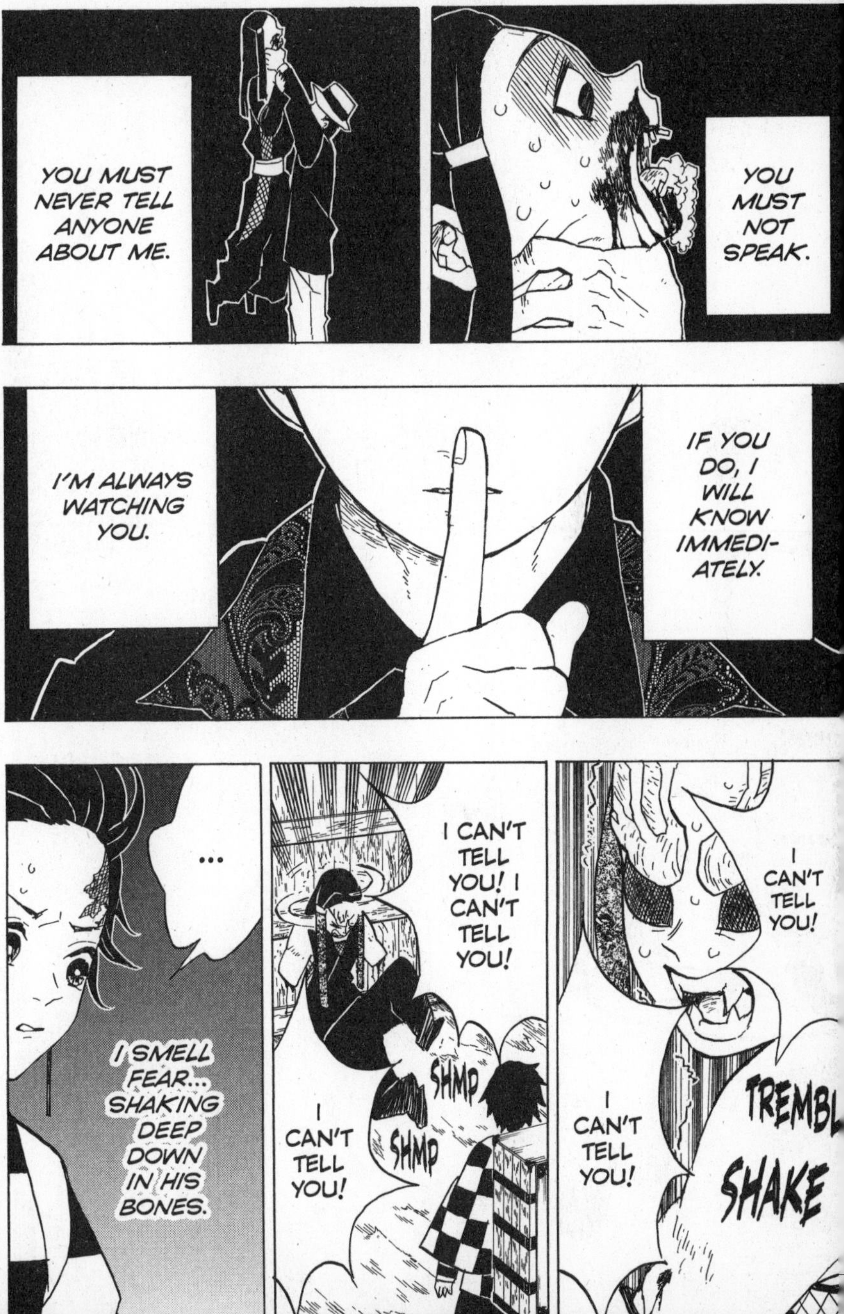

YOU MUST NOT SPEAK.
YOU MUST NEVER TELL ANYONE ABOUT ME.
IF YOU DO, I WILL KNOW IMMEDIATELY.
I'M ALWAYS WATCHING YOU.
I CAN'T TELL YOU!
TREMBL
SHAKE
I CAN'T TELL YOU!
I CAN'T TELL YOU! I CAN'T TELL YOU!
SHMP
SHMP
I CAN'T TELL YOU!
...
I SMELL FEAR... SHAKING DEEP DOWN IN HIS BONES.

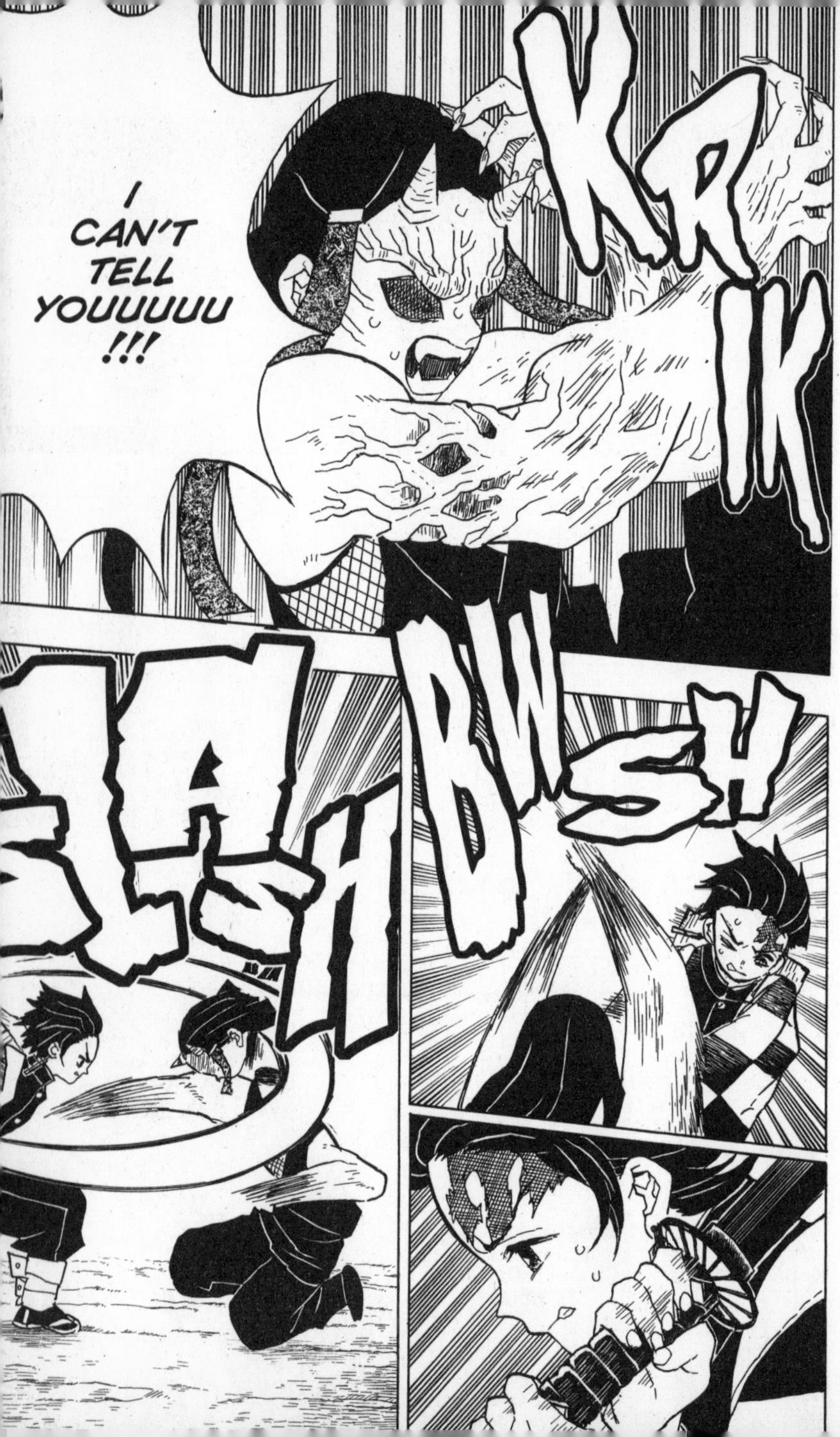
I CAN'T TELL YOUUUUUU!!!
KRIK
BWSH
SLASH

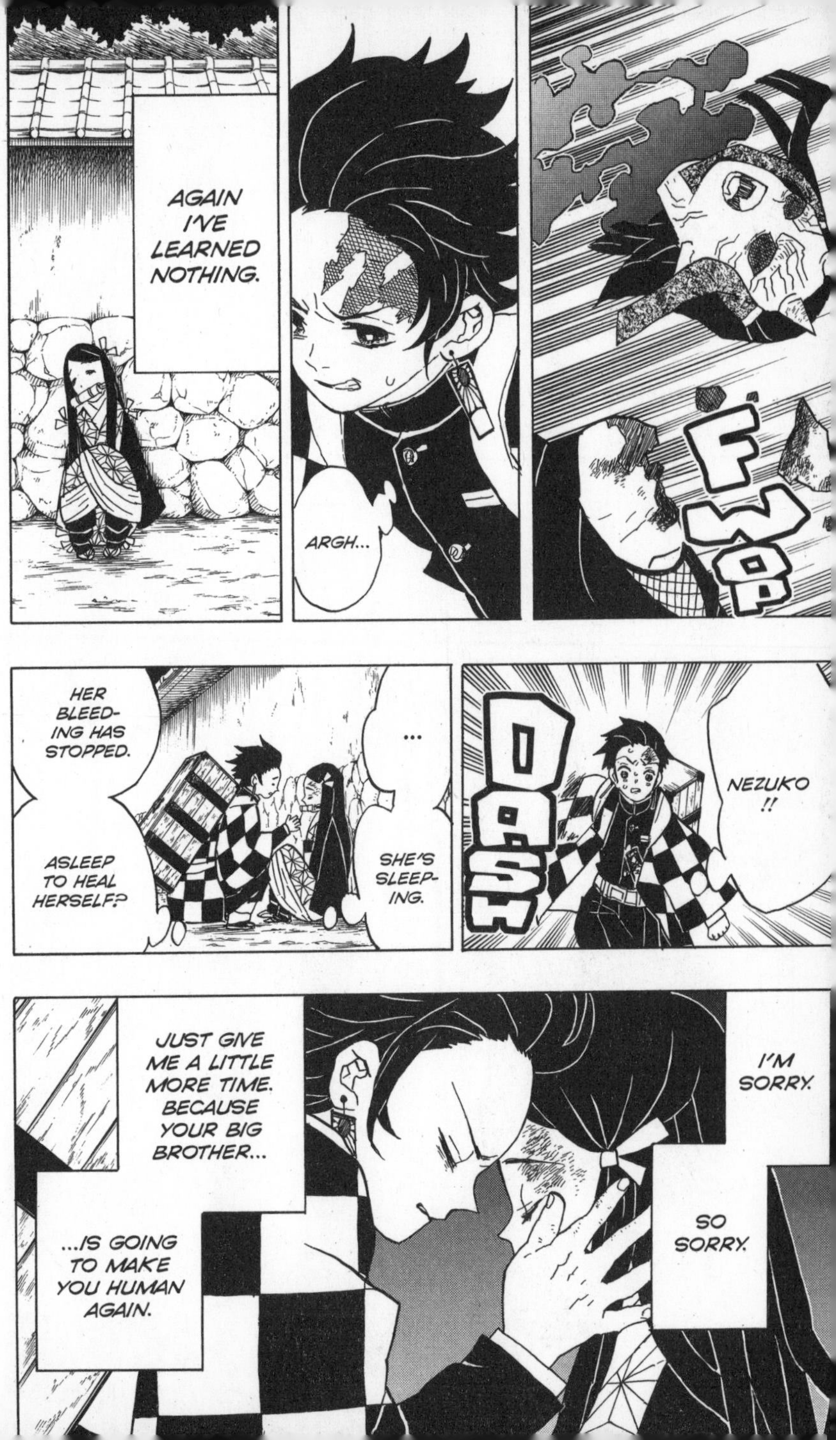
FWOP
ARGH...
AGAIN I'VE LEARNED NOTHING.
DASH
NEZUKO !!
...
HER BLEEDING HAS STOPPED.
SHE'S SLEEPING.
ASLEEP TO HEAL HERSELF?
I'M SORRY.
SO SORRY.
JUST GIVE ME A LITTLE MORE TIME. BECAUSE YOUR BIG BROTHER...
...IS GOING TO MAKE YOU HUMAN AGAIN.

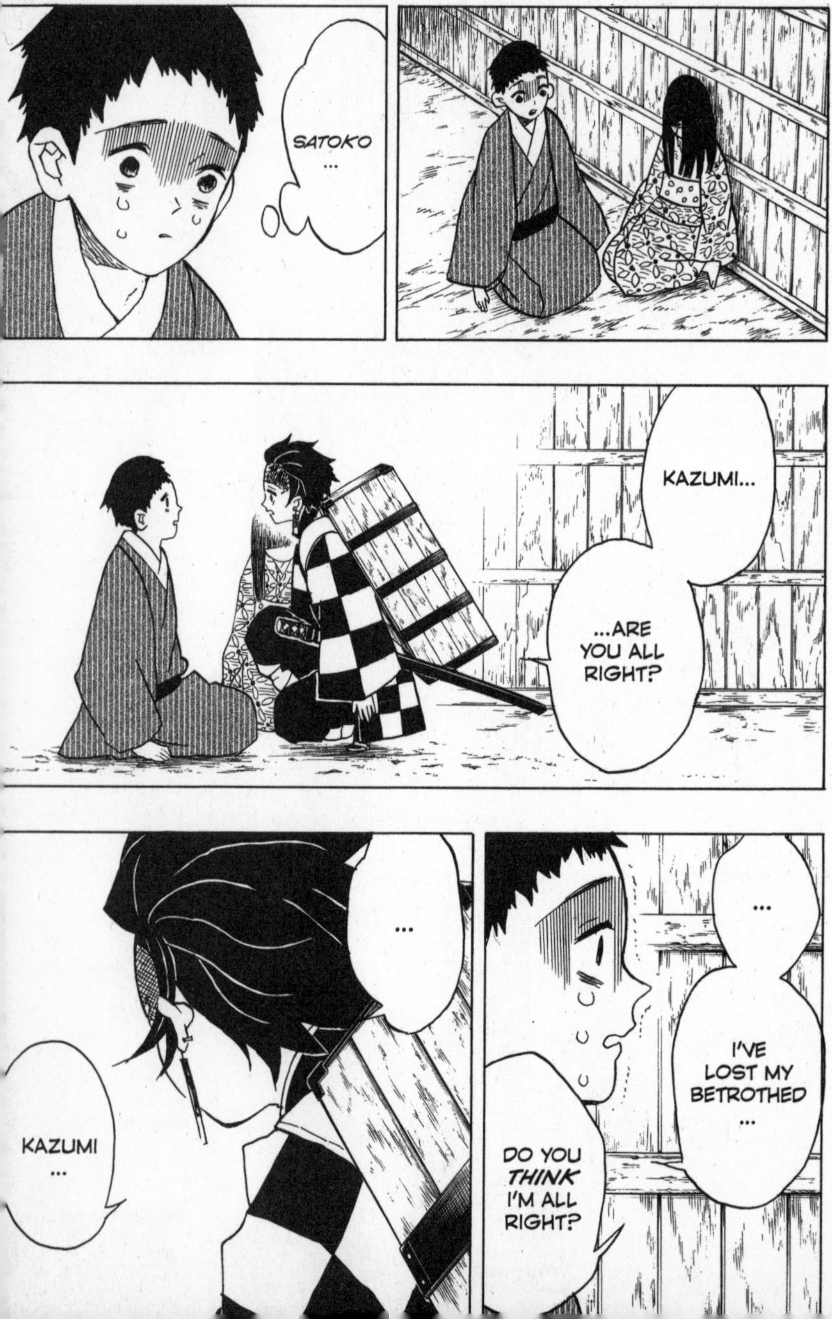
SATOKO ...
KAZUMI...
...ARE YOU ALL RIGHT?
...
I'VE LOST MY BETROTHED ...
DO YOU *THINK* I'M ALL RIGHT?
...
KAZUMI ...

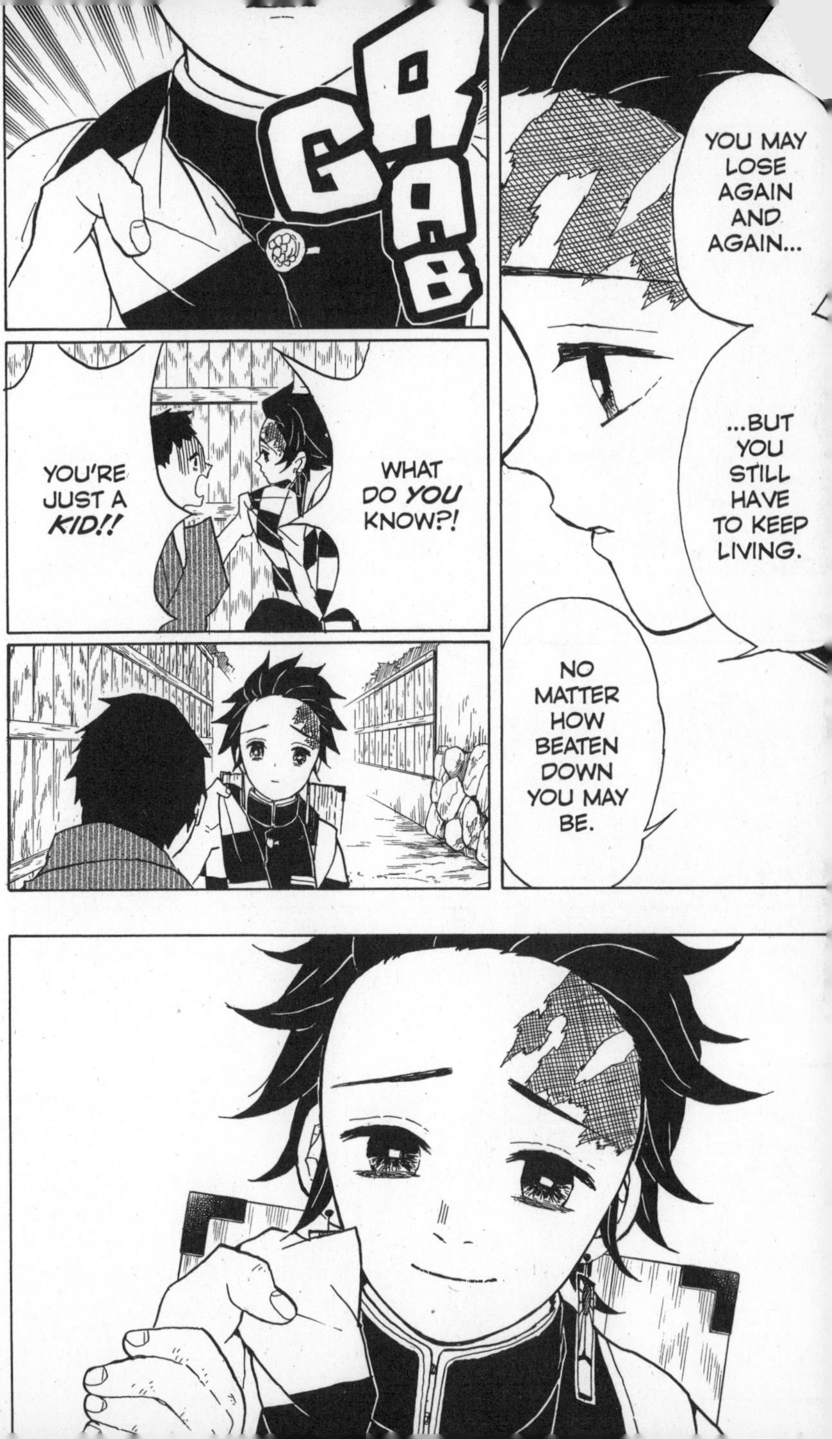
YOU MAY LOSE AGAIN AND AGAIN...
...BUT YOU STILL HAVE TO KEEP LIVING.
NO MATTER HOW BEATEN DOWN YOU MAY BE.
GRAB
WHAT DO *YOU* KNOW?!
YOU'RE JUST A *KID!!*

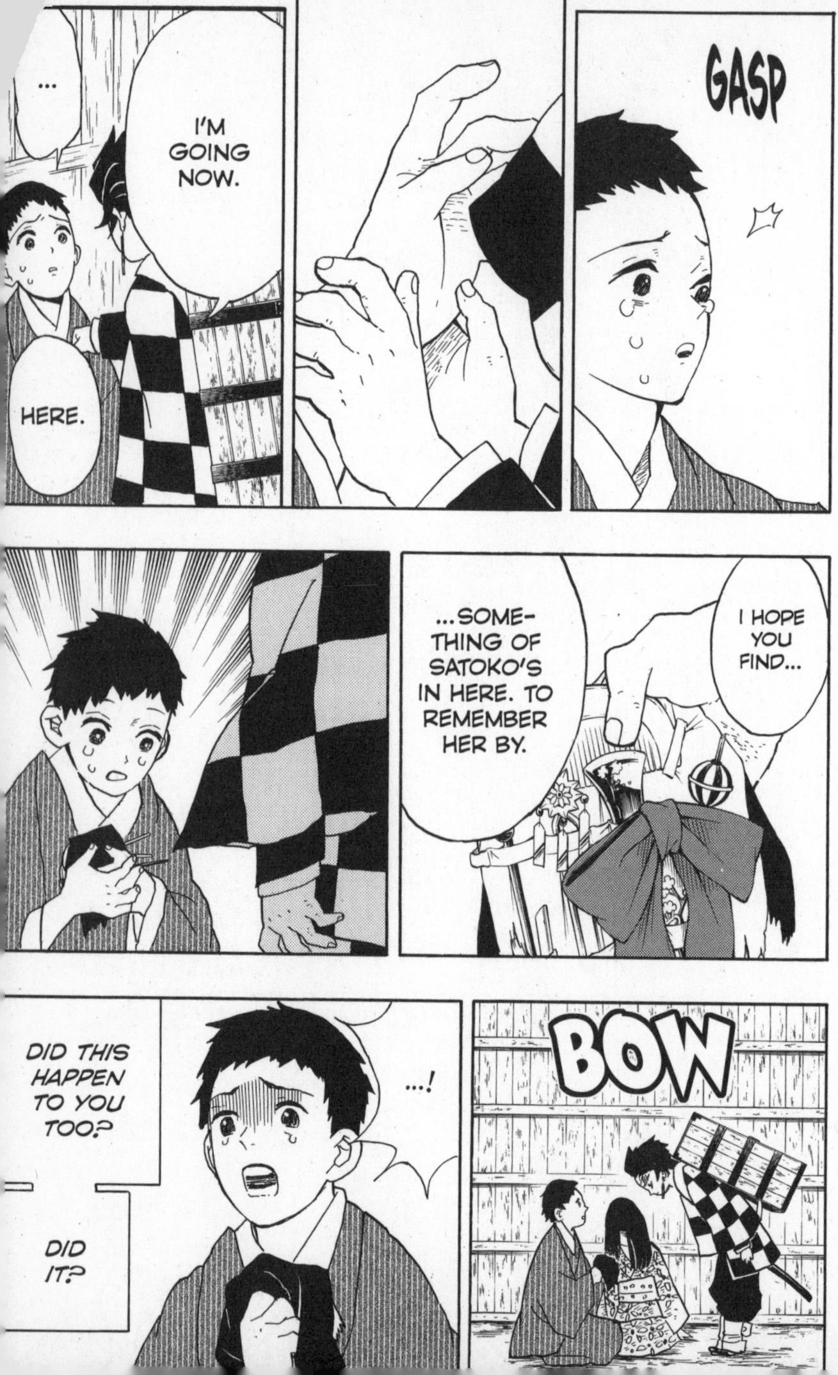
GASP
I'M GOING NOW.
...
HERE.
I HOPE YOU FIND...
...SOME-THING OF SATOKO'S IN HERE. TO REMEMBER HER BY.
BOW
...!
DID THIS HAPPEN TO YOU TOO?
DID IT?

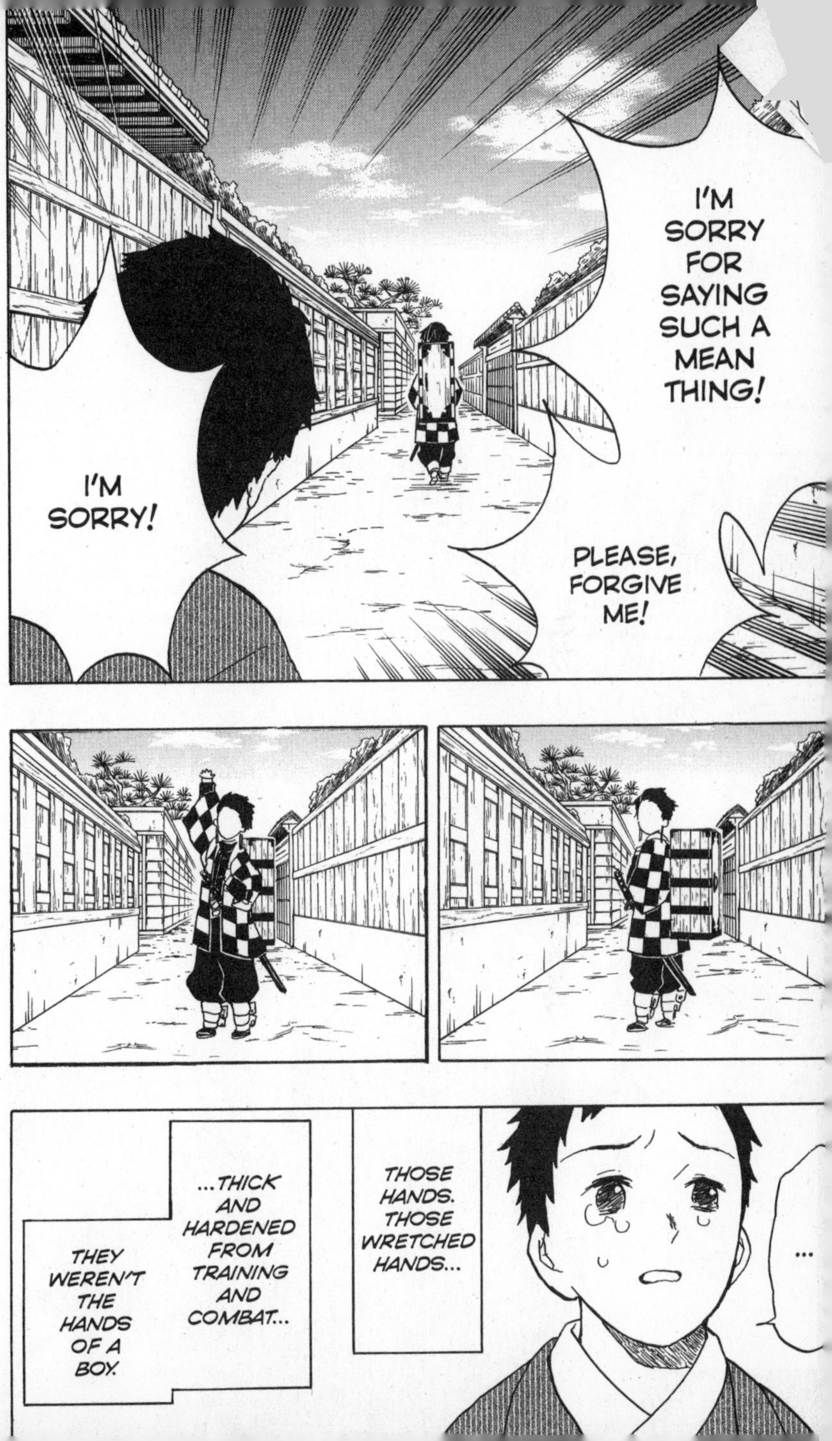
I'M SORRY FOR SAYING SUCH A MEAN THING!
PLEASE, FORGIVE ME!
I'M SORRY!
...
THOSE HANDS. THOSE WRETCHED HANDS...
...THICK AND HARDENED FROM TRAINING AND COMBAT...
THEY WEREN'T THE HANDS OF A BOY.

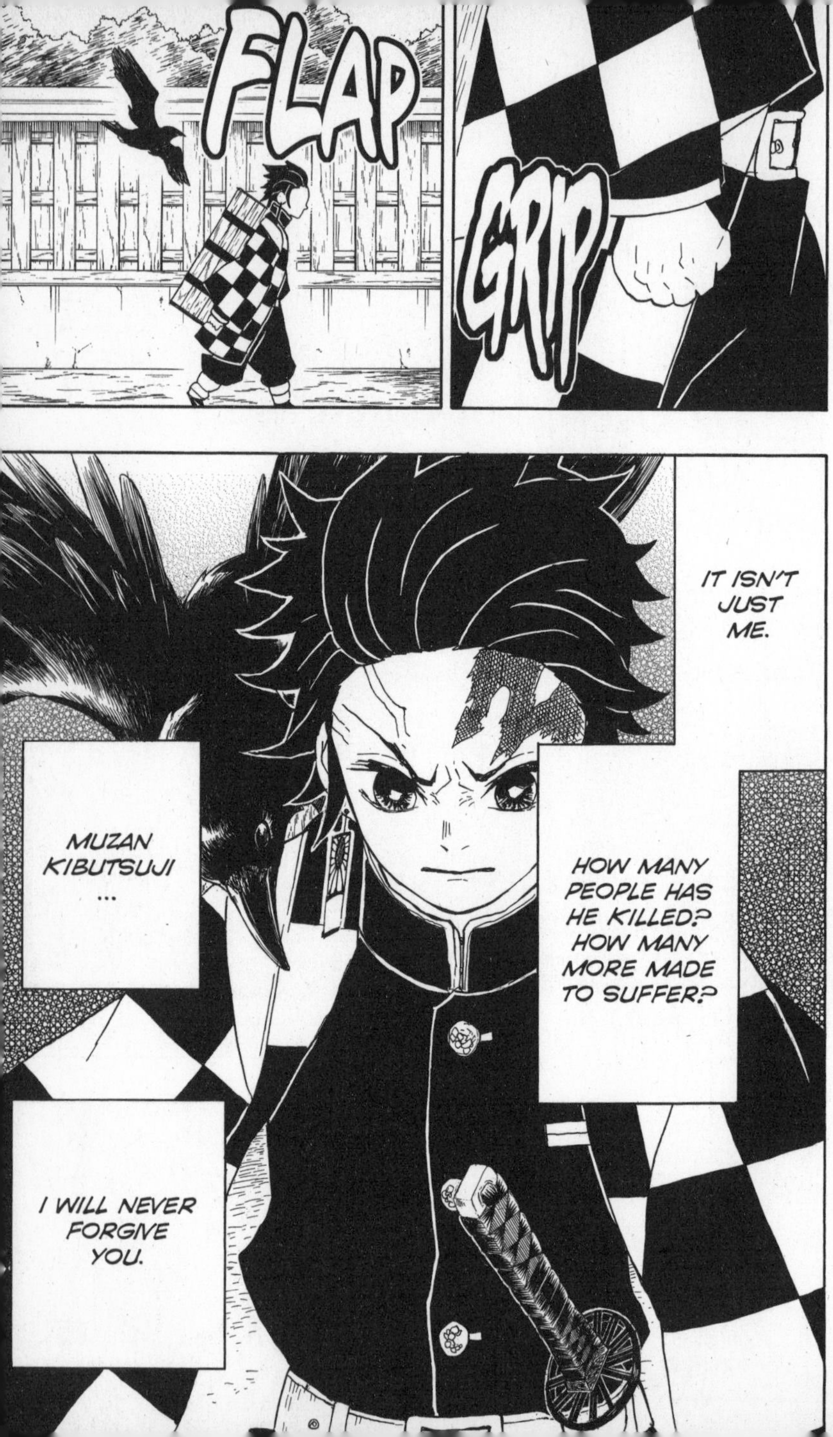
GRIP
FLAP
IT ISN'T JUST ME.
HOW MANY PEOPLE HAS HE KILLED? HOW MANY MORE MADE TO SUFFER?
MUZAN KIBUTSUJI ...
I WILL NEVER FORGIVE YOU.

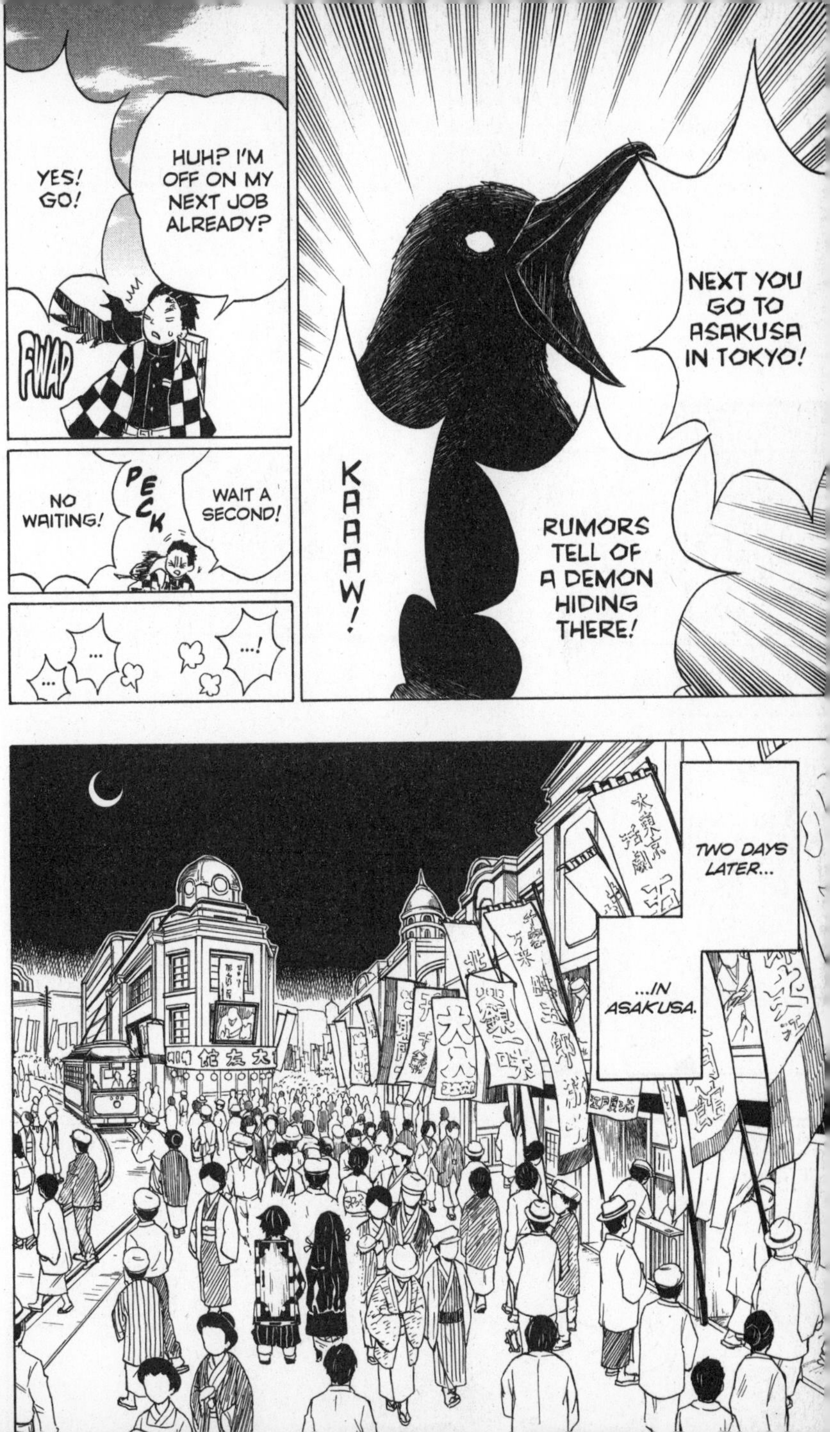
NEXT YOU GO TO ASAKUSA IN TOKYO!
KAAAAW!
RUMORS TELL OF A DEMON HIDING THERE!
HUH? I'M OFF ON MY NEXT JOB ALREADY?
YES! GO!
FWAP
WAIT A SECOND!
PECK
NO WAITING!
...!
...
...
TWO DAYS LATER...
...IN ASAKUSA.

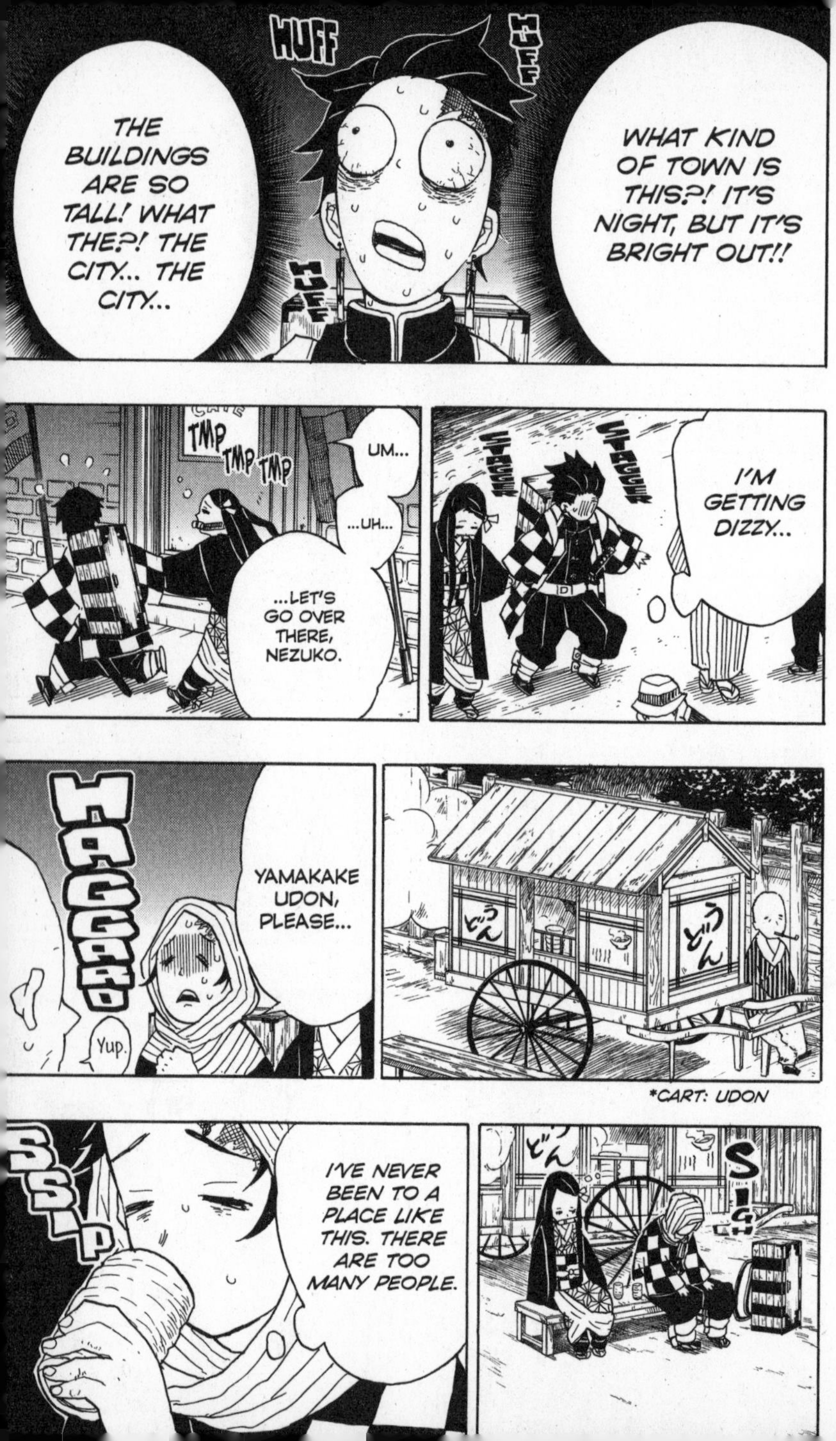
HUFF
HUFF
HUFF
WHAT KIND OF TOWN IS THIS?! IT'S NIGHT, BUT IT'S BRIGHT OUT!!
THE BUILDINGS ARE SO TALL! WHAT THE?! THE CITY... THE CITY...
STAGGER
STAGGER
I'M GETTING DIZZY...
TMP TMP TMP
UM...
...UH...
...LET'S GO OVER THERE, NEZUKO.
うどん
うどん
*CART: UDON
HAGGARD
YAMAKAKE UDON, PLEASE...
Yup.
SIGH
I'VE NEVER BEEN TO A PLACE LIKE THIS. THERE ARE TOO MANY PEOPLE.
SSIP

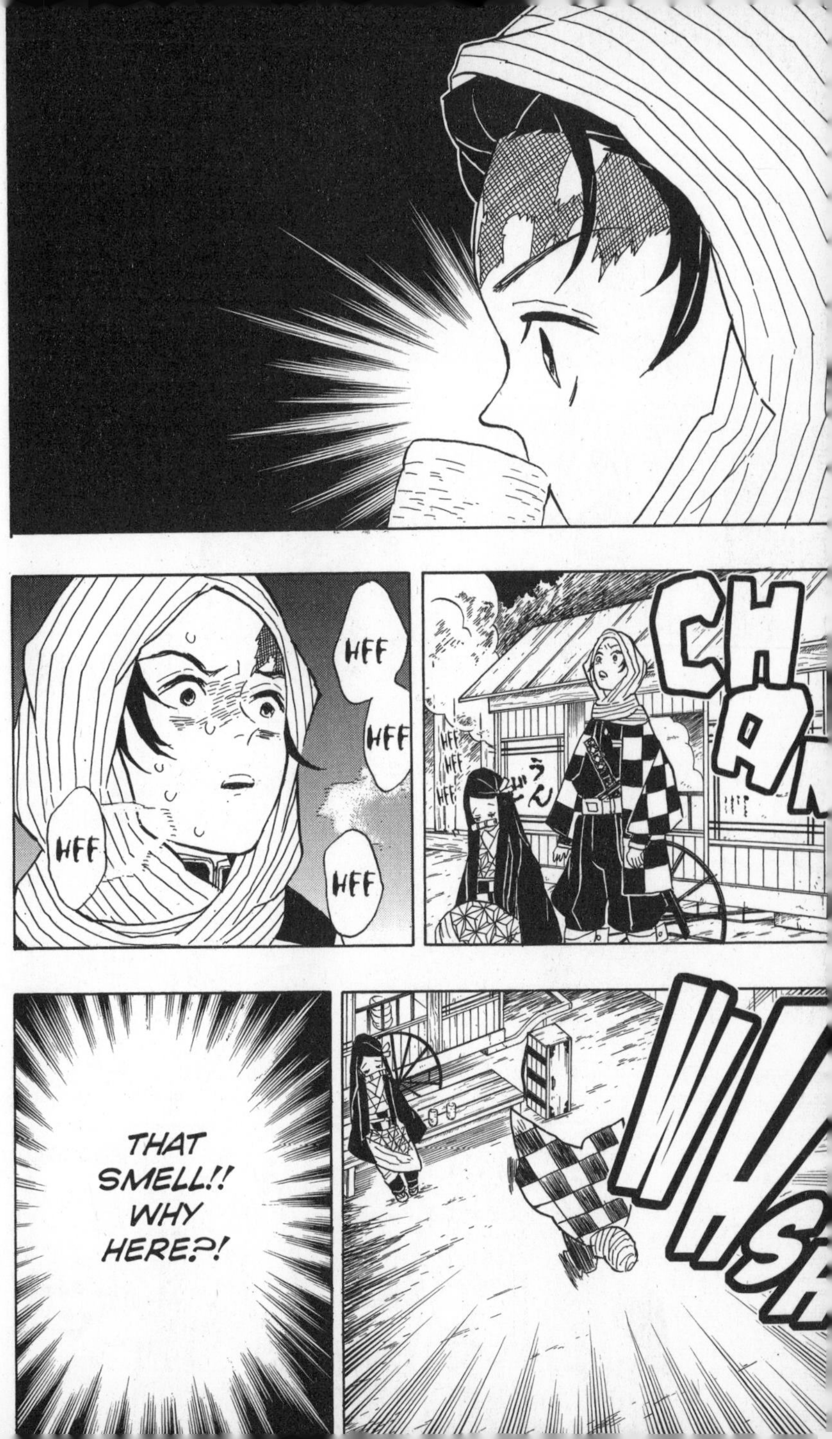
HFF
HFF
HFF
HFF
HFF
HFF
HFF
THAT SMELL!! WHY HERE?!

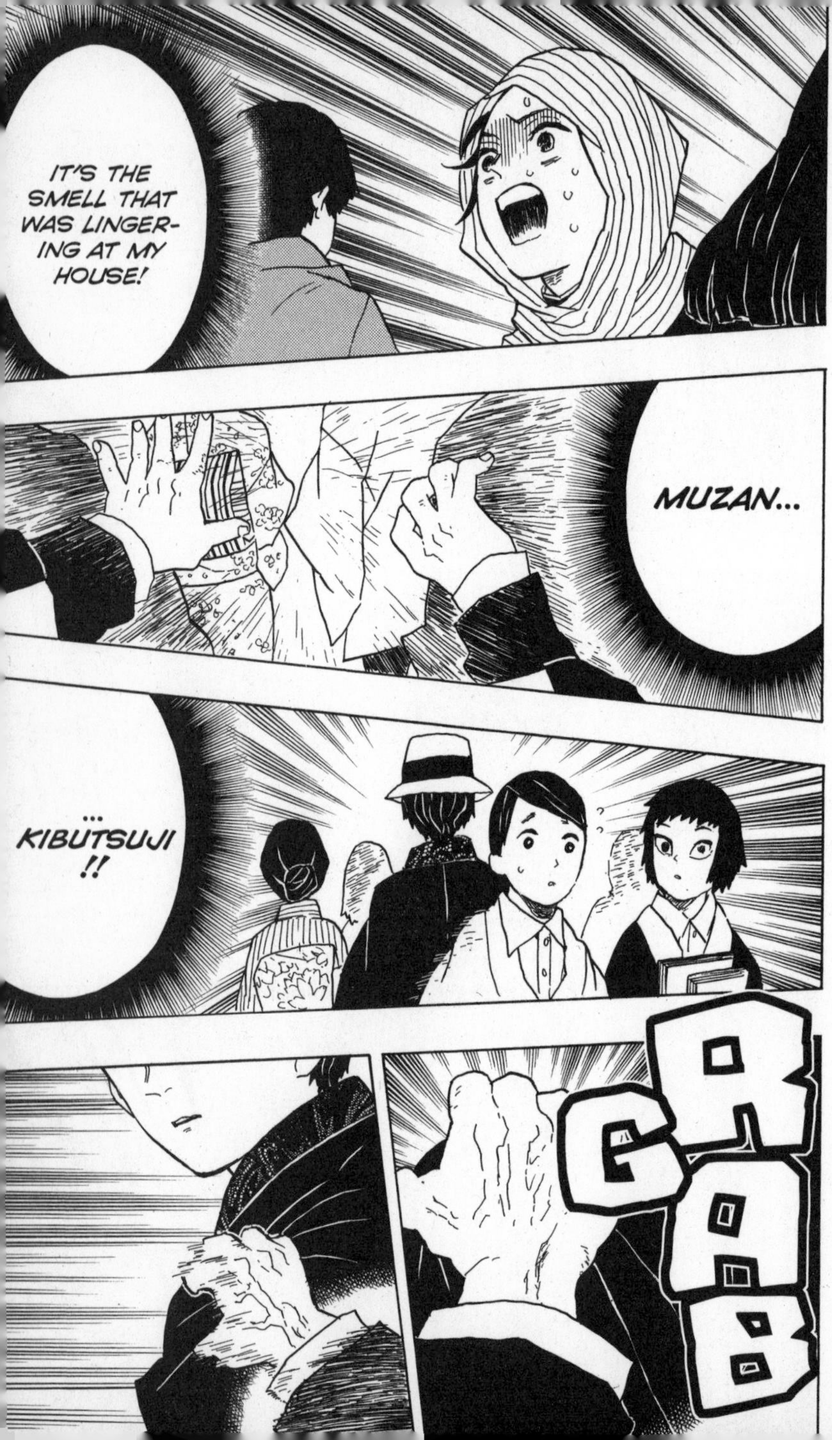
IT'S THE SMELL THAT WAS LINGER-ING AT MY HOUSE!
MUZAN...
...KIBUTSUJI!!
GRAB

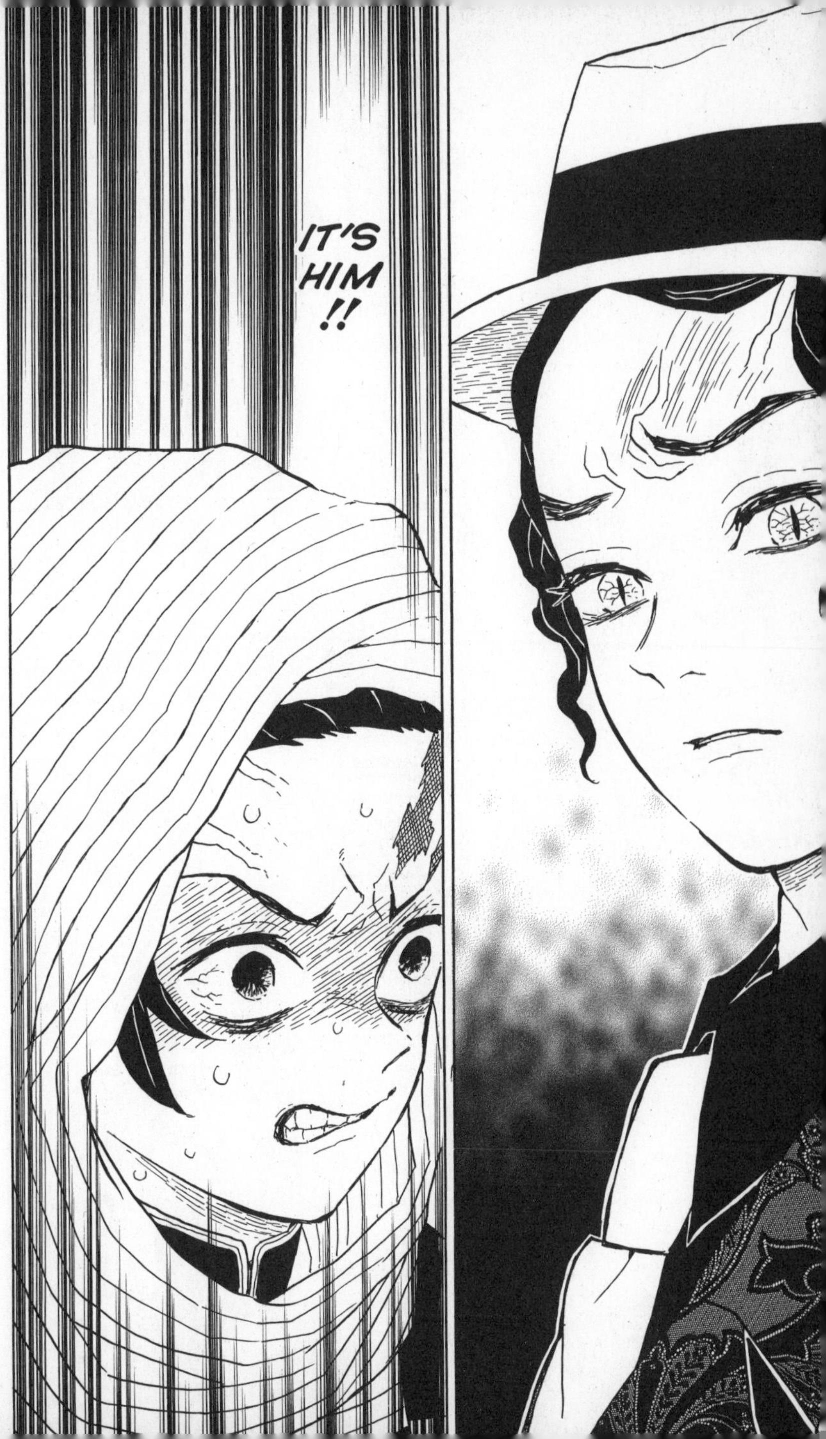
IT'S HIM !!

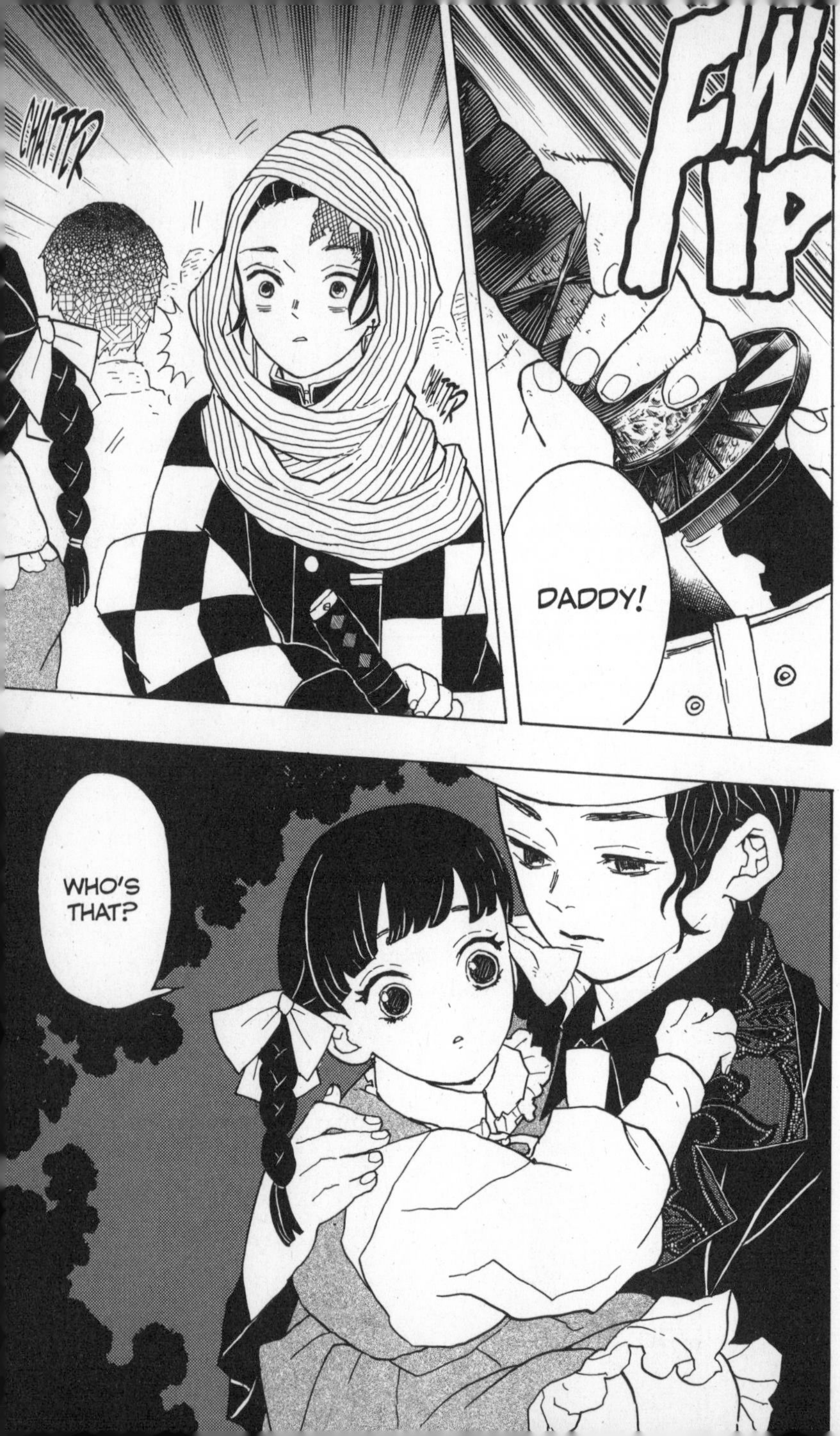
FWIP
DADDY!
CHATTER
CHATTER
WHO'S THAT?

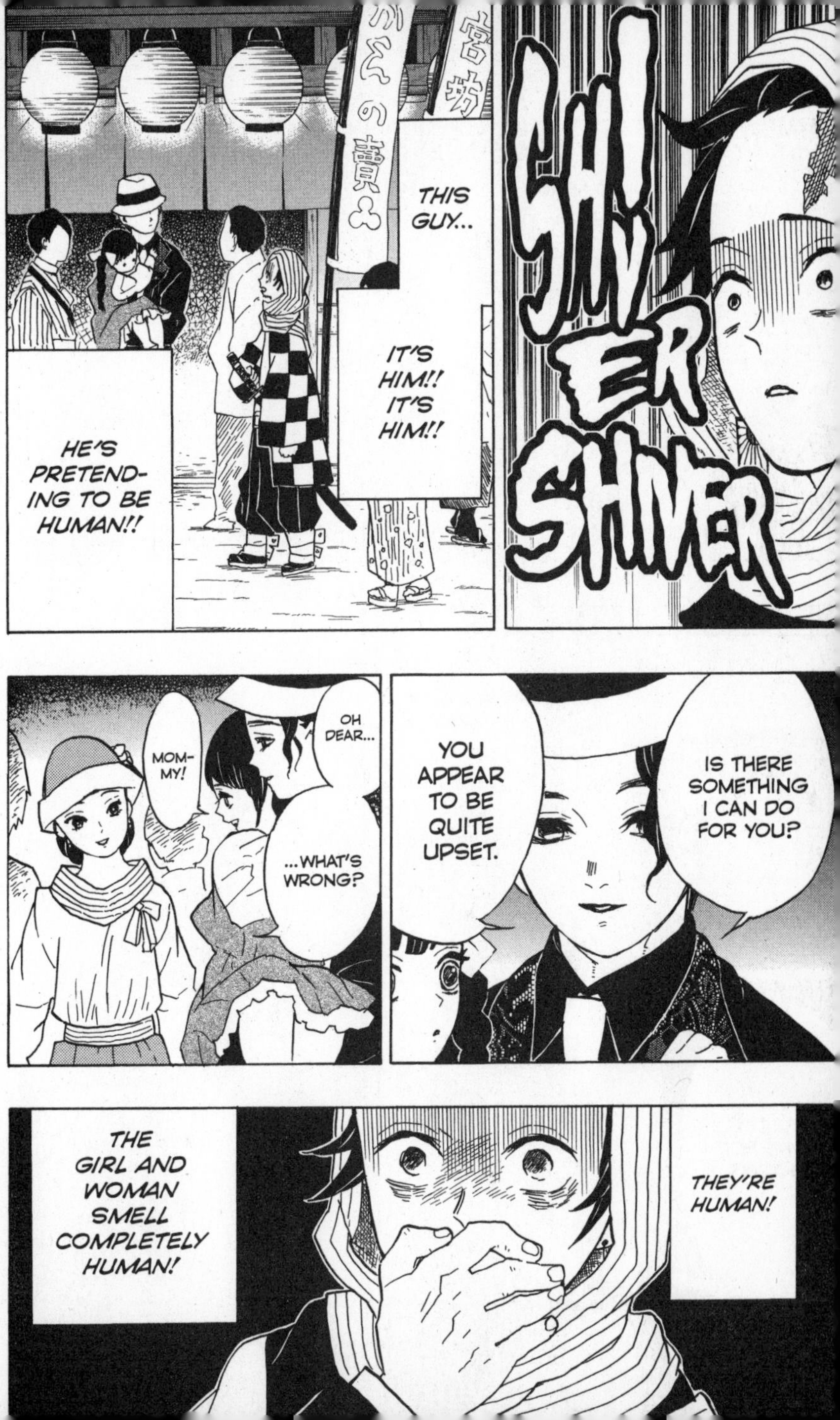
SHIVER SHIVER
THIS GUY...
IT'S HIM!! IT'S HIM!!
HE'S PRETEND-ING TO BE HUMAN!!
IS THERE SOMETHING I CAN DO FOR YOU?
YOU APPEAR TO BE QUITE UPSET.
OH DEAR...
...WHAT'S WRONG?
MOM-MY!
THEY'RE HUMAN!
THE GIRL AND WOMAN SMELL COMPLETELY HUMAN!

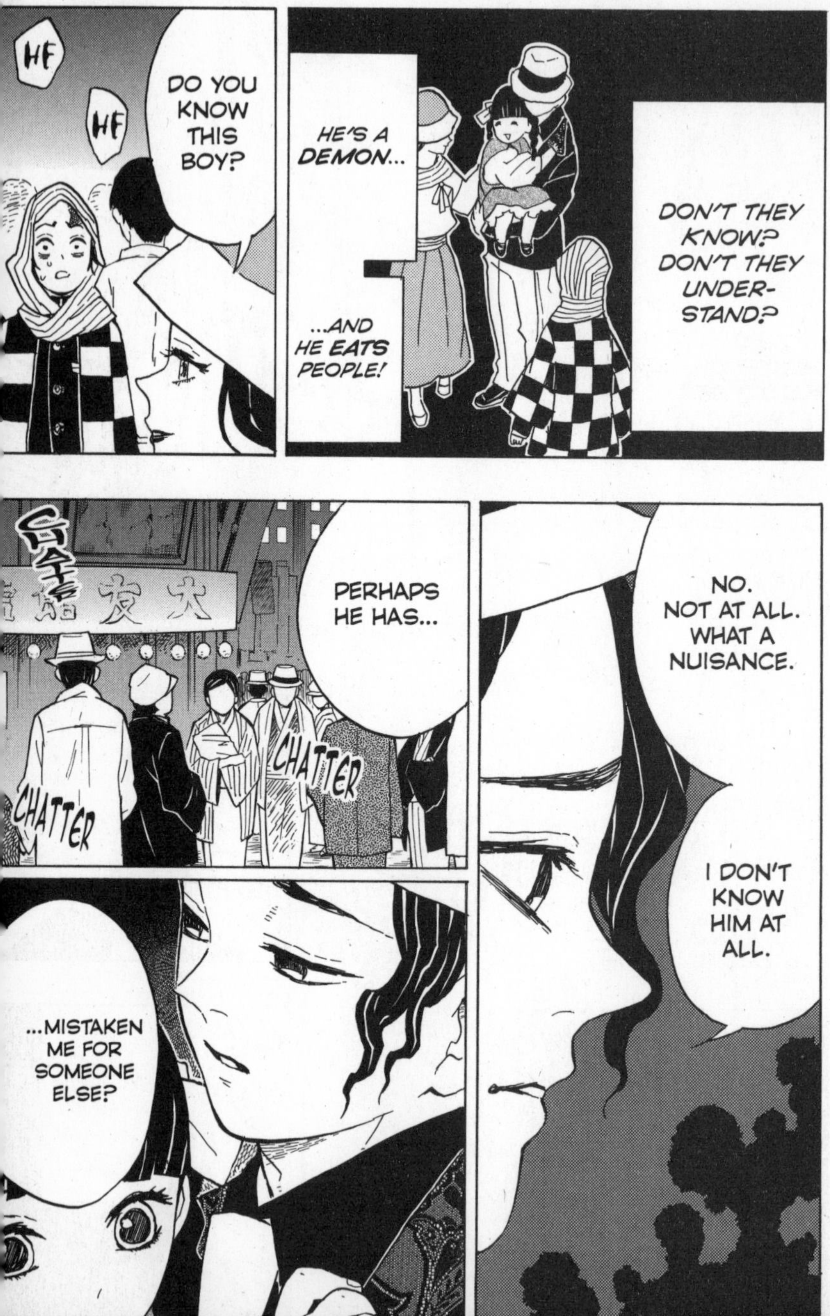
HE'S A DEMON...
...AND HE EATS PEOPLE!
DON'T THEY KNOW? DON'T THEY UNDER-STAND?
HF
HF
DO YOU KNOW THIS BOY?
NO. NOT AT ALL. WHAT A NUISANCE.
I DON'T KNOW HIM AT ALL.
PERHAPS HE HAS...
CHATTER
CHATTER
...MISTAKEN ME FOR SOMEONE ELSE?

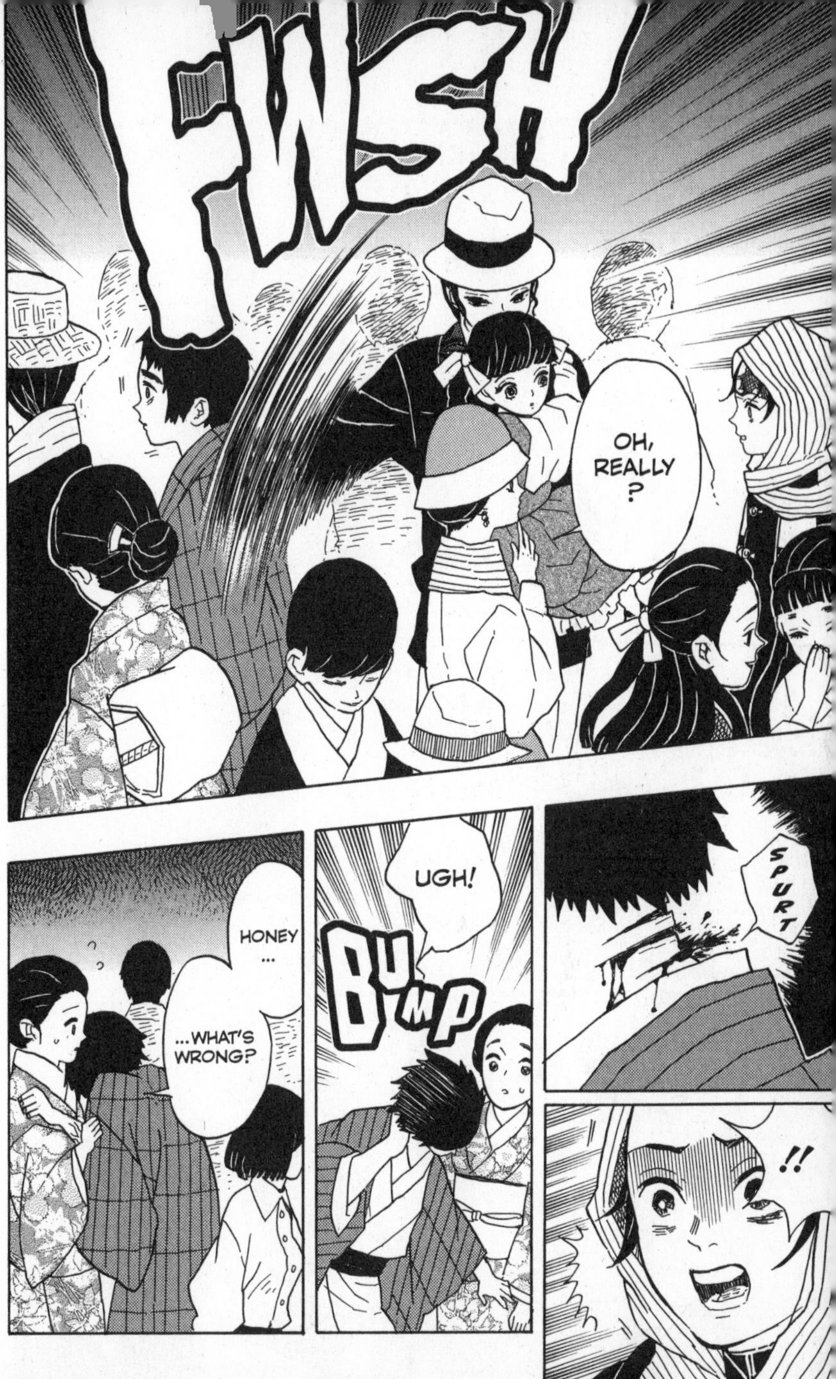
FWSH
OH, REALLY?
SPURT
!!
UGH!
BUMP
HONEY...
...WHAT'S WRONG?

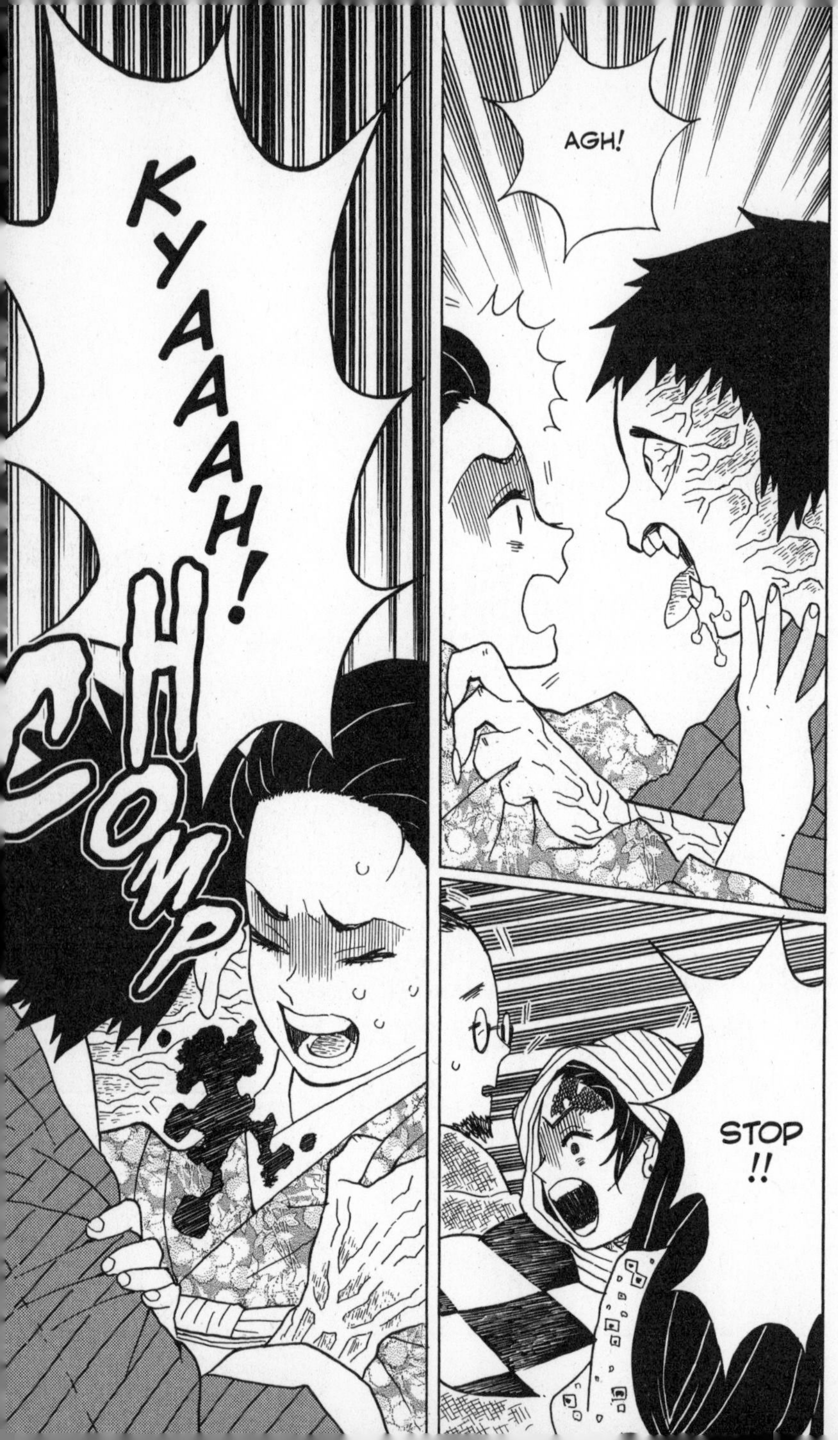
AGH!
STOP!!
KYAAAH!
CHOMP

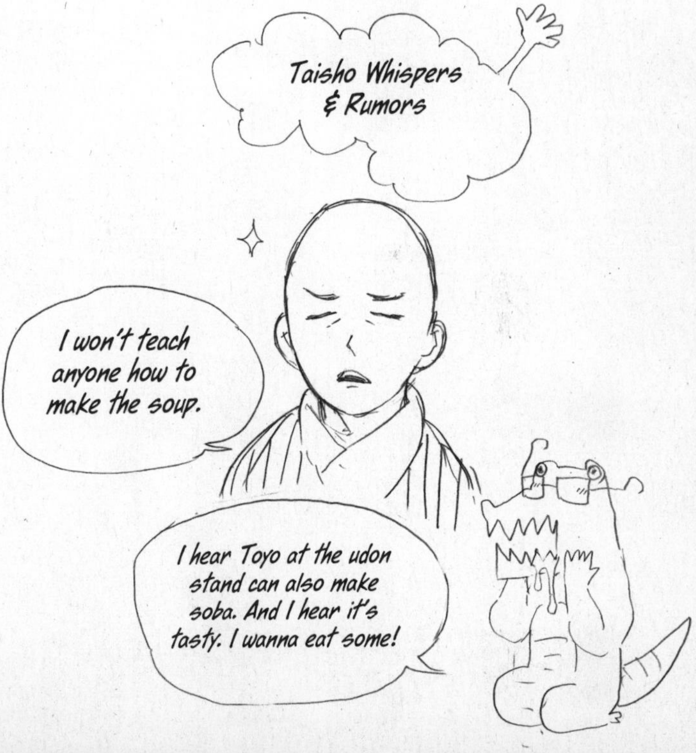
Taisho Whispers & Rumors
I won't teach anyone how to make the soup.
I hear Toyo at the udon stand can also make soba. And I hear it's tasty. I wanna eat some!

CHAPTER 14: KIBUTSUJI'S WRATH / THE SMELL OF ENCHANTING BLOOD

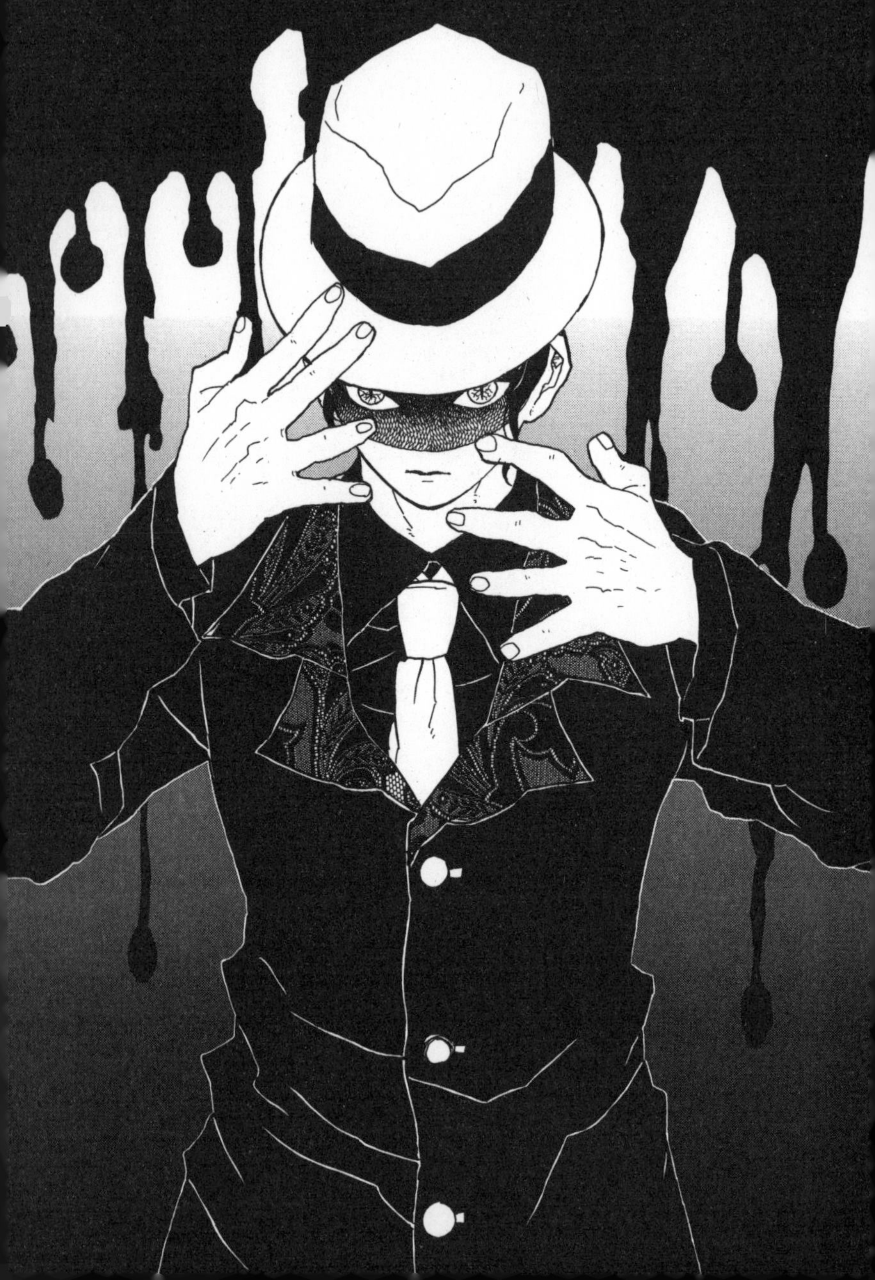

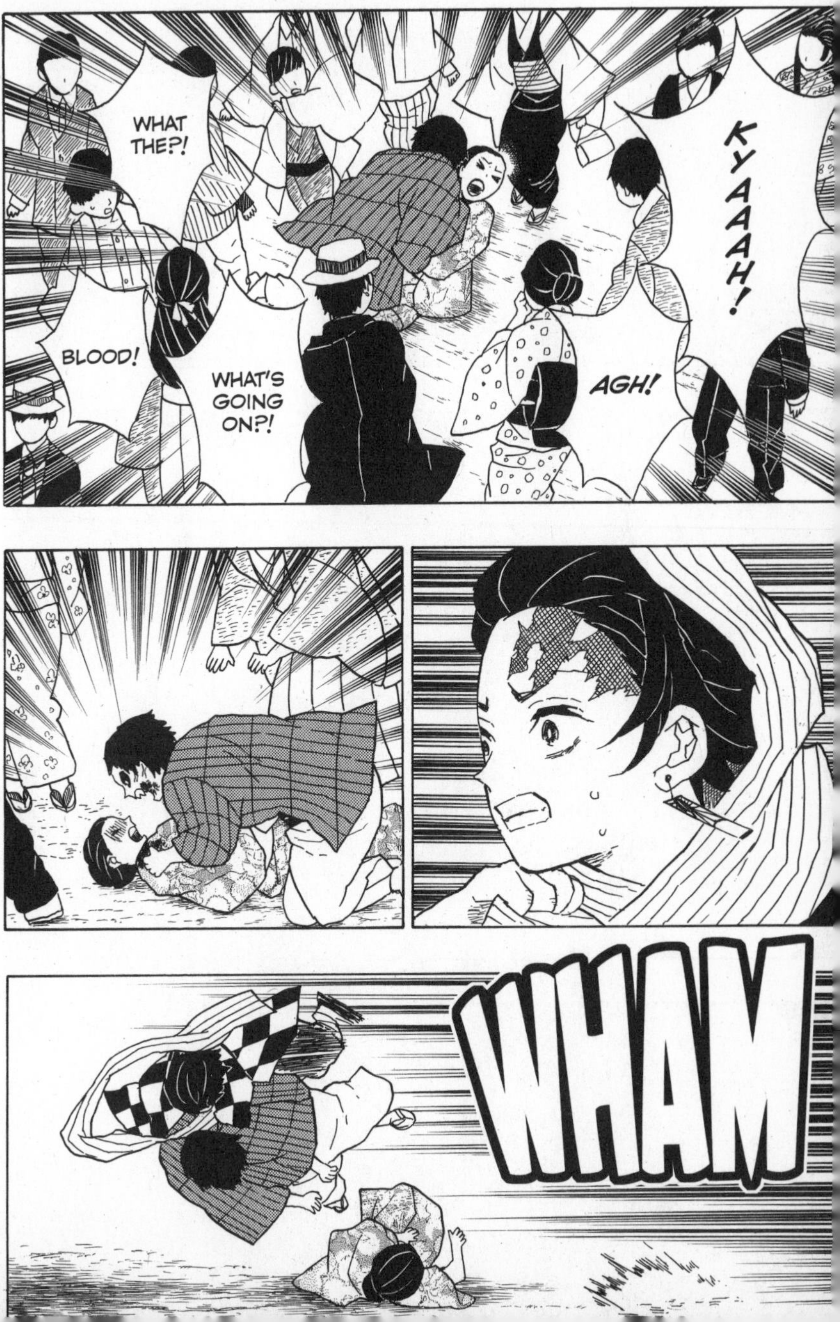
KYAAAAH!
WHAT THE?!
AGH!
WHAT'S GOING ON?!
BLOOD!
WHAM

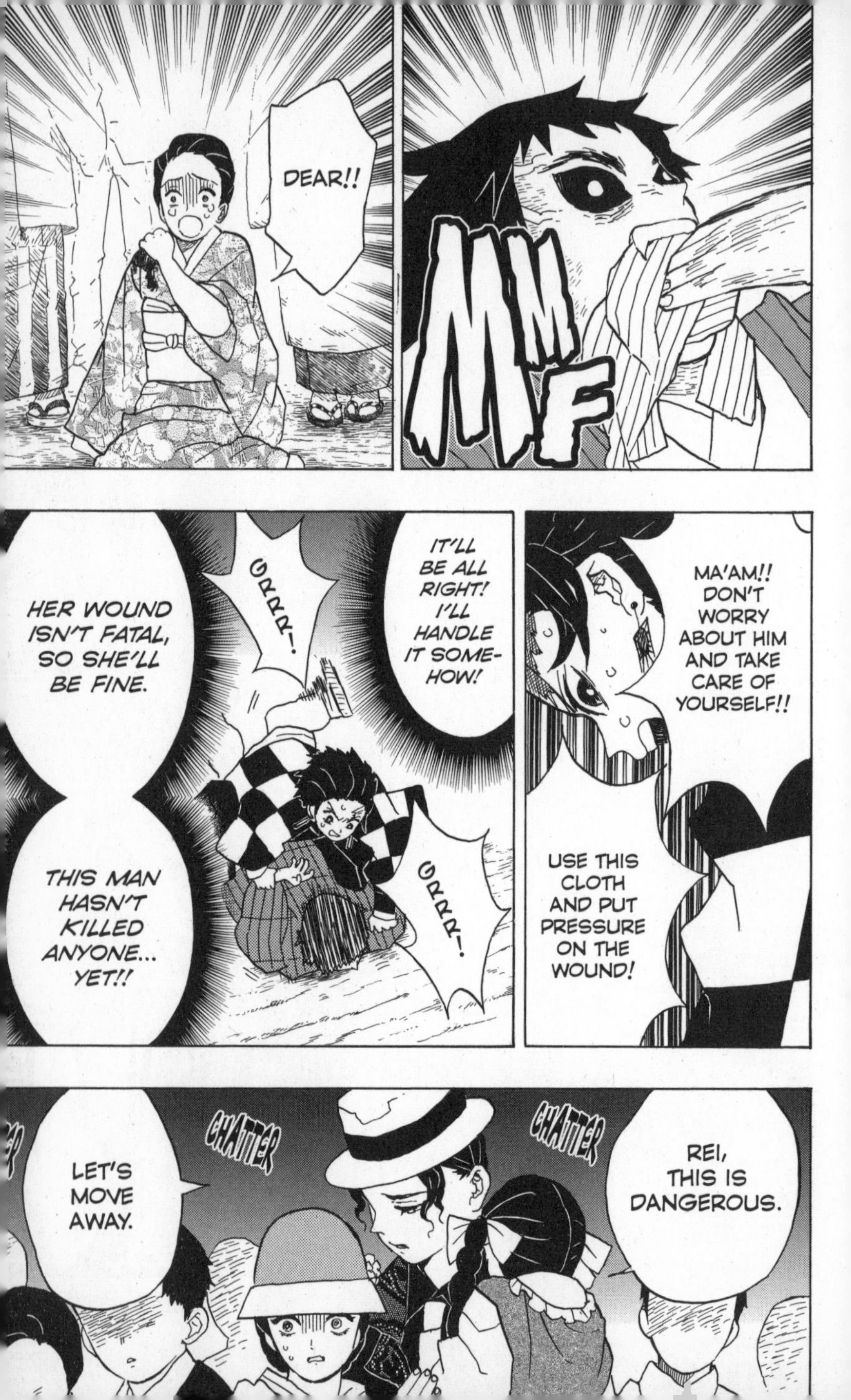
MMF
DEAR!!
MA'AM!! DON'T WORRY ABOUT HIM AND TAKE CARE OF YOURSELF!!
USE THIS CLOTH AND PUT PRESSURE ON THE WOUND!
IT'LL BE ALL RIGHT! I'LL HANDLE IT SOMEHOW!
GRRR!
HER WOUND ISN'T FATAL, SO SHE'LL BE FINE.
THIS MAN HASN'T KILLED ANYONE... YET!!
GRRR!
REI, THIS IS DANGEROUS.
CHATTER
CHATTER
LET'S MOVE AWAY.

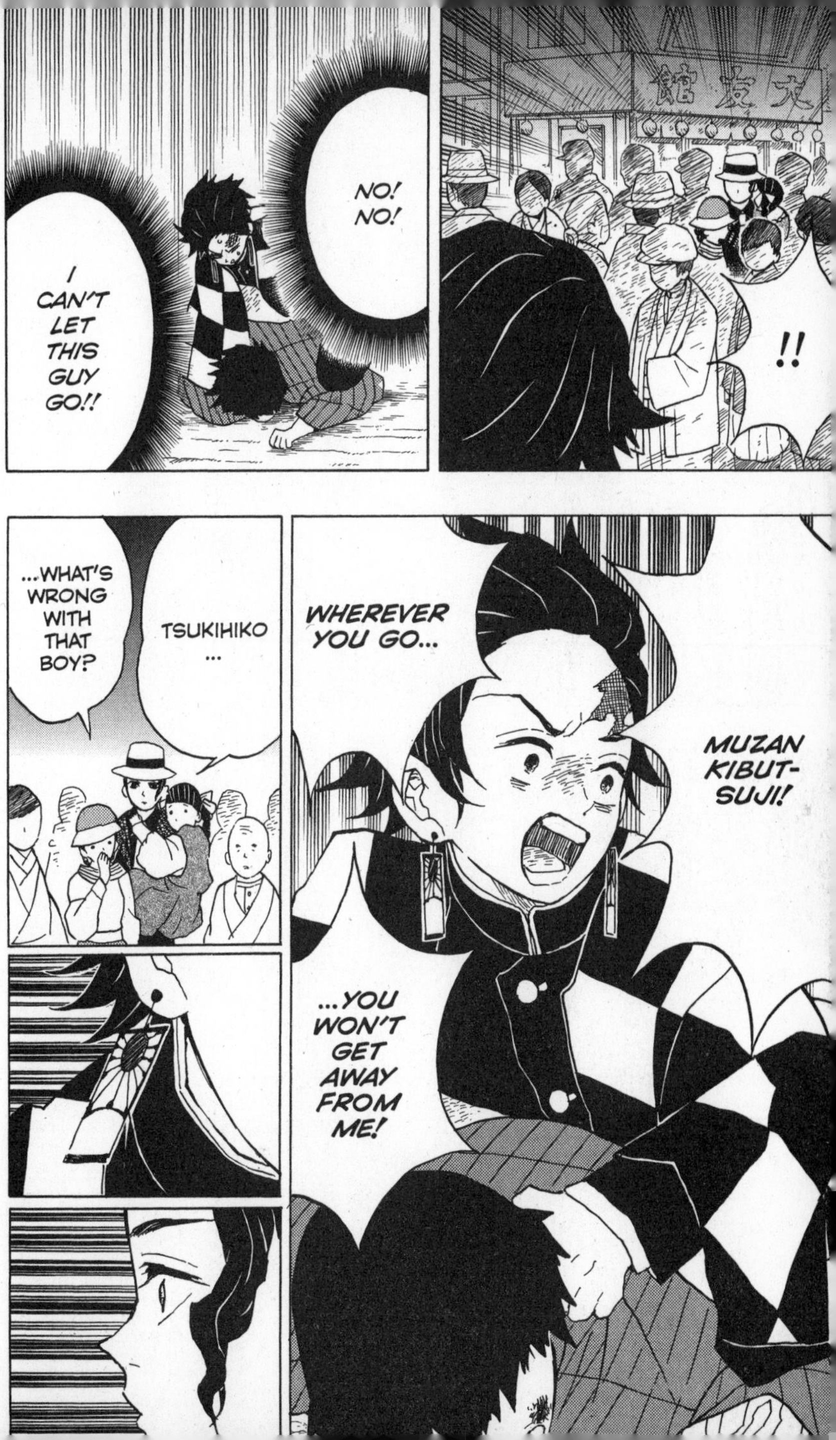
!!
NO! NO!
I CAN'T LET THIS GUY GO!!
WHEREVER YOU GO...
MUZAN KIBUTSUJI!
...YOU WON'T GET AWAY FROM ME!
TSUKIHIKO...
...WHAT'S WRONG WITH THAT BOY?

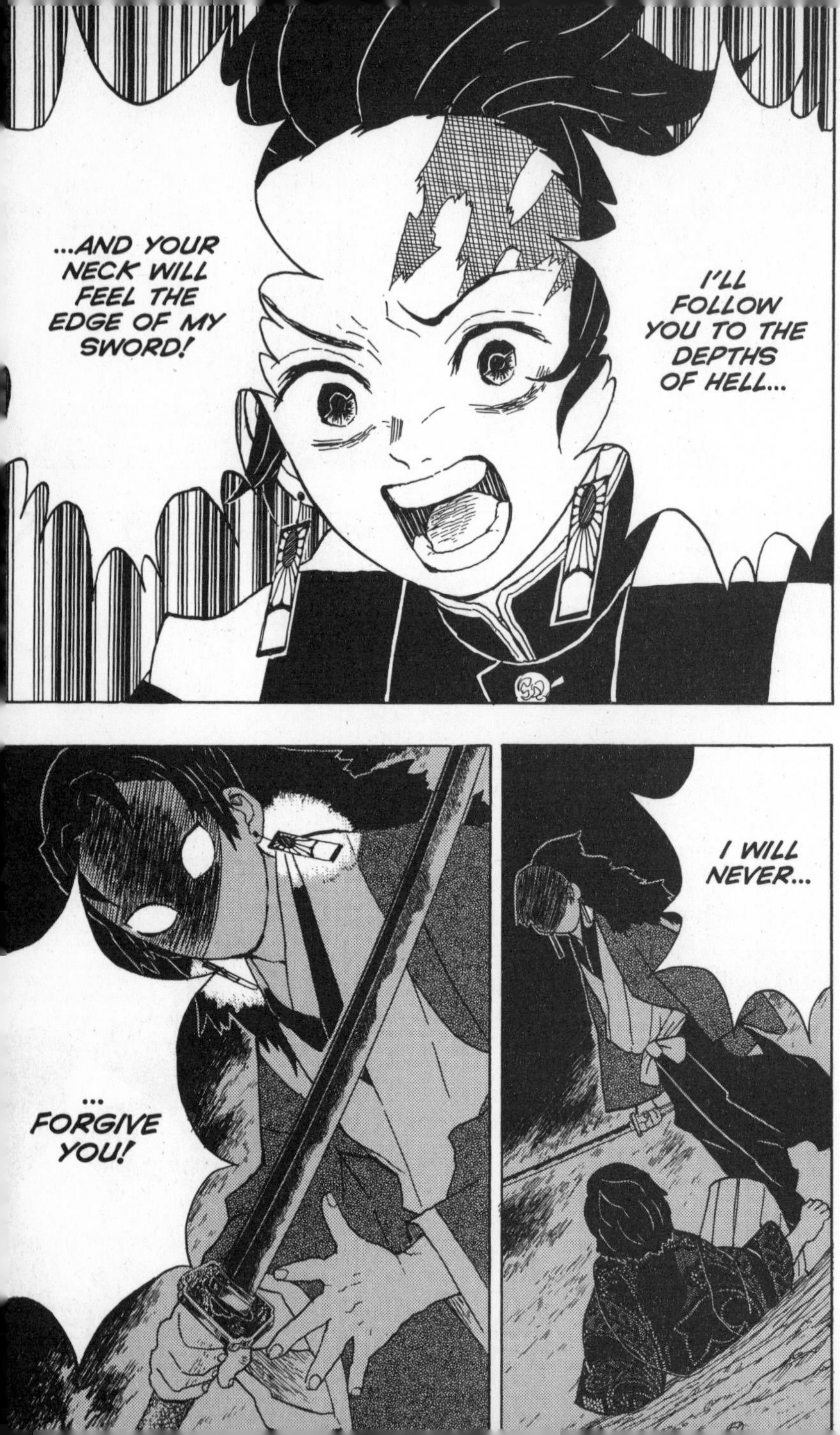
I'LL FOLLOW YOU TO THE DEPTHS OF HELL...
...AND YOUR NECK WILL FEEL THE EDGE OF MY SWORD!
I WILL NEVER...
... FORGIVE YOU!

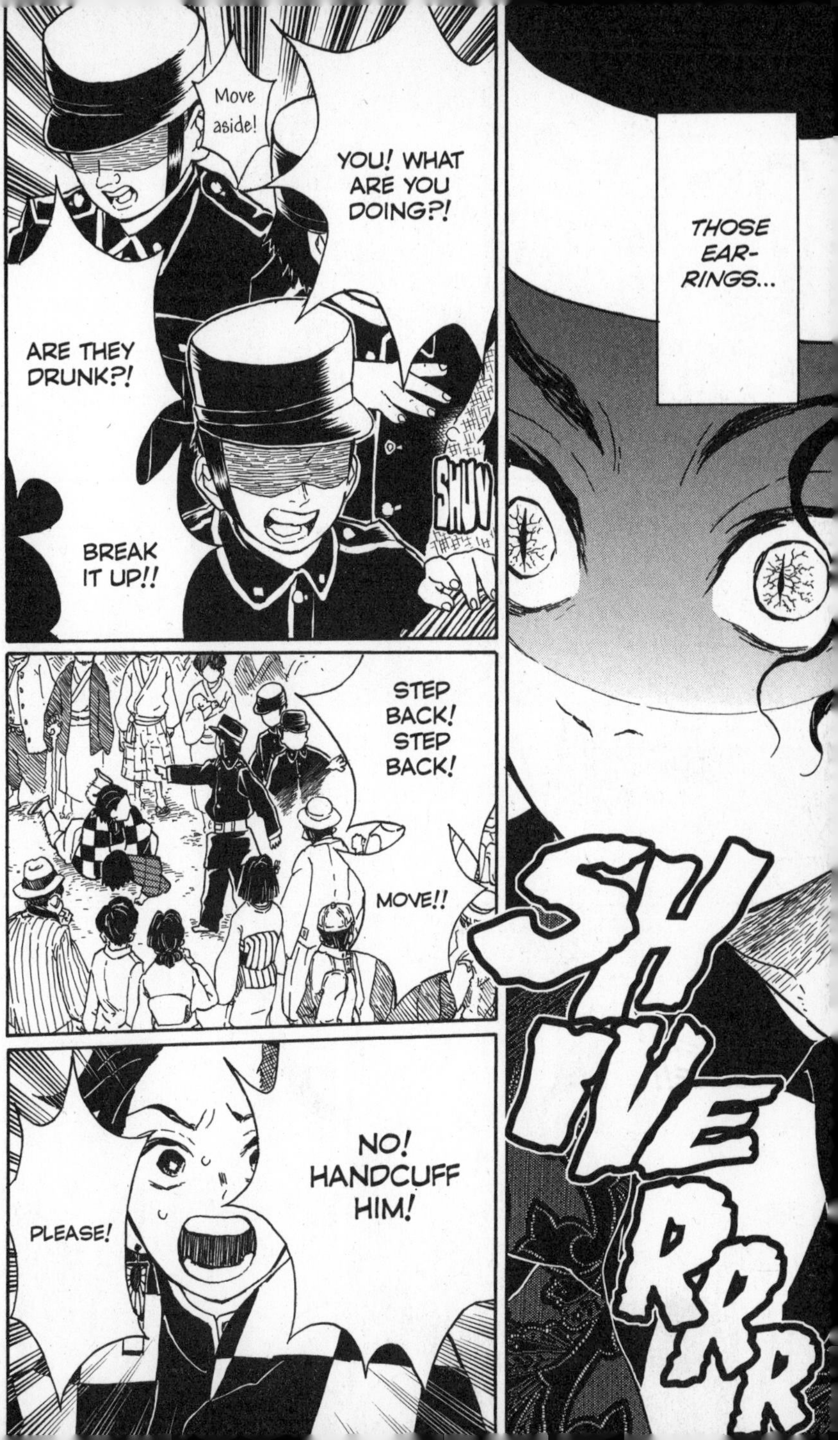
THOSE EAR-RINGS...
SHIVERRR
YOU! WHAT ARE YOU DOING?!
Move aside!
SHUV
ARE THEY DRUNK?!
BREAK IT UP!!
STEP BACK! STEP BACK!
MOVE!!
NO! HANDCUFF HIM!
PLEASE!

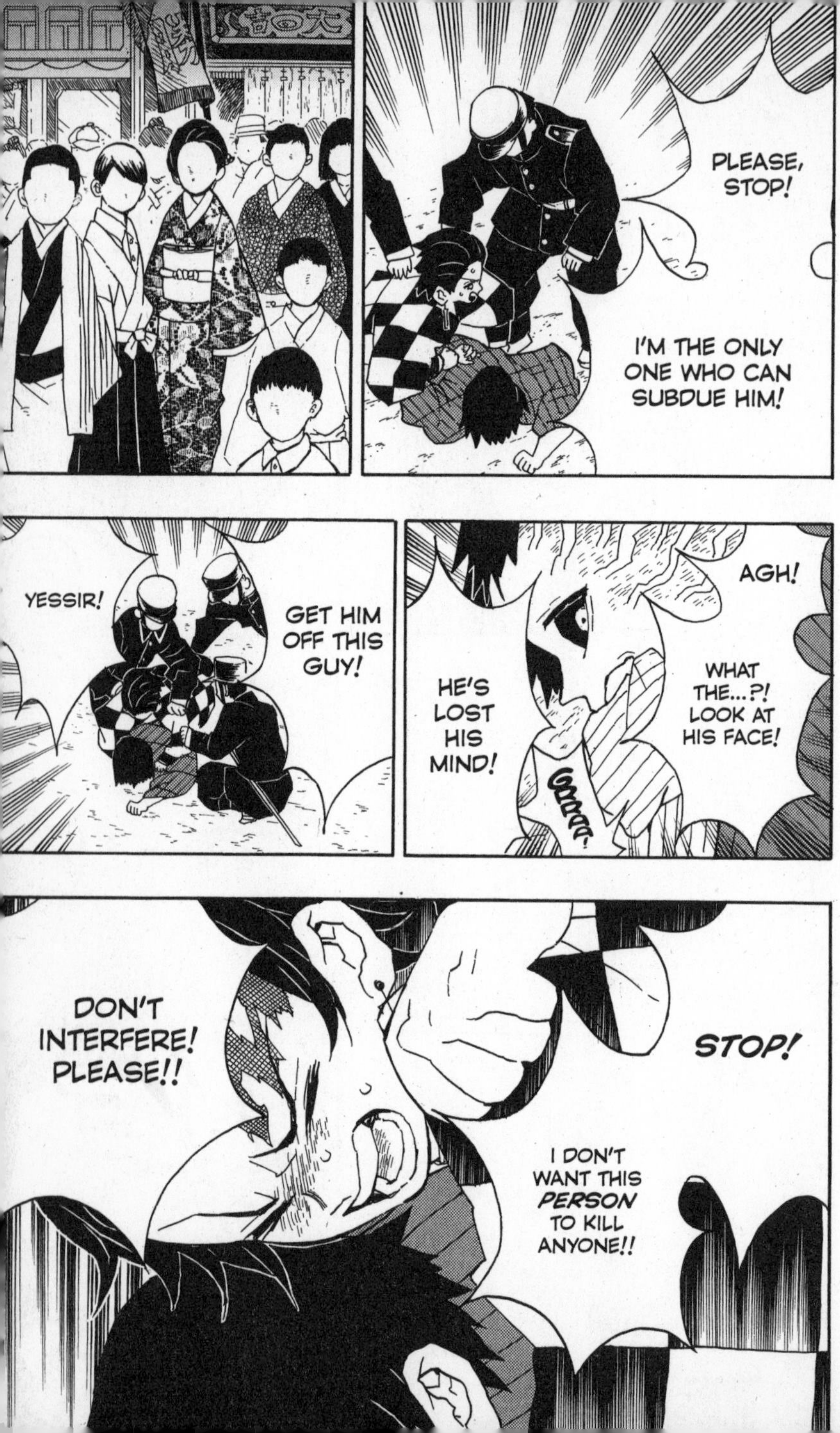
PLEASE, STOP!
I'M THE ONLY ONE WHO CAN SUBDUE HIM!
AGH!
WHAT THE...?! LOOK AT HIS FACE!
HE'S LOST HIS MIND!
GET HIM OFF THIS GUY!
YESSIR!
STOP!
I DON'T WANT THIS *PERSON* TO KILL ANYONE!!
DON'T INTERFERE! PLEASE!!

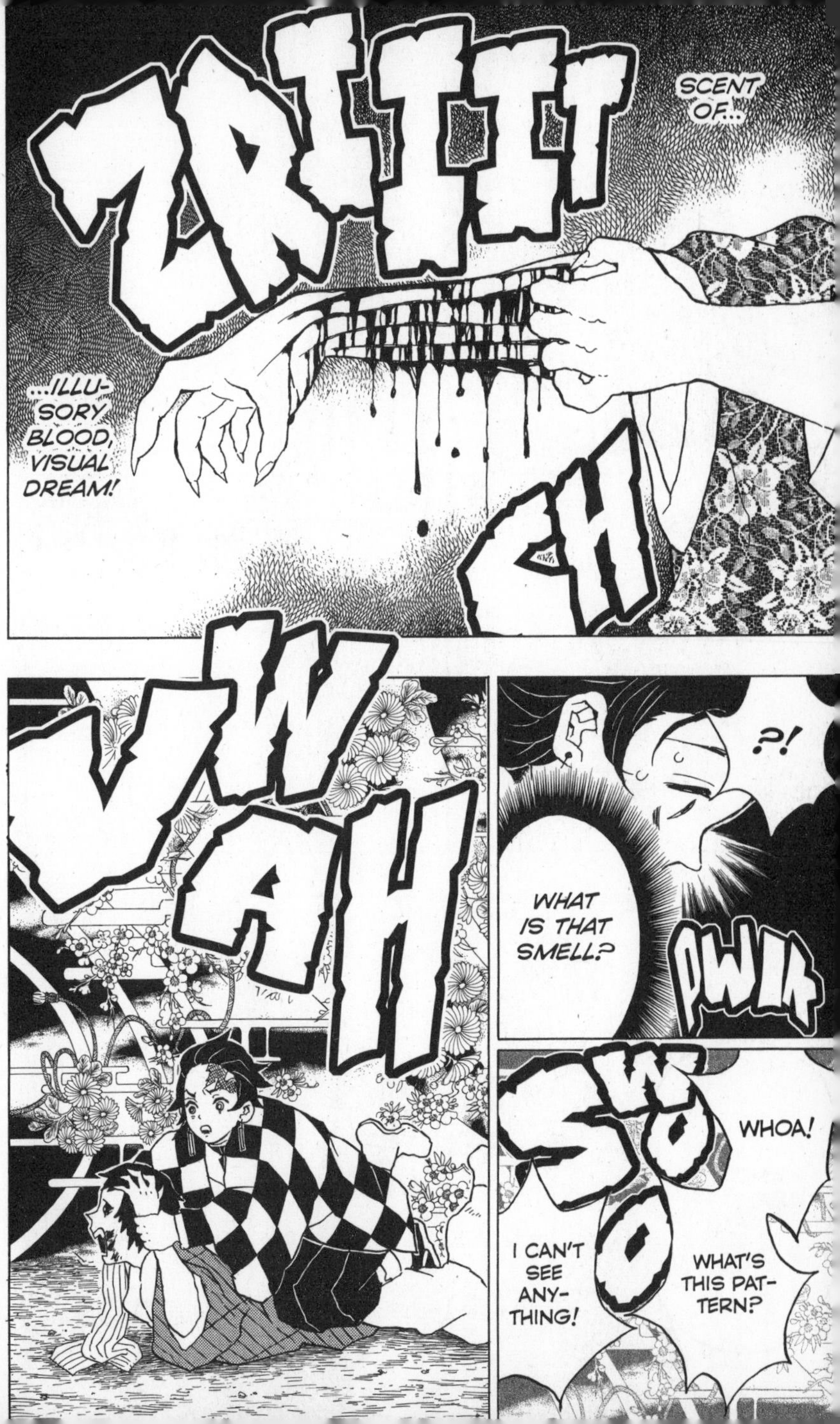
SCENT OF...
ZRIIIT
...ILLU-SORY BLOOD, VISUAL DREAM!
CH
?!
WHAT IS THAT SMELL?
PWIK
SWOO
WHOA!
WHAT'S THIS PAT-TERN?
I CAN'T SEE ANY-THING!
VWAH

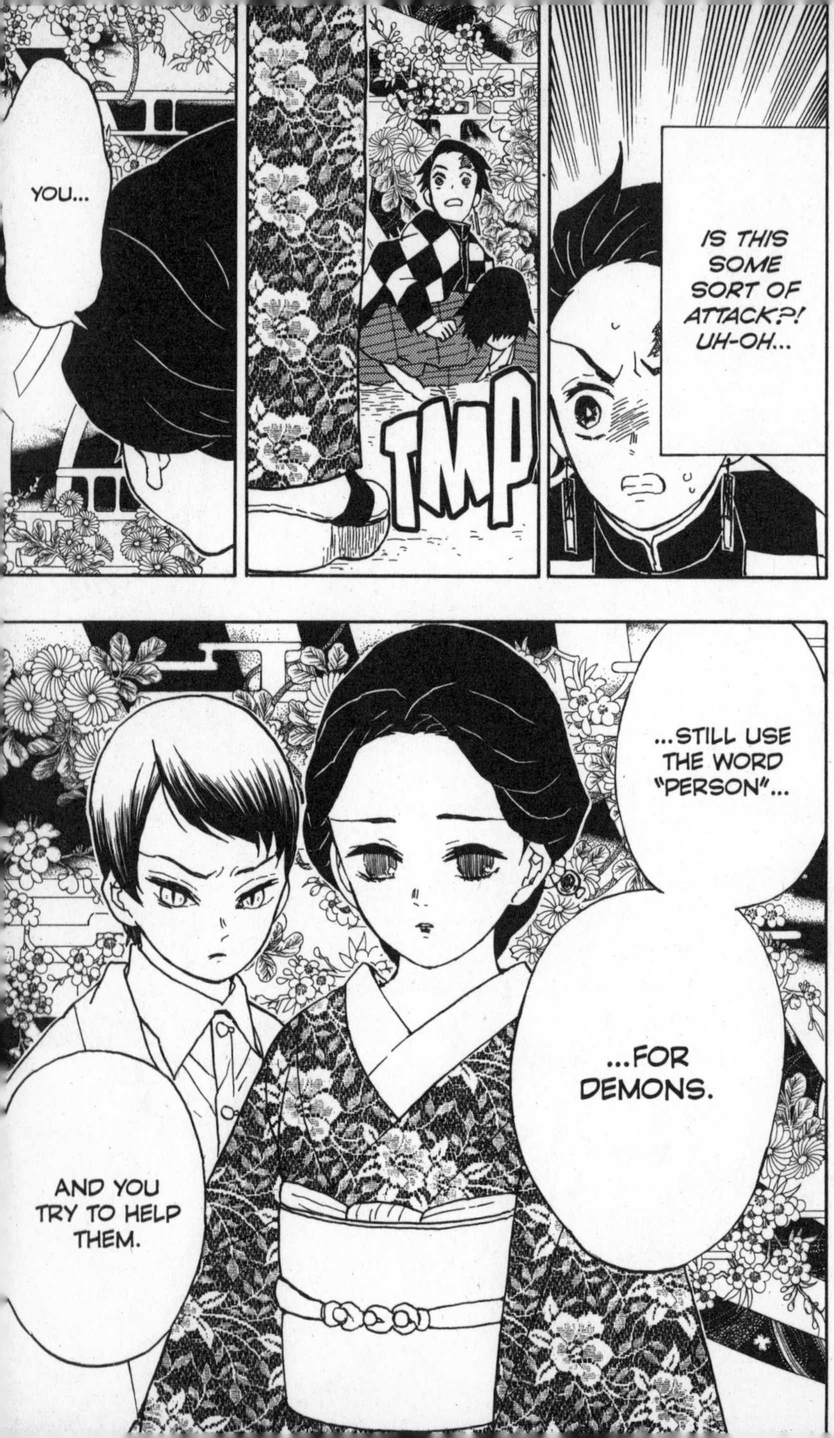
IS THIS SOME SORT OF ATTACK?! UH-OH...
TMP
YOU...
...STILL USE THE WORD "PERSON"...
...FOR DEMONS.
AND YOU TRY TO HELP THEM.

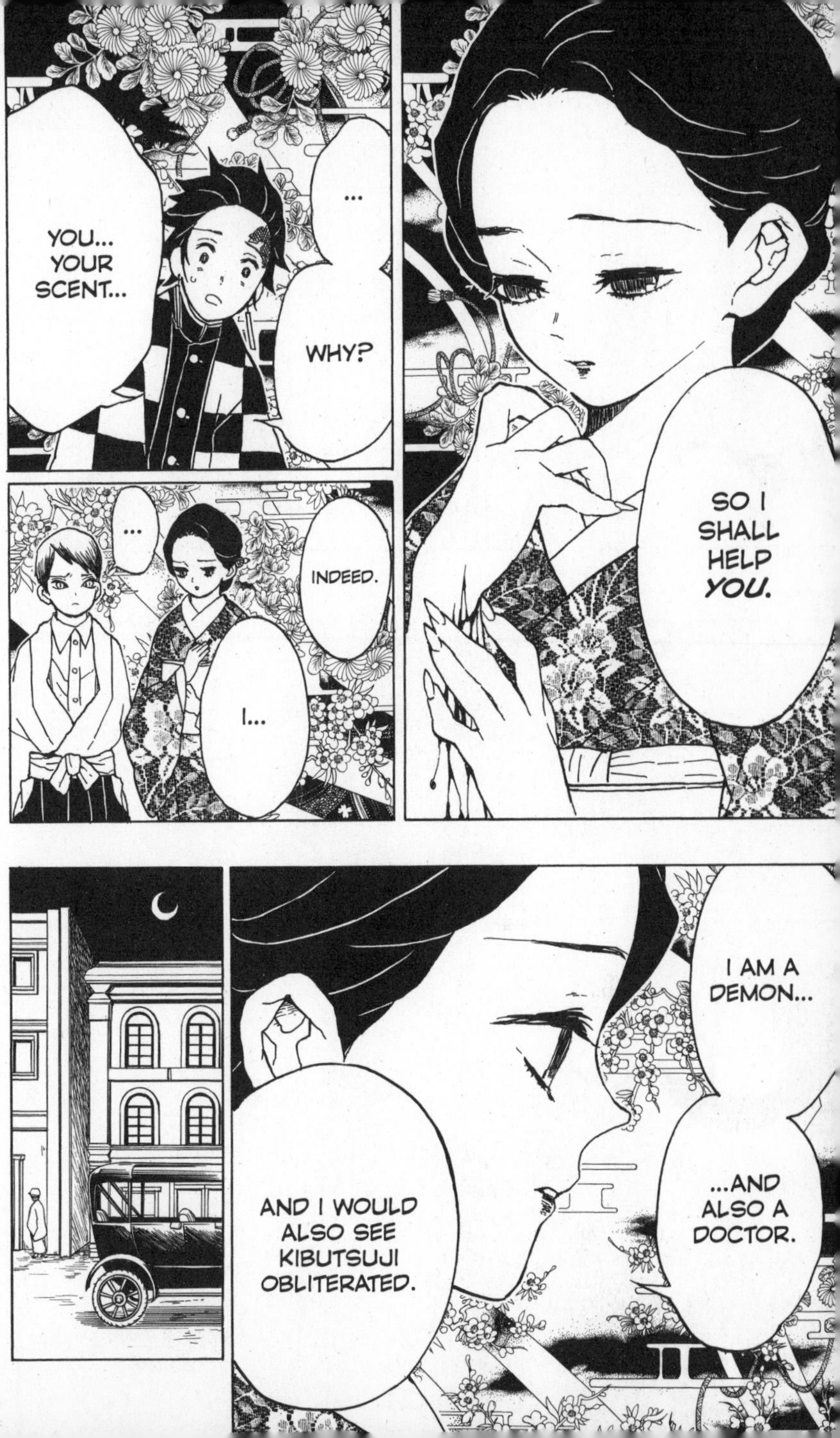
SO I SHALL HELP *YOU*.
...
WHY?
YOU... YOUR SCENT...
INDEED.
I...
...
I AM A DEMON...
...AND ALSO A DOCTOR.
AND I WOULD ALSO SEE KIBUTSUJI OBLITERATED.

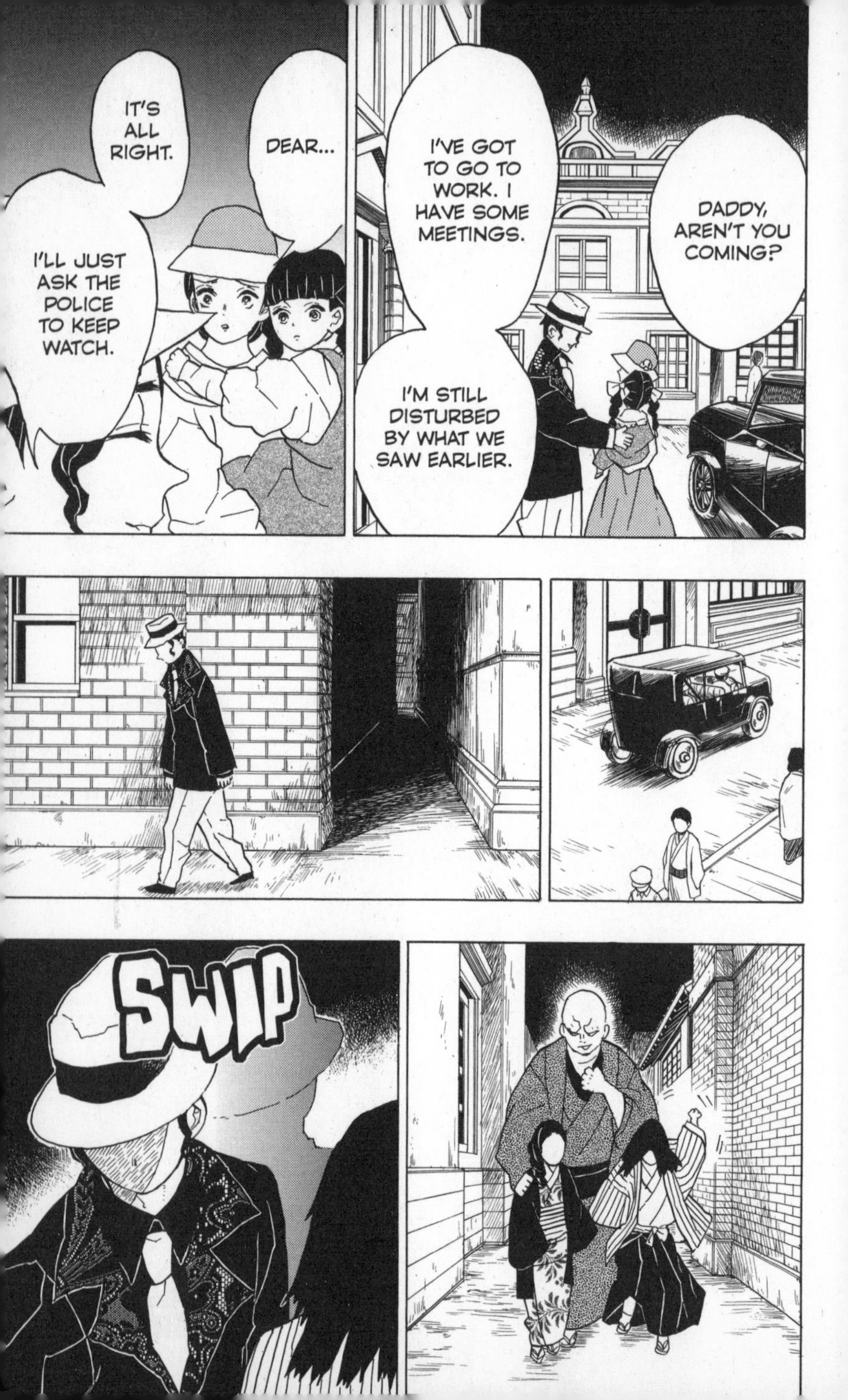
DADDY, AREN'T YOU COMING?
I'VE GOT TO GO TO WORK. I HAVE SOME MEETINGS.
I'M STILL DISTURBED BY WHAT WE SAW EARLIER.
DEAR...
IT'S ALL RIGHT.
I'LL JUST ASK THE POLICE TO KEEP WATCH.
SWIP

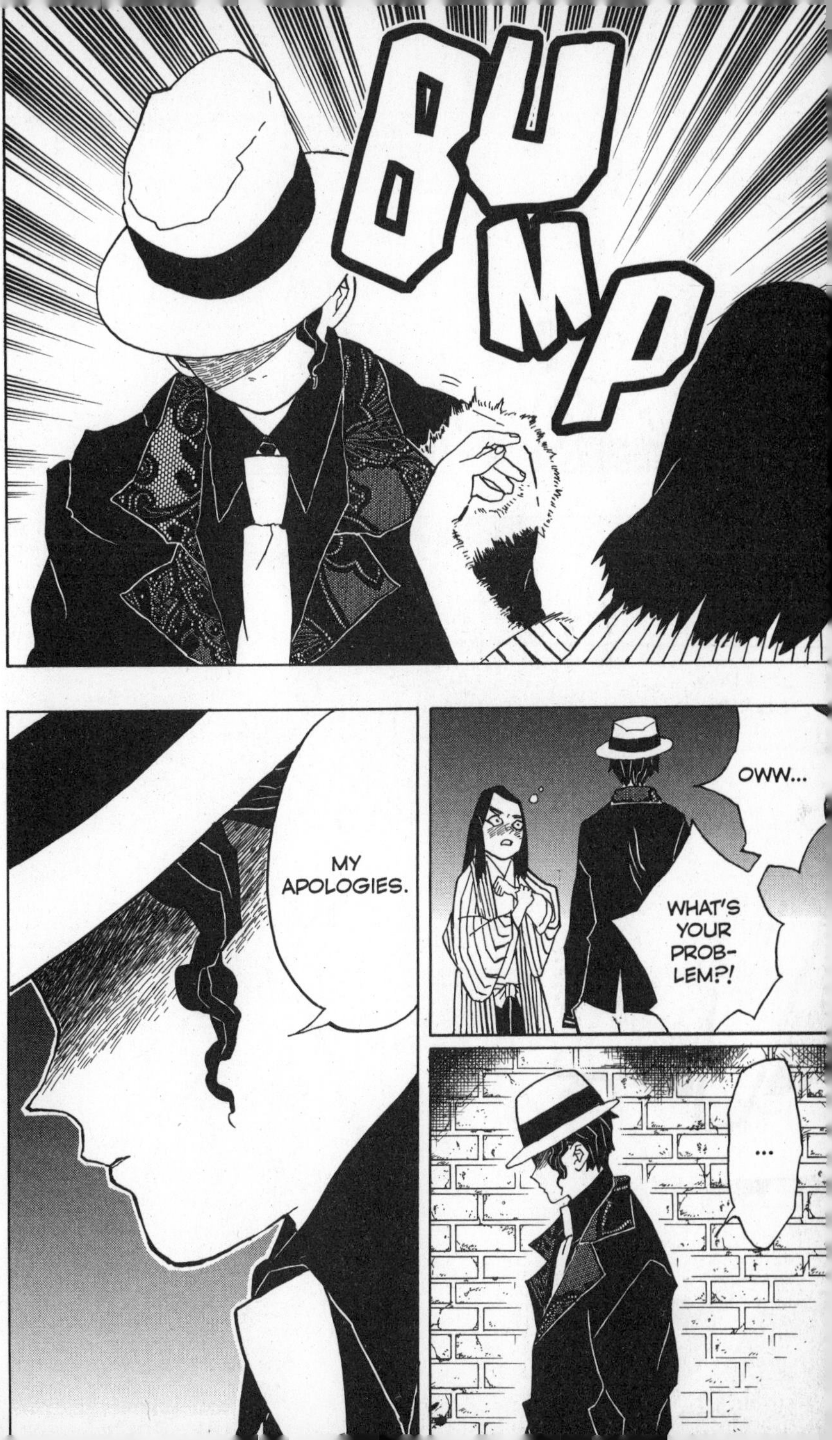
BUMP
OWW...
WHAT'S YOUR PROB-LEM?!
...
MY APOLOGIES.

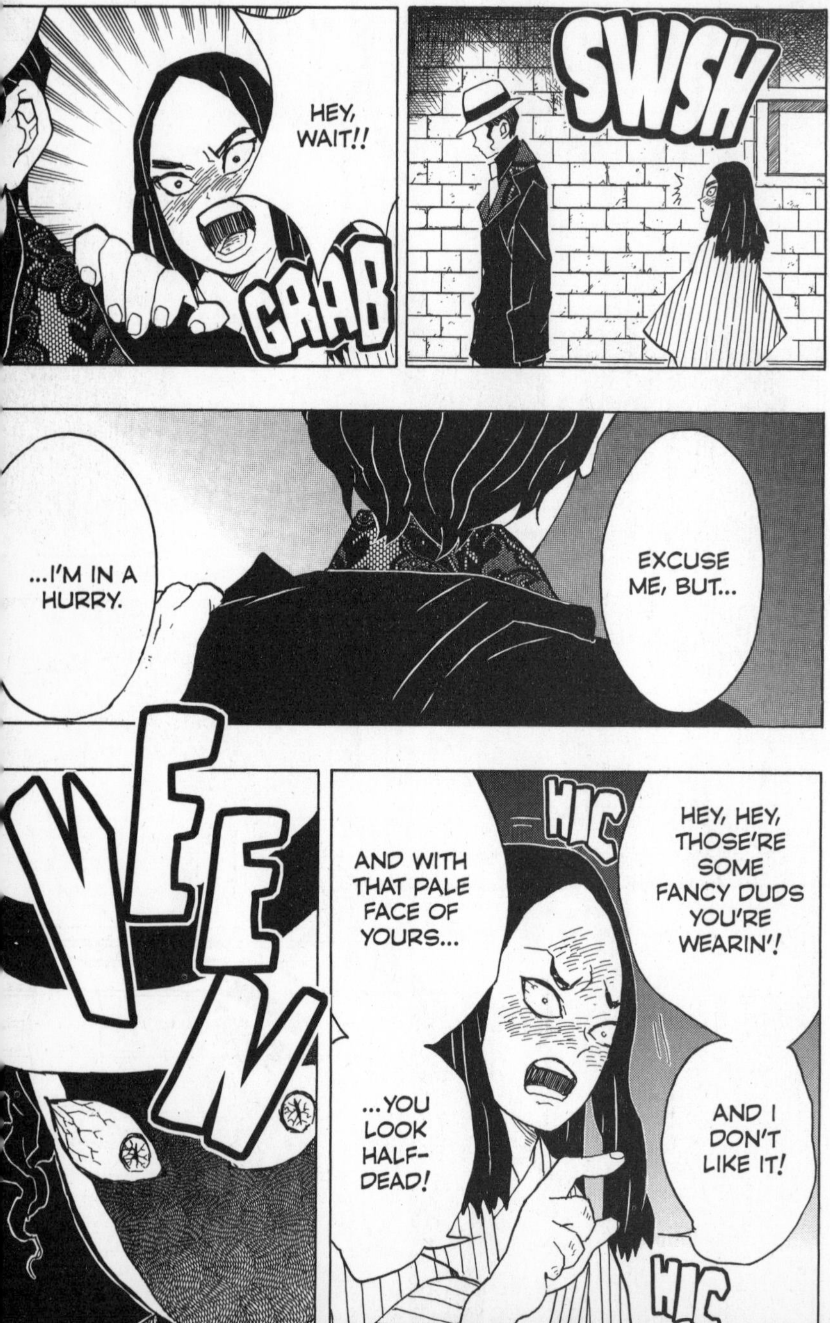
SWSH
HEY, WAIT!!
GRAB
EXCUSE ME, BUT...
...I'M IN A HURRY.
HIC
HEY, HEY, THOSE'RE SOME FANCY DUDS YOU'RE WEARIN'!
AND WITH THAT PALE FACE OF YOURS...
AND I DON'T LIKE IT!
...YOU LOOK HALF-DEAD!
HIC
VEEN

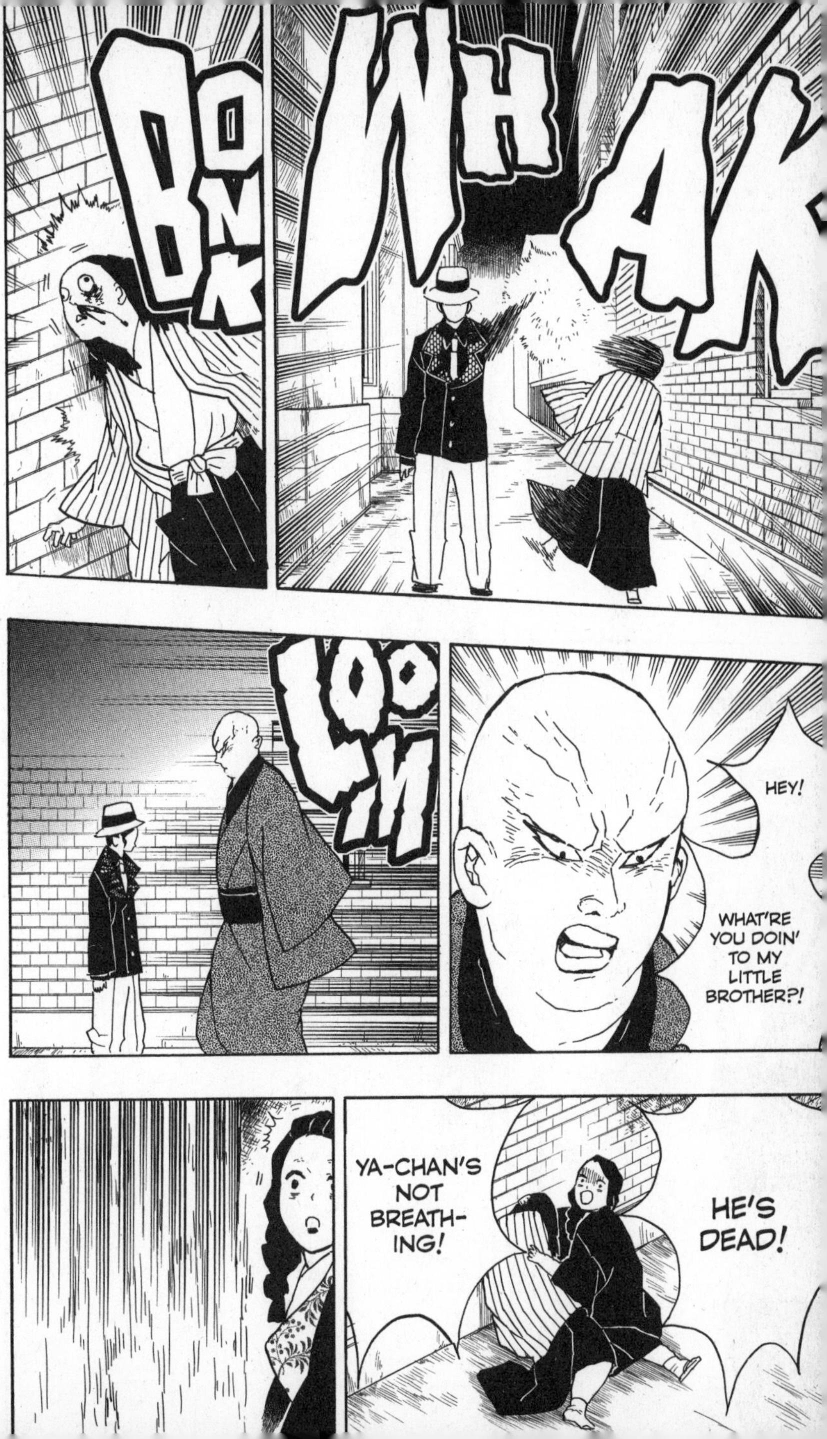
WHAK
BONK
HEY!
WHAT'RE YOU DOIN' TO MY LITTLE BROTHER?!
LOOM
HE'S DEAD!
YA-CHAN'S NOT BREATH-ING!

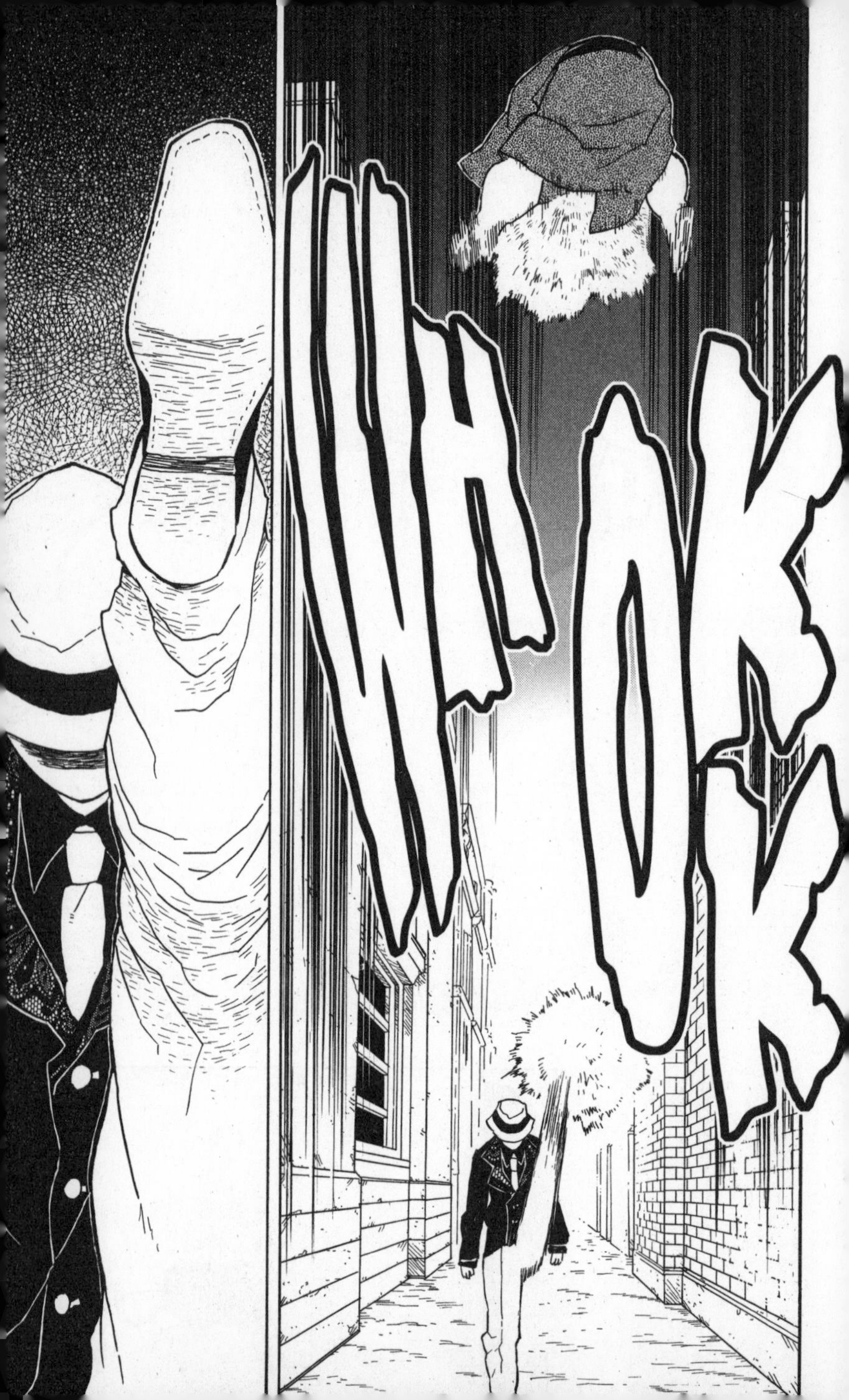
WHACK

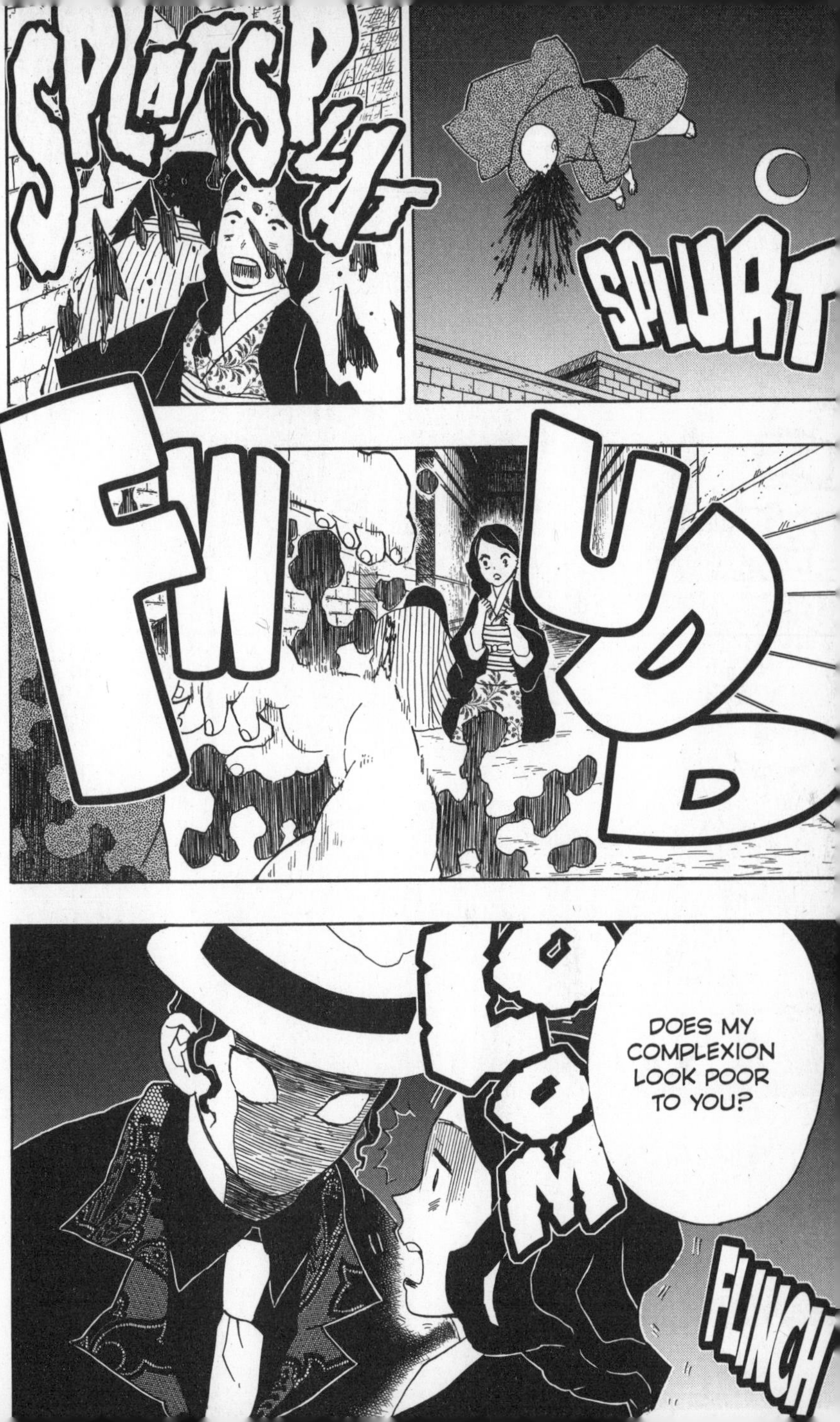
SPLURT
SPLAT SPLAT
FWUDD
DOES MY COMPLEXION LOOK POOR TO YOU?
FLINCH

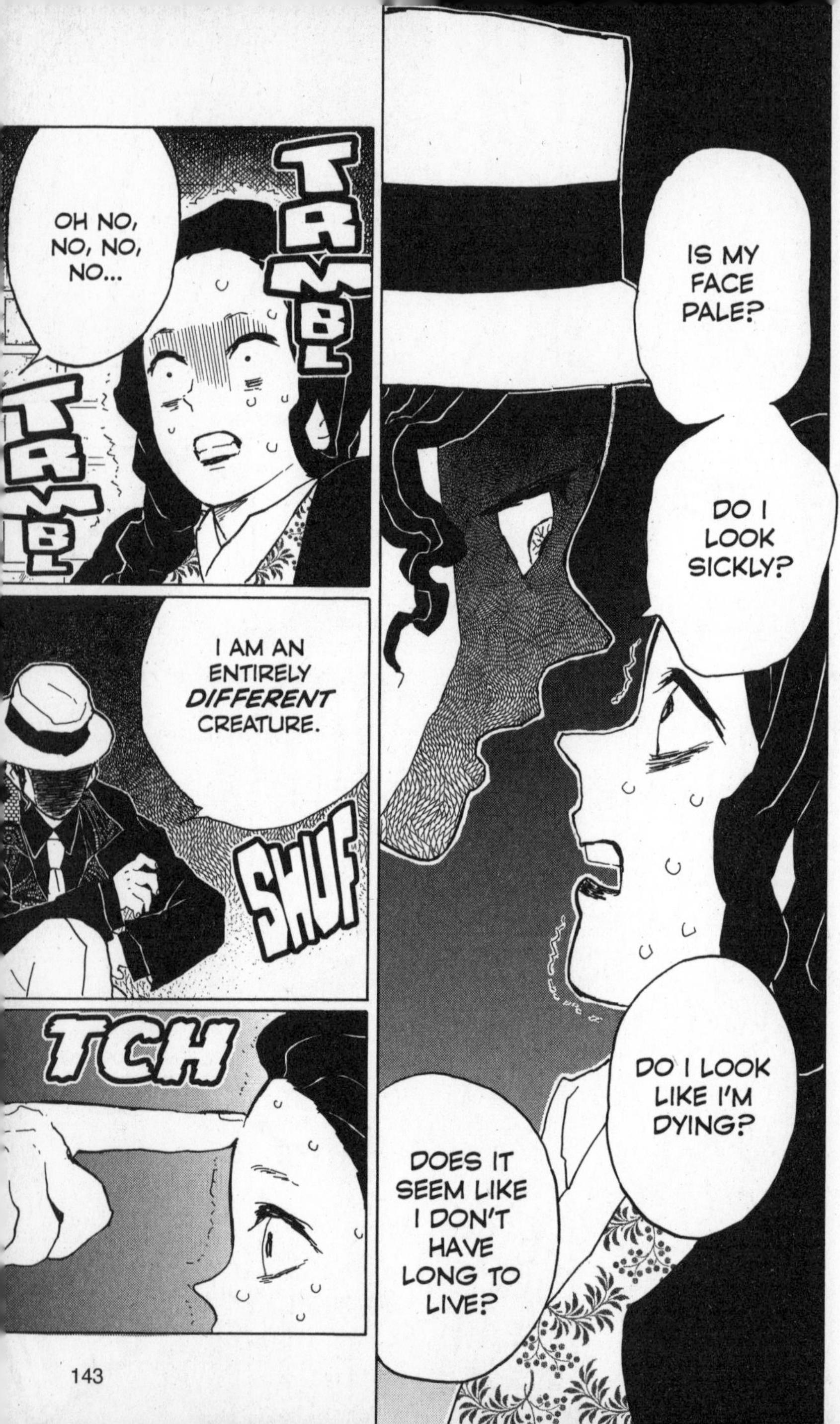
IS MY FACE PALE?
DO I LOOK SICKLY?
DO I LOOK LIKE I'M DYING?
DOES IT SEEM LIKE I DON'T HAVE LONG TO LIVE?
TRMBL
TRMBL
OH NO, NO, NO, NO...
I AM AN ENTIRELY *DIFFERENT* CREATURE.
SHUF
TCH

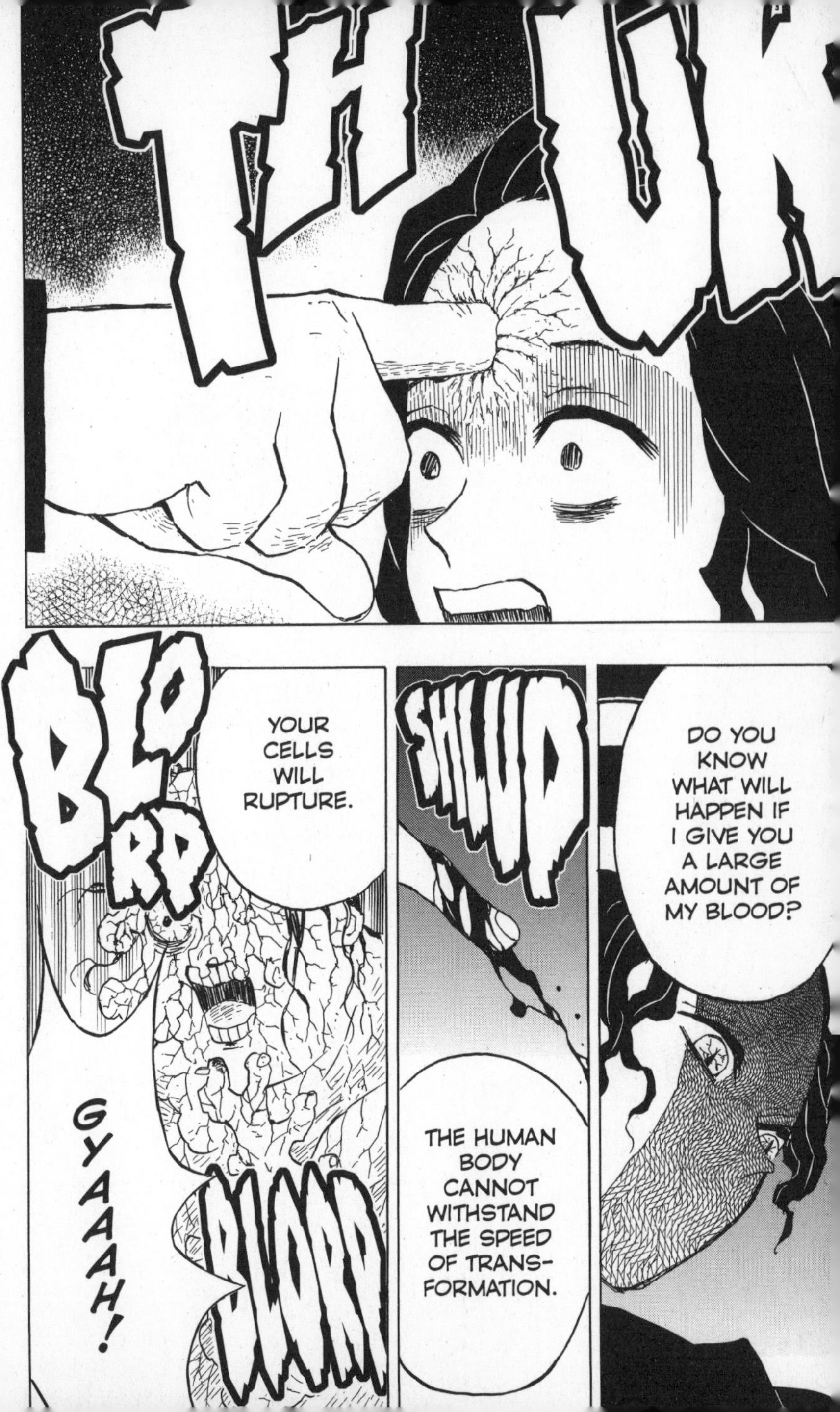
DO YOU KNOW WHAT WILL HAPPEN IF I GIVE YOU A LARGE AMOUNT OF MY BLOOD?
SHLUD
THE HUMAN BODY CANNOT WITHSTAND THE SPEED OF TRANS-FORMATION.
YOUR CELLS WILL RUPTURE.
GYAAAH!

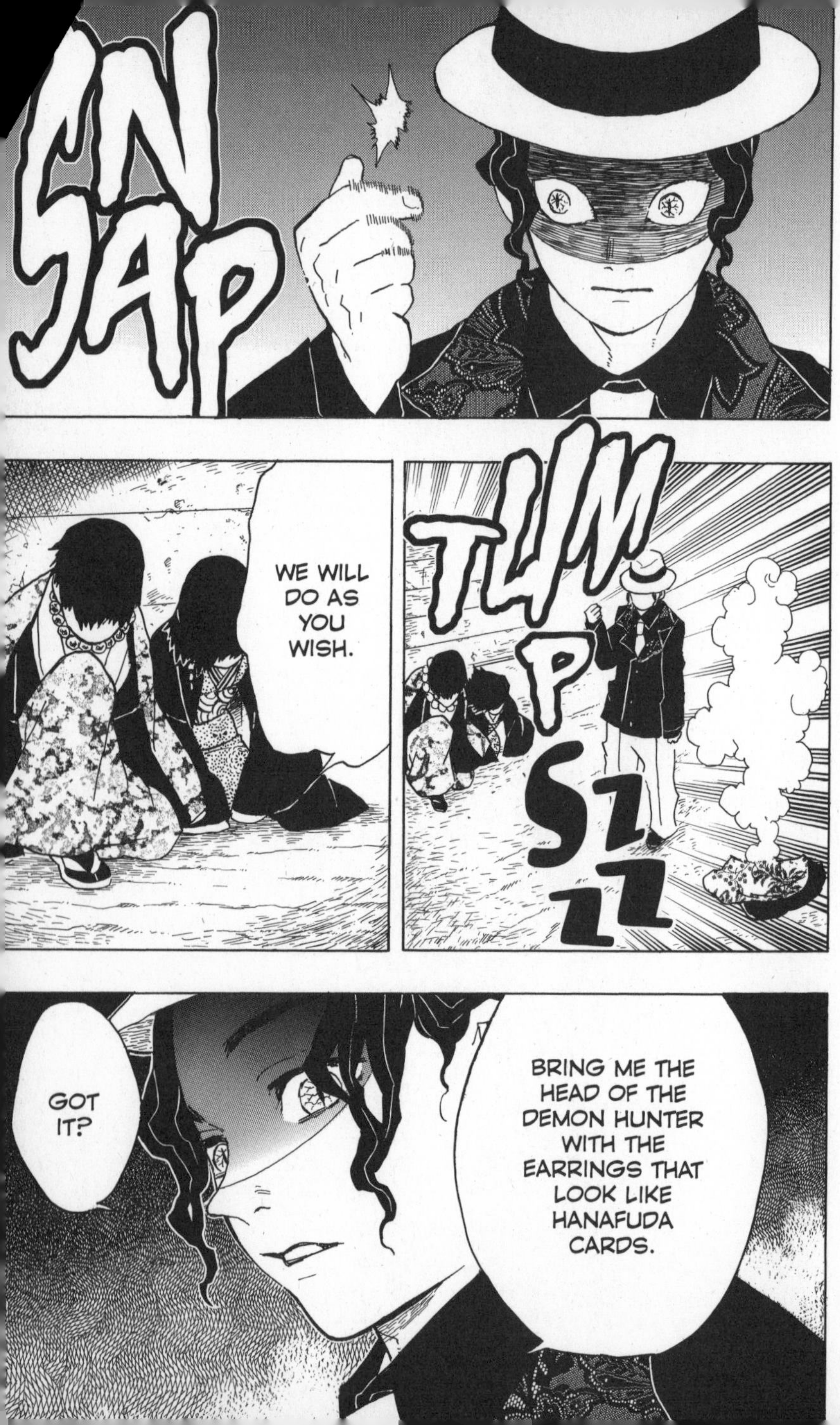
SNAP
THUMP
SZZZ
WE WILL DO AS YOU WISH.
BRING ME THE HEAD OF THE DEMON HUNTER WITH THE EARRINGS THAT LOOK LIKE HANAFUDA CARDS.
GOT IT?

Rejected Tanjiro / A.K.A. Botsujiro

I planned this for the cover of chapter 7, but it was no time for smiling, so...Botsujiro.

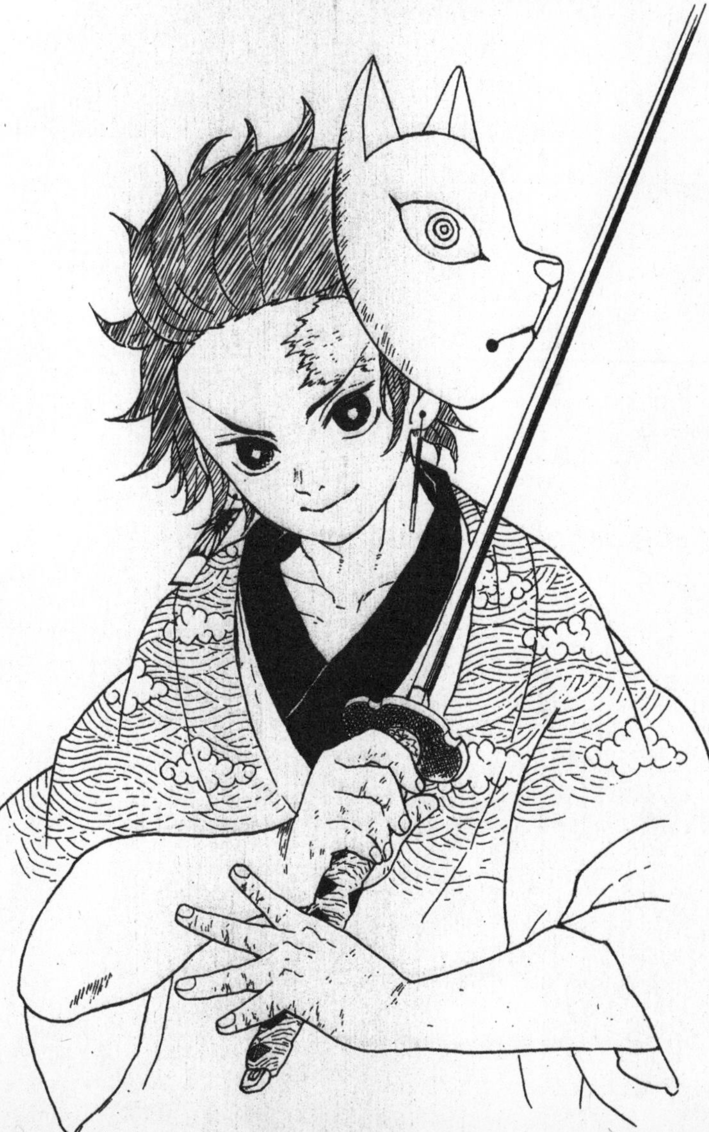

CHAPTER 15: THE DOCTOR'S OPINION

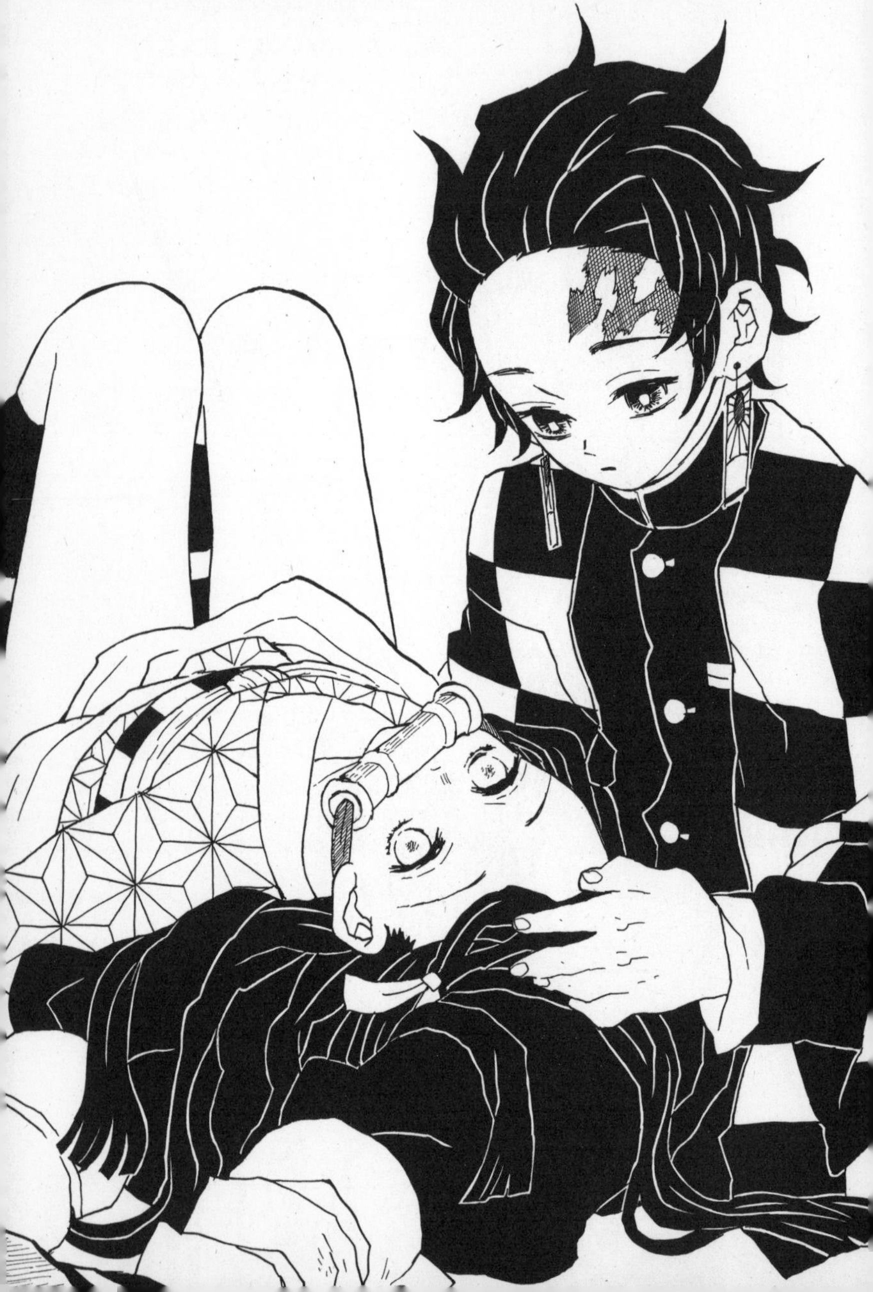

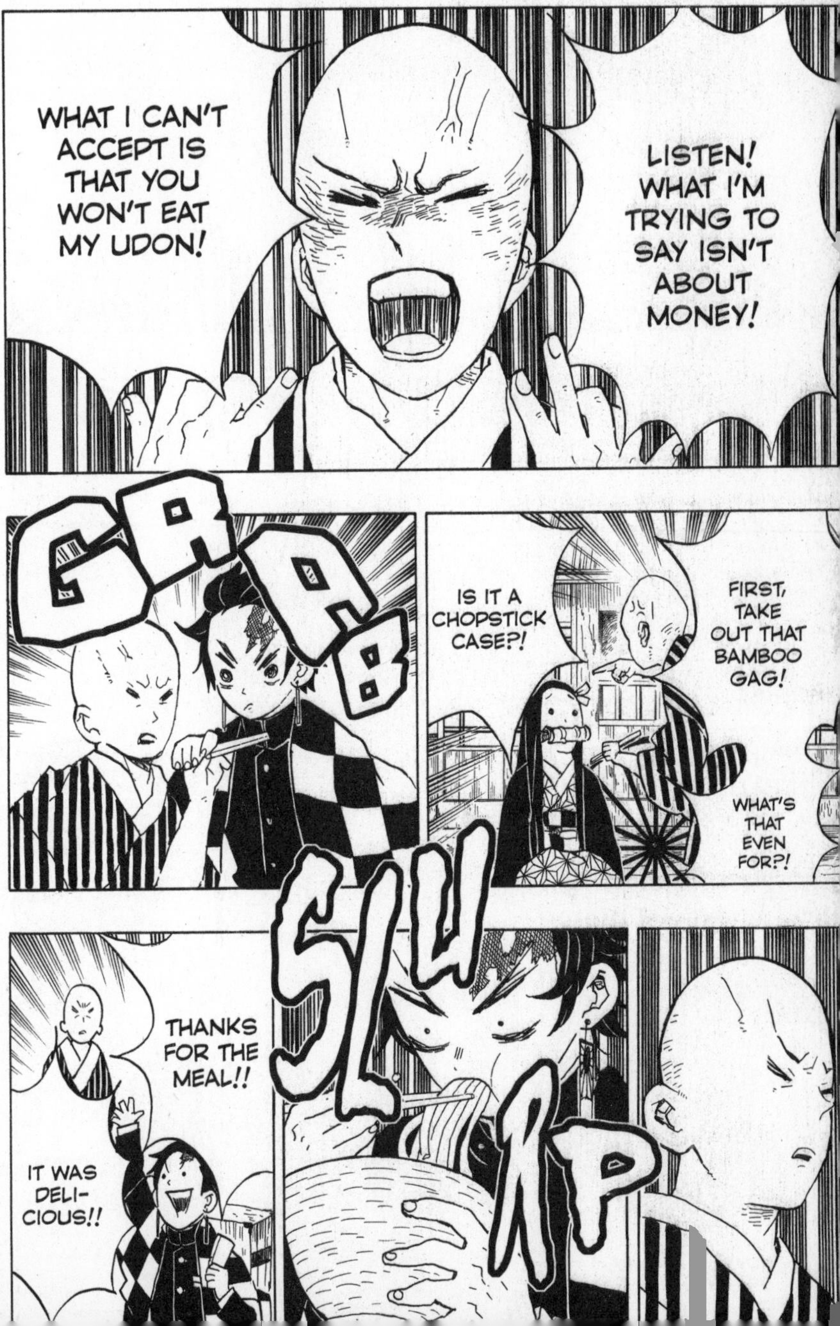
LISTEN! WHAT I'M TRYING TO SAY ISN'T ABOUT MONEY!
WHAT I CAN'T ACCEPT IS THAT YOU WON'T EAT MY UDON!
FIRST, TAKE OUT THAT BAMBOO GAG!
IS IT A CHOPSTICK CASE?!
WHAT'S THAT EVEN FOR?!
GRAB
SLURP
THANKS FOR THE MEAL!!
IT WAS DELI-CIOUS!!

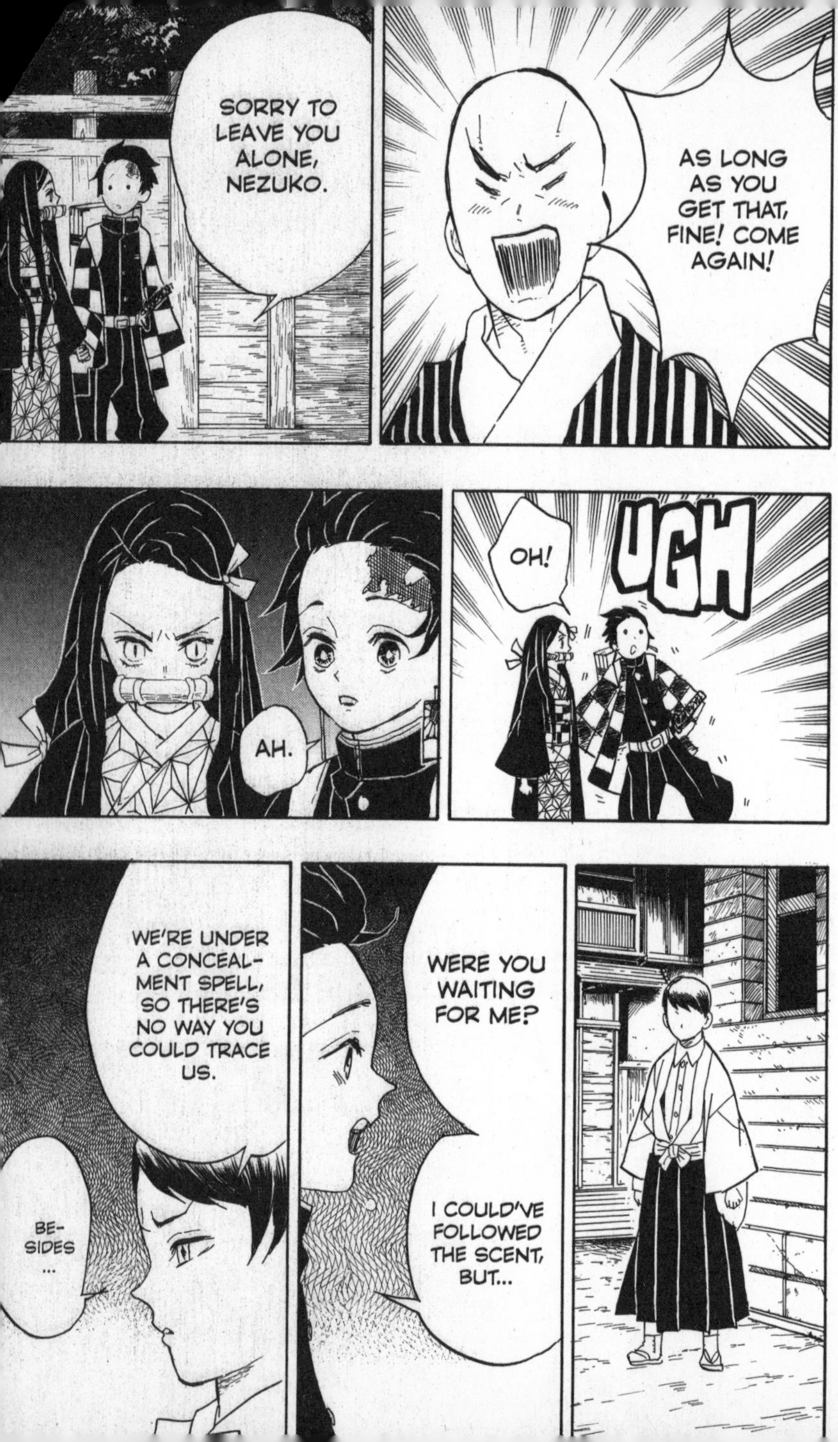
AS LONG AS YOU GET THAT, FINE! COME AGAIN!
SORRY TO LEAVE YOU ALONE, NEZUKO.
UGH
OH!
AH.
WERE YOU WAITING FOR ME?
I COULD'VE FOLLOWED THE SCENT, BUT...
WE'RE UNDER A CONCEAL-MENT SPELL, SO THERE'S NO WAY YOU COULD TRACE US.
BE-SIDES ...

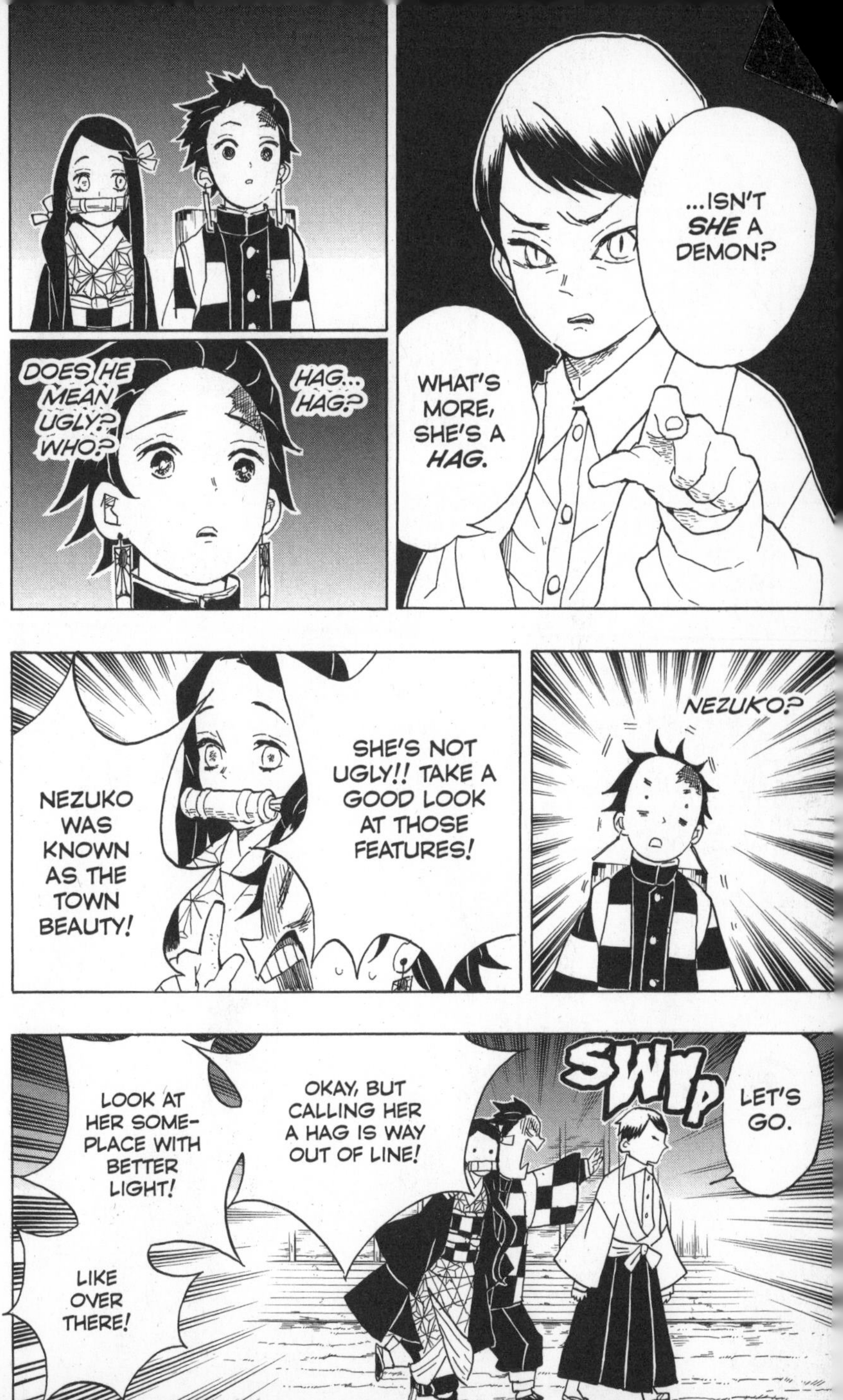
...ISN'T SHE A DEMON?
WHAT'S MORE, SHE'S A HAG.
HAG... HAG?
DOES HE MEAN UGLY? WHO?
NEZUKO?
SHE'S NOT UGLY!! TAKE A GOOD LOOK AT THOSE FEATURES!
NEZUKO WAS KNOWN AS THE TOWN BEAUTY!
LET'S GO.
SWIP
OKAY, BUT CALLING HER A HAG IS WAY OUT OF LINE!
LOOK AT HER SOME-PLACE WITH BETTER LIGHT!
LIKE OVER THERE!

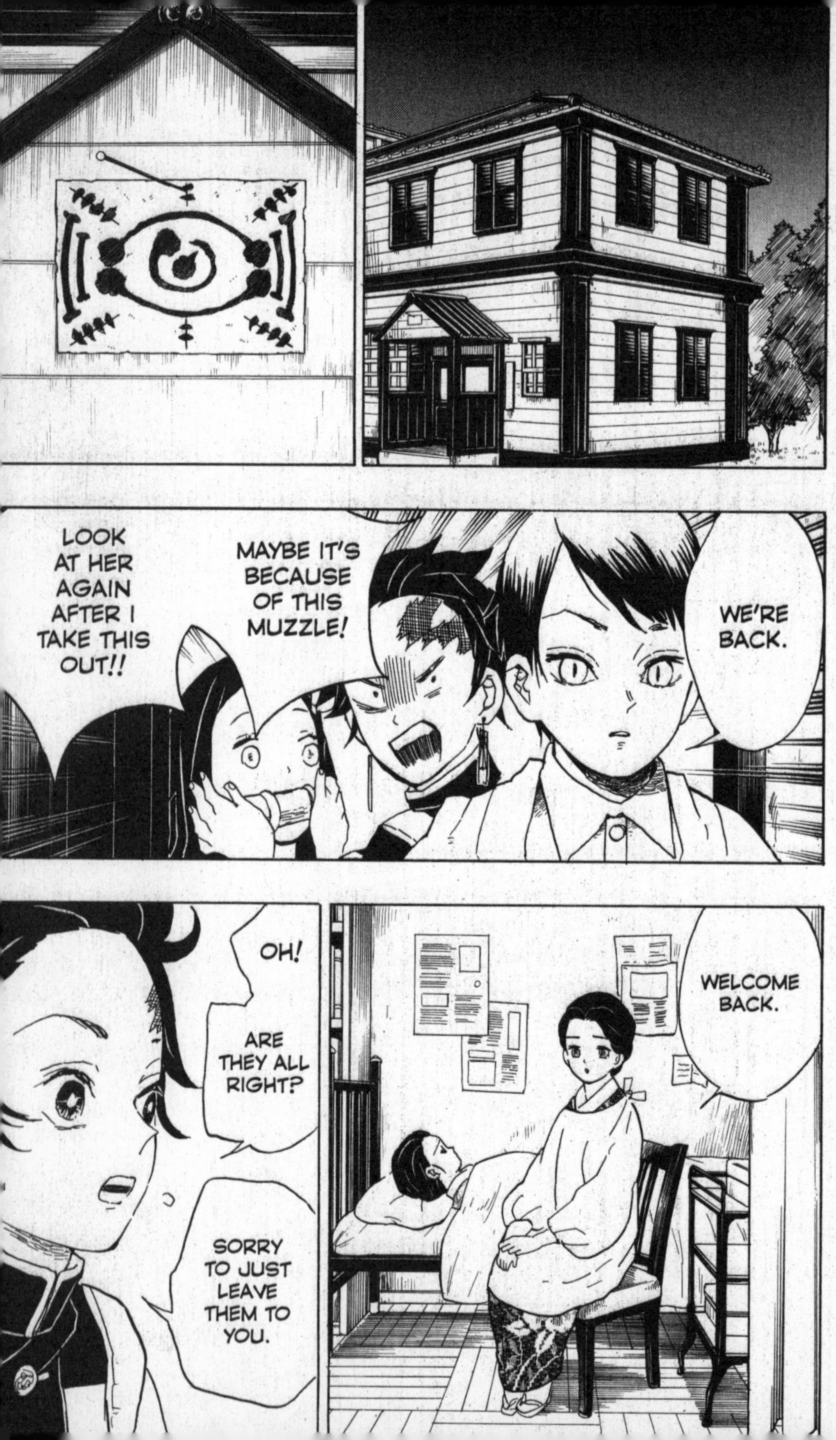
WE'RE BACK.
MAYBE IT'S BECAUSE OF THIS MUZZLE!
LOOK AT HER AGAIN AFTER I TAKE THIS OUT!!
WELCOME BACK.
OH!
ARE THEY ALL RIGHT?
SORRY TO JUST LEAVE THEM TO YOU.

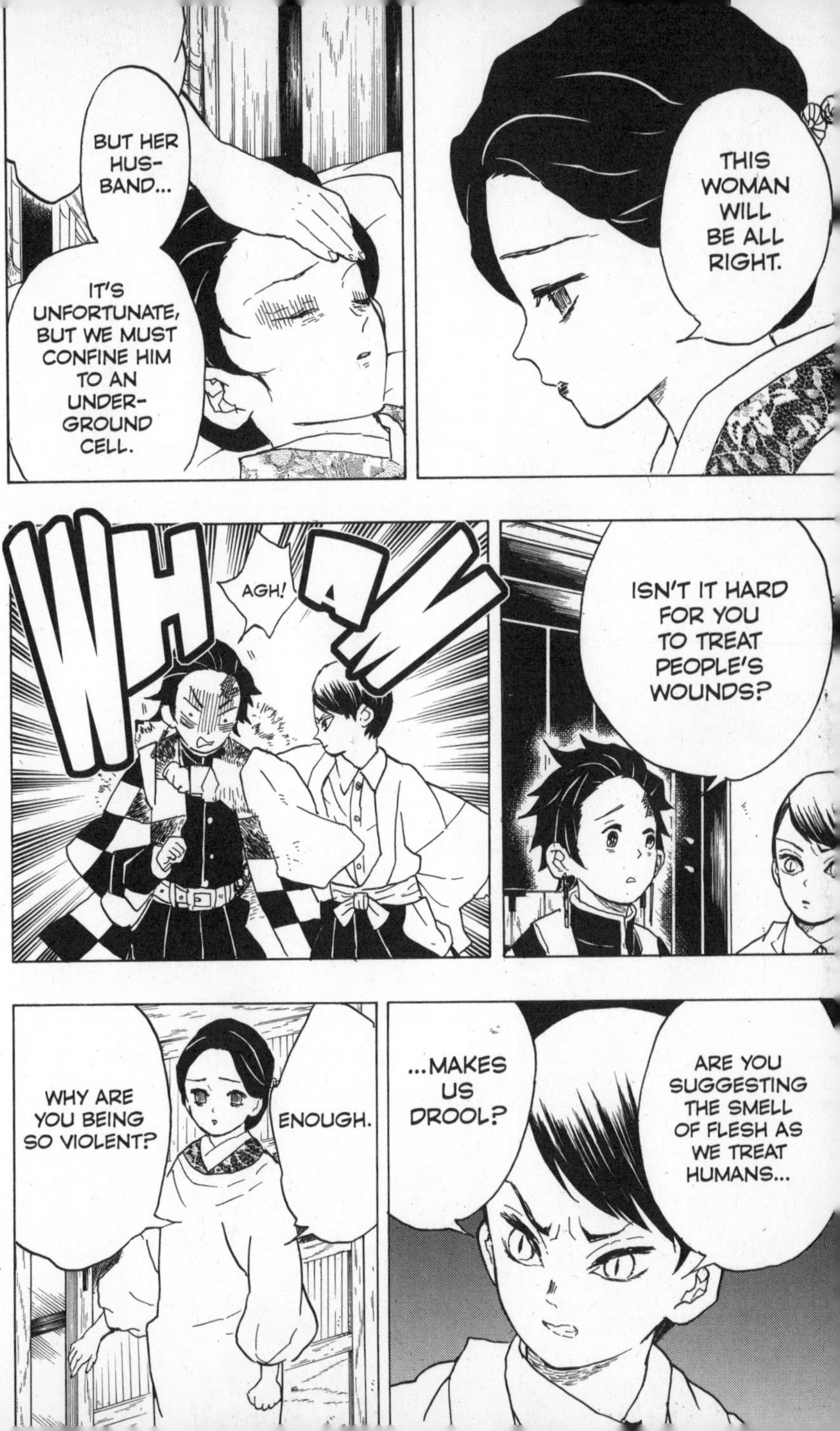
THIS WOMAN WILL BE ALL RIGHT.
BUT HER HUS-BAND...
IT'S UNFORTUNATE, BUT WE MUST CONFINE HIM TO AN UNDER-GROUND CELL.
ISN'T IT HARD FOR YOU TO TREAT PEOPLE'S WOUNDS?
WHAM
AGH!
ARE YOU SUGGESTING THE SMELL OF FLESH AS WE TREAT HUMANS...
...MAKES US DROOL?
ENOUGH.
WHY ARE YOU BEING SO VIOLENT?

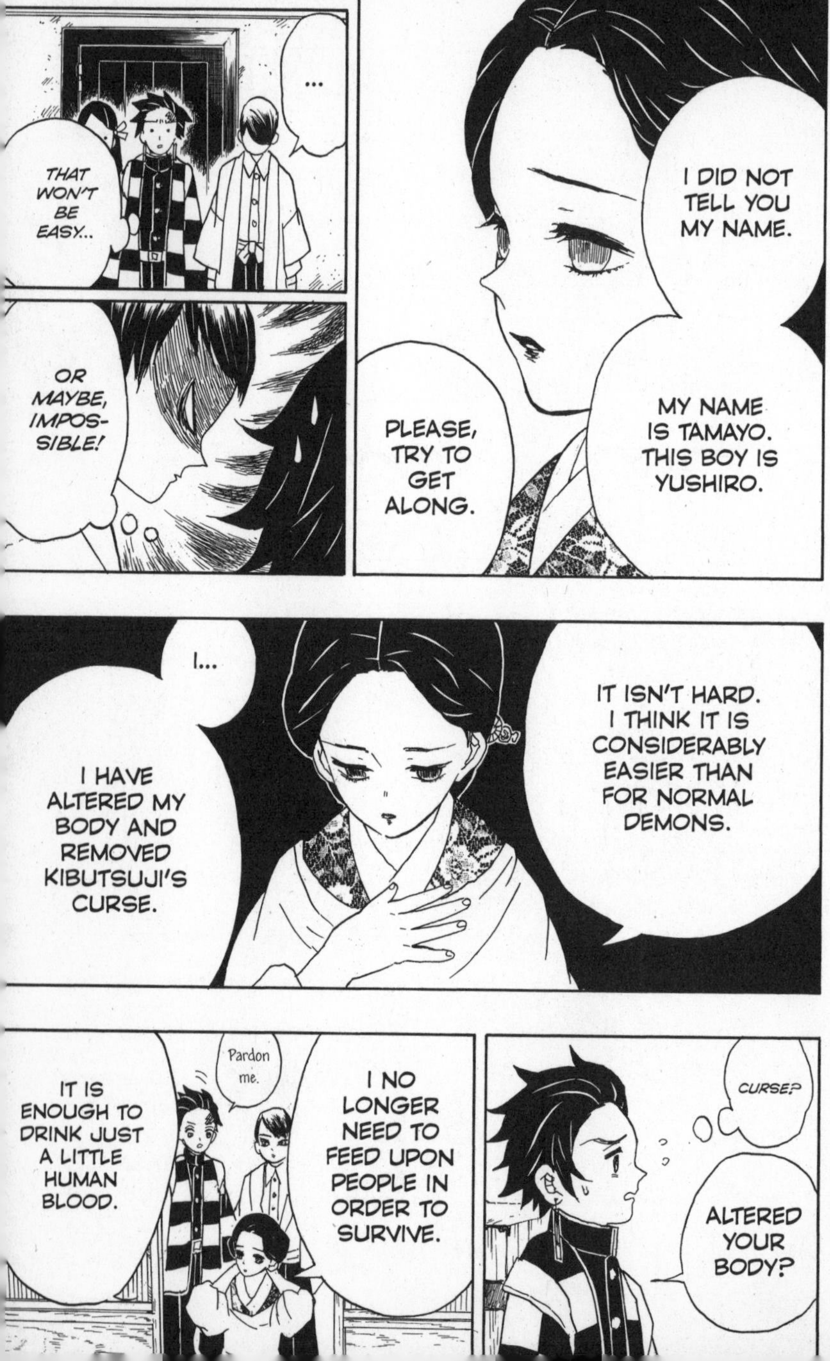
I DID NOT TELL YOU MY NAME.
MY NAME IS TAMAYO. THIS BOY IS YUSHIRO.
PLEASE, TRY TO GET ALONG.
...
THAT WON'T BE EASY...
OR MAYBE, IMPOSSIBLE!
IT ISN'T HARD. I THINK IT IS CONSIDERABLY EASIER THAN FOR NORMAL DEMONS.
I...
I HAVE ALTERED MY BODY AND REMOVED KIBUTSUJI'S CURSE.
CURSE?
ALTERED YOUR BODY?
I NO LONGER NEED TO FEED UPON PEOPLE IN ORDER TO SURVIVE.
Pardon me.
IT IS ENOUGH TO DRINK JUST A LITTLE HUMAN BLOOD.

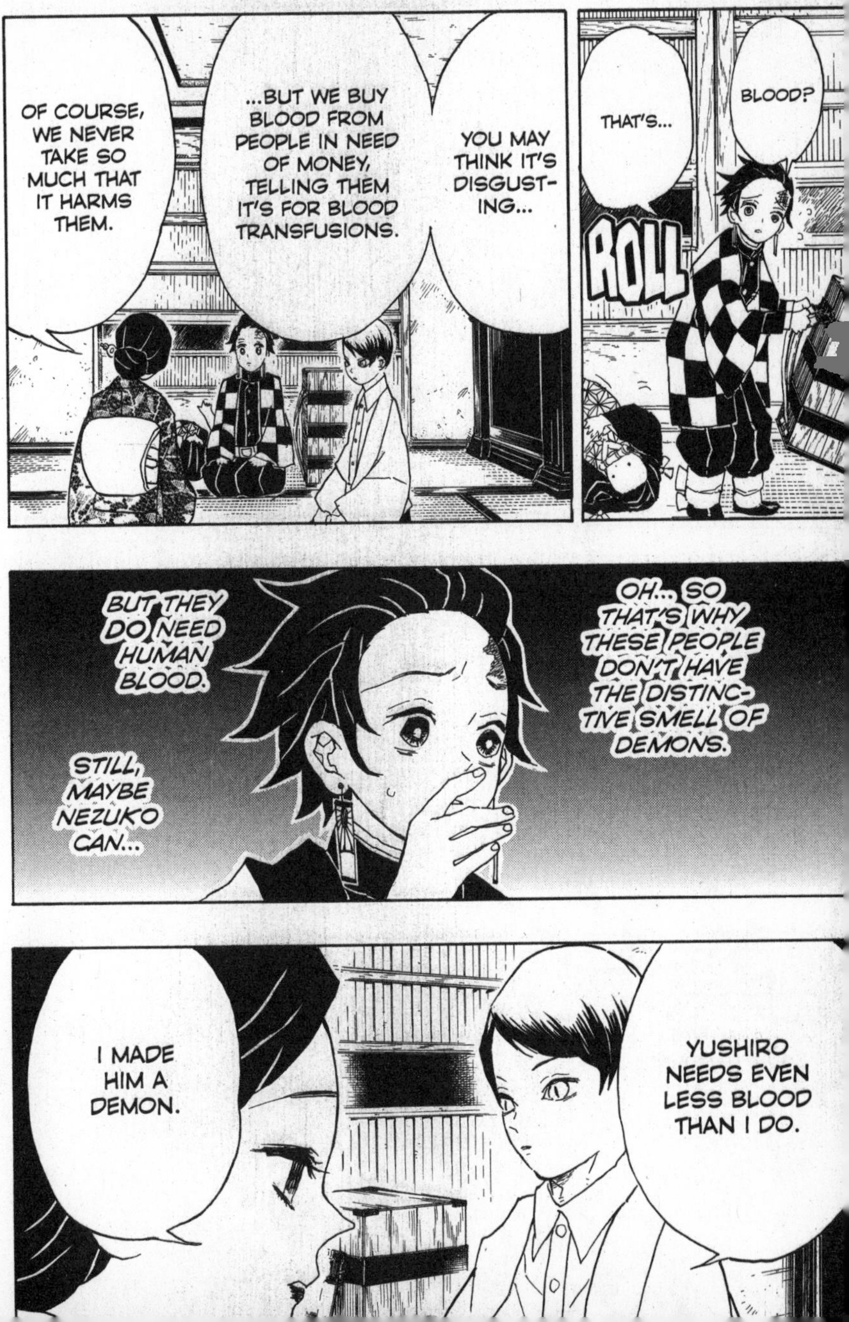
BLOOD?
THAT'S...
ROLL
YOU MAY THINK IT'S DISGUST-ING...
...BUT WE BUY BLOOD FROM PEOPLE IN NEED OF MONEY, TELLING THEM IT'S FOR BLOOD TRANSFUSIONS.
OF COURSE, WE NEVER TAKE SO MUCH THAT IT HARMS THEM.
OH... SO THAT'S WHY THESE PEOPLE DON'T HAVE THE DISTINC-TIVE SMELL OF DEMONS.
BUT THEY DO NEED HUMAN BLOOD.
STILL, MAYBE NEZUKO CAN...
YUSHIRO NEEDS EVEN LESS BLOOD THAN I DO.
I MADE HIM A DEMON.

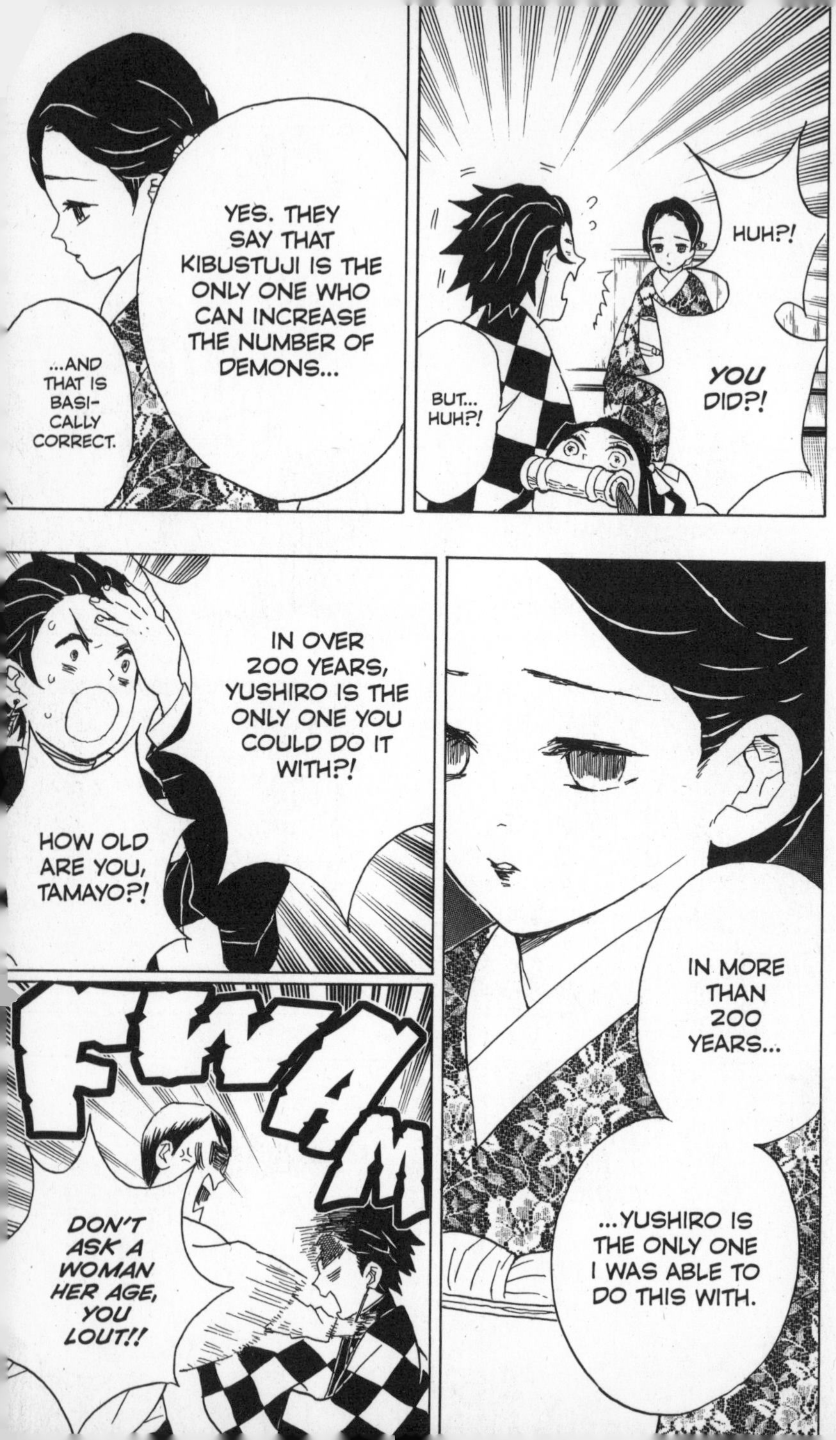
HUH?!
YOU DID?!
BUT... HUH?!
YES. THEY SAY THAT KIBUSTUJI IS THE ONLY ONE WHO CAN INCREASE THE NUMBER OF DEMONS...
...AND THAT IS BASI-CALLY CORRECT.
IN MORE THAN 200 YEARS...
...YUSHIRO IS THE ONLY ONE I WAS ABLE TO DO THIS WITH.
IN OVER 200 YEARS, YUSHIRO IS THE ONLY ONE YOU COULD DO IT WITH?!
HOW OLD ARE YOU, TAMAYO?!
FWAM
DON'T ASK A WOMAN HER AGE, YOU LOUT!!

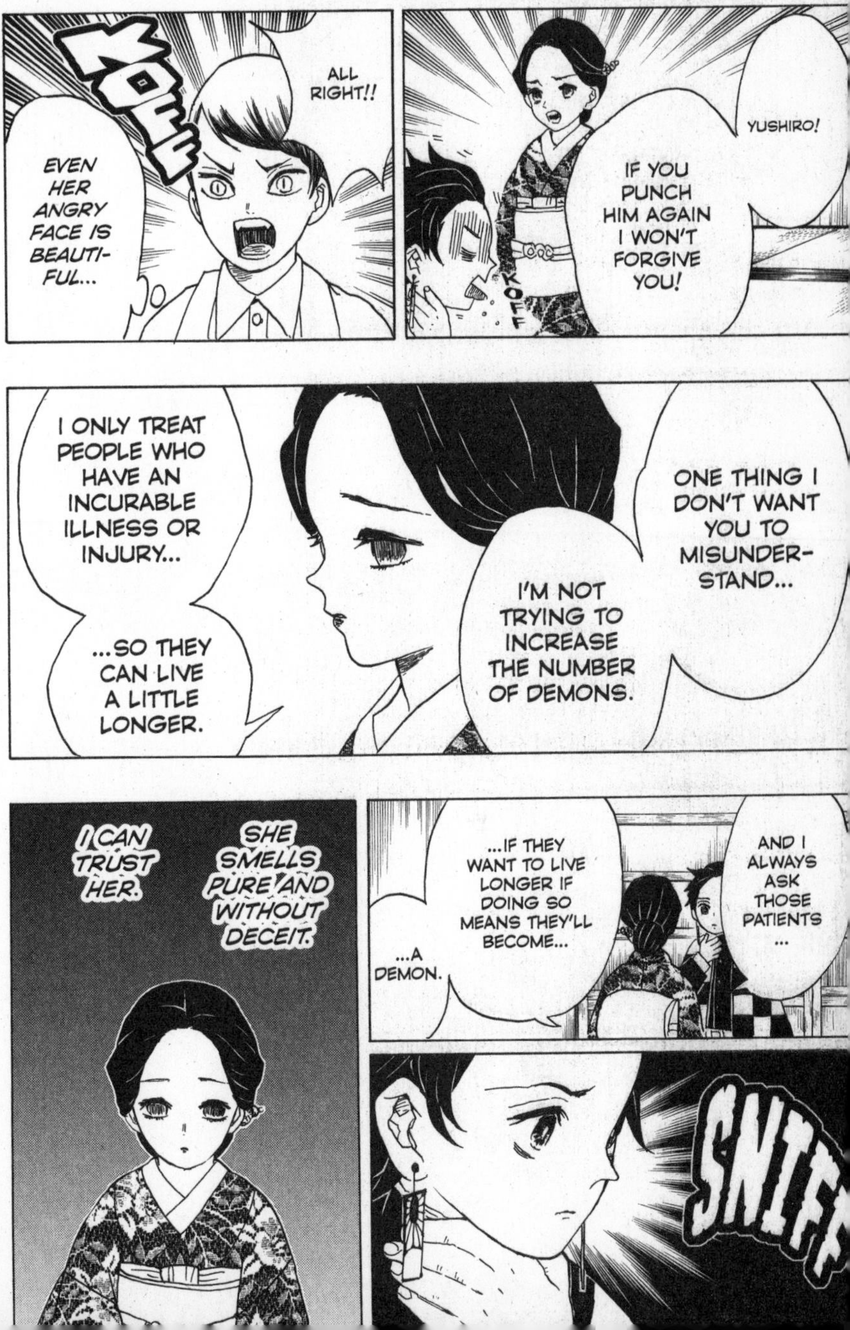
YUSHIRO!
IF YOU PUNCH HIM AGAIN I WON'T FORGIVE YOU!
KOFF
ALL RIGHT!!
EVEN HER ANGRY FACE IS BEAUTI-FUL...
ONE THING I DON'T WANT YOU TO MISUNDER-STAND...
I'M NOT TRYING TO INCREASE THE NUMBER OF DEMONS.
I ONLY TREAT PEOPLE WHO HAVE AN INCURABLE ILLNESS OR INJURY...
...SO THEY CAN LIVE A LITTLE LONGER.
AND I ALWAYS ASK THOSE PATIENTS ...
...IF THEY WANT TO LIVE LONGER IF DOING SO MEANS THEY'LL BECOME...
...A DEMON.
SNIFF
SHE SMELLS PURE AND WITHOUT DECEIT.
I CAN TRUST HER.

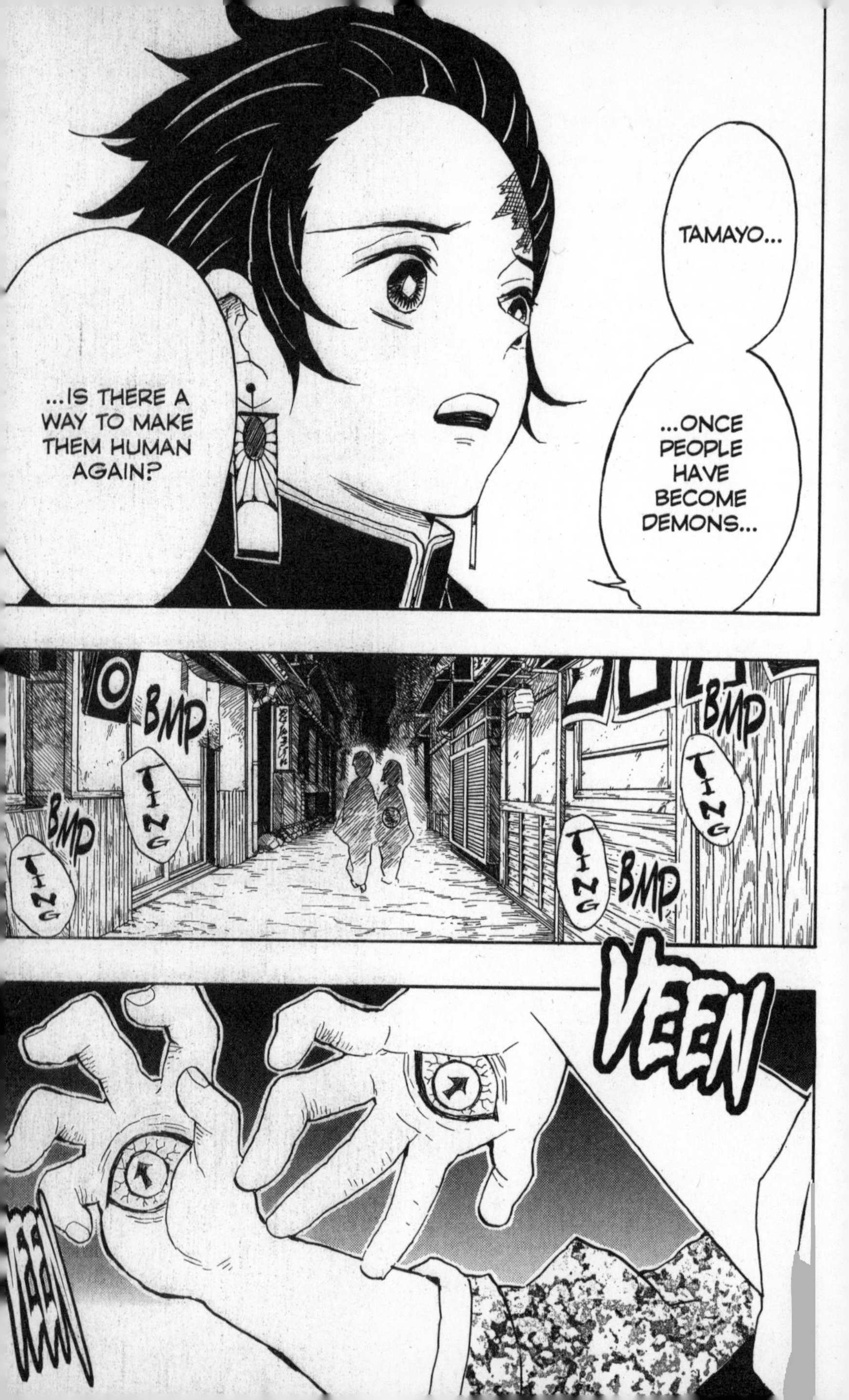
TAMAYO...
...ONCE PEOPLE HAVE BECOME DEMONS...
...IS THERE A WAY TO MAKE THEM HUMAN AGAIN?
BMP
TING
BMP
TING
BMP
TING
BMP
TING
VEEN

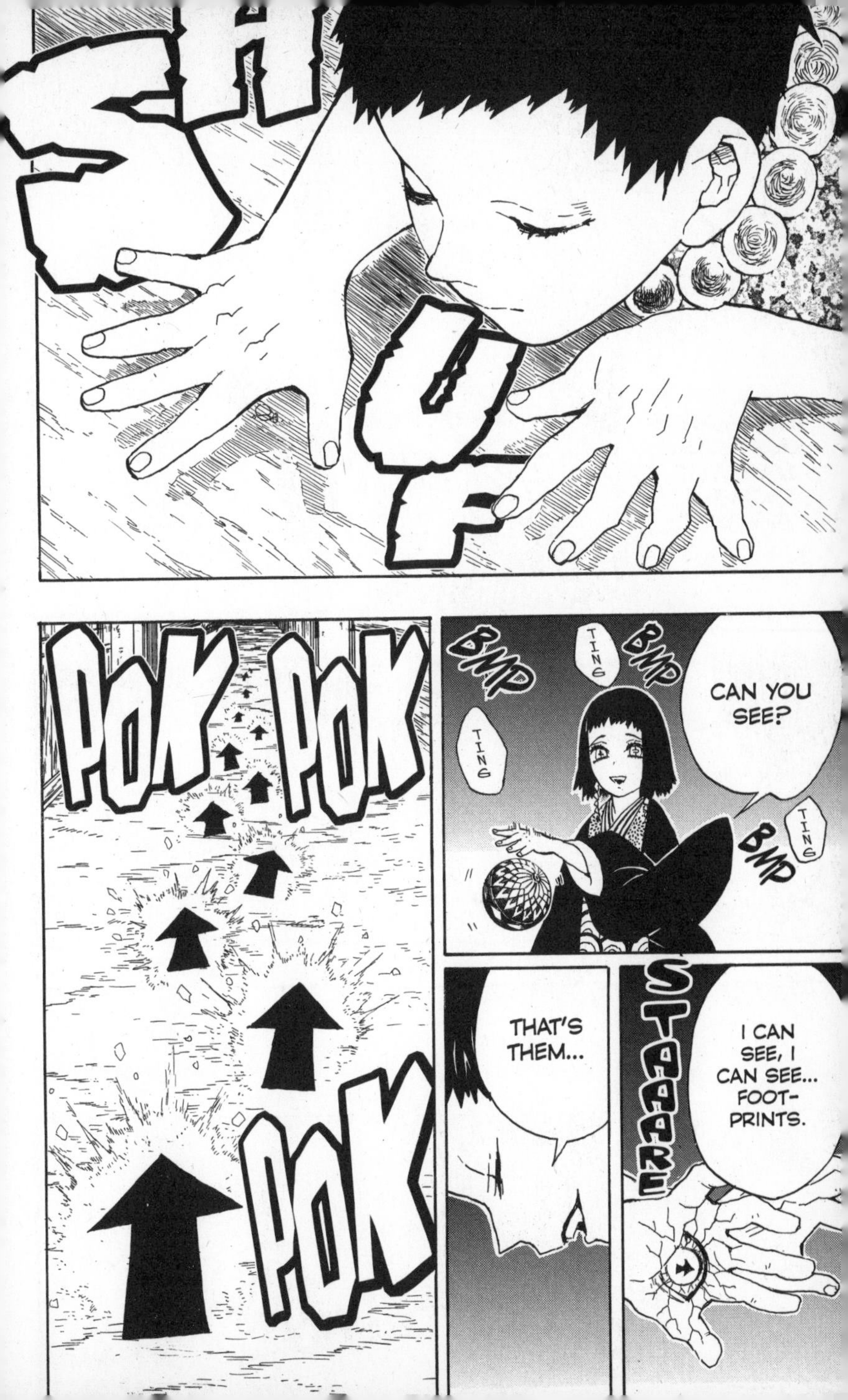
BMP
TING
BMP
CAN YOU SEE?
TING
TING
BMP
STAAARE
I CAN SEE, I CAN SEE... FOOT-PRINTS.
THAT'S THEM...
POK POK
POK

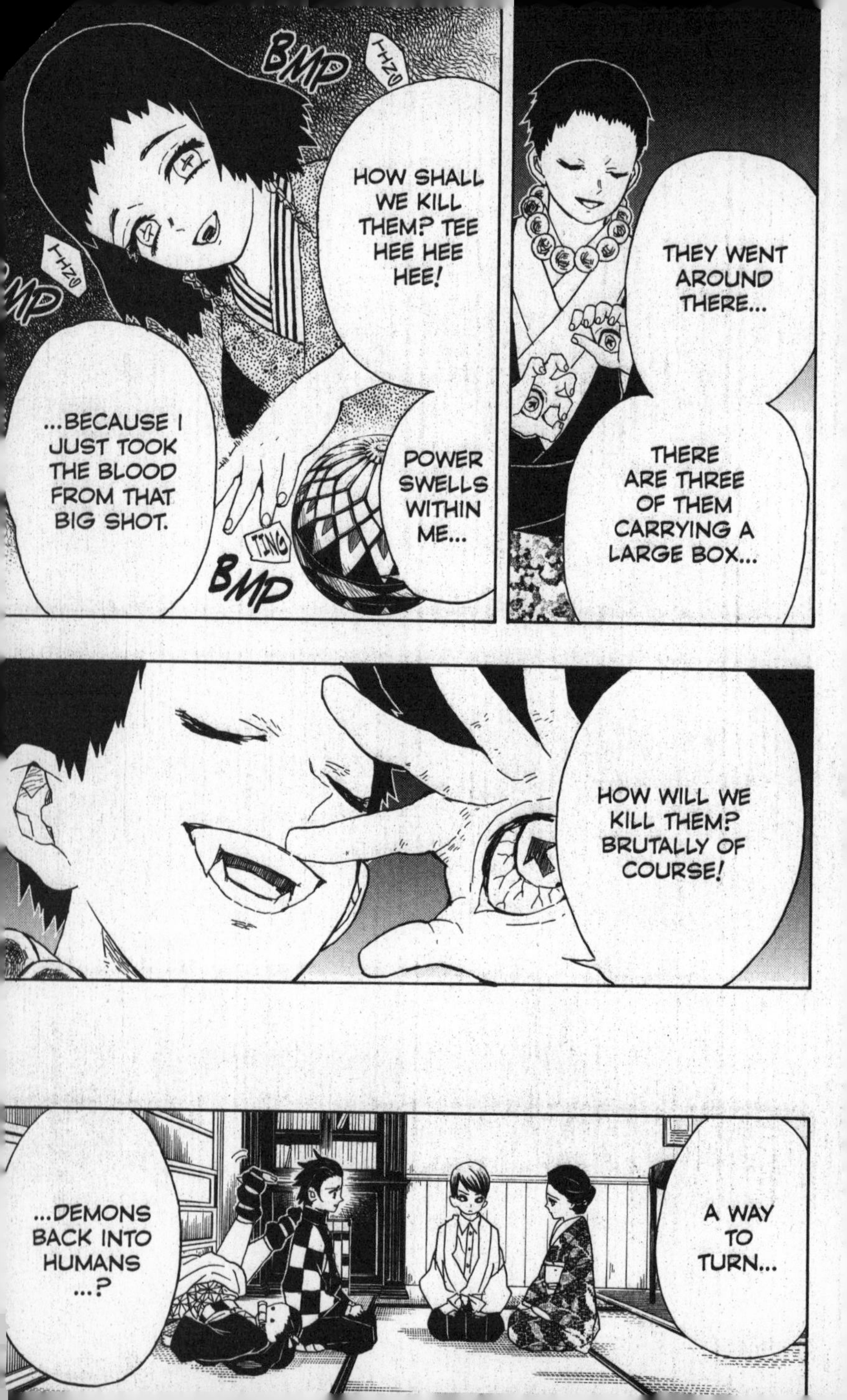
THEY WENT AROUND THERE...
THERE ARE THREE OF THEM CARRYING A LARGE BOX...
BMP
TING
HOW SHALL WE KILL THEM? TEE HEE HEE HEE!
BMP
TING
POWER SWELLS WITHIN ME...
BMP
TING
...BECAUSE I JUST TOOK THE BLOOD FROM THAT BIG SHOT.
HOW WILL WE KILL THEM? BRUTALLY OF COURSE!
A WAY TO TURN...
...DEMONS BACK INTO HUMANS ...?

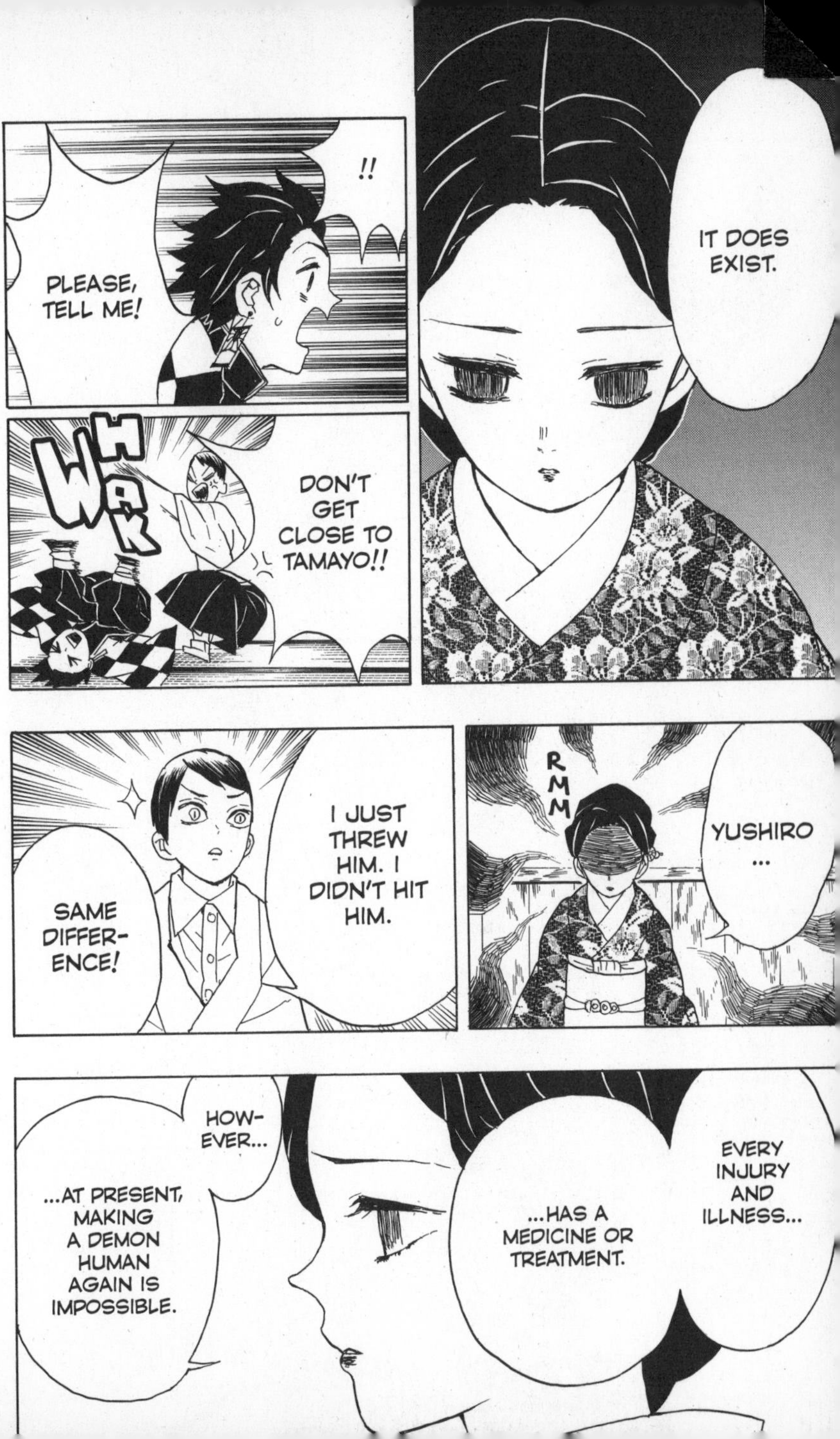
IT DOES EXIST.
!!
PLEASE, TELL ME!
WHAK
DON'T GET CLOSE TO TAMAYO!!
RMM
YUSHIRO ...
I JUST THREW HIM. I DIDN'T HIT HIM.
SAME DIFFERENCE!
EVERY INJURY AND ILLNESS...
...HAS A MEDICINE OR TREATMENT.
HOW-EVER...
...AT PRESENT, MAKING A DEMON HUMAN AGAIN IS IMPOSSIBLE.

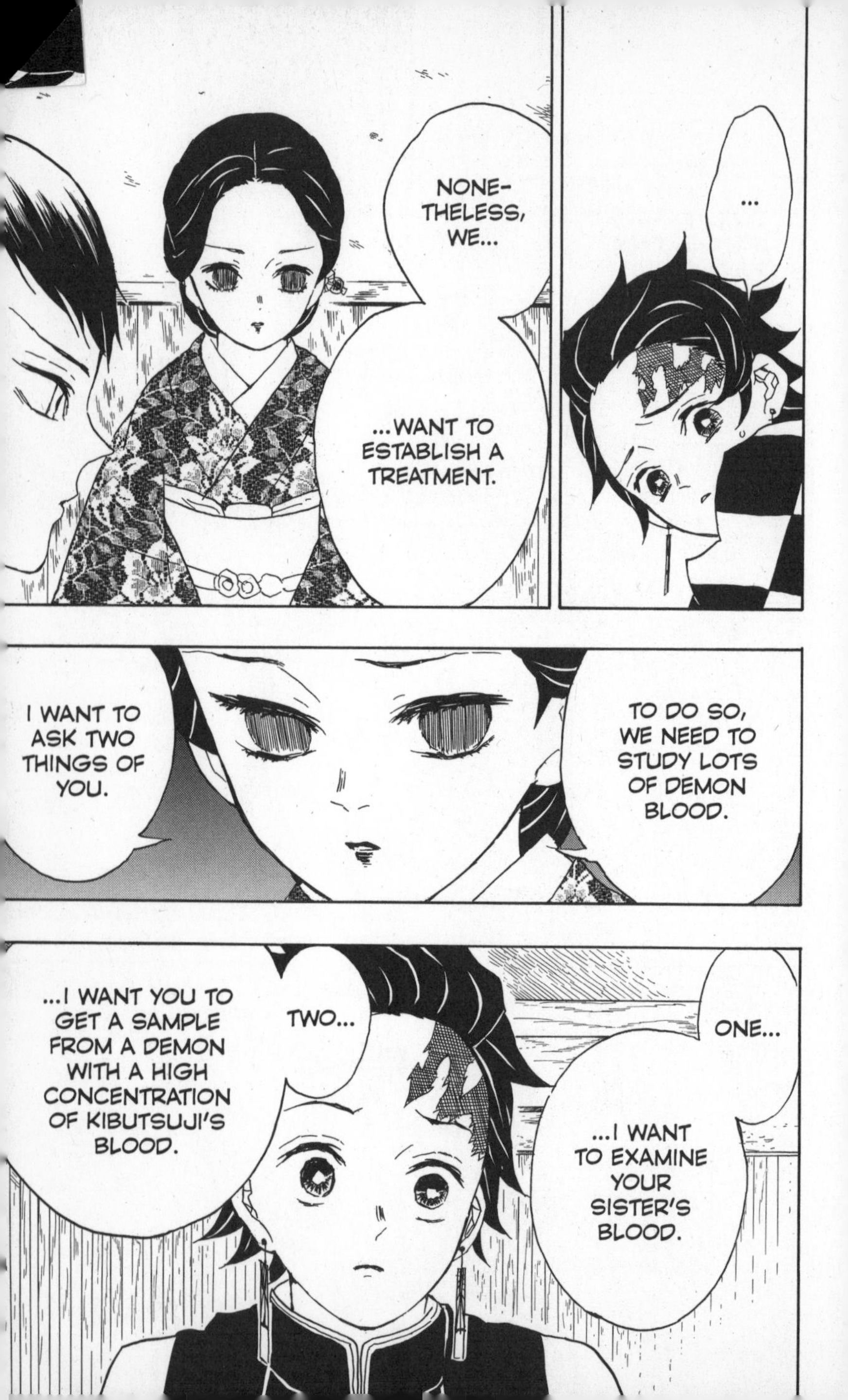
...
NONE-THELESS, WE...
...WANT TO ESTABLISH A TREATMENT.
TO DO SO, WE NEED TO STUDY LOTS OF DEMON BLOOD.
I WANT TO ASK TWO THINGS OF YOU.
ONE...
...I WANT TO EXAMINE YOUR SISTER'S BLOOD.
TWO...
...I WANT YOU TO GET A SAMPLE FROM A DEMON WITH A HIGH CONCENTRATION OF KIBUTSUJI'S BLOOD.

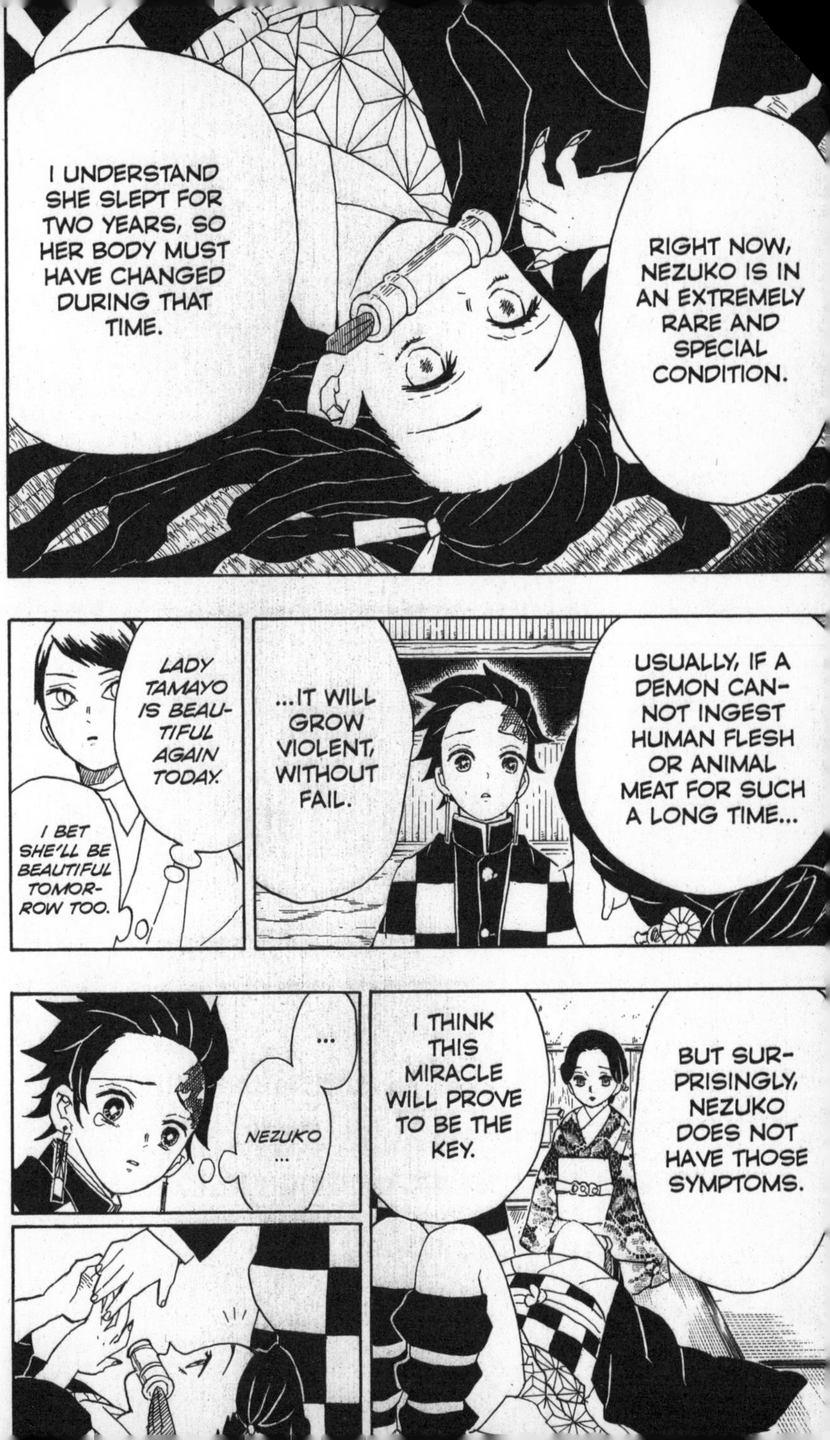
RIGHT NOW, NEZUKO IS IN AN EXTREMELY RARE AND SPECIAL CONDITION.
I UNDERSTAND SHE SLEPT FOR TWO YEARS, SO HER BODY MUST HAVE CHANGED DURING THAT TIME.
USUALLY, IF A DEMON CANNOT INGEST HUMAN FLESH OR ANIMAL MEAT FOR SUCH A LONG TIME...
...IT WILL GROW VIOLENT, WITHOUT FAIL.
LADY TAMAYO IS BEAUTIFUL AGAIN TODAY.
I BET SHE'LL BE BEAUTIFUL TOMORROW TOO.
BUT SURPRISINGLY, NEZUKO DOES NOT HAVE THOSE SYMPTOMS.
I THINK THIS MIRACLE WILL PROVE TO BE THE KEY.
...
NEZUKO ...

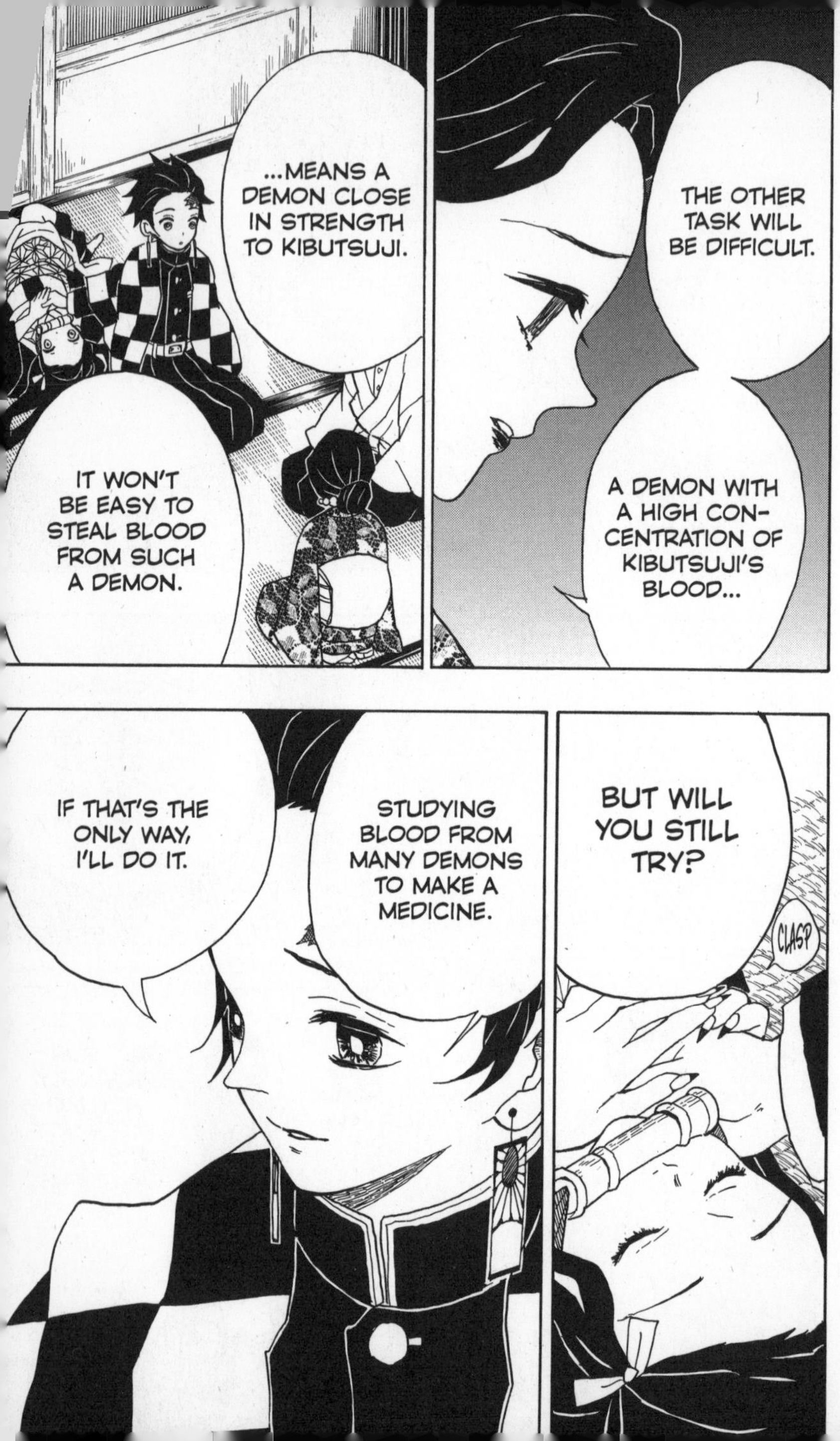
THE OTHER TASK WILL BE DIFFICULT.
A DEMON WITH A HIGH CON-CENTRATION OF KIBUTSUJI'S BLOOD...
...MEANS A DEMON CLOSE IN STRENGTH TO KIBUTSUJI.
IT WON'T BE EASY TO STEAL BLOOD FROM SUCH A DEMON.
BUT WILL YOU STILL TRY?
CLASP
STUDYING BLOOD FROM MANY DEMONS TO MAKE A MEDICINE.
IF THAT'S THE ONLY WAY, I'LL DO IT.

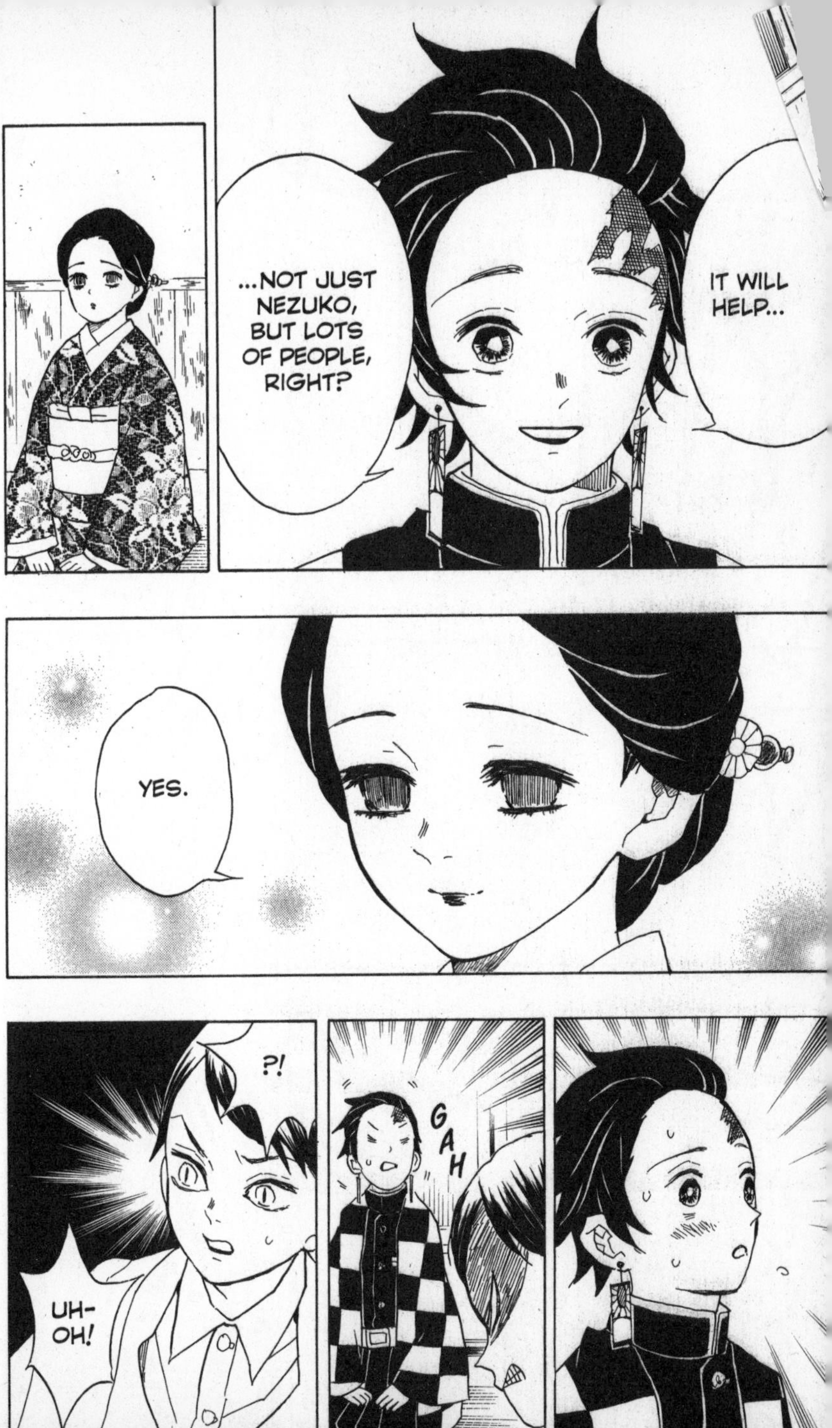
IT WILL HELP...
...NOT JUST NEZUKO, BUT LOTS OF PEOPLE, RIGHT?
YES.
GAH
?!
UH-OH!

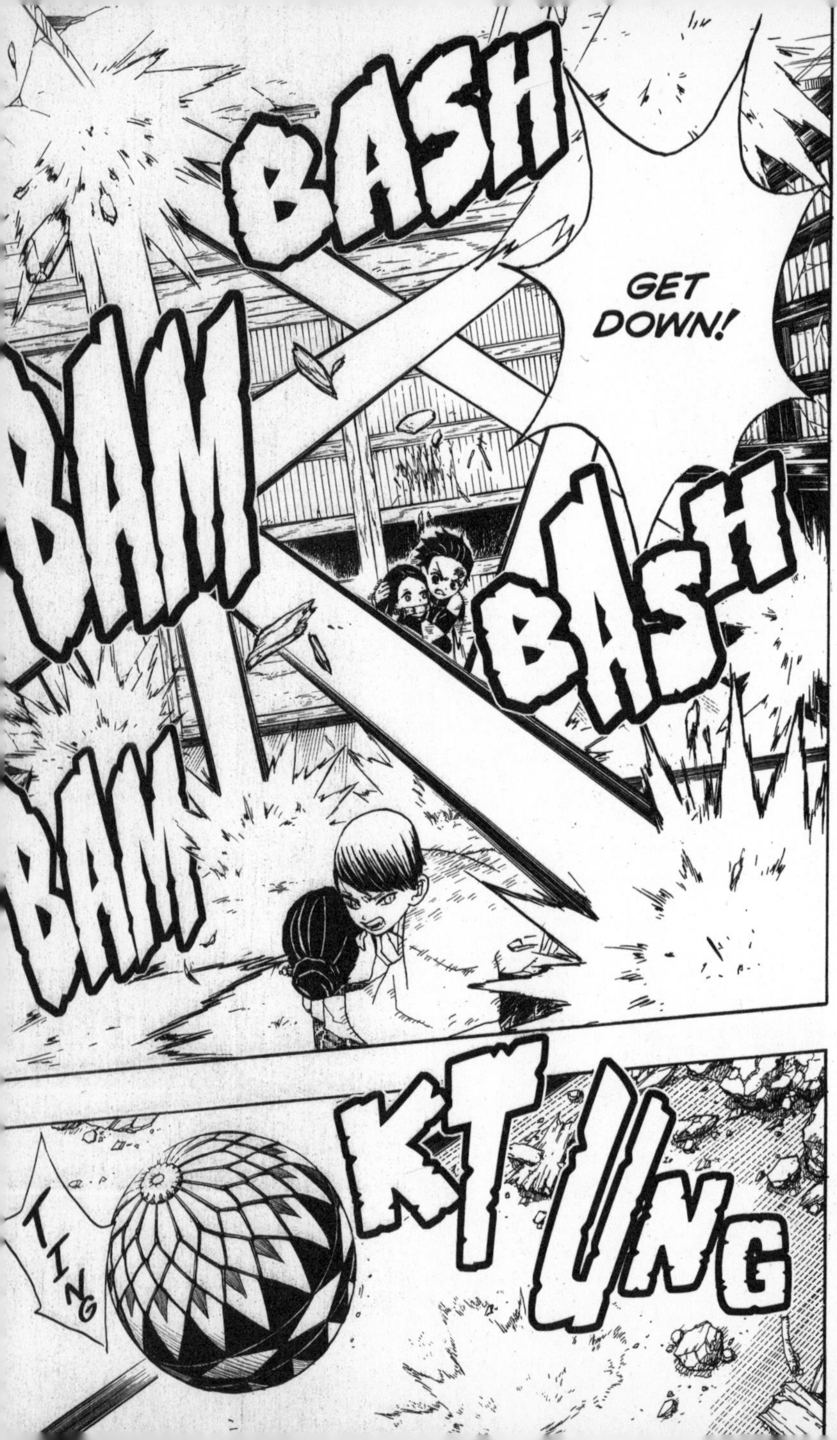
GET DOWN!
BASH
BASH
BAM
BAM
KTUNG
TING

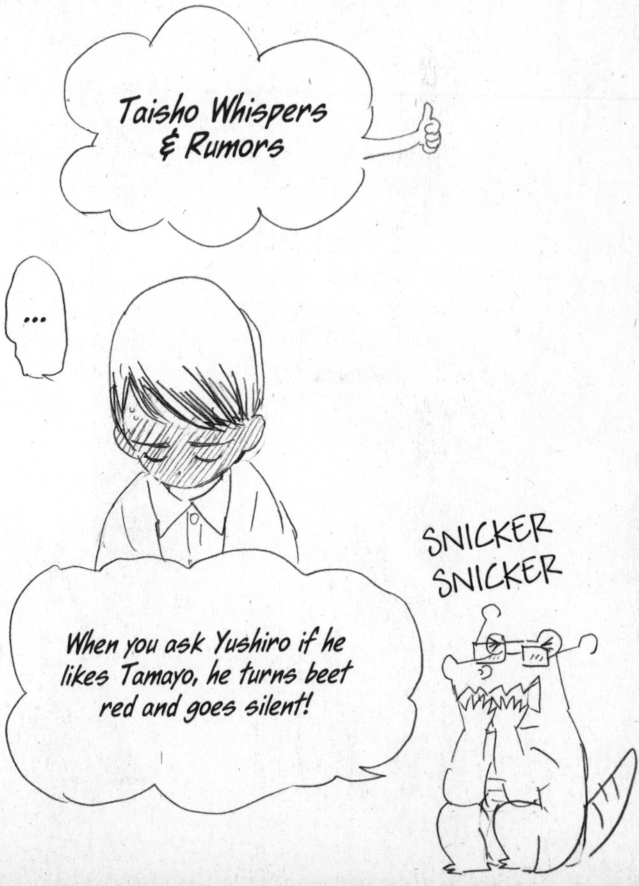

Taisho Whispers & Rumors
...
SNICKER SNICKER
When you ask Yushiro if he likes Tamayo, he turns beet red and goes silent!

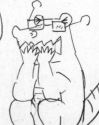

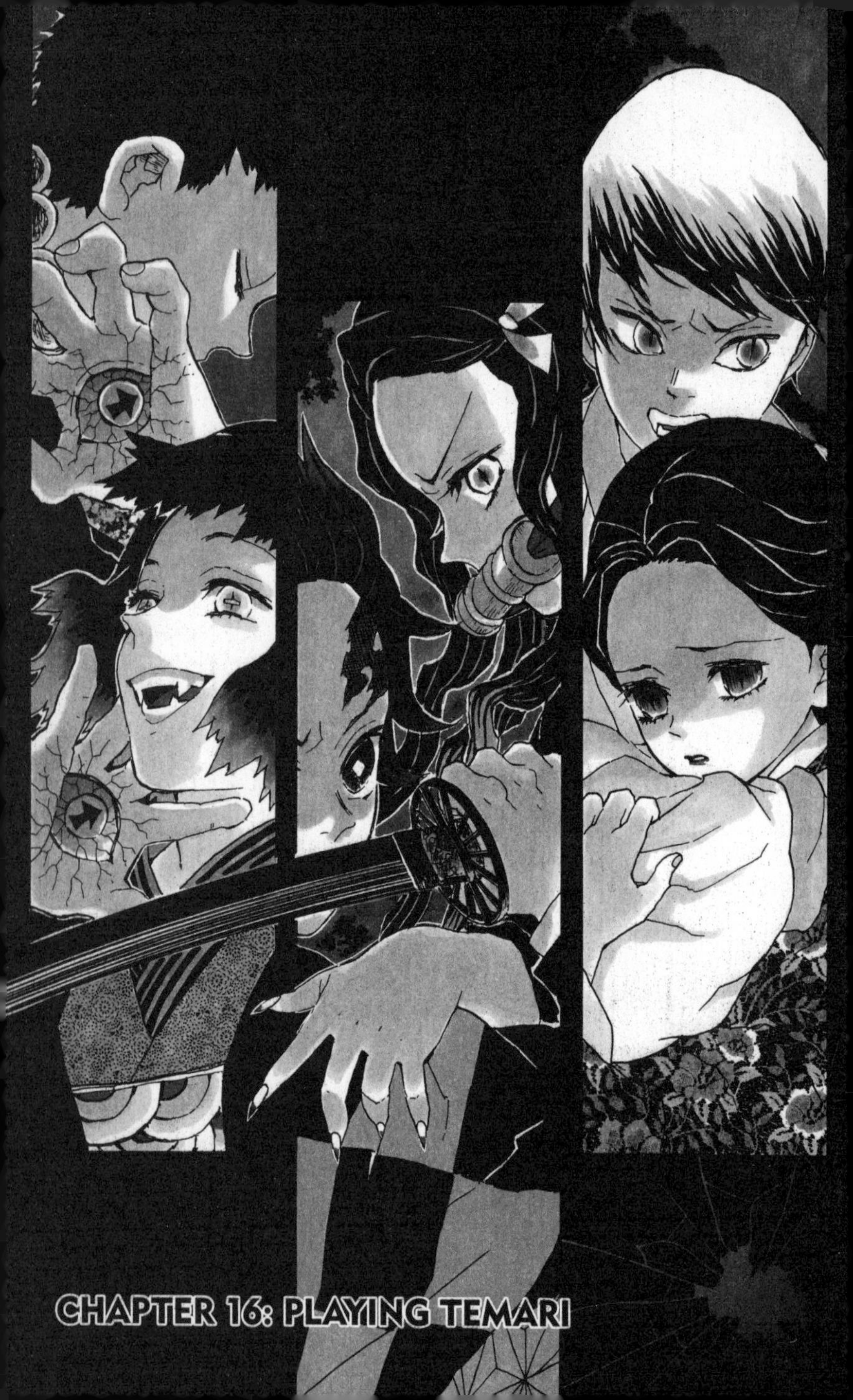

CHAPTER 16: PLAYING TEMARI

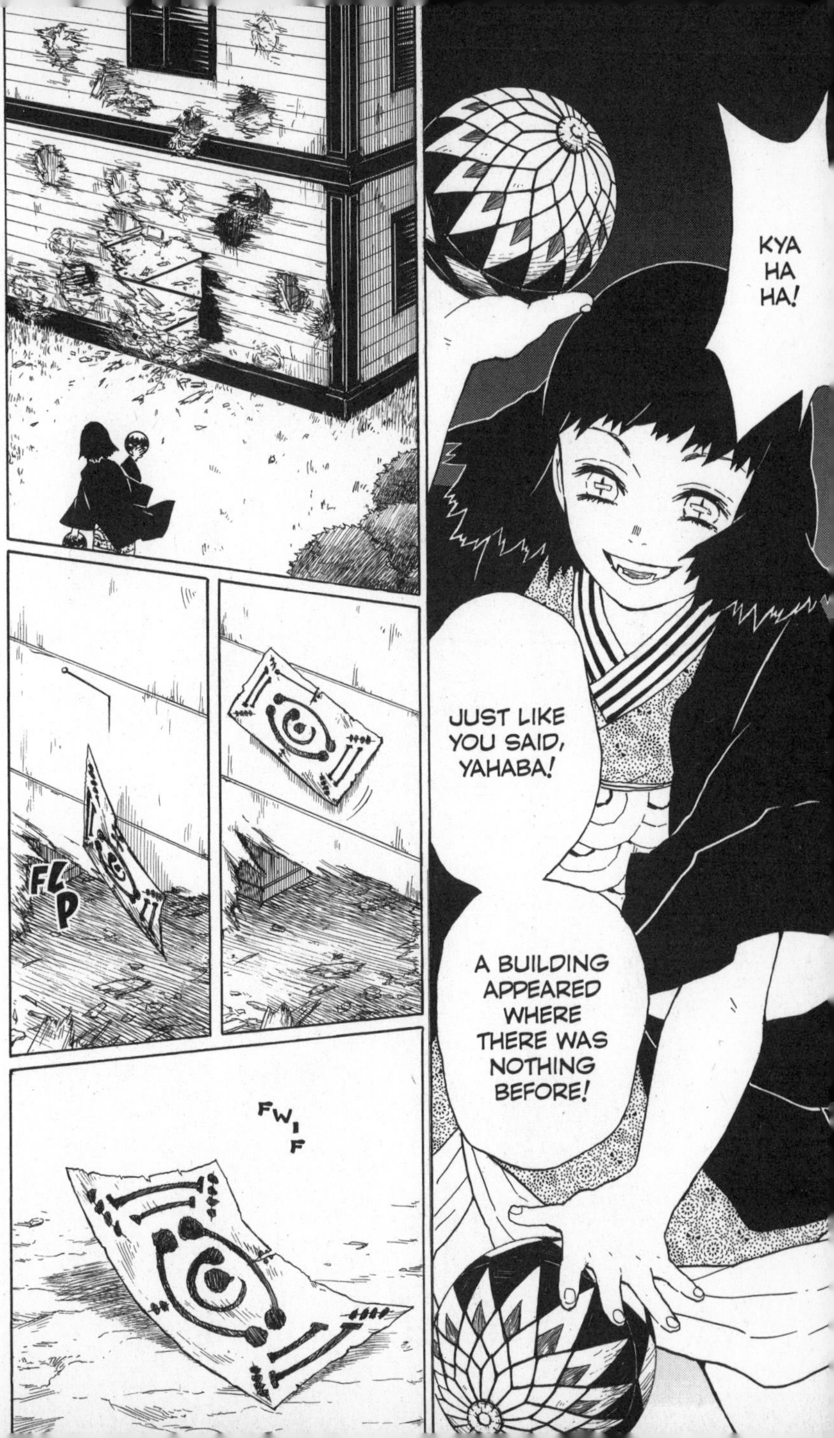
KYA HA HA!
JUST LIKE YOU SAID, YAHABA!
A BUILDING APPEARED WHERE THERE WAS NOTHING BEFORE!
FLP
FWIF

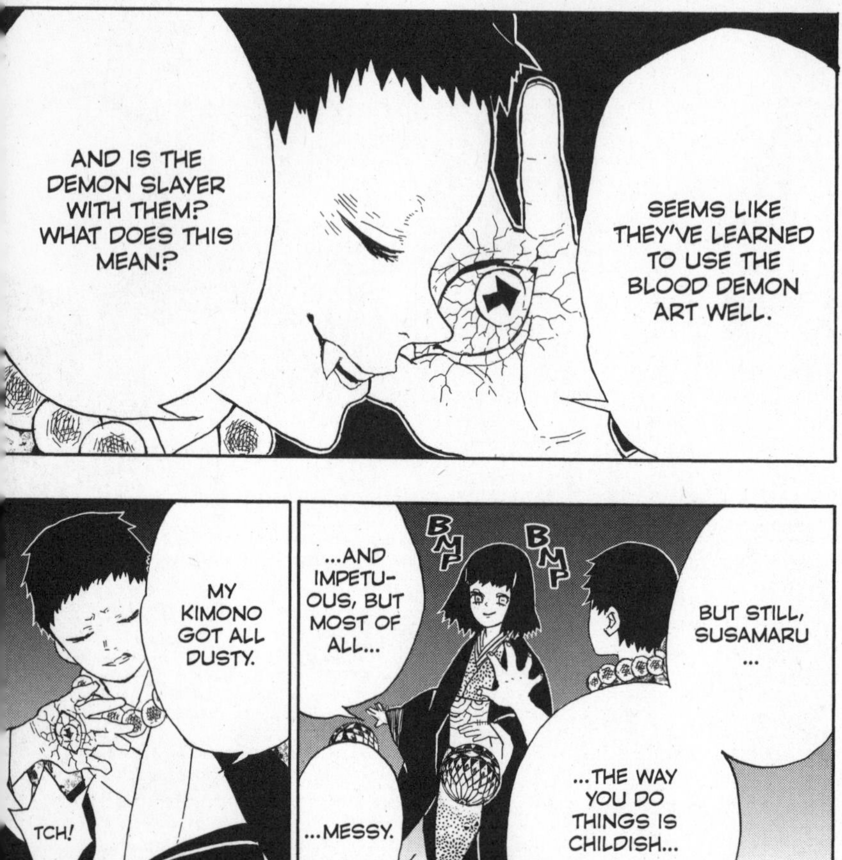
SEEMS LIKE THEY'VE LEARNED TO USE THE BLOOD DEMON ART WELL.
AND IS THE DEMON SLAYER WITH THEM? WHAT DOES THIS MEAN?
BUT STILL, SUSAMARU ...
...THE WAY YOU DO THINGS IS CHILDISH...
BMP
BMP
...AND IMPETUOUS, BUT MOST OF ALL...
...MESSY.
MY KIMONO GOT ALL DUSTY.
TCH!

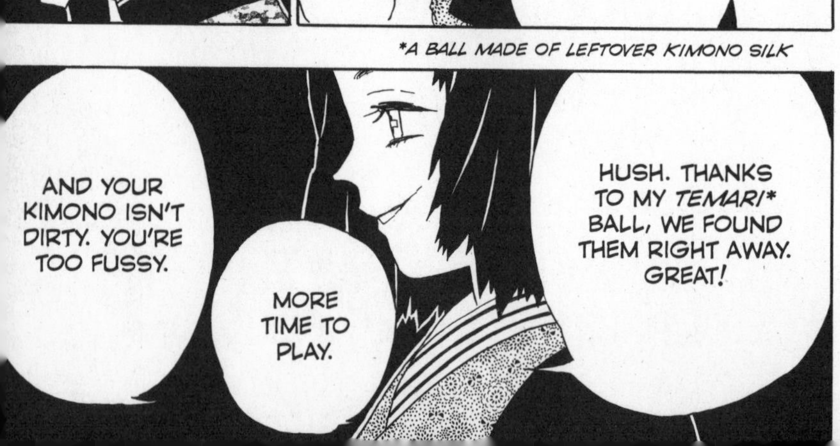
HUSH. THANKS TO MY *TEMARI** BALL, WE FOUND THEM RIGHT AWAY. GREAT!
MORE TIME TO PLAY.
AND YOUR KIMONO ISN'T DIRTY. YOU'RE TOO FUSSY.

**A BALL MADE OF LEFTOVER KIMONO SILK*

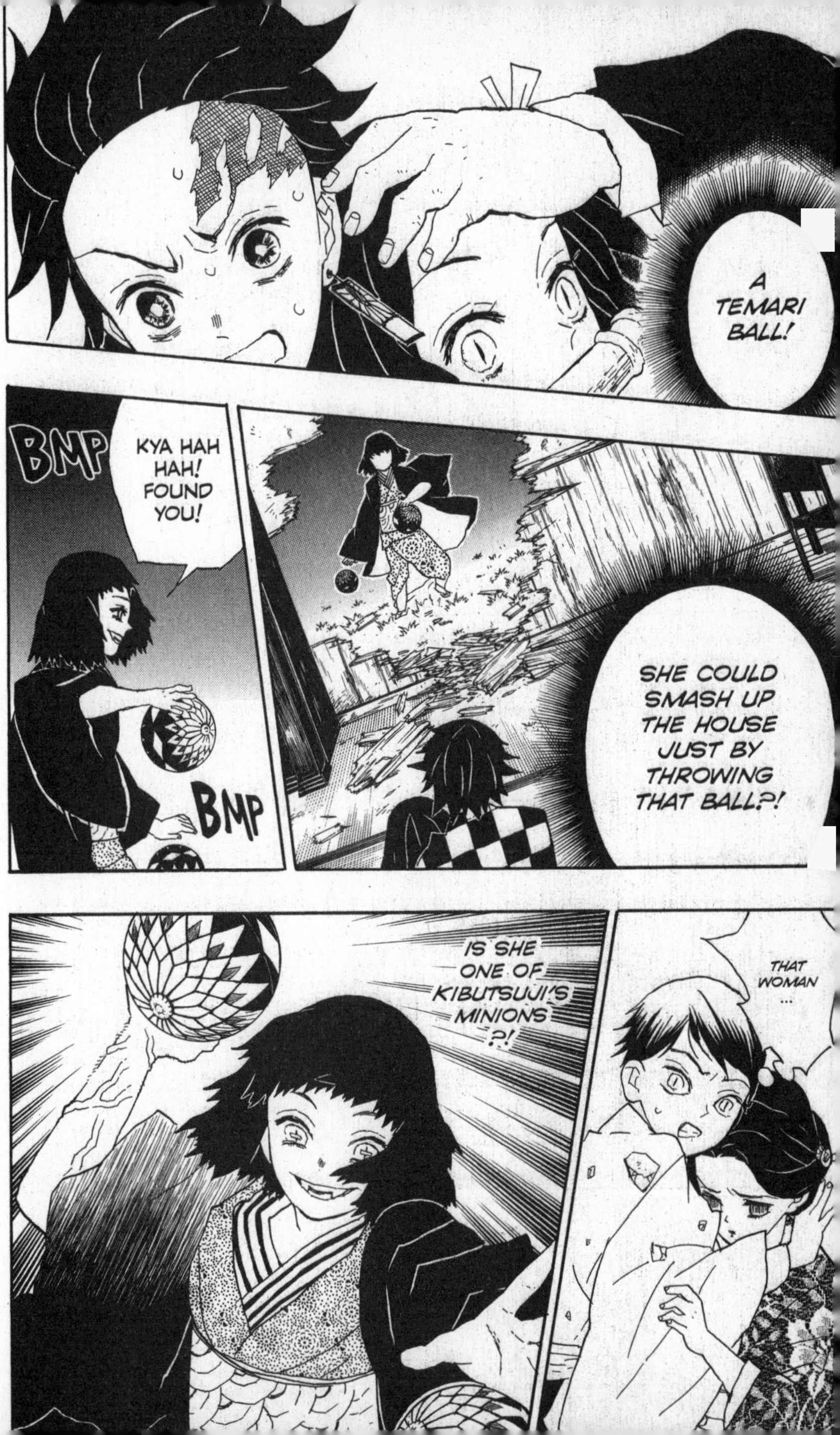
A TEMARI BALL!
SHE COULD SMASH UP THE HOUSE JUST BY THROWING THAT BALL?!
KYA HAH HAH! FOUND YOU!
BMP
BMP
THAT WOMAN ...
IS SHE ONE OF KIBUTSUJI'S MINIONS ?!

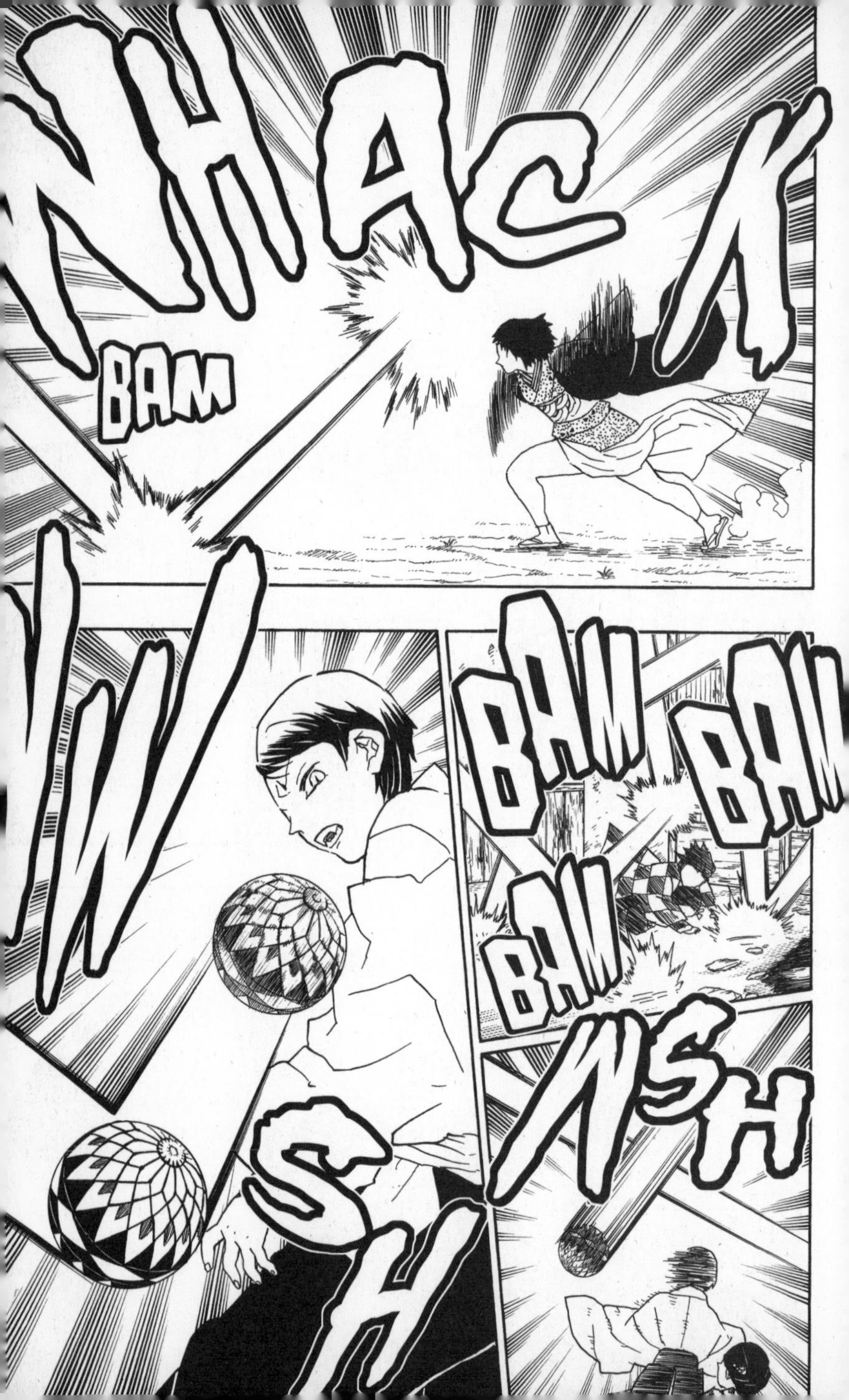
WHACK
BAM
BAM
BAM
BAM

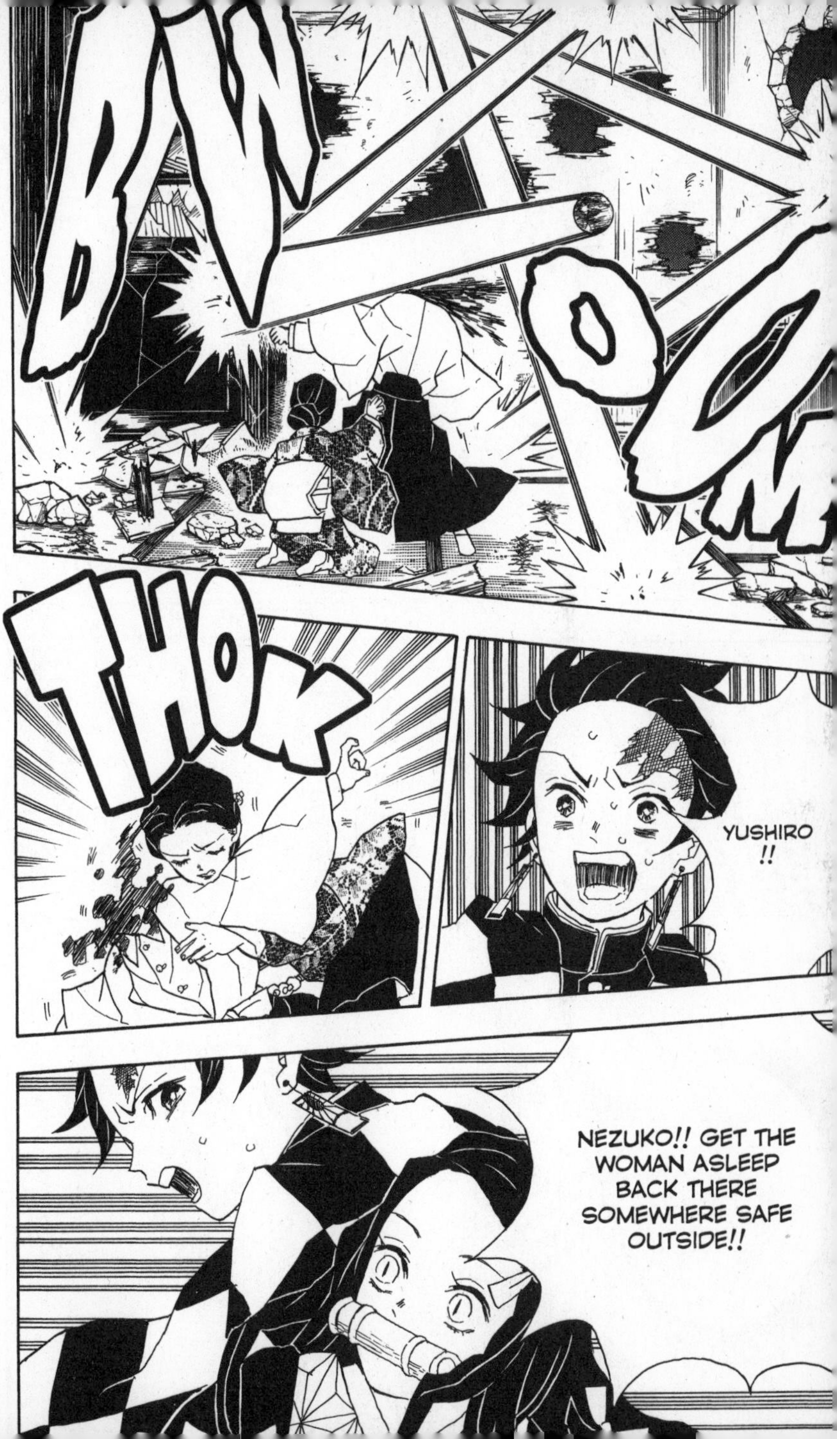
BOOM
BAM
YUSHIRO!!
THOK
NEZUKO!! GET THE WOMAN ASLEEP BACK THERE SOMEWHERE SAFE OUTSIDE!!

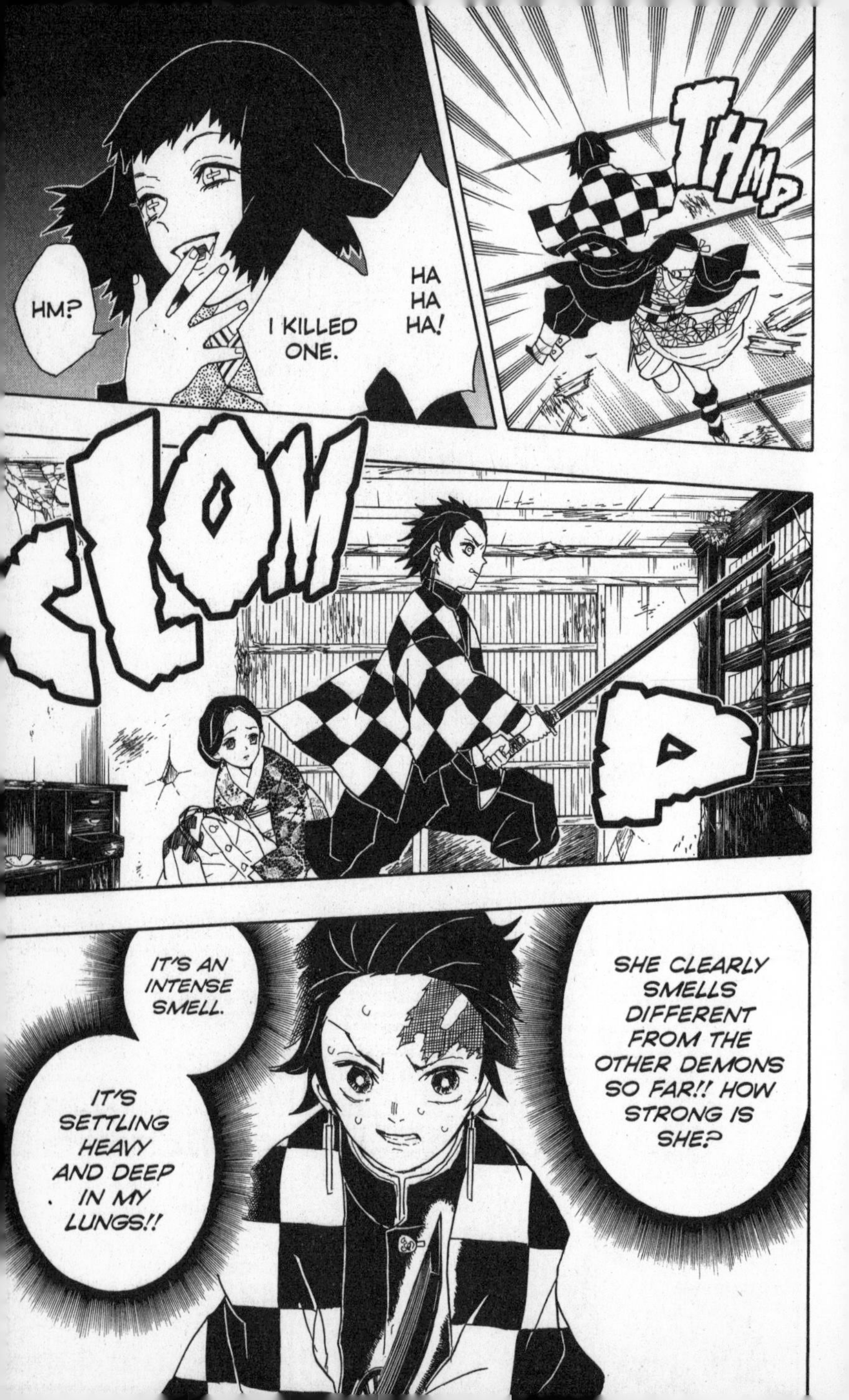
THMP
HA HA HA!
I KILLED ONE.
HM?
CLOMP
SHE CLEARLY SMELLS DIFFERENT FROM THE OTHER DEMONS SO FAR!! HOW STRONG IS SHE?
IT'S AN INTENSE SMELL.
IT'S SETTLING HEAVY AND DEEP IN MY LUNGS!!

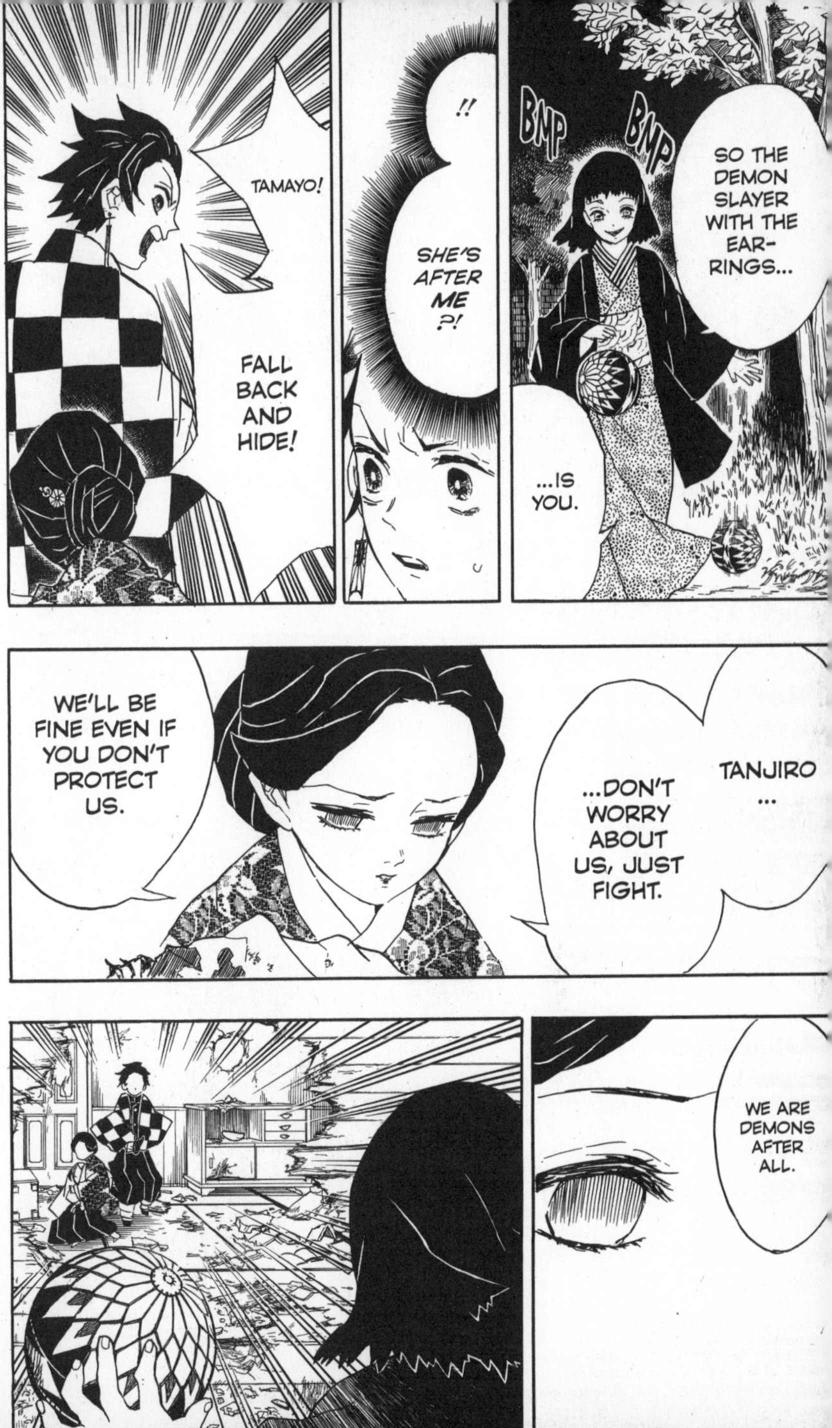
BMP
BMP
SO THE DEMON SLAYER WITH THE EAR-RINGS...
...IS YOU.
!!
SHE'S AFTER ME ?!
TAMAYO!
FALL BACK AND HIDE!
TANJIRO ...
...DON'T WORRY ABOUT US, JUST FIGHT.
WE'LL BE FINE EVEN IF YOU DON'T PROTECT US.
WE ARE DEMONS AFTER ALL.

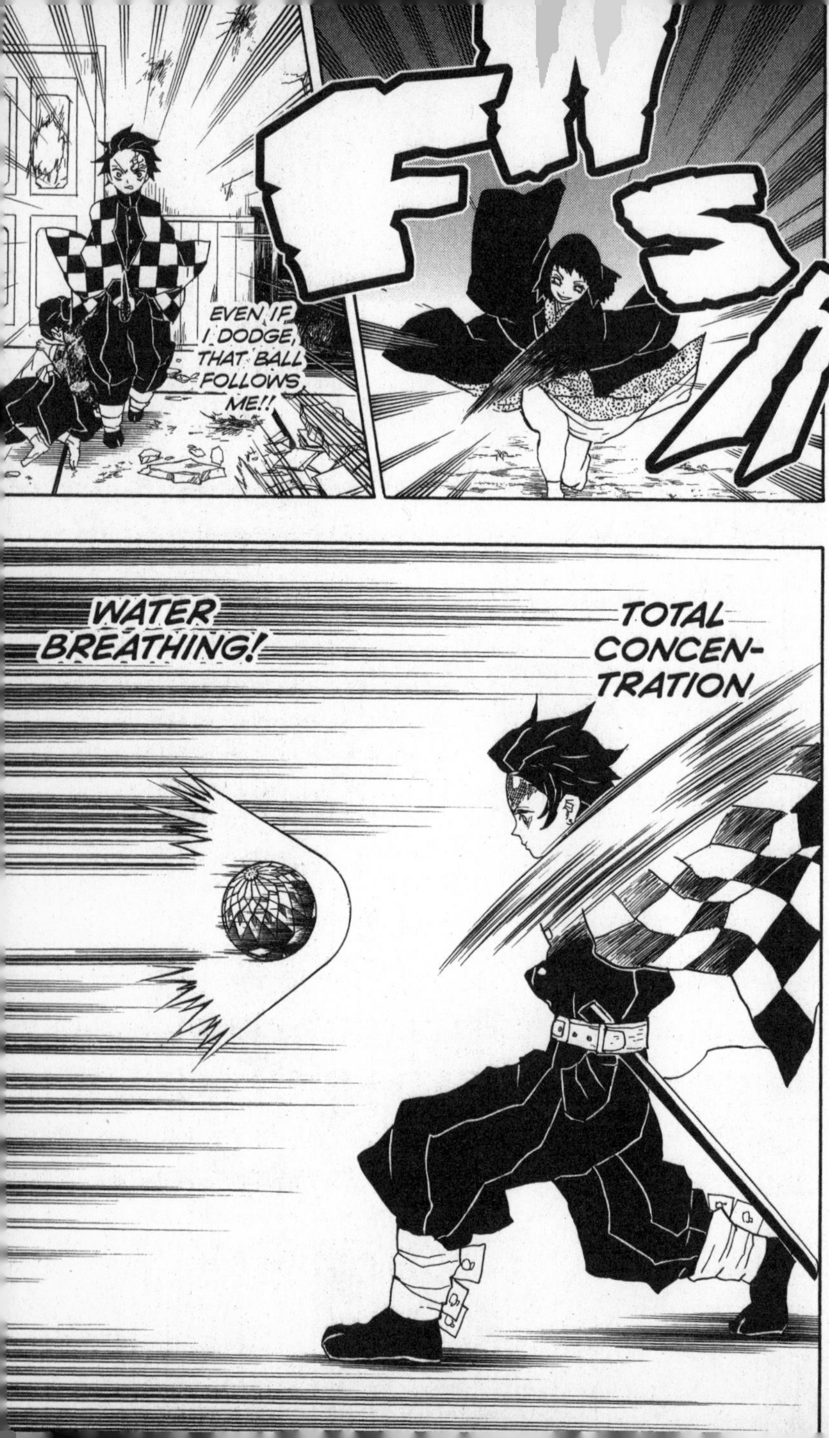
FWSH
EVEN IF I DODGE, THAT BALL FOLLOWS ME!!
TOTAL CONCEN-TRATION
WATER BREATHING!

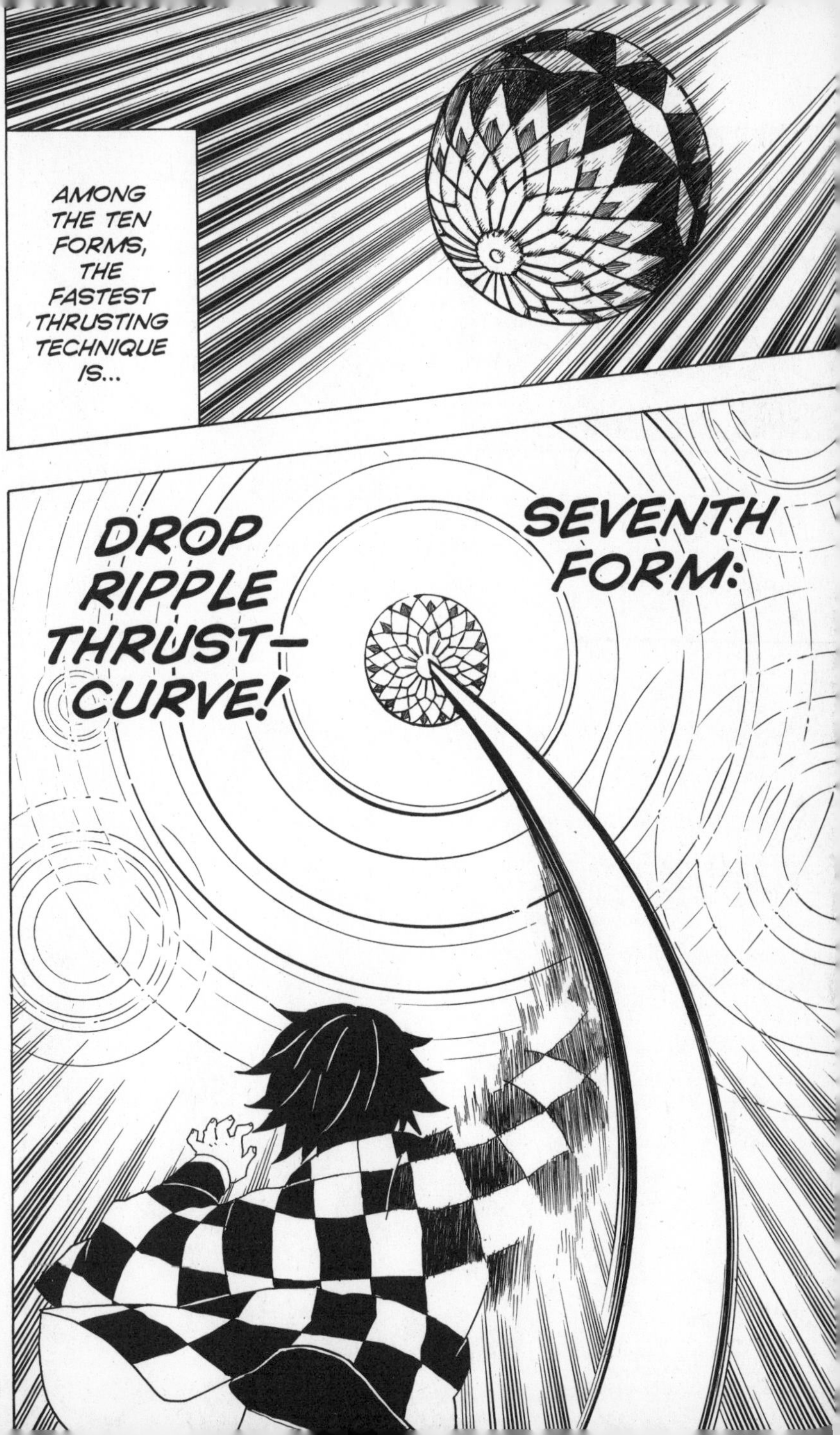
AMONG THE TEN FORMS, THE FASTEST THRUSTING TECHNIQUE IS...
SEVENTH FORM:
DROP RIPPLE THRUST—CURVE!

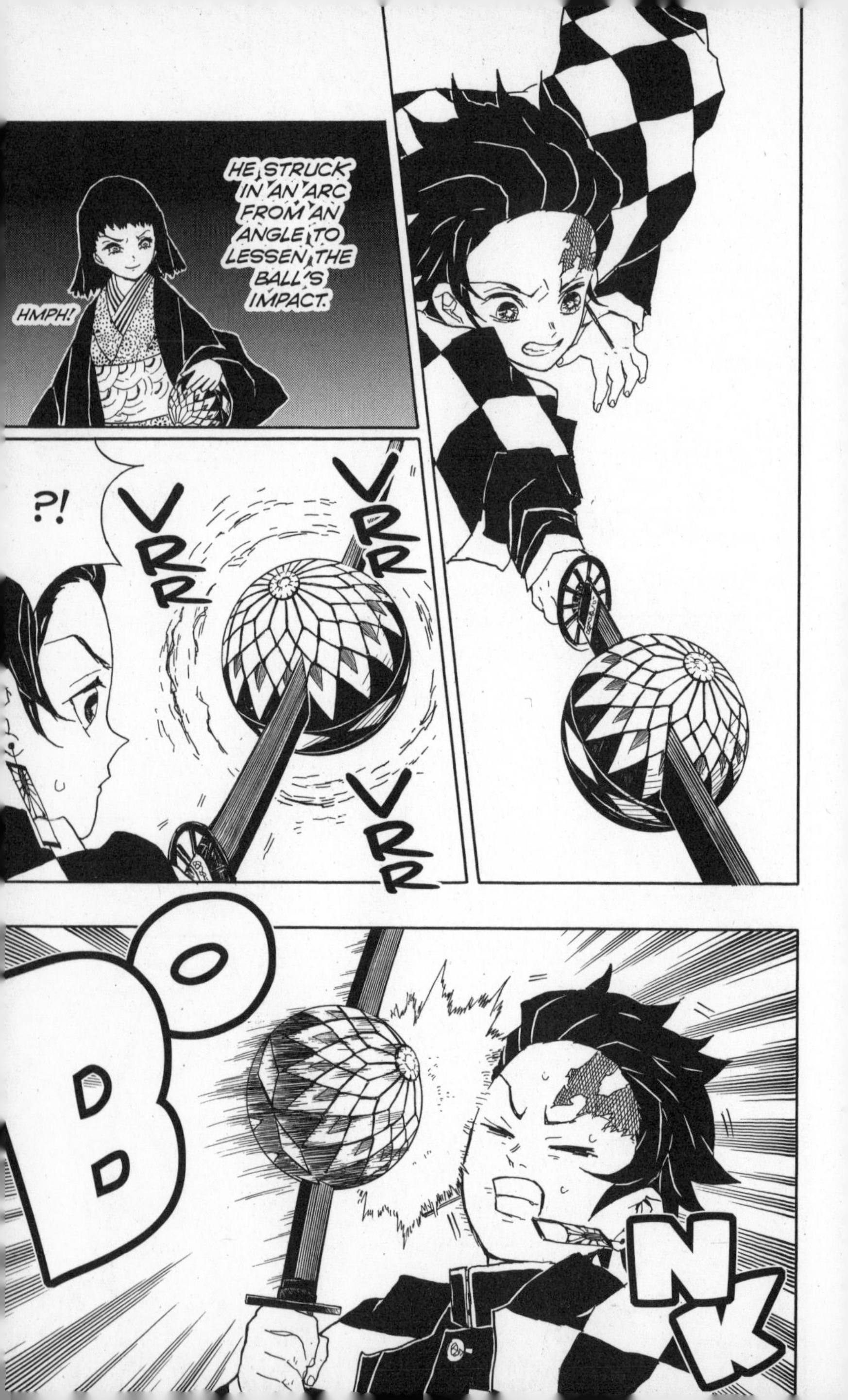
HE STRUCK IN AN ARC FROM AN ANGLE TO LESSEN THE BALL'S IMPACT.
HMPH!
VRRR
VRRR
VRR
?!
BOOONK

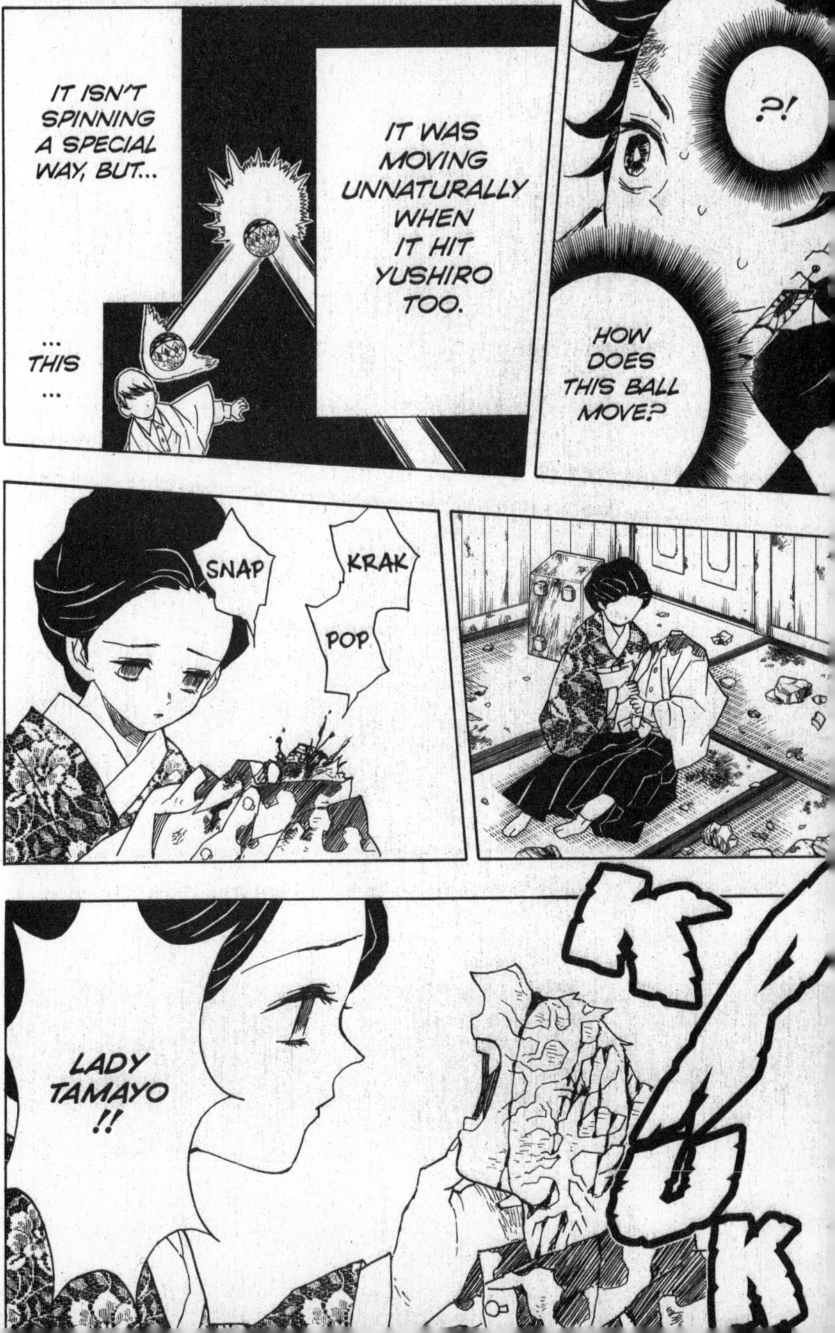
?!
HOW DOES THIS BALL MOVE?
IT WAS MOVING UNNATURALLY WHEN IT HIT YUSHIRO TOO.
IT ISN'T SPINNING A SPECIAL WAY, BUT...
... THIS ...
KRAK
SNAP
POP
LADY TAMAYO!!

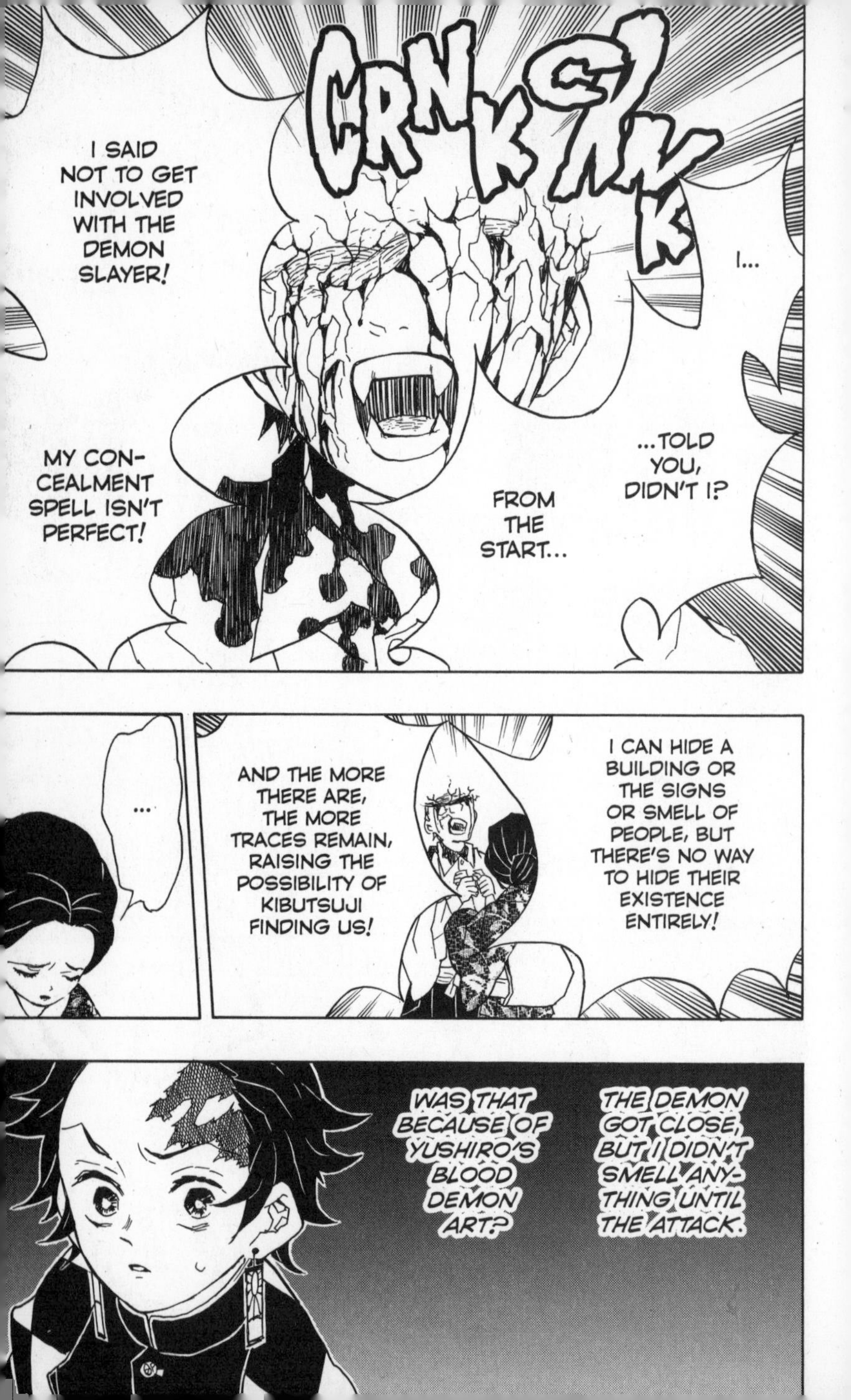
CRNK CRNK
I...
...TOLD YOU, DIDN'T I?
FROM THE START...
I SAID NOT TO GET INVOLVED WITH THE DEMON SLAYER!
MY CON-CEALMENT SPELL ISN'T PERFECT!
I CAN HIDE A BUILDING OR THE SIGNS OR SMELL OF PEOPLE, BUT THERE'S NO WAY TO HIDE THEIR EXISTENCE ENTIRELY!
AND THE MORE THERE ARE, THE MORE TRACES REMAIN, RAISING THE POSSIBILITY OF KIBUTSUJI FINDING US!
...
THE DEMON GOT CLOSE, BUT I DIDN'T SMELL ANY-THING UNTIL THE ATTACK.
WAS THAT BECAUSE OF YUSHIRO'S BLOOD DEMON ART?

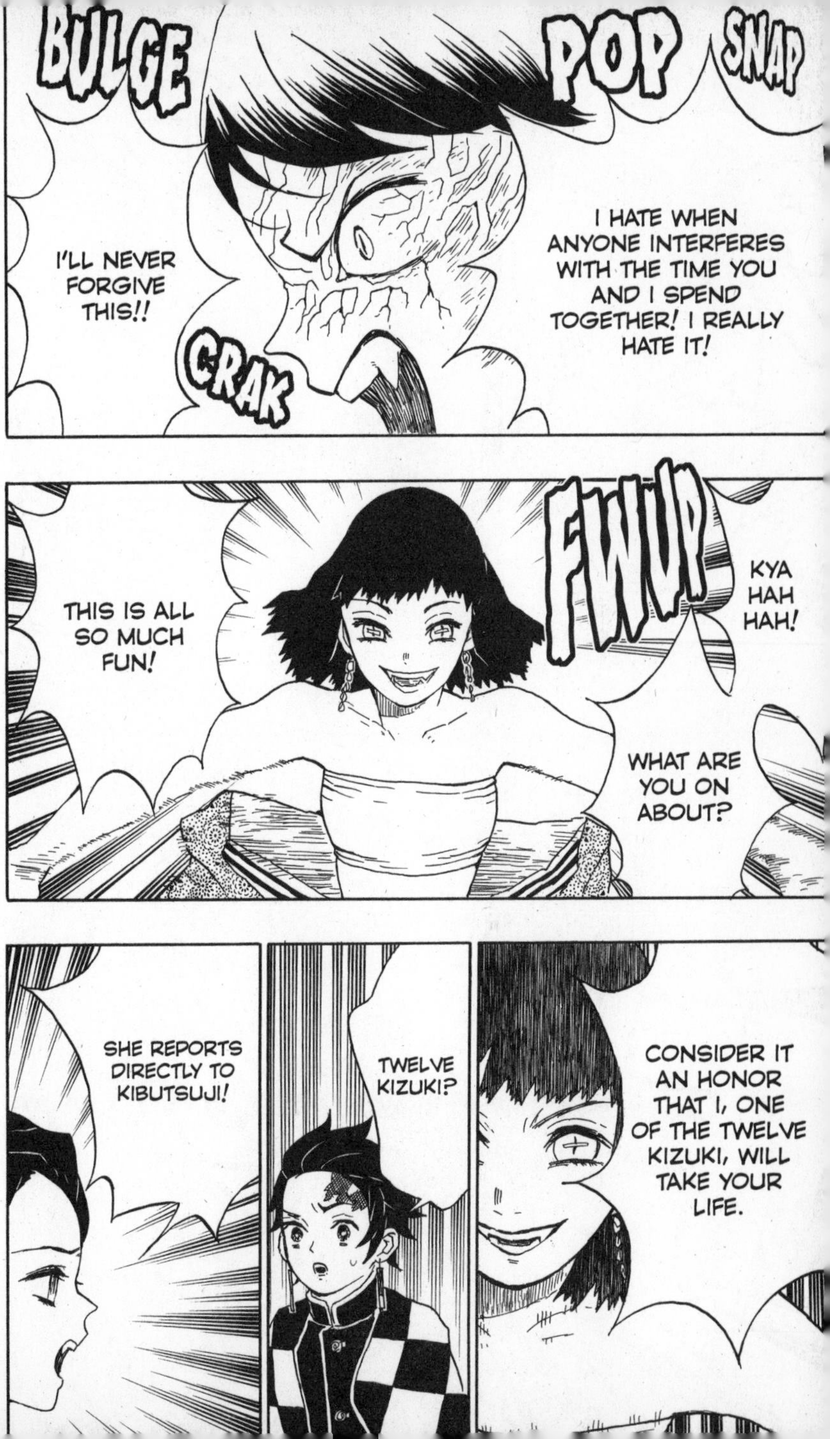
SNAP
POP
I HATE WHEN ANYONE INTERFERES WITH THE TIME YOU AND I SPEND TOGETHER! I REALLY HATE IT!
BULGE
I'LL NEVER FORGIVE THIS!!
CRAK
FWUP
KYA HAH HAH!
THIS IS ALL SO MUCH FUN!
WHAT ARE YOU ON ABOUT?
CONSIDER IT AN HONOR THAT I, ONE OF THE TWELVE KIZUKI, WILL TAKE YOUR LIFE.
TWELVE KIZUKI?
SHE REPORTS DIRECTLY TO KIBUTSUJI!

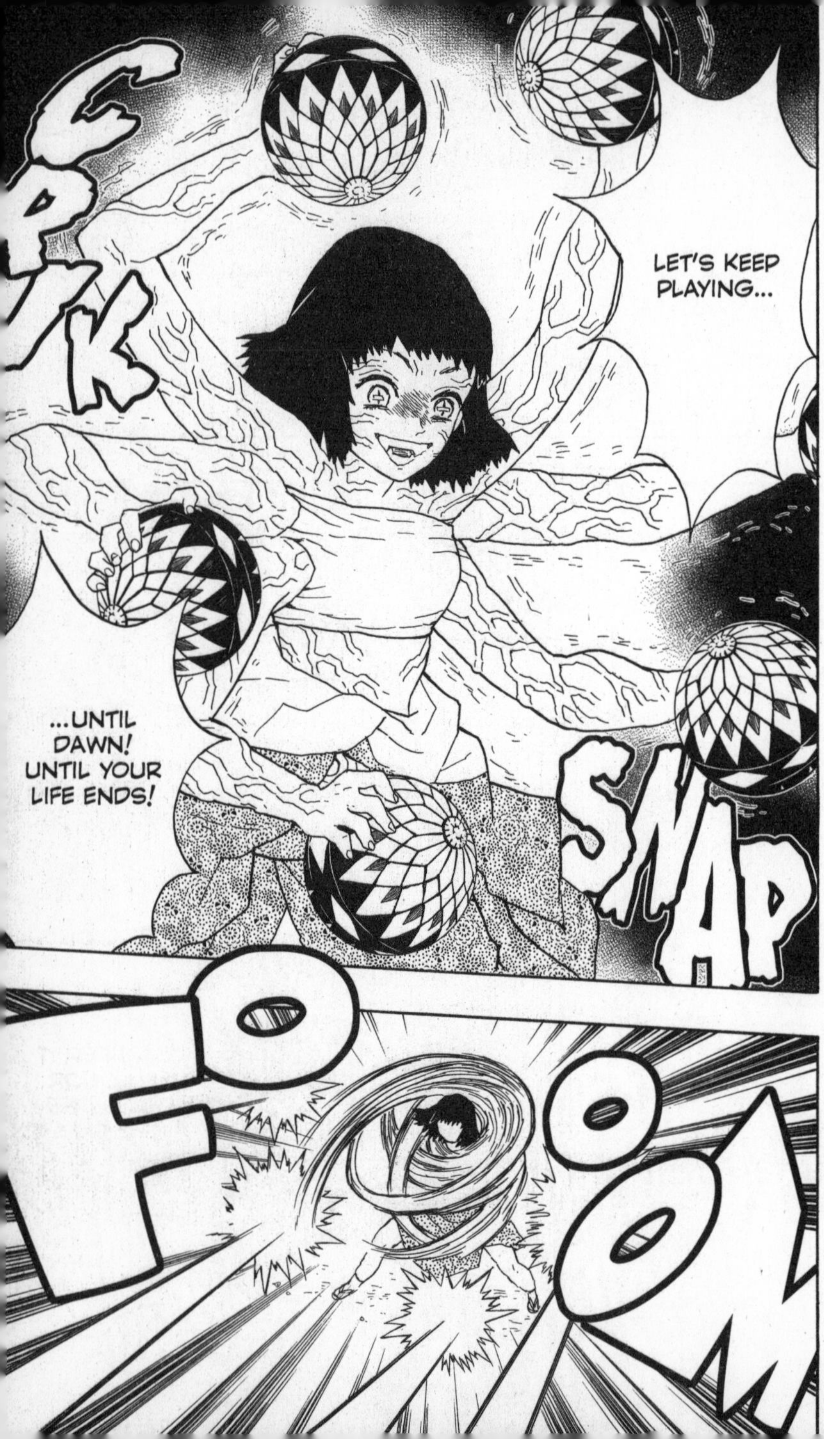
LET'S KEEP PLAYING...
...UNTIL DAWN! UNTIL YOUR LIFE ENDS!
SNAP
FOOOM

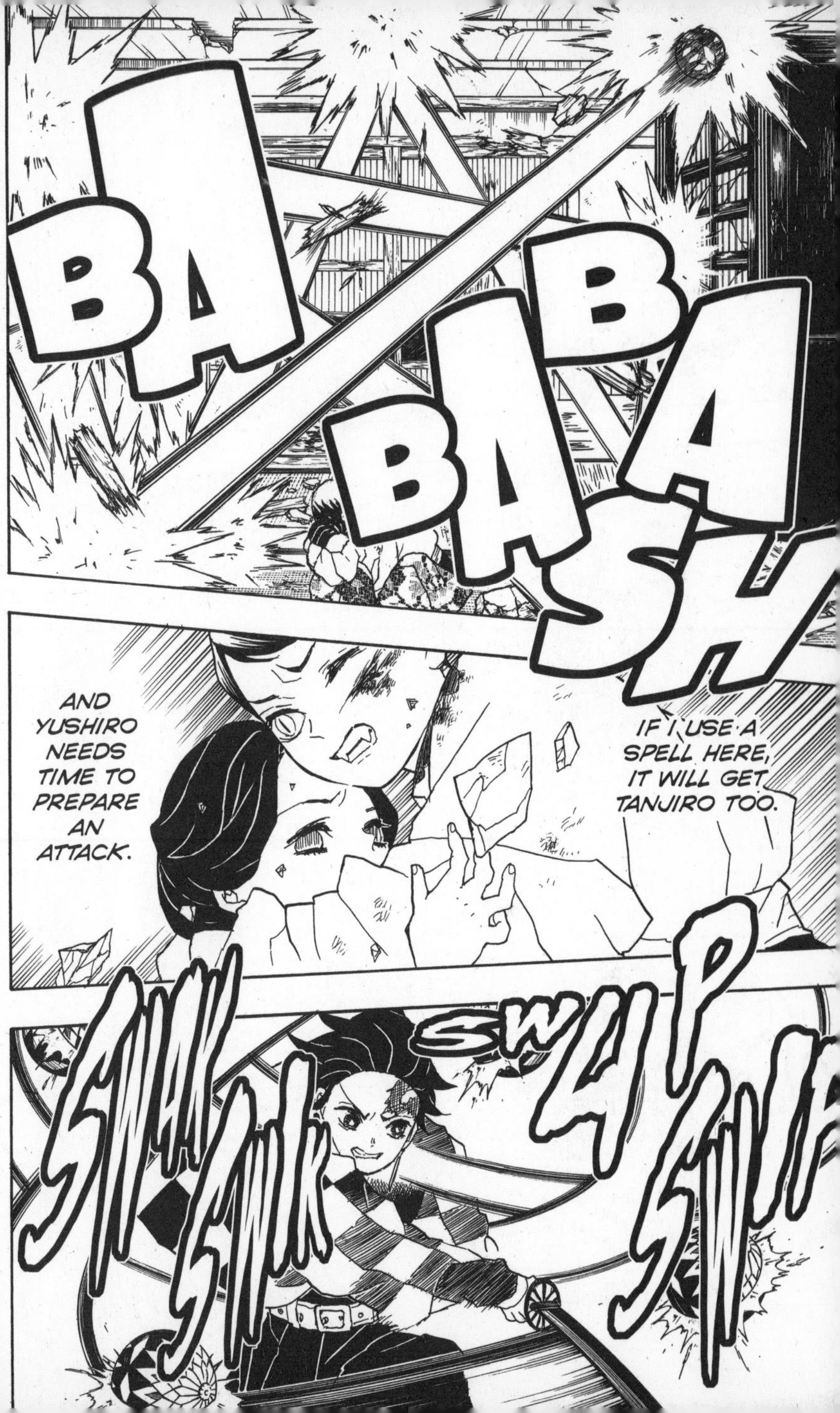
BA BA BASH
IF I USE A SPELL HERE, IT WILL GET TANJIRO TOO.
AND YUSHIRO NEEDS TIME TO PREPARE AN ATTACK.
SWIP
SHNK
SHNK

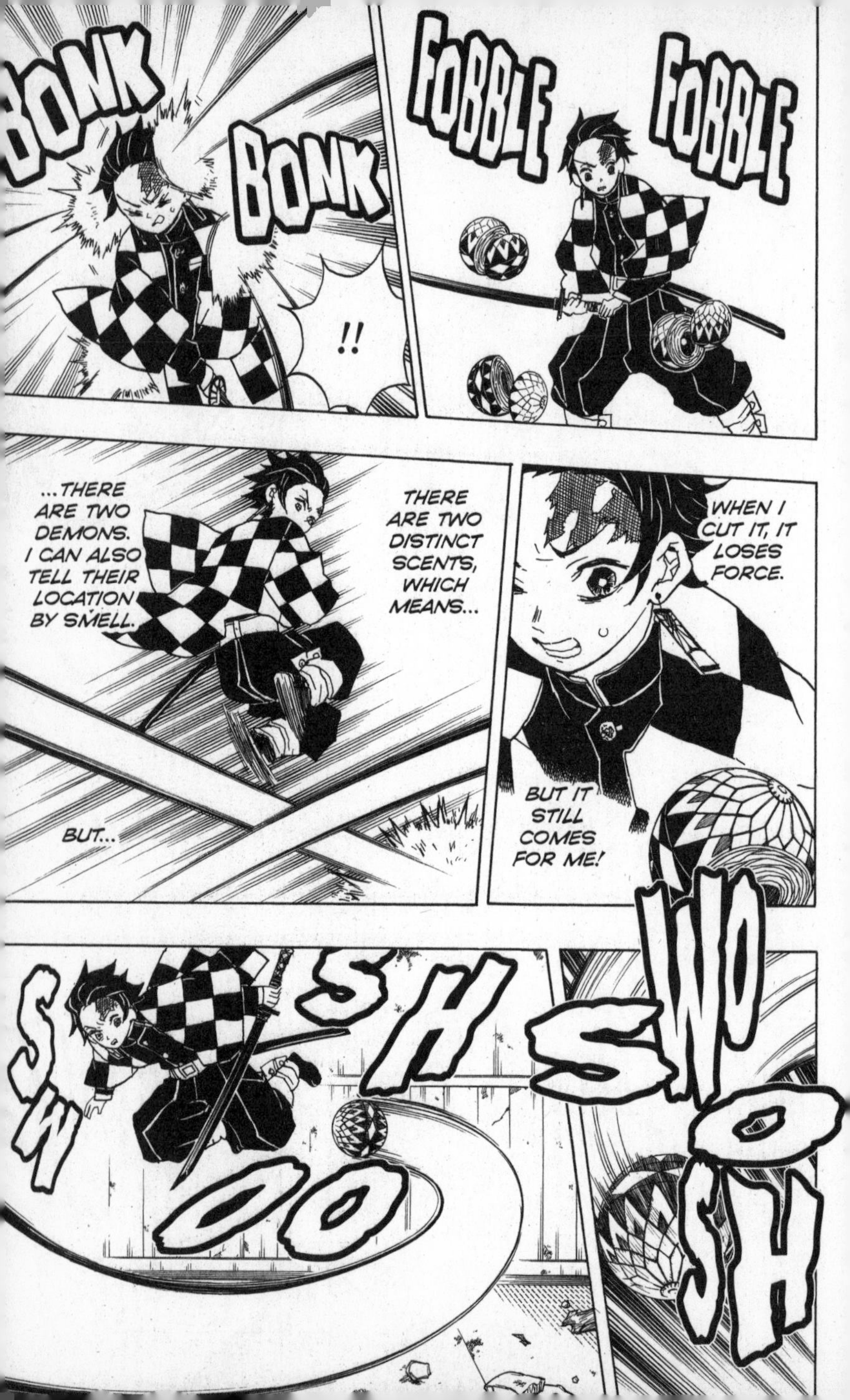
FOBBLE
FOBBLE
BONK
BONK
!!
WHEN I CUT IT, IT LOSES FORCE.
BUT IT STILL COMES FOR ME!
THERE ARE TWO DISTINCT SCENTS, WHICH MEANS...
...THERE ARE TWO DEMONS. I CAN ALSO TELL THEIR LOCATION BY SMELL.
BUT...
SWOOSH
SWOOSH

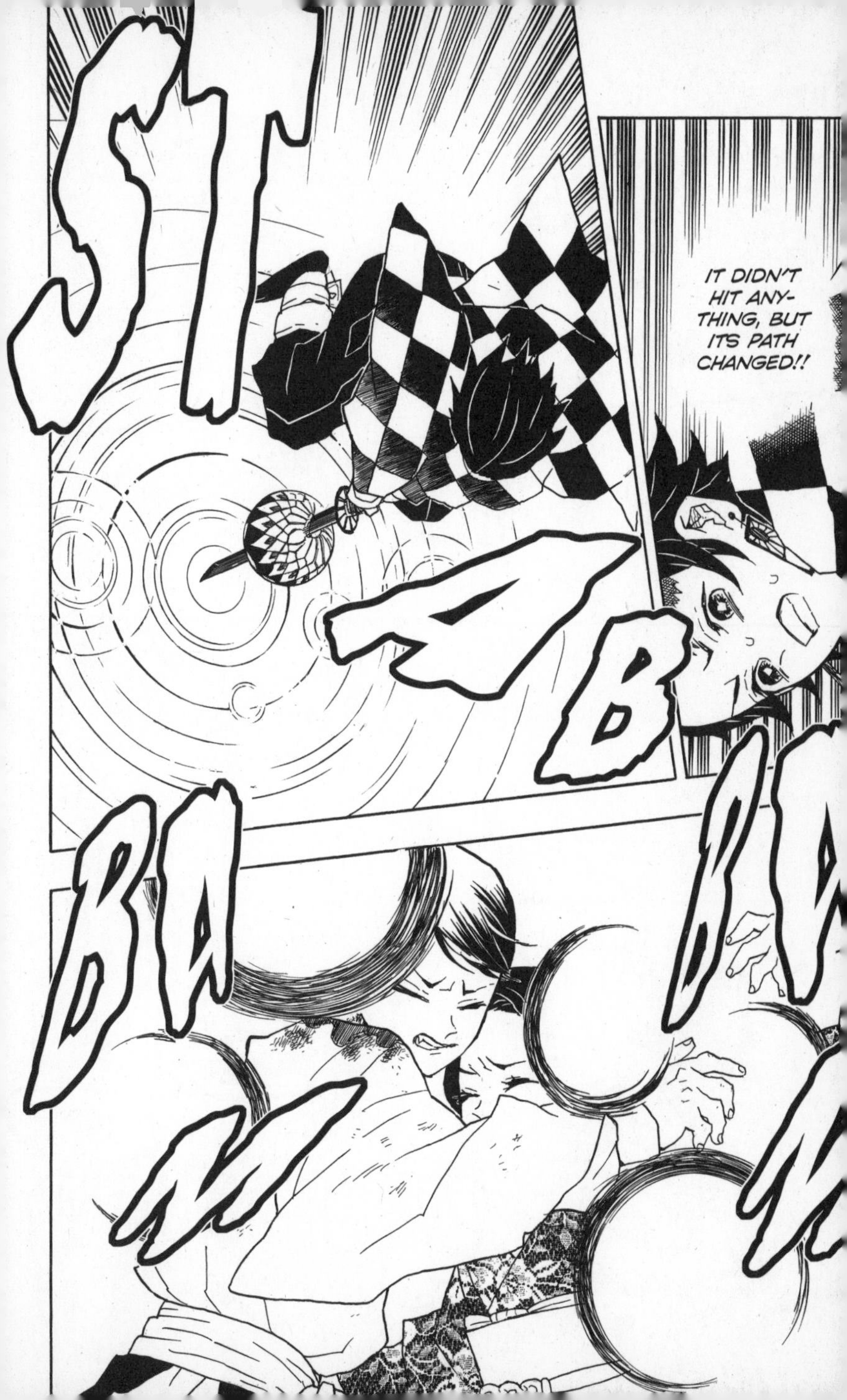
IT DIDN'T HIT ANY-THING, BUT ITS PATH CHANGED!!
STAB
BAM

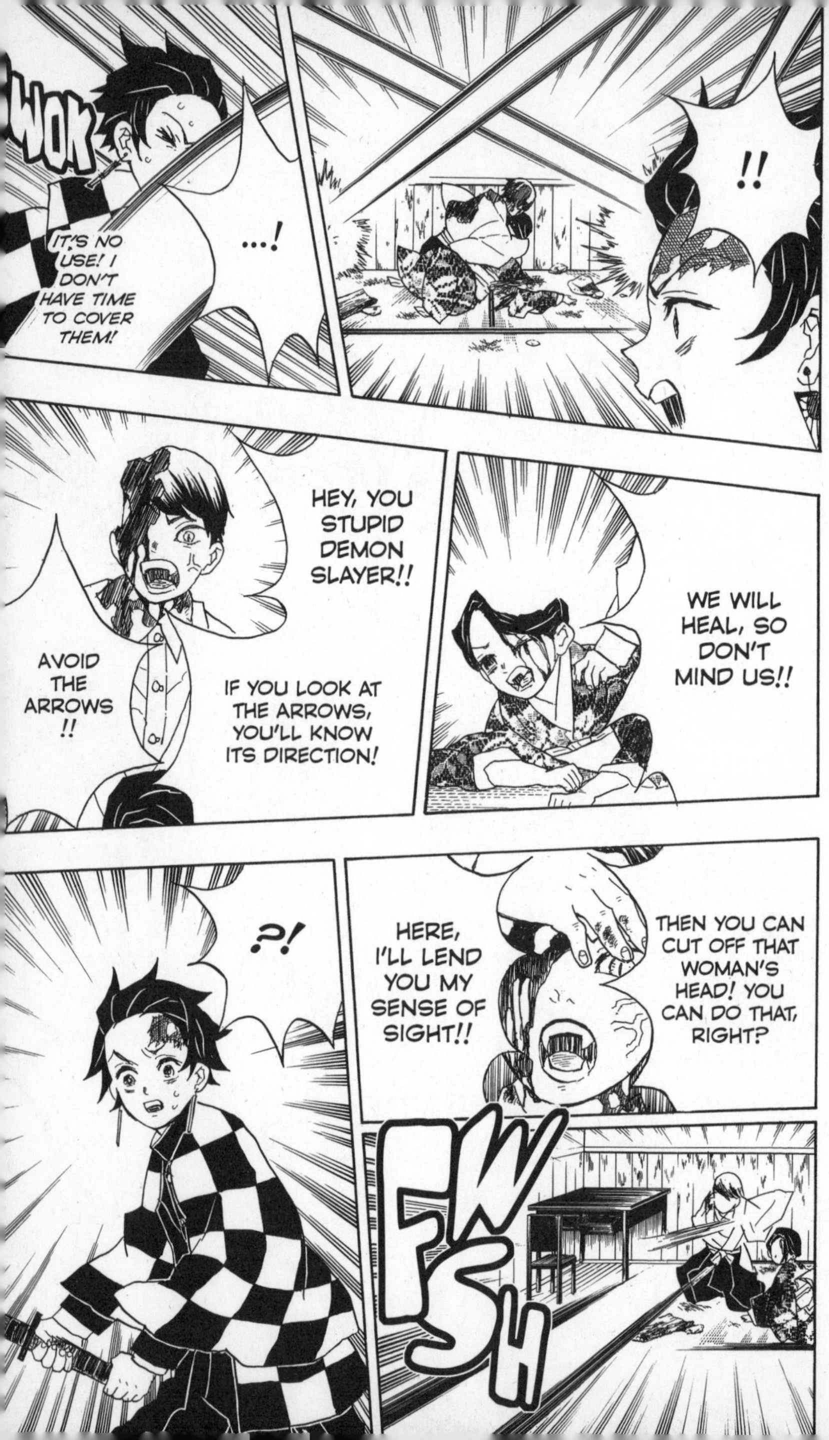
!!
...!
WOK
IT'S NO USE! I DON'T HAVE TIME TO COVER THEM!
WE WILL HEAL, SO DON'T MIND US!!
HEY, YOU STUPID DEMON SLAYER!!
IF YOU LOOK AT THE ARROWS, YOU'LL KNOW ITS DIRECTION!
AVOID THE ARROWS!!
THEN YOU CAN CUT OFF THAT WOMAN'S HEAD! YOU CAN DO THAT, RIGHT?
HERE, I'LL LEND YOU MY SENSE OF SIGHT!!
FWSH
?!

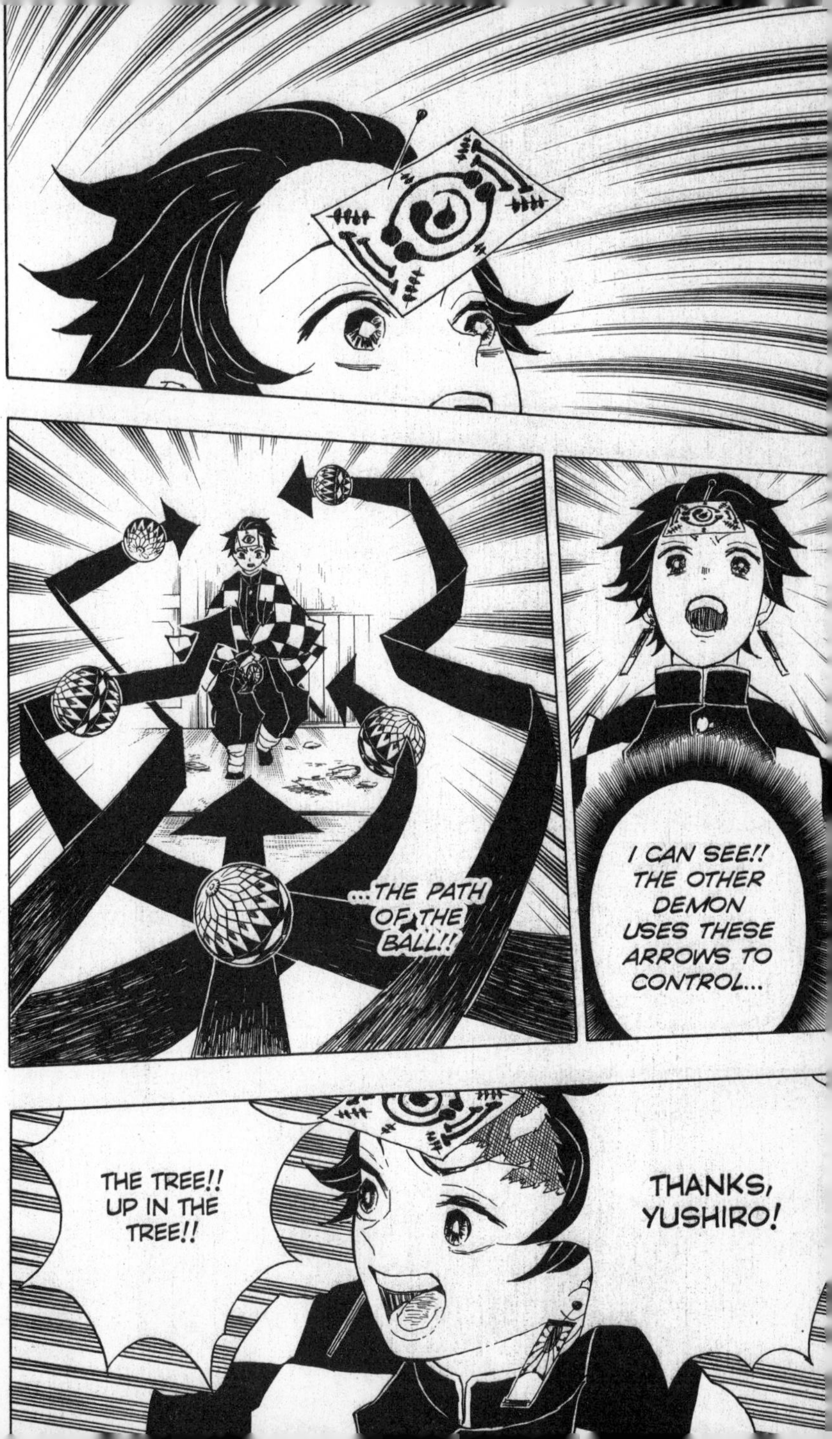
I CAN SEE!! THE OTHER DEMON USES THESE ARROWS TO CONTROL...
...THE PATH OF THE BALL!!
THANKS, YUSHIRO!
THE TREE!! UP IN THE TREE!!

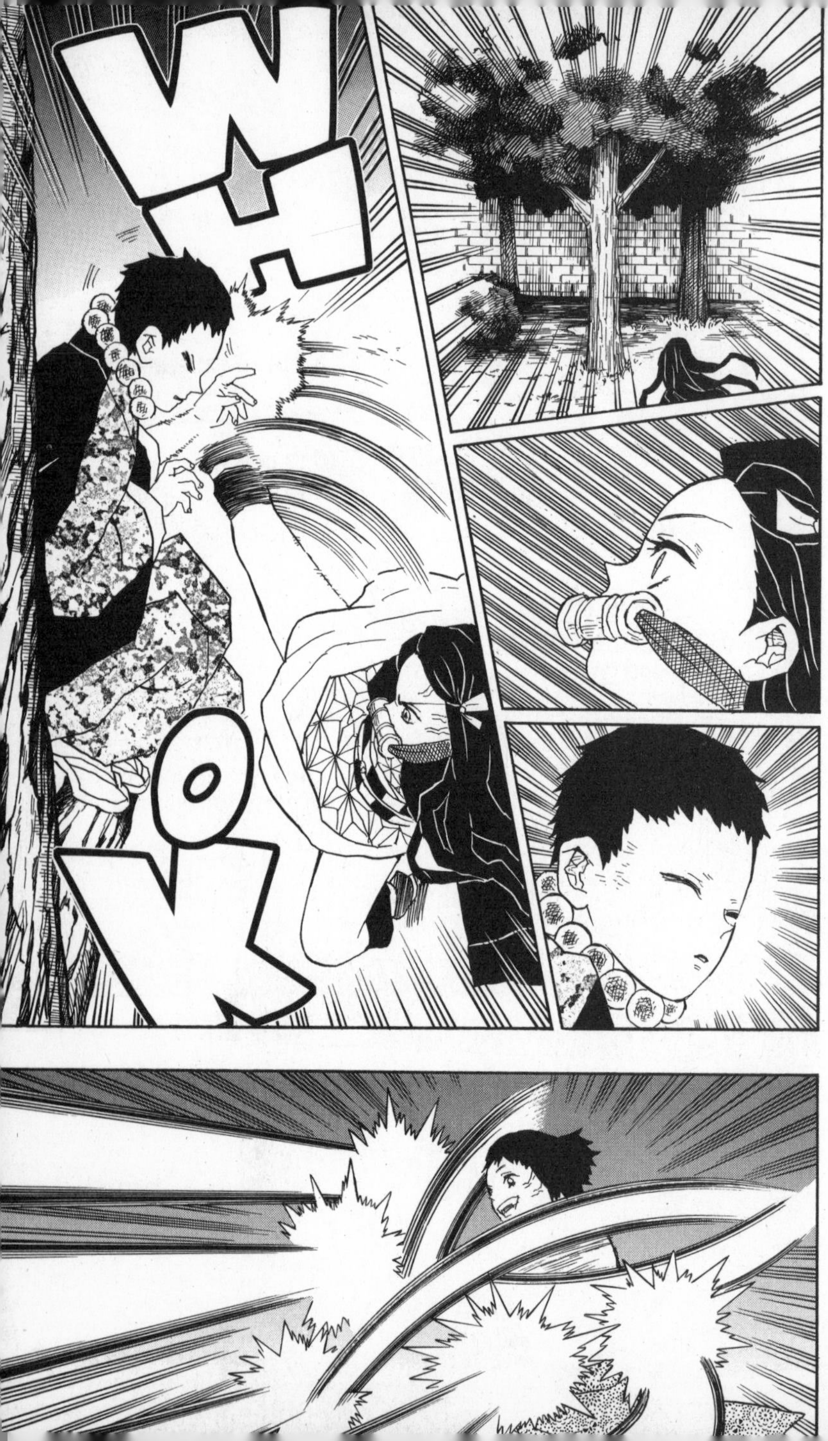

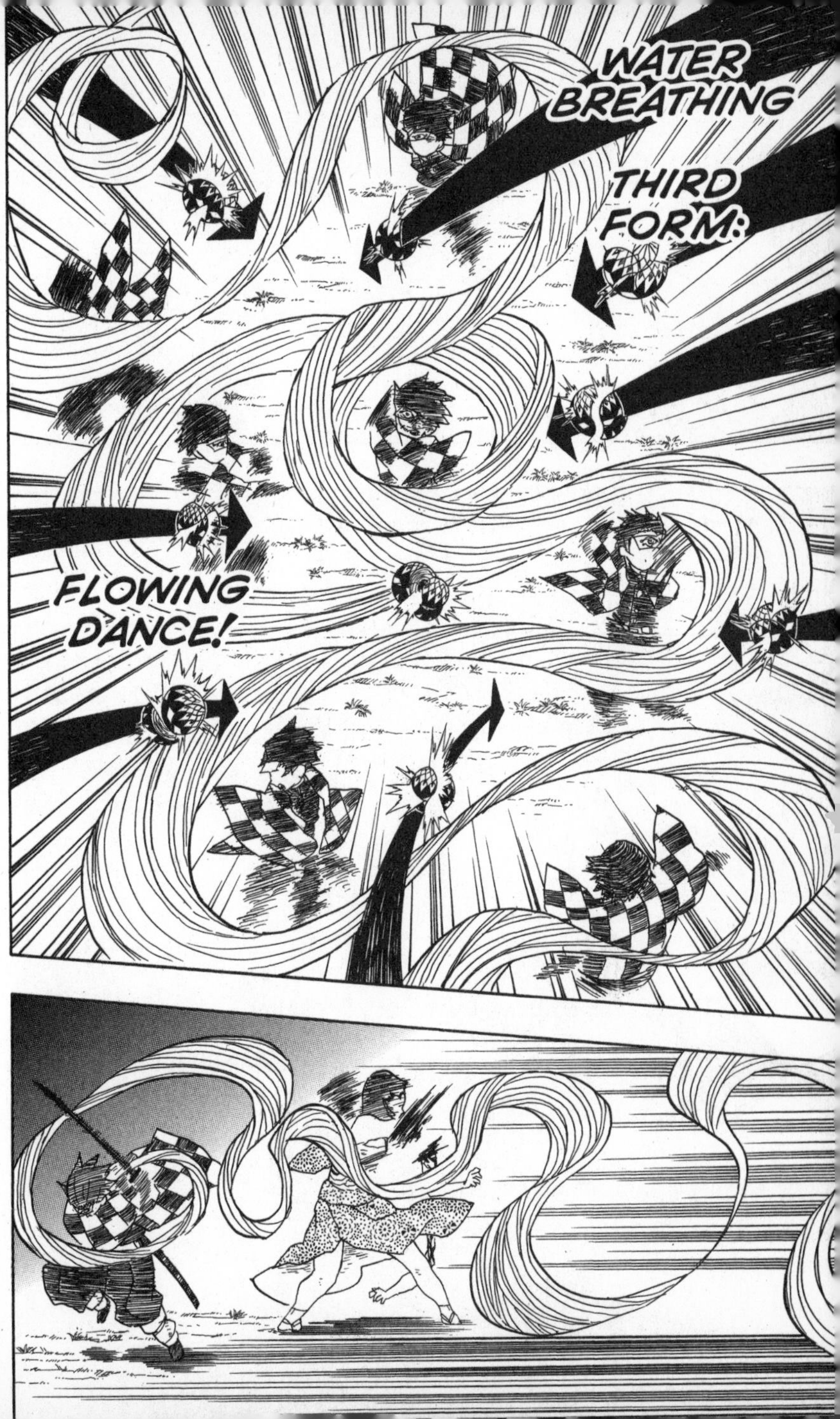
WATER BREATHING
THIRD FORM:
FLOWING DANCE!

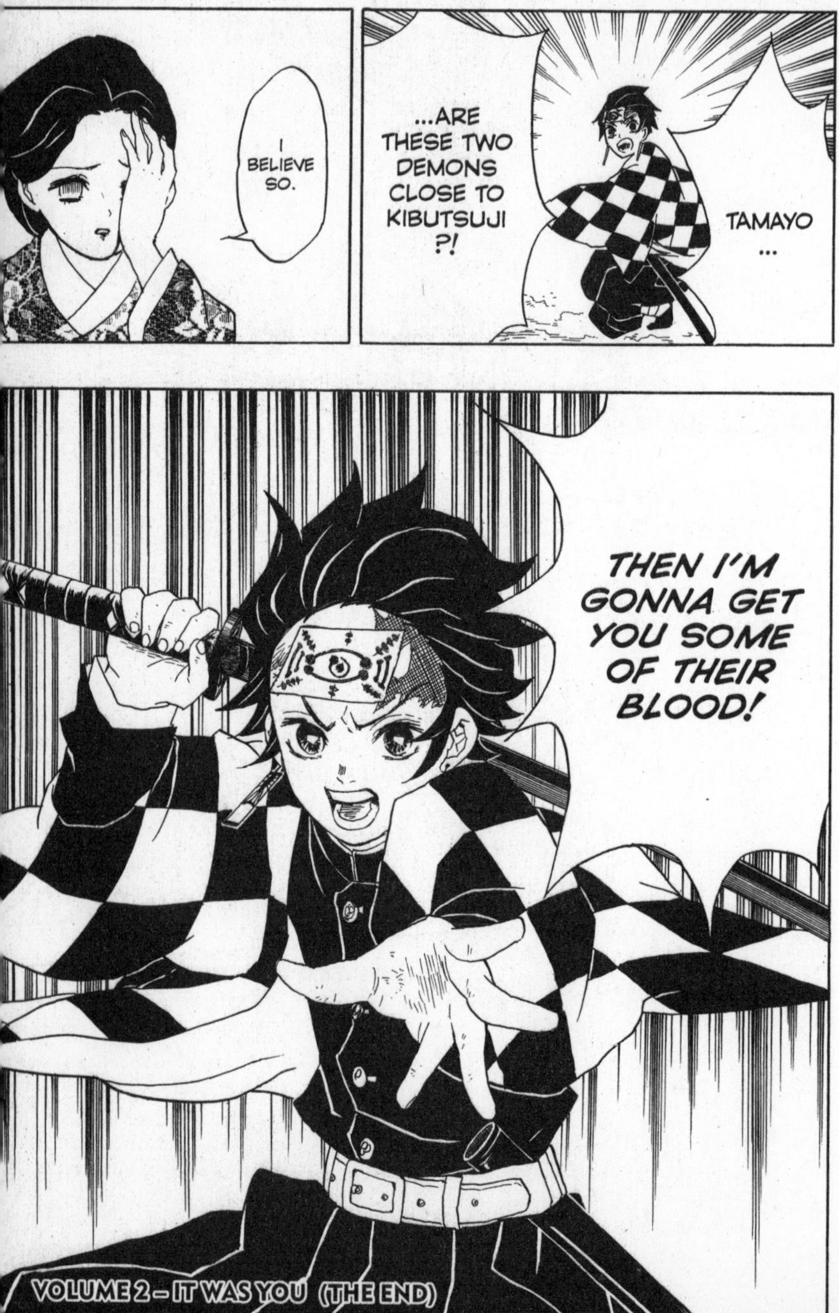
TAMAYO ...
...ARE THESE TWO DEMONS CLOSE TO KIBUTSUJI ?!
I BELIEVE SO.
THEN I'M GONNA GET YOU SOME OF THEIR BLOOD!
VOLUME 2 – IT WAS YOU (THE END)

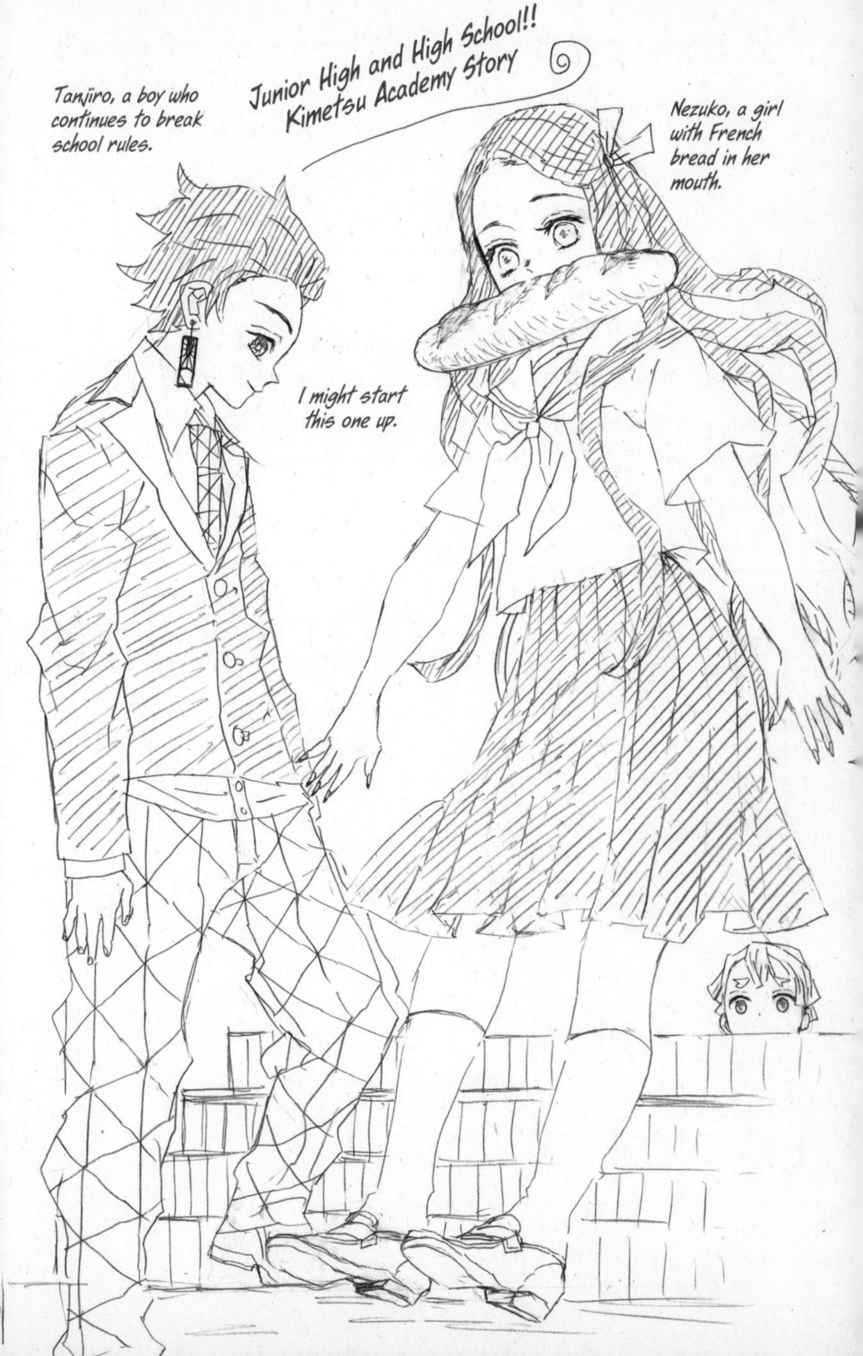
Junior High and High School!!
Kimetsu Academy Story
Nezuko, a girl with French bread in her mouth.
Tanjiro, a boy who continues to break school rules.
I might start this one up.

Words of Gratitude

Hello, I'm Gotouge. Volume 2 is out! Thank you. I'm causing trouble for a lot of people and getting help from a lot of people too. Thanks to everyone in the editorial department, my editor and assistants, and everyone reading and cheering for Kimetsu, I'm able to draw manga again today. I've failed so many times that a day doesn't pass when I don't worry about whether it's okay for me to draw manga, but I plan to give my best!
Thanks!!

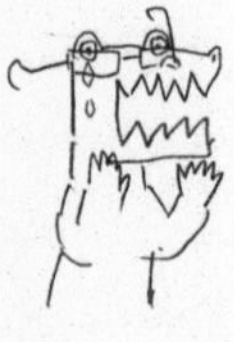
Arigato!!

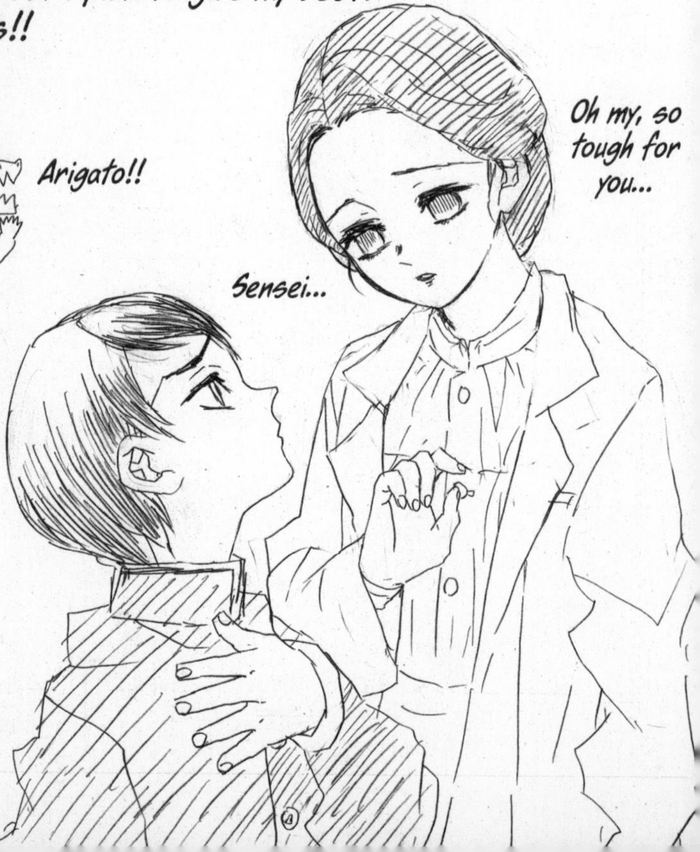
Oh my, so tough for you...
Sensei...
...my heart aches.

YOU'RE READING THE
WRONG WAY!

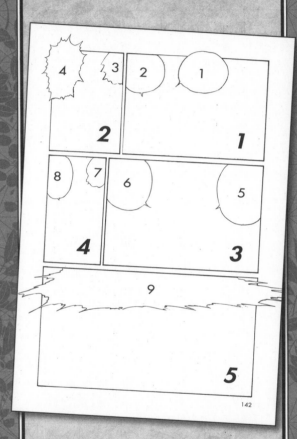

DEMON SLAYER: KIMETSU NO YAIBA reads from right to left, starting in the upper-right corner. Japanese is read from right to left, meaning that action, sound effects and word-balloon order are completely reversed from English order.